Britain and the Armenian Question
1915-1923

Akaby Nassibian

CROOM HELM
London & Sydney

ST. MARTIN'S PRESS
New York

© 1984 Akaby Nassibian
Croom Helm Ltd, Provident House, Burrell Row,
Beckenham, Kent BR3 1AT
Croom Helm Australia Pty Ltd, First Floor,
139 King Street, Sydney, NSW 2001, Australia

British Library Cataloguing in Publication Data

Nassibian, Akaby
    Britain and the Armenian question 1915-1923.
    1. Armenia – Politics and government
    2. Great Britain – Foreign relations – Turkey
    3. Turkey – Foreign relations – Great Britain
    I. Title
    956.6'2   DS175.3

    ISBN 0-7099-1820-8

All rights reserved. For information, write:
St. Martin's Press, Inc., 175 Fifth Avenue, New York, NY 10010
Printed in Great Britain
First published in the United States of America in 1984

Library of Congress Cataloging in Publication Data

Nassibian, Akaby.
    Britain and the Armenian question, 1915–1923.

    Bibliography: p. 272.
    Includes index.
    1. Armenian question. 2. Great Britain – Foreign
relations – 1910–1936. I. Title.
DS195.5.N29 1984   956.6'2   84–8358
ISBN 0-312-09809-X

Printed and bound in Great Britain

Contents

Maps

Abbreviations

The following abbreviations have been used throughout:

Arm. Nat. Deleg. Papers, microf.	Armenian National Delegation Papers, microfilm (at the Armenian General Benevolent Union Library, Saddle Brook, New Jersey)
BAC	British Armenia Committee
BDOW	*British Documents on the Origins of the War 1898–1914* (ed. G.P. Gooch and H. Temperley)
CAB	Cabinet
CIGS	Chief of the Imperial General Staff
C. in C.	Commander-in-Chief
CO	Colonial Office
DBFP	*Documents on British Foreign Policy 1919–1939* (The 1st Series has been used throughout)
DMI	Director of Military Intelligence
EC	Eastern Committee (of the War Cabinet)
fn	footnote
FO	Foreign Office
IDCE	Inter-Departmental Conference on the Middle East
MP	Member of Parliament
min.	minute
n.	note
n.d.	no date
PP	Parliamentary Papers
PRO	Public Record Office, London
Rep. of Arm. Archives	Archives of the Republic of Armenia (at the Archive Centre of Dashnaktsutiun, Boston, Massachusetts)
S.S.	Secretary of State
WO	War Office

British official documents have been cited first by series, then by volume number, file number and document number. For example, FO 371/2488/51009/123491 refers to Foreign Office series 371 (political), volume 2488, file 51009, document 123491.

TO
MY FATHER AND MOTHER

Preface

This book is a discussion of Britain's attitude both towards the Armenian people after Turkey's entry into the First World War on the opposite side to her, and towards the Republic of Armenia created consequent to the break-up of the Russian Empire. It necessarily examines the policy of the British government as shaped by the evolving strategic, political, imperial and economic considerations. It pays close attention not only to Cabinet minutes and Foreign Office despatches, but also to the views of the India Office, since Britain was the greatest Moslem power in the world; to the War Office which had assumed a heightened influence because of the War; and to Lloyd George who often conducted a personal diplomacy, superseding the Foreign Office. The book also examines, through documents hitherto unused, the activities of pro-Armenian groups, all following a strong British humanitarian tradition, and trying to influence the government during this period of transition from the old 'aristocratic' notion of foreign policy to the 'democratic'.

Such a discussion was best served by a thematic approach — without neglecting chronology — in order to give to the themes unity of thought and clarity. On the other hand, despite the care taken, some overlapping and repetition was unavoidable. The book has naturally drawn heavily on British manuscript sources. But use has also been made of important Armenian archival material in Boston and New Jersey, USA. The internal history of both Britian and Armenia lies beyond the scope of this study and no attempt has been made to deal with it except where essential to an understanding of the central theme.

The pro-Armenian groups often referred, during 1915–23, to past British responsibility as regards Armenia. It was necessary, therefore, to have an introductory chapter tracing Britain's involvement in the Armenian Question since 1878. The British interest, before the First World War, was to prevent Russian influence in the Armenian territories. Reforms to benefit the Armenian people, therefore, were considered much less important than the strategically valuable Armenian territories. Chapter 2 outlines the work and the unfailing devotion of the pro-Armenian pressure groups and relief organisations up to 1918. Chapter 3 documents for the first time the use the British Foreign Office made, for the war effort, of the Armenian holocausts of 1915, and examines the background of the British 'pledges' to the liberation of Armenia. Chapter 4 outlines Britain's post-war dilemmas: her inability to reconcile her sympathetic statements about Armenia with her reluctance to assume responsibility for a territory in which she had now lost her interest — once she had secured predominance in the Persian Gulf. It also considers her contradictory policy in the Caucasus and the disproportion between her objectives and her financial resources. Chapter 5 discusses Britain's illusions — both as regards Anatolia and the Caucasus — , the result of her unprecedented prestige acquired under world conditions at a time when her armies and power were shrinking under domestic pressures: illusions which proved to be disastrous for Armenia. Chapter 6 describes the post-war efforts of the pro-Armenian humanitarian groups to force the British government into giving effective help to Armenia and their bitter disappointment in its response. Their pressure could only induce the British government to *show* what it was doing; thus, they indirectly contributed to the illusory hopes of the Armenian people who preferred to depend on far-away Europe instead of following a determined policy of accommodation in the Caucasus. The book concludes that Britain's sympathy with the Armenian people and her strategic interests were never moulded into a single policy forming a rounded whole.

This book would have been impossible without the help of many people. But as the greater part of it is based on my doctoral thesis for the University of Oxford, I am grateful above all to my supervisor, Dr Agatha Ramm, D. Litt., whose guidance and advice at all stages have been invaluable. She has given of her deep knowledge of, and experience in, diplomatic history, and of her time for the discussion of my drafts, both as regards substance and style, most generously. I am also indebted to Professor M.S. Anderson for his constructive suggestions and to Dr Albert Hourani who has always kindly shared with me his profound understanding of the history and people of the Near East. Dr A. Beylerian, in Paris, has been unfailing in replying to my queries about the Armenian history of this period, and I wish to express my sincere thanks to him. I am also greatly indebted to the Principal and Fellows of Lady Margaret Hall, my college in Oxford, for the great kindness and encouragement I enjoyed there at all times as a research student.

I am most grateful for the help given to me by the staff of: the Archive Centre of Dashnaktsutiun, Boston, Massachusetts; the Armenian General Benevolent Union Library, Saddle Brook, New Jersey; the Bodleian Library, Oxford, where the greater part of my work was done; the Bristol University Library; the British Library, London; the Churchill College Library, Cambridge; the History Faculty Library, University of Oxford; the House of Lords Record Office; the Imperial War Museum; the India Office Library; the Labour Party Archives, London; Lambeth Palace Library; the Public Record Office; the Religious Society of Friends, London; Rhodes House Library, Oxford; St Antony's College Middle East Centre, Oxford; St Deiniol's Library, Hawarden; and Trinity College Library, Cambridge.

The Hon. Mrs Hogg of Brenchley, Kent; Mrs Elizabeth Brooks of

Dawson Place, London, and Mr Robin Hodgkin of Bareppa House near Falmouth, not only made available for me the private papers in their possession of Noel Buxton, Aneurin Williams and Thomas Hodgkin respectively, but also showed their great kindness in various other ways. It is with pleasure that I wish to express my warmest thanks to them. Mr Ronald de Bunsen of Waltham Abbey, Essex, shared with me his personal impressions of the Reverend Harold Buxton, for which I am indeed grateful.

I realise that it is impossible to name here all those friends whose interest in my work and unfailing kindness have been a great source of encouragement for me. I thank them all most warmly.

A.N.

1 Introduction:
Britain and the Armenian Question
on the Eve of the First World War

The earliest references to the inhabitants of Armenia, a region lying to the east of the bulge of the river Euphrates and south of the Caucasian mountains, are found on Hittite tablets dating from the fourteenth century BC. They mention the kinglets of Hayasa and the tribes of Azzi. Later, an Assyrian inscription of Sargon I (980-48 BC) refers to the tribes of Armeni and Shubria. But the first unitary and strong kingdom of this area, established in the ninth century BC, was that of Urartu, whose city Erebuni survives in the modern Erevan. By the sixth century BC, the Urartians, weakened by the wars of Assyria, Media and Achaemenid Persia, were penetrated by the tribes of Hayasa-Azzi and Armeni-Shubria, who imposed on them Armenian, an Indo-European language. Thereafter the name of Urartu was gradually superseded by Armenia, as mentioned in the inscription of Behistun (recounting the wars of Darius the Great) and in the works of Herodotus and Xenophon. The word Armenia, derived from the Armeni-Shubria grouping, has prevailed to this day except among the Armenians themselves, who call their country Hayastan and themselves Hay, originating from the people of Hayasa. Armenians, therefore, have inhabited Armenia or Hayastan since earliest times.

The most brilliant period in the history of ancient Armenia was the reign of Tigran II (95-56 BC) when his vast empire stretched from the Caspian Sea to the Mediterranean. Being situated, however, on crossroads, Armenia has suffered bitter rivalry at the hands of Western and Eastern powers and invasion from wild tribes in central Asia.

The first major dispersion of the Armenian people occurred in the eleventh century when the Seljuk Turks overthrew the Armenian kingdom. Subsequently, Armenia was successively invaded, first by Mongols in the thirteenth century . . . and finally by Ottoman Turks in the early sixteenth century. Thousands of Armenians went to settle in the Balkans, Poland, Russia, Persia and as far as India.

A large number of Armenians also went to Cilicia, on the Mediterranean coast, and in due course founded there, in the eleventh century, a new kingdom. The important help given to the Crusaders by the Cilician Armenians has been acknowledged by Pope Gregory XIII. But towards the end of the fourteenth century this little Armenian kingdom also was destroyed by the Mamluks and the emigration movement received a further impetus. Many Armenians went to settle in Cyprus, Rhodes and Crete and thence to Egypt and to many parts of Europe.

1

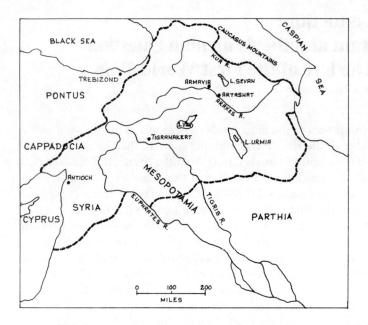

Map 1: The Empire of Tigram II

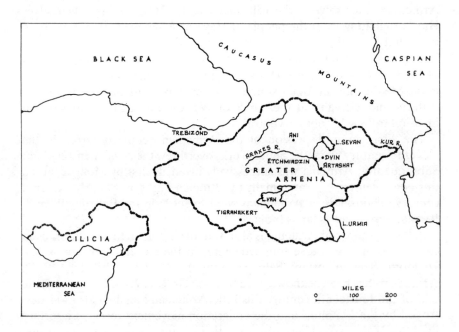

Map 2: Armenia in Ancient and Medieval Times

In Armenia proper the wars between Persia and Ottoman Turkey resulted in Eastern Armenia passing eventually to Persia in 1746. By 1828, however, Russia had acquired the *khanates* (provinces) of Erevan and Nakhichevan (Eastern Armenia) from Persia, following her victorious wars with the latter. The river Araxes became Russia's frontier with Persia.

In 1828 Russia also engaged in war with Turkey and gained some territory. She acquired further territory following the Crimean and the 1876-7 wars. Thus, before the First World War historic Armenia was divided between Turkey and Russia and the bulk of the Armenian people lived in Western or Turkish Armenia and Eastern or Russian Armenia. But there also were Armenian communities as far away as the United States of America, the movement of dispersion having continued during the 1895-6 Armenian massacres in Turkey and the 1909 massacres in Cilicia.[1]

Just before 1914 the total world population of Armenians was reckoned to be about four and a half millions. In Russian Armenia, comprising the provinces of Kars, Erevan, the highlands of Karabagh and the southern parts of the province of Tiflis, there were about one and a half million Armenians. But the Armenian population in the Ottoman Empire still remains a hotly disputed point. According to the official Turkish statistics there were only 1,300,000 Armenians in the whole Empire of whom 628,000 lived in the 'six (Eastern) *vilayets*'[2] or provinces — the Armenian homelands — forming a mere 12.53 per cent of the population (5,010,594) in the region. Oddly enough, the Ottoman statistics do not provide separate figures for the Turks and the Kurds of the region: they are grouped as a single entity under the name of 'Moslems'. On the other hand, in 1912, the Armenian Patriarchate of Constantinople gave the number of Armenians in the Empire as 2,100,000. There were 1,018,000 Armenians in the 'six *vilayets*' forming 38.9 per cent of the population of the region — a relative majority (against 25.4 per cent Turks and 16.3 per cent Kurds). Considering the big discrepancy between the official Turkish and Armenian figures one wonders whether both sides have deliberately resorted to exaggeration in order to refute or justify Armenian national aspirations. However, according to a view expressed in 1920 by the Historical Section of the Foreign Office, it is probable that the figures for the Armenians given by the Patriarchate are 'too low rather than too high', since the existence of a capitation tax tended to make the Armenians conceal rather than exagger-

1. For the peoples and history of ancient Armenia, see Charles Burney and D.M. Lang, *The Peoples of the Hills* (London, 1971); Sirarpie Der Nersessian, *Armenian Art* (London, 1978); D.M. Lang, *The Armenians: A People in Exile* (London, 1981); Archag Tchobanian, *The People of Armenia* (transl. G.M. Gregory, London, 1914); Aram Raffi, 'Armenia: Historical Background' in Noel Buxton and Harold Buxton, *Travel and Politics in Armenia* (London, 1914).

2. Erzerum, Van, Bitlis, Kharput, Diarbekir and Sivas. The Patriarchate has excluded from its statistics the following regions not inhabited by Armenians: Hakkiari, and those regions situated south of Sighert, Diarbekir, Malatia and to the north-west of Sivas.

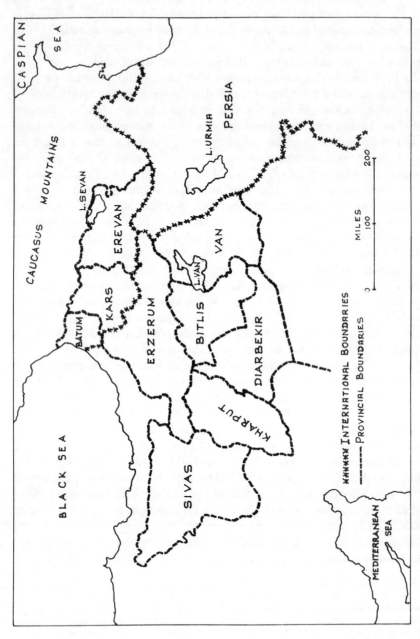

Map 3: The Administrative Divisions in Turkish Armenia in 1914

rate their own numbers. The debate still continues and, in 1982, an article in the *Spectator* referred to 'a flourishing academic industry' in Turkey which aims at minimising the size of the pre-1914 Armenian population.[3]

Contact between the Armenian and English kings had existed since the Middle Ages. Thus the Cilician King Leon II had acted as chief best man at the wedding of Richard the Lion-Heart in Cyprus in 1191. And Leon VI, the last king of the Armenians, went to France and England in 1386 to mediate between Richard II and the King of France, then at war.[4] But it was the decline of the Ottoman Empire and the victories of Russia in Asia in the nineteenth century which first brought Armenia into British politics. In an effort to bolster up Turkey, the Western powers forced the Emperor of Russia in 1856 to restore to the Sultan the town and citadel of Kars, as well as those other parts of Ottoman territory which the Russian troops had occupied during the Crimean War. Moreover, the sovereigns of Britain, Austria, France, Prussia, Russia and Sardinia engaged 'to respect the independence and territorial integrity of the Ottoman Empire'.[5]

British officers on the spot, in the 1870s especially, stressed — it seems in an exaggerated way — the strategic importance of Armenia, which should on no account be allowed to fall into Russian hands. It was assumed that by holding Armenia and the Kurdish mountains Russia could threaten the head of the Persian Gulf by way of the valleys of the Euphrates and Tigris. The British government was warned, at the outbreak of the Russo-Turkish War, that were the Russian forces to conquer the Armenian Plateau, they would have the command of the 'whole of Asia Minor'. In his turn, Sir A.H. Layard, the British ambassador, also commented upon the immense advantages to Russia and the moral effect on Britain's Mohammedan subjects in India of a Russian conquest of Armenia. The consequence would be the greatest blow ever struck at the British Empire, he wrote.[6]

Russia was Britain's greatest rival in the east and India was Britain's most precious possession. On the other hand Turkey's geographical position with regard to Russia and India was unique: her integrity, therefore, had to be supported by Britain at all costs. India weighed so heavily in the scale of values in the British Empire that the first Report of the Committee of Imperial Defence had stated:

---

3. FO 371/2116/4947; FO 371/1773/16927; FO Handbook no. 62, *Armenia and Kurdistan*, pp. 6-7; Norman Ravitch, 'The Armenian Catastrophe', *Encounter*, vol. LVII, no. 6 (Dec. 1981), p. 71; Roger Cooper, 'Armenian Aspirations', *Spectator*, 28 Aug. 1982, p. 11, col. 3.

4. Raffi, 'Armenia: Historical Background', pp. 192-4.

5. Parliamentary Papers (hereafter PP), 1877, XCII (Turkey no. 4), p. 1003: Treaty of Paris, 30 Mar. 1856, Articles III, VII.

6. Dwight E. Lee, *Great Britain and the Cyprus Convention Policy of 1878* (Cambridge/ Harvard, 1934), pp. 39, 62-3, quoting R. Home, Intell. Dept., WO, Feb. 1877; Simmons, 17 Apr. 1877; Layard, 30 May, 13 June 1877.

The British Empire is pre-eminently a great Naval, Indian and Colonial Power.[7]

Thus, India ranked second only in importance, immediately after the navy, in the factors making up the strength of the Empire and occupied a vital position in the considerations shaping British attitudes towards Turkey. Hence, Turkey was of strategic importance for Britain as regards both India and Russia. In addition, it was definitely to the advantage of Britain to be on friendly terms with the Sultan of Turkey, the Khalif, since Britain was the greatest colonial power in the Moslem world. Nor could Britain disregard her very considerable economic and financial interests in the Turkish Empire. According to G.N. Curzon (later Lord Curzon),

> In the furious commercial competition that now rages like a hurricane throughout the world, the loss of a market is a retrograde step that cannot be recovered; the gain of a market is a positive addition to the national strength.[8]

The threat to British trade and finance served as part of the background to political rivalry in the Levant.

During the 1877 war, Russia occupied Kars, Batum and Ardahan, as well as Bayazit and Alashkert, to the intense dislike of Britain. The Preliminary Treaty of Peace between victorious Russia and Turkey, signed at San Stefano on 19 February/3 March 1878,[9] was definitely not acceptable to the Western powers. In his circular to the powers of 1 April 1878, Lord Salisbury, the Foreign Secretary, argued that the acquisition of the strongholds of Armenia would place the population of that province under the immediate influence of Russia, while the 'extensive' European trade which passed from Trebizond to Persia would, in consequence of the Russian occupation of Alashkert and Bayazit, be liable to be arrested by prohibitory barriers.[10]

During the ensuing confidential negotiations between Britain and Russia it was manifest that the latter power might probably accept modifications in the Articles concerning European Turkey. As to Alashkert and Bayazit, although Prince Gorchakov, the Imperial Chancellor, retorted that

> It is carrying distrust to an extreme to affirm that they would place Russia

---

7. In 1904, M.P.A. Hankey, *The Supreme Command 1914-1918* (London, 1961), I, p. 46.

8. G.N. Curzon, *Persia and the Persian Question* (London, 1892), II, p. 604, quoted in D.C.M. Platt, 'Economic Factors in British Policy During the "New Imperialism" ', *Past and Present*, no. 39 (Apr. 1968), p. 134.

9. PP, 1878, LXXXIII (Turkey no. 22), pp. 239-65.

10. H. Temperley and L.M. Penson, *Foundations of British Foreign Policy* (Cambridge, 1938), p. 378.

'in a position to impede by prohibitive obstacles the commercial system of Europe',

they were eventually restored to Turkey. But as regards Batum, described by Gorchakov as the only good port in those parts, and the fortresses of Kars and Ardahan, which only possessed a defensive value,[11] the government of Russia was definitely not prepared to recede from the stipulations to which defeated Turkey had consented.

On his part Lord Salisbury considered it 'impossible' that the British government should look with indifference upon these changes in Asiatic Turkey. The government of the Ottoman dynasty was that of a still alien conqueror, resting more upon power than upon the sympathies of common nationality. The defeat of Turkish arms and the mere retention by Russia of Batum, Kars and Ardahan would produce, among the population of Syria, Asia Minor and Mesopotamia, a general belief in the decadence of Turkey, and a devotion to Russia — the power which was in the ascendant. Such a state of feeling would not be welcome to Britain:

> It is impossible for Her Majesty's Government to accept, without making an effort to avert it, the effect which such a state of feeling would produce upon regions whose political condition deeply concerns the Oriental interests of Great Britain . . .

Salisbury maintained. The only provision which could furnish a substantial security for the stability of Ottoman rule in Asiatic Turkey was an engagement on the part of a strong power 'that any further encroachments by Russia upon Turkish territory in Asia will be prevented by force of arms'. Such an undertaking would give to the populations of the Asiatic provinces the requisite confidence that Turkish rule in Asia was not destined to a speedy fall. Britain could give such an assurance on two conditions. The British government was 'not prepared to sanction misgovernment and oppression' and, therefore, they should be 'formally assured' of the intention of the Porte to introduce the necessary reforms into the government of Turkey's provinces. The second requirement was the lease of Cyprus.[12]

Article I of the Cyprus Convention, signed on 4 June 1878, read:

> If Batoum, Ardahan, Kars, or any of them shall be retained by Russia, and if any attempt shall be made at any future time by Russia to take possession of any further territories of His Imperial Majesty the Sultan in Asia, as fixed by the Definitive Treaty of Peace, England engages to join His Imperial Majesty the Sultan in defending them by force of arms.

11. PP, 1878, LXXXIII (Turkey no. 27), pp. 276-7: Gorchakov to Shuvalov, 28 Mar. 1878, comm. to Salisbury, 13 Apr. 1878.
12. Ibid., LXXXII (Turkey no. 36), pp. 3-4: Salisbury to Layard, 30 May 1878.

In return, His Imperial Majesty the Sultan promises to England to introduce necessary reforms, to be agreed upon later between the two Powers, into the government, and for the protection, of the Christian and other subjects of the Porte in these territories; and in order to enable England to make necessary provision for executing her engagement, His Imperial Majesty the Sultan further consents to assign the Island of Cyprus to be occupied and administered by England.[13]

As pointed out by William L. Langer, it is perfectly clear that the British government was much less concerned with the Armenians than with the country they inhabited: a fact which could not have escaped the Sultan's notice. They were interested in bolstering up the Turkish rule in north-eastern Anatolia by the method of reforming the system of government. According to the historians H. Temperley and L.M. Penson, Salisbury was 'genuinely' set on Asiatic reform.[14] But his project failed because the Sultan was not really interested in reform. On the other hand as the initiative of bolstering up the Ottoman Empire was undertaken by Britain, she ran the risk of incurring the jealousy and resistance of Russia and France, who because of their position and traditions, were the opponents of Britain. Even during the Congress of Berlin, the publication by the London *Globe* of the secret Cyprus Convention between Britain and Turkey, resulted in almost breaking up the Congress. The French and Russian ambassadors declared themselves 'outraged at the English ill-faith'.[15]

The Treaty of Berlin, signed on 13 July 1878, revised the Treaty of San Stefano. Writing from Berlin on the day it was signed, Salisbury admitted with satisfaction that the alterations made were 'very large'. Their general effect had been to restore 'a very large territory' — including the district of Bayazit — to the government of the Sultan and they tended 'powerfully to secure' the stability and independence of his Empire.

The Article which most concerned the Armenians in the new Treaty of Berlin was 61, which read:

The Sublime Porte undertakes to carry out, without further delay, the ameliorations and reforms demanded by local requirements in the provinces inhabited by the Armenians, and to guarantee their security against the Circassians and Kurds.

---

13. Ibid., pp. 5-6: Convention of Defensive Alliance Between Great Britain and Turkey, signed 4 June 1878; E. Hertslet, *The Map of Europe by Treaty* (London, 1891), IV, pp. 2722-3.

14. W.L. Langer, *The Diplomacy of Imperialism 1890-1902* (New York, 1956), p. 151. Temperley and Penson, *Foundations of British Foreign Policy*, p. 383.

15. Wilfrid Scawen Blunt, 'Turkish Misgovernment', *Nineteenth Century*, no. 40 (Nov. 1896), p. 839, quoted in C.J. Walker, *Armenia: The Survival of a Nation* (London, 1980), p. 114. Lee, *Great Britain and the Cyprus Convention Policy of 1878*, pp. 162-3.

It will periodically make known the steps taken to this effect to the Powers, who will superintend their application.[16]

Article 61 of the Treaty of Berlin had replaced Article 16 of the Treaty of San Stefano which had stipulated:

> As the evacuation by the Russian troops of the territory which they occupy in Armenia, and which is to be restored to Turkey, might give rise to conflicts and complications detrimental to the maintenance of good relations between the two countries, the Sublime Porte engages to carry into effect, without further delay, the improvements and reforms demanded by local requirements in the provinces inhabited by Armenians, and to guarantee their security from Kurds and Circassians.[17]

On the face of it there was not much difference between Article 16 of the Treaty of San Stefano and Article 61 of the Treaty of Berlin. In both cases the Sublime Porte undertook, or engaged, to carry out reforms in the provinces inhabited by Armenians and to guarantee their security against the Kurds and Circassians. In reality, however, the difference was of momentous significance. In the first case Turkey gave her undertaking to Russia who had decisively defeated her, whose military power was effective and whose armies were on the spot. In the second case, the undertaking was given to all the signatory powers who would 'superintend' the application of these reforms. But as the shrewd Duke of Argyll was to point out, 'What was everybody's business was nobody's business.'[18] No power bothered much about reform in Armenia, a far-away country; and vast economic and financial interests and mutual jealousies precluded the powers from ever acting together and putting pressure on Turkey. So the promises of reform remained on paper.

British pro-Armenian and humanitarian groups strongly believed that Britain had a special responsibility for good government in Armenia on account of her being a signatory to both the Cyprus Convention and the Treaty of Berlin. In both agreements the Sultan had promised or undertaken to introduce reforms. Britain should therefore see that he carried out these written provisions.

However, replying to a letter from Lady Frederick Cavendish,[19] Sir Edward Grey, the Foreign Secretary, did not admit that Britain was *'doubly pledged'* to protect the Armenians. As regards the Treaty of Berlin, the obligations of the British government were 'of course exactly the same' as those of the other signatory powers of the Treaty. As regards the Cyprus

16. PP, 1878, LXXXIII (Turkey no. 38), p. 384: copy of Treaty signed in Berlin, 13 July 1878.

17. Ibid., (Turkey no. 22), p. 262: Prelim. Treaty of Peace between Russia and Turkey signed at San Stefano 19 Feb./3 Mar. 1878, comm. to Derby by Shuvalov, 23 Mar. 1878.

18. Duke of Argyll, *Our Responsibilities for Turkey* (London, 1896), p. 68.

19. See below, pp. 40-1 and 44-5.

Convention, Grey pointed out that Britain bound herself to support Turkey against Russia under certain conditions. Cyprus was occupied by Britain in order to enable her to execute her engagement. In return the Sultan had undertaken to introduce reforms. But it was 'needless to add' that the Sultan and his successor had not fulfilled their undertaking. Grey believed that it was a common misapprehension that Britain was 'bound' by agreement to insist on the introduction of reforms. He wished to make it clear that the party which had 'failed to fulfil its undertakings' was not Great Britain but Turkey.[20]

It appears that Grey was technically right. Britain was not 'bound' to insist on reforms. Moreover, as pointed out sharply by the Duke of Argyll, no security whatever was asked in the agreements for Turkey's promises to introduce reforms.[21]

It seems that Britain's responsibility — and a heavy one indeed — arose not so much from the wording of the agreements but from her major share in substituting the relevant clauses of the Treaty of San Stefano by arrangements which left the bulk of the Armenian population under Turkish rule with no solid provision whatsoever for their security.

At the Congress of Berlin when Russia agreed — under concerted pressure — to make the concession of Bayazit and the valley of Alashkert to Turkey, Disraeli, the Prime Minister, felt 'happy' on behalf of his Delegation, to record a conciliatory step 'of so high value'. Salisbury, in his turn, indicated that he was prepared to accept the last part of Article 16 of the Treaty of San Stefano, aiming at the reforms to be granted to the Armenians, 'provided' the Congress agreed to the suppression of its first part which appeared to make the evacuation of the Russian troops dependent on the concession of reforms by the Sultan. In vain did Count Shuvalov, the Russian ambassador to Britain, express his fear that the evacuation of the Russian troops could be the signal for serious disturbances, were it to take place 'before the establishment of the promised reforms'. Salisbury strongly insisted, however, that the new Article 61 should be adopted so as 'to disconnect the engagements to be taken by the Sultan with regard to reforms in Armenia from any promises given specially to Russia, . . . '[22] Disconnected from any effective pressure, the Sultan simply ignored his promises. Salisbury did not care sufficiently to substitute for the Russian pressure any other real pressure and proper supervision. Here lay Britain's heavy responsibility. Eventually both the Cyprus Convention and the Treaty of Berlin utterly failed Armenia.

'It was the action of this country' which deprived the Armenians of the Russian protection guaranteed by the Treaty of San Stefano, James Bryce,

20. FO 371/1773/6585: Grey to F. Cavendish, copy, 4 Mar. 1913.
21. Argyll, *Responsibilities*, p. 74.
22. PP, 1878, LXXXIII (Turkey no. 39) pp. 599, 578: Congress of Berlin, 6 and 4 July 1878. See also ibid., pp. 579, 602, 617: Salisbury to FO, 8 July 1878 and sitting 6, 8 July 1878.

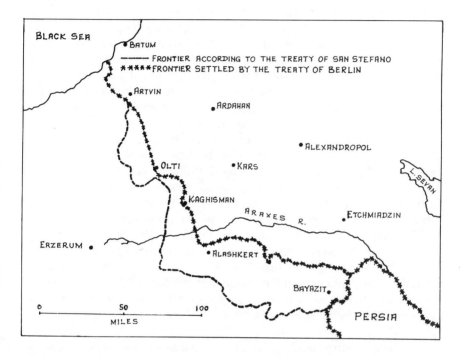

Map 4: The Ottoman Frontier According to the Treaties of San Stefano and Berlin

MP for Aberdeen and a former Minister, reminded Parliament during the massacres of the 1890s. In November 1918, a Foreign Office memorandum maintained that Britain was 'bound, perhaps juridically and certainly morally' by Article 61 of the Berlin Treaty. David Lloyd George, the Prime Minister, starkly admitted later:

> Had it not been for our sinister intervention, the great majority of the Armenians would have been placed, by the Treaty of San Stefano in 1878, under the protection of the Russian flag . . . The action of the British Government led inevitably to the terrible massacres of 1895-7, 1909 and worst of all to the holocausts of 1915.[23]

23. Bodleian Library, Bryce Papers, UB 63: cutting from *Hansard*, 11 Feb. 1896; see also MS Bryce 12, ff. 181-2: 'Some Observations . . . ', encl. in Bryce to Gladstone, 2 Aug. 1895; CAB 27/37, EC 2525, memo., FO 21 Nov. 1918 (see below, p. 143, note 79); D. Lloyd George, *The Truth About the Peace Treaties* (London, 1938), pp. 1256-7.

Arthur James Balfour, another Prime Minister, who had acted as Private Secretary to Salisbury at Berlin, to the end of his days unswervingly believed that 'the Turk was not capable of ruling';[24] and during the period covered by this study, few persons worked for the Armenian people with such zeal as Lord Robert Cecil, Under Secretary of State for Foreign Affairs, 1915-18 and Assistant Foreign Minister, 1918-19, the very son of Salisbury.

But at Berlin, the aim of the British diplomats was to check Russian influence in the Middle East. Indeed, the primary task of the British Military Consuls despatched to eastern Anatolia soon after the agreements of 1878, was to maintain posts of observation on the frontiers and provide information about the military defences of the area, as shown by the detailed 'Report on the Defence of Erzerum' by Sir William Everett.[25] Only secondly were they concerned to try and make the Sultan keep his promises of reform. Still, they reported back conscientiously from time to time, about the hopeless conditions there. But neither their representations, nor those of the British government in London, ever resulted in the actual improvement of conditions. Representations without effective force simply irritated the Sultan: 'We alone of the Great Powers adhere to the old system of acting Schoolmaster', commented the British ambassador in 1885.[26] It is true that Britain, by bolstering Turkey, was safeguarding her own strategic and commercial interests, but her relations with Turkey did not improve.

> . . . this country could not have bid for the alliance of the present Sultan [the notorious Abdul Hamid] without losing its self-respect, which is a greater asset to it than any alliance,

Sir Edward Grey wrote.[27] Thus, successive British governments found themselves in an impossible situation, pursuing two lines of policy 'diametrically opposed and consequently incompatible with one another': attempting

> . . . the impossible task of furthering our commercial interests while pursuing a course (in Macedonia, Armenia, Turco-Persian Boundary &c.) which the Sultan interprets as pre-eminently hostile in aim and tendency.[28]

24. CAB 23/24/14, App. 1, Conf. of Ministers, 18 Feb. 1921, quoted in C.J. Lowe and M.L. Dockrill, *The Mirage of Power* (London, 1972), II, p. 373.

25. St Antony's College, Middle East Centre, Everett Papers, Box 2, File 3, 1883.

26. C.L. Smith, *The Embassy of Sir William White at Constantinople* (1957), p. 160, quoted in Elizabeth Monroe, *Britain's Moment in the Middle East 1914-1956* (London, 1963), p. 16.

27. G.M. Trevelyan, *Grey of Fallodon* (London, 1940), p. 223, quoting Grey to Morley, 11 Dec. 1906.

28. G.P. Gooch and H. Temperley (eds.), *British Documents on the Origins of the War 1898-1914* (hereafter *BDOW*) (London, 1928-38), V, p. 247, Fitzmaurice, Const. to Tyrrell, 12 Apr. 1908. See also J.A.S. Grenville, *Lord Salisbury and Foreign Policy: The Close of the Nineteenth Century* (London, 1964), pp. 28, 46.

British policy was 'deadlock and failure', Grey would write later on. Public opinion in Britain demanded that representations should be made about the Armenian massacres. These the British government made, with the result that Britain was 'hated, but not feared'.[29]

The hopeless situation of the government was revealed by an absurd scheme put forward by the Foreign Office in 1908. It aimed at the relief of 'destitution' in Armenia, caused by the 'abuses' of administration, by the emigration and settlement of Armenian agriculturists in the British African Protectorates on a large scale.[30] But nothing came of it.

Britain must be satisfied with half-measures, a British diplomat wrote from Constantinople, unless the governments interested in the fate of the Armenians were willing to use 'the only argument' that would deflect the Sultan from his policy of 'gradually eliminating' the Armenian element in the Asiatic regions — 'the argument of force persistently and effectively applied'.[31]

In 1913 when Enver, a leading member of the Committee of Union and Progress, shot Nazim Pasha, the Minister of War, and forced the Cabinet to resign, grave fears of widespread massacres were expressed by Dr C.A. Gates, one of the Principals of Robert College. A member of the Foreign Office staff aptly minuted the insoluble dilemma of the British government:

> What Dr. Gates says is probably quite true, but it is quite impossible to prevent massacres in Armenia except by the occupation of those provinces by Russian troops which is undesirable for other reasons.[32]

Thus it was recognised that the only power which might stop the massacres was Russia. But she would not be allowed to intervene. A Russian occupation of the Armenian provinces might break the *status quo* and might spark off a process of partition. Turkey, called the 'sick man of Europe' in the nineteenth century might die and her Empire be divided. But as the division of a personal inheritance generally causes bad feelings among the heirs, so there was the danger that the partition of the Empire might result in strained relations between the powers.[33] Supporting the independence and integrity of the Ottoman Empire was considered a safer course for Britain to follow than trying to agree with other powers on a division of Turkey, since this might land her in unforeseen and unpredictable difficulties.

On the eve of the War, Britain warmly supported the Scheme of Reforms for the 'Eastern Provinces' initiated by Russia. When the Turkish government asked for seventeen British advisers and inspectors for these pro-

29. Grey of Fallodon, *Twenty-Five Years 1892-1916* (London, 1925), I, pp. 131-3
30. FO 371/533/599: FO to CO draft, 17 Jan. 1908; ibid., minutes.
31. Ibid., no 2889: Sir N. O'Conor to Grey, 17 Jan. 1908.
32. FO 371/1773/4961: Gates, 24 Jan. 1913, enc. in Symonds to Grey, 30 Jan. 1913; min. by ?H.N., 3 Feb. 1913.
33. *Hansard*, 5th Ser., 1911, XXII, 1300 (Noel Buxton, MP).

vinces, Grey, mainly on the advice of the British officials in Constantinople, rejected the request. They suspected that the Turkish proposals seemed designed to provoke maximum friction between Britain, Russia and France.[34] The Scheme might fail.

Still, 'the only policy' to which Britain could become a party, Grey maintained before the war, was 'one directed to avoid [the] collapse and partition of Asiatic Turkey'. Otherwise the effect of the opposite course would produce complications between the European powers and would be 'disastrous' *vis-à-vis* Britain's 'own Mussulmans in India'. In considering the Armenian reforms, Sir Arthur Nicolson, the Under Secretary of State for Foreign Affairs, could not help being sceptical as to their efficacy: it would always be difficult to find Turkish officials who were competent and trustworthy. All the same, he also believed that Britain should do all in her power, especially in view of the feelings of the Moslems in India, to strengthen the Turkish government.[35]

In the pre-war years, Britain was concerned with the fate of the Armenian people, but she was much more concerned with their land — *en route* to India — which, she believed, should on no account fall into the hands of a major rival power.

As to the Armenians themselves, it would be easy, by being selective, to point to a few overstatements and rash acts made by some members of the Armenian 'revolutionary' parties, and blame them for all the misfortunes of the people as a whole. Such statements have been quoted: as, for example, one by a leading member of a party, about its purpose, which was allegedly to bring about

> . . . a long drawn-out fight against the Ottoman tyranny, to create in the country a continuous revolutionary state, always having before our eyes the intervention of the third factor — the European factor.

A proclamation from another party paper has also been mentioned:

> The cup is full. Prepare for the inevitable . . . Yes, in truth, it is better to live as a free man for a day, for an hour, and to die fighting, than to live a life of slavery for generations . . .[36]

But almost all political parties sometimes use exaggerated language. Is it not, however, the case that basically strong, efficient and civilised govern-

34. *BDOW*, X,I, p. 447, Lowther to Grey, 6 June 1913. Ibid, pp. 471, 518, Marling to Grey, 2 July and 7 Oct. 1913 and min. by Eyre Crowe. See also pp. 427-30, 432, 436-7, 520, 523.

35. Ibid., p. 481, Grey to Buchanan, 4 July 1913; p. 489, Nicolson to Marling, 9 July 1913.

36. Langer, *Diplomacy of Imperialism*, p. 155, quoting M. Varandian of Dashnaktsutiun and p. 159 quoting from *Hunchak*, V, no. 7 (July 1892); see also S.J. Shaw and E.K. Shaw, *History of the Ottoman Empire and Modern Turkey* (Cambridge, 1977), II, pp. 203-5.

ments will differentiate between the seditious and the innocent and not resort to mass reprisals indiscriminately? It seems to be impossible to justify a government which wreaks its vengeance on whole communities for the statements, acts and even 'plots' of some of the members of these communities mainly operating from abroad.

The founders of the two main revolutionary parties were not Turkish Armenians. The Hunchakian Revolutionary Party was formed in Geneva in 1887 by seven Russian Armenian students, all in their twenties, who had left Russia to continue their higher education in Western Europe. None of them had ever lived under the Turkish flag, yet they were concerned with the living conditions of the Armenians in Turkey. The Armenian Revolutionary Federation, or Dashnaktsutiun, a merger of various Armenian groups, primarily in Russia, was founded in Tiflis in 1890.[37]

The stirrings of revolutionary activity among Armenians may be related to a national awakening coinciding with the growing intolerance of the Ottoman authorities (especially in the provinces) and to total disappointment regarding the non-implementation of reforms formally promised, after the generation of hopes by the Cyprus Convention and the Treaty of Berlin. It was not the activities of the revolutionary parties which made the living conditions of the Armenians, especially in the Asiatic provinces, unbearable. Conditions were far from satisfactory long before these parties were organised. It was the plight of the people which to a great extent kindled revolutionary activity.

General Fenwick Williams, the British officer sent to Kars during the Crimean War to organise its defence against Russia, had in 1855 described the machinery of Turkish government in the Asiatic provinces as 'an engine of tyranny perhaps unequalled in the world'.[38] In 1858 it was reported that the 'harsh and vexatious' treatment of Christians by the Turkish authorities in Trebizond was driving them to resort to Russian protection across the border. According to Consul J.G. Taylor, so severe was the oppression of Christians in Diarbekir that large numbers would probably join the Latin Church in order to obtain the protection of the French Consulate. In addition, about 1,400 families were preparing to emigrate to Russian Armenia.[39] In 1869 Consul Taylor stated that, during the last three years, because of the extortionate system of the collection of tithes, 'of the 106 villages then existing, 76 only now remain' in the *vilayet* of Erzerum. One unbearable custom was the *kishlak,* by which the Kurds exercised the extraordinary right of quartering themselves and their flocks in the Christian

37. L. Nalbandian, *The Armenian Revolutionary Movement: The Development of Armenian Political Parties through the Nineteenth Century* (Berkeley/Los Angeles, 1963), pp. 104, 151.

38. PP, 1877, XCII (Turkey no. 17), p. 781: Williams, Erzerum, to Clarendon, 25 Feb. 1855; Argyll, *Responsibilities,* p. 28; Duke of Argyll, *The Eastern Question* (London, 1879), I, pp. 42-5.

39. PP, 1877, XCII (Turkey no. 17) pp. 858, 859: Malmesbury to Bulwer, 29 Nov. 1858, 9 June 1859; p. 888: Russell to Bulwer, 13 Aug. 1863.

villages during winter. Complaints to the government had not remedied this evil. In the region of Mush, within the last six years, 750 families had emigrated to Russia and 500 more had in the current year sent representatives to negotiate a similar step. Everywhere throughout these districts, continued Taylor, Armenians were bitter in their complaints against the Turkish government. Were it 'really' to carry out the spirit of its numerous *firmans* in favour of Christians, it would remove the existing disaffection. But without such a programme the Christians would be

> . . . forced into bankruptcy; that sooner or later must give rise to emigration or open downright rebellion. I cannot exaggerate the gravity of the situation . . .[40]

Consul Taylor's diagnosis made on the spot and his grim predictions proved only too accurate. Armenians regularly emigrated; and within twenty years Armenian revolutionary groups agitated — in order to gain the sympathy and help of Europe.

The humiliating military defeats which the Ottoman Empire had suffered from the late seventeenth century, the rebellions of Moslem chieftains in Egypt, Syria, Baghdad and Basra, and later, the revolts of the Balkan peoples, had promoted growing intolerance on the part of the Turkish government (mainly manifest in the provinces). Ottoman power was in decline. The European discovery of new lands and new routes had turned the eastern Mediterranean into a backwater and had resulted in the loss of Ottoman trade; the flow of cheap American silver and the rise in the price of gold brought about the ruin of some sections of the population; the changed conditions of warfare necessitated the maintenance of ever larger paid professional armies, caused a shrinking economy and a costly superstructure resulting in the harsher taxation of the rural population.[41]

This decline of Ottoman power, fostering intolerance and reaction, co-incided with the awakening of Armenian national consciousness, which made conditions look worse than before. The activities, first of the Roman Catholic, and later of the Protestant missionaries, the foundation of the Mekhitarist Order in the Island of St Lazarus in Venice in the eighteenth century, the impact of the French Revolution, especially on Armenians studying in European universities, the works of Khachatur Abovian, Raffi, Mikayel Nalbandian and Rapayel Patkanian and the activity of Mkrtich Khrimian, called 'Hayrik' (Father), awakened Armenians to a new nationalism. Armenians also wanted to be treated with justice and humanity. In March 1872 a group of Armenians in Van met and decided to act together for self-protection, arguing:

40. Ibid. (Turkey no. 16), pp. 636-8: Taylor, Erzerum, to Clarendon, 19 Mar. 1869; ibid., pp. 651-2.
41. See B. Lewis, *The Emergence of Modern Turkey* (Oxford, 1961), pp. 36-7, 27-33.

. . . gone is our honour; our churches have been violated; they have kidnapped our brides and our youth; they take away our rights and try to exterminate our nation . . . let us find a way of salvation . . . if not, we will soon lose everything.[42]

In September 1876, Sir H. Elliot, the British ambassador, reported that the Armenians had forwarded a statement of their grievances to the Porte. Their complaints chiefly referred to the exactions of the tax-gatherers, and to the depredations which they suffered from the Kurds, against whom the government afforded them no protection. On 10 May 1878, Mkrtich Khrimian, Archbishop of Daron and ex-Patriarch of the Turkish Armenians, asked, calling upon Salisbury, that at the Congress of Berlin measures be taken to ensure the Armenians of the blessings of good government.[43]

It seems that the majority of the Armenians of the nineteenth century were not prepared to propose independence. Physical security, unhindered cultural development and regional autonomy were deemed the maximal and ideal conditions for which they should strive. Self-administration within the framework of the Ottoman Empire would be the most desirable improvement.[44]

Armenians were naturally disappointed that the Treaty of San Stefano was revised. Yet the Cyprus Convention and the Treaty of Berlin aroused unbounded hopes: the Great powers and especially Great Britain had at least undertaken to be interested in Armenia. Thus, on 14 November 1880, 940 Armenians in Van addressed a letter to Captain Emilius Clayton, expressing their joy that 'the Divine Providence at last began to pity' them and sent him, who represented Britain, to Van. They stressed their gratitude to the 'magnanimous English nation' and to the British government for 'the high protection and sympathy' they intended to grant to Armenia.[45]

However, despite the formal undertakings Turkey had given in both the Cyprus Convention and the Berlin Treaty, the conditions of the Armenians did not improve. The Armenians appealed to the Great powers; however, out of their special interests and mutual jealousies, these were not prepared to exert pressure unanimously. They only made futile and infuriating exhortations to Turkey to reform. The plight of the Armenians worsened.

It appeared to be 'impossible' that things could go on as they were, George Goschen, the ambassador, told Abedine Pasha in July 1880. In his turn, Vice-Consul William Everett wrote, while travelling in the south-

42. Nalbandian. *The Armenian Revolutionary Movement*, pp. 30-66, 80.

43. PP, 1877, XV (Turkey no. 1), p. 375: Elliott to Derby, 23 Sept., 1876. Ibid., 1878, LXXXIII (Turkey no. 31), p. 345: Salisbury to Layard, 11 May 1878.

44. R.G. Hovannisian, *Armenia on the Road to Independence, 1918* (Berkeley/Los Angeles 1967), p. 16.

45. PP, 1881, C (Turkey no. 6), pp. 748-9: translation enc. in Clayton to Major Trotter, 16 Nov. 1880.

eastern areas of the *vilayet* of Erzerum, that at no time since his arrival in the country had life and property been so insecure as at present. Major Henry Trotter ended a long memorandum about the people in the eastern *vilayets* of Turkey significantly: he could not believe that the people would much longer submit to the rule of a government which did nothing for its subjects but bled them and otherwise maltreated them. Influential Armenians told Captain Clayton, in Van, that the people were beginning to think that 'it would be better to die than to remain longer in their present condition'.[46]

Thus, it was only the failure of the Ottoman government to initiate genuine reforms in the Asiatic provinces and the inability of the Great Powers to put pressure on Turkey that forced some groups to resort to 'revolutionary' or terroristic methods. It has already been seen that the Hunchakian Revolutionary Party was formed in 1887, that is a full nine years after the Cyprus Convention and the Berlin Treaty, and the Armenian Revolutionary Federation or Dashnaktsutiun twelve years later, in 1890. The objective of the Hunchakian Party was the political independence of Turkish Armenia. The purpose of Dashnaktsutiun was the political and economic freedom of Turkish Armenia within the framework of the Ottoman Empire.[47] In vain had Sir W. White, the ambassador, 'endeavoured to impress' in April 1888 both the Grand Vizier and the Minister of Foreign Affairs with the importance of avoiding apparently arbitrary acts and of not 'irritating' a population 'hitherto docile and laborious', amongst whom revolutionary principles were 'not likely to find access' unless they were 'driven to desperation'. Winning the sympathy of the *raya* (subject) by conciliation and equal justice would be more efficacious than adopting repressive measures, Vice-Consul G.P. Devey reported from Van in April 1889. Armenians were being constantly arrested and questioned on somewhat frivolous counts. They were far from having any disloyal views or sentiments, and sore feeling was being created by unmerited suspicion and consequent persecution, Devey concluded.[48]

The demonstration of Kum Kapu in Constantinople in 1890, the 'rebellion' of Sasun in 1894, when the peasants of Sasun simply refused to pay the additional tribute — *hafir* — to the Kurds and resisted the Turkish forces who supported the Kurds, the demonstration of Bab Ali in Constantinople in 1895, the rebellion at Zeitun in 1895-6 and the seizure in 1896 of the Ottoman Bank in Constantinople, were mainly aimed at arousing European interest for the implementation of Article 61 of the Treaty of Berlin.[49]

---

46. Ibid., p. 465: Goschen to Granville, 13 July 1880; p. 636: Everett to Trotter, 7 Sept. 1880; p. 657: Trotter to Goschen, 2 Oct. 1880; p. 752: Clayton to Trotter, 29 Nov. 1880.
47. See above, p. 15. Nalbandian, *The Armenian Revolutionary Movement*, pp. 108, 167, 182.
48. PP, 1889, LXXXVII (Turkey no. 1), p. 157: White to Salisbury, 26 Apr. 1888; pp. 220-2: Devey to Chermside, 13 Apr. 1889.
49. Nalbandian, *The Armenian Revolutionary Movement*, pp. 118-28, 176-8; Walker, *Armenia*, pp. 132-73.

But the Armenian revolutionary groups were under somewhat of an illusion that demonstrations or terroristic acts might result in the intervention of the European powers. The period of the precarious 'concert' of the Europe of 1878 had long passed. The Great powers could not agree on a specific policy. On the other hand, the Sultan was a past master at playing off one against the other. The only result of these demonstrations and terroristic acts was widespread massacre. On the pretext of 'sedition' and 'revolution', the Ottoman government massacred some 200,000 Armenians[50] all over the country — the innocent and the guilty, women and children, old and young.

The Armenian revolutionaries were mostly young, romantic idealists who did not always have the co-operation of the conservative-minded leaders of the older generation. Moreover, although the older intelligentsia had been instrumental in propagating enlightened ideas of freedom and national consciousness, they did not join the revolutionary parties. Nor did the well-to-do wish to be committed to illegal methods. The clergy were, on the whole, apathetic towards political developments. So too were the majority of the peasantry in the eastern provinces. According to Ahmed Rustem Bey, only 'une infime minorité' (a tiny minority) of the Armenians were in the revolutionary movement. In addition, the parties were further handicapped by a lack of cohesiveness. All such weaknesses, however, might have been overcome if the revolutionaries had received assistance from the European powers — a vital factor in the programme. They did not. They were persistently naïve in their evaluation of European politics and diplomacy.[51] On the other hand it seems that the Ottoman government deliberately exaggerated the scope of the activities and the influence of these revolutionary groups. The Hunchaks were strong in Cilicia, yet they represented 'but a fraction of the people'.[52]

Was all the agitation and disorder between 1894 and 1897 caused by the Armenian revolutionaries?

There certainly was some provocation on their part in a few instances. But it seems that it was the Ottoman government's choice to exaggerate their activities and to use them as pretexts and justification for penalising not only the perpetrators, but also the mass of the Armenian population. According to Ambassador Sir P. Currie, 'the charge against the Armenians of having been the first to offer provocation cannot be sustained'. On his part, Consul R.W. Graves reported that there was reason to believe that the Turkish authorities at Sasun had secretly encouraged the Kurds to pick a quarrel and

50. See FO 371/1773/16926: Lowther to Grey, 6 Apr. 1913; E. Pears, *Turkey and Its People* (London, 1911), p. 270: 'probably at least two hundred and fifty thousand of them were killed or died from exposure'.

51. Nalbandian, *The Armenian Revolutionary Movement,* pp. 182-4; Ahmed Rustem Bey, *La Guerre Mondiale et La Question Turco-Arménienne* (Berne, 1918), pp. 26, 35; Langer, *Diplomacy of Imperialism,* p. 160.

52. PPJ 1889, LXXXVII (Turkey no. 1), p. 237, Devey, Van, to Sir. W. White, 9 July 1889; FO 371/772/17612, Vice-Cons. Doughty-Wylie, Adana, to Lowther, 21 Apr. 1909.

attack the Armenians in force. Neither were the massacres simply the work of the Kurds, nor were they provoked by mobs. 'The participation of the soldiers in the massacres [is] in many places established beyond doubt.'[53] Having read 'in full' the despatches of the British Consuls, James Bryce was convinced that the Turk 'deliberately' desired to reduce the Armenian population. The Turk remembered Bulgaria only to regret that his methods were not more effective there.[54] Again, it was the Ottoman government's choice not to allow C.M. Hallward, the British Vice-Consul, to visit the disturbed districts of Sasun on the pretext that his presence there would raise expectations of British intervention and encourage insurrection. The Turkish government's object, evidently is 'to stave off any close enquiry into the matter' retorted Hallward. The Sultan's government went on finding pretexts. The Turkish amabassador in London renewed his 'often-repeated complaints' at the Foreign Office that Britain was giving encouragement to the malcontent Armenians. Foreign Secretary Earl of Kimberley's answer was:

> The danger to the Turkish Government did not [I observed], arise from agitators, but from corrupt and vicious administration.[55]

When, a year later, the Sultan himself chose to blame the delay in reforms on the 'intrigues and sedition' of the Armenians and asked Britain to threaten that reforms could not be carried out as long as they continued to agitate and create disorder, Lord Salisbury was apparently exasperated. He cabled tartly the same day: the reports which had reached him showed that

> . . the Sultan is mistaken in his belief that the Armenians have pro- voked these disorders. We are informed that on nearly every occasion this was not the case, and that in too many instances the Turkish authori- ties and troops have encouraged and even take part in the outrages which have occurred.

The British government, continued Salisbury, was not encouraged to feel 'any confidence' in the earnestness of the Sultan's intention to give effect to the promised reforms.[56]

At the end of 1895, and even before the renewed massacres of 1896,

53. PP, 1896, XCV (Turkey no. 2), p. 540: Currie to Salisbury, 13 Dec. 1895; ibid. 1895, CIX (Turkey no. 1), p. 263: Currie to Kimberley, 15 Oct. 1894; ibid. 1896, XCV (Turkey no. 2), p. 540: Currie to Salisbury, 13 Dec. 1895.

54. Bryce Papers, MS Bryce 12, ff. 158-9, Bryce to Gladstone, 5 Jan.1895; see also ibid., ff. 155-6, 169-72, Bryce to Gladstone, 23 Dec. 1894, 9 June 1895; ibid., ff. 181-2 'Observations' enc. in Bryce to Gladstone, 2 Aug. 1895.

55. PP, 1895, CIX (Turkey no. 1) p. 261: Currie to Kimberley, 9 Oct. 1894; p. 269: Hallward, Mush, to Currie, 9 Oct. 1894; p. 270: Kimberley to Currie, 7 Nov. 1894.

56. Ibid., 1896, XCV (Turkey no 2), p. 452: Salisbury to M.H. Herbert, 11 Nov. 1895.

tated, as far as the Armenians were concerned, 'the whole of the provinces to which the scheme of reforms was intended to apply'.[57] Thus, it was not by the method of reform, promised from time to time, that the Ottoman government chose to solve the Armenian question, but by the method of devastating and depopulating the area where the reforms were meant to be applied.

Writing from Urfa, the scene of some of the most terrible massacres, Vice-Consul G.H. Fitzmaurice referred to 'trumped-up charges, would-be seditious documents and imaginary reports and lists of revolutionary Committees'. He deplored that the Ottoman government had committed the 'fatal error' of confounding the guilty with the innocent. Instead of using its just rights to punish such Armenians who had engaged in treasonable action, it had committed the further blunder of allowing the Moslem population to usurp the prerogatives of government by wreaking their blind fury on a, 'to a great extent, guiltless section' of the Sultan's most intelligent, hard-working and useful subjects.[58]

It seems that the 'seditious' acts of the Armenian revolutionaries were the pretext for, rather than the cause of, the widespread 1894-6 massacres. It was the decline and weakness of the Ottoman Empire, resulting in suspicion, fear and hatred towards the national awakening of the subject peoples, that made the Ottoman government overact to the statements and actions of Armenian revolutionaries and to resort to radical measures involving almost the whole population.

No effective help had come from Europe. Article 61 proved 'an absolute dead letter' and the Turks never introduced any reforms in the provinces inhabited by Armenians.[59]

So, when the Sultan's regime was toppled by the Young Turks' Revolution of 1908, no community in the Ottoman Empire was more hopeful than the Armenian. Mateos Izmirlian, the Patriarch of the Armenians in Constantinople, told Fitzmaurice, now First Dragoman at the British Embassy, of his firm conviction that the only safe course for the Armenians, their only chance of pulling themselves together and making good their terrible losses during the old Palace regime, lay in working in loyal union with the Turks on the lines of prudence and moderation. Furthermore, the Armenian Revolutionary Federation or Dashnaktsutiun entered into an 'understanding' for co-operation with the Young Turks Committee.[60]

However, the Adana massacres of 1909 in Cilicia came as a terrible shock. The Turkish side of the question was that the Armenians had armed themselves, that certain members of the Hunchakian Revolutionary Party and

57. Ibid., p. 540: Currie to Salisbury, 13 Dec. 1895.
58. Ibid., XCVI (Turkey no. 5), pp. 10, 15: Fitzmaurice to Currie, 16 Mar. 1896.
59. FO 371/557/42608, FO min., initials illegible, n.d. (Dec. 1908).
60. FO 371/546/30952/30969, Lowther to Grey, 26 Aug., 1 Sept. 1908; FO 371/557/42608, Fitzmaurice to Lowther, 30 Nov. 1908; FO 371/1242/1657: Marling to Grey, 11 Jan. 1911; Feroz Ahmad, *The Young Turks* (Oxford, 1969), p. 27n5.

the Armenian Bishop had openly urged the people to fight the Turks and set up a Principality. Major C.H.M. Doughty-Wylie, the Vice-Consul at Mersina, who had rushed to Adana, admitted that among the Armenians there was 'much vain boasting and wordy provocation'. But he could not think that 'such widespread destruction was without some secret preparation on the Turkish side':

> The massacres began in very distant places, on the same day and at nearly the same hour. The local provocation at Adana could not have effected this. I am inclined to think that some, at any rate, of the authorities knew of the intended massacre beforehand.

In his account of the massacres given to the court-martial at their request, Major Doughty-Wylie totally dismissed the idea, disseminated among the Moslem population, of a plot by the Armenians:

> . . . Going through the town I saw not a single attack originating from the Armenian side . . . I have every reason to believe that it was the Turks who were doing the attacking.

Hagop Babikian, although an Armenian deputy affiliated to the Committee of Union and Progress, was convinced that the Committee had 'organised' the Adana massacres. Sir Gerard Lowther, the ambassador, told Grey that Babikian had been a member of the Parliamentary Commission sent to enquire into the massacres, but in his report had been less open for prudential reasons. This report of 7 June 1909, which Lowther considered 'a document of historical interest', had none the less clearly ascribed the responsibility to the Committee; and soon afterwards Babikian had died. The Adana massacres of some 20,000 were a rude disillusionment to the Armenians who had welcomed the new regime.[61]

Yet the Armenian question would disappear to a great extent if only the Turkish government 'really provided justice and security to the people', as Colonel Hawker, the British Instructor to the Ottoman Gendarmerie, maintained after his tour of the Asiatic provinces lasting nearly a month and a half in 1913. There would 'no longer be any Armenian question' if the Turks abolished the Hamidie regiments and governed the Kurds with firmness and justice, a Vice-Consul almost repeated from Van.[62]

The limited character of Armenian claims, as sought by the majority of the Armenian people, was clearly indicated in two letters written by Boghos

---

61. FO 371/772/17612, FO 371/773/27100, Doughty-Wylie to Lowther, 21 Apr., 6 July 1909; FO 371/1773/16926, Lowther to Grey, 6 Apr. 1913, also enc. in dupl., copies of three printed pamphlets.

62. Ibid., no. 50846, Hawker to British ambassador, 1 Nov. 1913; ibid., no. 35485, L. Molyneux-Seel to Lowther, 9 July 1913.

Nubar to *The Times* on the eve of the war. The son of a former Prime Minister of Egypt and the founder of the Armenian General Benevolent Union, he had been appointed, in 1912 by the Catholicos of All Armenians, as President of the Armenian National Delegation in Paris, to represent the Armenian claims in Europe. In his first letter he explained the aims of his Delegation which asked for 'neither separation, nor independence, nor political autonomy' but only the application of the reforms promised by Article 61 of the Treaty of Berlin. About a year later, in February 1914, when at long last the Reform Scheme, agreed and put forward by the Great powers, was, after modifications, accepted by the Turkish government, Boghos Nubar wrote again. He expressed his gratitude to both the powers and the government of the Sultan for this agreement and reiterated that 'the population of the Armenian Provinces only asked to remain Ottoman', provided that the reforms stipulated in the Treaty of Berlin were carried out. Boghos Nubar concluded his letter by stressing that there would no longer be an Armenian question if only the reforms were implemented sincerely and without reservation.[63] A. Tchobanian, a leading Armenian intellectual, shared these views in public. The pro-Armenian Balkan Committee had also told Grey in 1912 that neither they nor the Armenians themselves asked for Armenia's 'absolute independence or severance' from the Turkish Empire. What they desired was good government. In its turn, *The Times* argued, in a leading article, that the loyalty with which Armenians had fought for the Sultan in the Balkan wars proved that they had no desire to throw off the Turkish yoke as such. But they should obtain safety for their lives and for their homes.[64]

Thus, despite the occasional overstatements of Armenian party leaders, it seems that to the last the majority of the Armenian people simply wanted the security and reforms which Turkey had promised. The Ottoman government, however, clearly showed its bad faith by abandoning the Reform Scheme even before the country entered the European war at the end of October 1914. Westenek, one of the European Inspectors-General over the Armenian provinces, just appointed by the Sultan under the stipulations of the Reform Scheme, was given leave on half pay and Hoff, the other (European) Inspector-General, was recalled in September.[65]

It seems that the crux of the problem, insoluble for Turkey, was the unfeasibility of application of the modern ideas of 'equality and justice'. Were real equality to be given to the subject races, who had hitherto been considered second-class citizens, Turkish hegemony and supremacy would be lost. According to the seasoned Fitzmaurice, the Turk felt that he would 'go to

63. *The Times*, 23 May 1913, p. 7, col. 2; ibid., 20 Feb. 1914, p. 5, col. 2.
64. Tchobanian, *The People of Armenia*, pp. 63-4. FO 371/1520/51157, memo. by Balkan Comm., enc. in Symonds to Grey, 29 Nov. 1912; *The Times*, 31 Oct. 1913, p. 9, cols. 4-5.
65. FO 371/2116/56207, Sir L. Mallet to Grey, 23 Sept. 1914.

the wall' under the Western conditions of equality and justice, while the subject races would progress and become his superiors. Apparently the Turkish rulers could not solve this conflict between their instinct for self-preservation in the matter of hegemony and the implementation of the new ideas of equality and justice. A Handbook by the Historical Section of the Foreign Office observed that the determination at all costs to maintain 'the dominance' of the Moslem over the more progressive Christian nationalities was actually one of the major 'real motives' of the massacres.[66] The fanatical sections of the Moslems jibbed at the idea of equality, reported Sir G. Lowther in 1908. The Young Turks wanted to be 'the upper dog' he confided privately in 1909; and a British military attaché asserted that Turkish supremacy had only been maintained by force and massacres from time to time; that once the non-Moslems were allowed to expand freely, the Turk would be driven to the wall. Thus, naturally he was loath to cede this supremacy.[67] In 1913 it was pointed out that there were at least 500,000 Ottoman non-Moslems in Constantinople out of a population of about 1,250,000 and yet, after five years of 'equality', not even one per cent of the police and gendarmerie were non-Moslems.[68]

It seems, therefore, that successive Turkish governments were beset, from the beginning of the nineteenth century, by this fear of equality and by the fear of consequently losing their supremacy. The centuries-old Turkish hegemony on one hand and the modern idea of equality on the other were incompatible. The conflict could not be solved peacefully. It was either evaded or solved by force. It was perhaps this fear, conscious or unconscious, that had been the cause of the repeated failures to carry out the reforms stipulated by the Cyprus Convention and the Treaty of Berlin. The negative results in Turkish government did not come from the lack of reform schemes. Most bookshelves in Turkey were littered with laws and projects for reforms. What were lacking were 'men, not measures', men among the Turks with a sense of impartiality, really meaning to carry out reforms.[69]

Again, perhaps it was this fear of equality and a tendency towards discrimination that had prompted the Ottoman government to make changes in the administrative boundaries in eastern Turkey. Most of it — the Armenian Plateau — had constituted the 'eyalet' or province of Erzerum. According to Fitzmaurice, this area was 'designedly' broken up into exceptionally small units in 1878, in order to enable the Ottoman government to deal more effectually with the Armenian population by the process of

---

66. *BDOW*, X, I, pp. 511-12, Fitzmaurice, memo., 10 Aug. 1913. The memo. was described as 'admirable' by Sir Eyre Crowe, p. 516. FO Handbook no. 59, *Anatolia*, p. 36.

67. FO 371/546/30969, Lowther to Grey, 1 Sept. 1908; Bryce Papers, UB 64, Lowther to Tyrrell, 30 Aug. 1909, copy enc. in Tyrrell to Bryce, 6 Sept. 1909; FO 371/776/23991: Col. Surtees to Lowther, 20 June 1909.

68. *BDOW*, X, I, p. 512: Fitzmaurice, memo, 10 Aug. 1913.

69. Ibid., p. 507, Fitzmaurice. See A. Hourani, *A Vision of History* (Beirut, 1961), pp. 82-3 for a discussion of nationalism and equality.

elimination. Thus several districts of Armenian concentration were hived off from Erzerum, while at the same time surrounding Moslem-populated regions were joined to the eastern provinces so that in each of them the Armenians would constitute a minority.[70]

Certainly a policy of discrimination had characterised the attitudes of the successive Turkish governments towards the Armenian peasantry and the land question. The restitution of, or compensation for lands usurped by the Kurds, and persistently evaded both by the old regime and by the Young Turks, was, to a great extent, the touchstone of Armeno-Turkish relations. Shrewdly realising that the peasantry were to a significant degree the guardians of nationality, the Turkish governments had, by making use of the Kurds, persistently manoeuvred to uproot the Armenian peasantry from the soil. The subtle Fitzmaurice remarked:

> The Turkish Government, after the Treaty of Berlin, realising that a sense of nationality cannot easily live without a peasantry, and that if it suc- ceeded in uprooting the Armenian peasantry from the soil and driving them into the towns or out of the country, it would in great part rid itself of the Armenians and the Armenian question, condoned and encouraged Kurdish usurpation of Armenian lands.

This 'retail process' was repeated on a 'wholesale scale' after the massacres of the 1890s. Large numbers of Armenians returned from the Caucasus especially after 1908, but, despite the promises of the Young Turks, nothing was done.[71]

Thus, the Western ideas of equality and justice were incompatible with the preservation of Moslem-Turkish hegemony and were persistently evaded by successive governments. But they presented yet another conflict. They were essential if the Turkish governments meant to keep their Empire and not lose all enlightened public opinion in Europe. Despite the advan- tages for Turkey of the fickleness of European diplomacy, Turkish patriots could not disregard the change of attitude especially in Britain, the power which had staunchly supported their country in both 1856 and 1878. It would be difficult to induce the British people to support a government which they so thoroughly detested, Salisbury wrote in 1897. Gloomily concluding that unless Turkey was reformed the Ottoman Empire would disintegrate, Salis- bury suggested to the Tsar in 1896 that reforms should be forced on the Sultan, and if he refused, he should be deposed.[72]

Neither the Conference at Reval, nor the Anglo-Russian Convention of 1907 between Britain, the power which had been Turkey's supporter, and

70. *BDOW*, X, I, p. 508; Hovannisian, *Independence*, p. 34.

71. *BDOW*, X, I, pp. 513-14.

72. Temperley and Penson, *Foundations of British Foreign Policy*, pp. 497-8, Salisbury to Rumbold, 20 Jan. 1897; Grenville, *Lord Salisbury and Foreign Policy* pp. 79, 80, 82.

Russia, the power which was her ancient and inexorable enemy, were viewed by Turkey with favour. According to Ahmed Emin, the Young Turks had the impression that the country would be treated as so much lifeless prey unless quick action was taken. The revolution of 1908 was mainly dictated by acute external dangers. It was, therefore, a nationalist revolution. Its prime objective was to save and secure the survival of the Ottoman state.[73] Evidently, its liberalism and constitutionalism were subordinated to its nationalistic aims.

The Young Turks, however, dismally failed in their aims to stop the decay and dismemberment of the Empire. Soon afterwards Austria annexed Bosnia and Herzegovina. Bulgaria declared her complete independence. Italy conquered Tripoli. In Albania the rule of Turkey was smashed. Finally the Balkan League almost drove her out of Europe. In all she lost territory of about 424,000 square miles. Turkey was sore and despoiled. She therefore held fast to Anatolia.[74]

Neither could the Young Turks redeem their country from her position of economic servility to the Great powers of Europe:

> Turkey is today barred from enjoying the right accorded to all independent states of increasing its revenues by indirect taxation . . .

had stated the British president of the Council of Public Debt Administration, Sir Adam Block, in his Special Report for 1907-8. Until April 1907 the Turkish customs duties had been 8 per cent. The powers had then assented to an increase of 3 per cent, namely to 11 per cent, but not to a further increase of 4 per cent as asked for by the Turkish government.[75]

This economic subservience had started in the mid-nineteenth century. In 1879, the Ottoman government was forced, through bankruptcy and financial chaos, to assign six sources of revenue to the service of the national debt; and to hand over their collection to the Public Debt Administration, managed by foreign, European representatives. Turkey permanently suffered from deficits. Just before the war she was regarded as an 'almost bankrupt' state.[76] This state of affairs made her economy an easy prey for domination and even exploitation by the Great powers.

Sir Ernest Cassel had founded and controlled the National Bank of Turkey. Seventy-five per cent of the shares in the Turkish Petroleum Company, which had exclusive rights over the oil deposits in the *vilayets* of Baghdad and Mosul, were held by British interests. Vickers and Armstrong

---

73. W.S. Churchill, *The World Crisis — The Aftermath* (London, 1929), p. 355; Ahmed Emin, *Turkey in the World War* (Yale/Oxford, 1930), p. 41; Lewis, *Emergence of Modern Turkey*, p. 208.

74. Ahmad, *The Young Turks*, pp. 152-3; Grey, *Twenty-Five Years*, I, pp. 263, 177.

75. D.C. Blaisdell, *European Financial Control in the Ottoman Empire* (New York, 1929), p. 178; *Hansard*, 5th Ser. 1912, XXXIX, 2083.

76. Andrew Ryan, *The Last of the Dragomans* (London, 1951), p. 86.

owned the Imperial Ottoman Company of Docks, Arsenals and Naval Constructions, together with the Turkish government. Ernest Abbott was the most influential of the holders of concessions in the deposits of emery in the *vilayet* of Aidin which was by far the most important source of the world's supply. 'The trade of the world with Turkey is preponderatingly British', the Earl of Ronaldshay stated in 1911. Out of all the imports of foreign goods into Turkey during 1909, 30 per cent represented British goods.[77]

French capital investments in Turkey surpassed those of any other country, including British and German. Within the territorial limits of present-day Turkey, they amounted in 1914, to about 900 million gold francs or approximately 4½ billion paper francs. Of the Ottoman Public Debt, 62.9 per cent was due to France and 22.3 per cent to Britain. The Imperial Ottoman Bank, which enjoyed the prerogatives of a State Bank, was Franco-British owned, with mainly French capital. It controlled the Tobacco Monopoly and various undertakings. Other enterprises dependent wholly or in great part upon French capital included the Bank of Salonika; the Wharves, Docks and Warehouses at Constantinople; the Waterworks at Constantinople; the Electricity and Tramways at Constantinople; the Wharves at Smyrna and the Heraclea Mines.[78]

Germany had been gaining ground on the earlier arrivals since the 1880s. By 1914, while France accounted for 25.9 per cent and Britain for 16.9 per cent of the foreign money invested in Turkish enterprises — apart from the Ottoman Public Debt — Germany alone attained 45.4 per cent. In 1888 and 1903 concessions had been granted respectively to the Deutsche Bank of Berlin for the extension of the railway from Constantinople to Angora and to Germany for the extension of the Anatolian Railway to the Persian Gulf. Berlin finance, together with the Wiener Bankverein, was responsible for the Oriental Railway connecting Constantinople with Central Europe. By 1914 German concerns controlled the passenger service of the Golden Horn, the Metropolitan Railway of Constantinople, the port at Haidar Pasha and the Constantinople Tramways.[79]

The economic, financial and military domination of the Great powers was reflected in Turkey's government services. The Inspector-General of Finance and the Directors of the Police and of the Tobacco Monopoly were Frenchmen. A British Naval Mission tried to help in reorganising the Navy.

77. FO Handbook no. 16, *Turkey in Europe*, pp. 133-4, 78; W.W. Gottlieb, *Studies in Secret Diplomacy During the First World War* (London, 1957), p. 19; H. Nicolson, *Curzon: The Last Phase 1919-1925* (London, 1934), p. 330; FO Handbook, no. 59, *Anatolia*, pp. 90-1; *Hansard*, 5th Ser. 1911, XXIII, pp. 629, 632.

78. H.H. Cumming, *Franco-British Rivalry in the Post-War Near East* (Oxford, 1938) p. 11; Gottlieb, ibid., p. 20; FO Handbook no. 16, *Turkey in Europe*, p. 133; R. de Gontaut-Biron et L. Le Reverend, *d'Angora a Lausanne, Les Etapes d'une Decheance* (Paris, 1924), pp. 224-5 quoted in Cumming, pp. 11-12.

79. Gottlieb, *Studies in Secret Diplomacy*, pp. 21-3; Blaisdell, *European Financial Control*, pp. 3-4; FO Handbook no. 16, *Turkey in Europe*, pp. 63-8, 80, 103.

The Director-General of the Ottoman Bank and the Inspector-General of the Ministry of Justice were British. All the above posts and the arrival of General von Sanders's Military Mission in December 1913, and his command of the Sultan's army,[80] went far to show that the sprawling Turkish Empire had, by 1914, become a semi-colony of the exploiting Great powers. According to Blaisdell, the Council of Public Debt Administration, managed by European representatives, controlled approximately 'a quarter' of the Turkish revenue and more significantly the liquid resources of the country.[81]

The Young Turks failed, therefore, to redeem Turkey from her economic subservience to foreign interests. Neither could they lift her from the morass of backwardness and poverty.

Municipal enterprise, power plants, harbours and sea transport were run by, and for, European capital. External trade was monopolised by foreigners or by Greek, Armenian and Jewish agents. Of more than a thousand merchants registered in Constantinople in 1911, not more than seventy were Turks. The peasantry fared no better. Writing about 'Turkey's unbearable rural conditions', Ahmed Emin has referred to a report made by the chief medical officer of the Third Army in the eastern provinces, according to which 72 per cent of the inhabitants were verminous and those who could read and write constituted only 0.7 per cent of the total — in the villages inhabited by Christian majorities they reached 21 per cent.[82]

Thus the Young Turks disastrously failed in their efforts on both political and economic terms to save the Empire. They could stop neither its dismemberment nor its decay.

They had professed the intention of saving the Empire through Ottomanism, that is, by recruiting all the forces, all the races in the Empire, by arousing Ottoman consciousness and by stressing common Ottoman citizenship. But the idea of Ottoman consciousness or Ottoman citizenship did not prevail. According to Henry Morgenthau, the American ambassador, the races which had been maltreated and massacred by the Turks for centuries could not transform themselves overnight into brothers.[83] They were more likely to be alive to strong feelings of nationalism — their own nationalism. They withstood all blandishments. The Balkan wars blighted the doctrine of Ottomanism. In their turn the Young Turks also abandoned Ottomanism, adopted the concept of national uniformity and indulged in 'Turkification'.

One section of the Young Turks had been imbued, from the very beginning, with Turkish nationalism, which tended to chauvinism.[84] It seems that

80. Gottlieb, ibid, pp. 21, 24; Ryan, *The Last of the Dragomans*, pp. 67, 92, 93.
81. Blaisdell, *European Financial Control*, p. 151.
82. FO Handbook no. 16, *Turkey in Europe*, p. 104; Gottlieb, *Studies in Secret Diplomacy*, pp. 25-6. Emin, *Turkey in the World War*, pp. 83, 81.
83. Henry Morgenthau, *Secrets of the Bosphorus* (London, 1918a), p. 7.
84. See Ryan, *The Last of the Dragomans*, pp. 68, 71; Edwin Pears, *Forty Years in Constantinople*, 2nd edn (London, 1916), pp. 306, 310.

when the aim of regenerating Turkey 'miscarried', and when the nation was, as Morgenthau discovered on his arrival in 1913, more degraded, more impoverished and more dismembered than ever before,[85] the majority of the Young Turks took refuge in extreme nationalist dreams. Indeed, only extreme nationalism amounting to racism could compensate for the failures, degradations and humiliations of the regime. Only Pan-Turanianism or Turkism as a concept of Turkish racial superiority could satisfy the national pride of both the Young Turks and the Turkish people. According to information derived by the British Vice-Consul at Monastir from an 'un-impeachable source', Talaat, the Minister of the Interior, told a secret meeting in 1910 that contrary to the Constitution, equality was an unrealis-able ideal. There could be no question of equality. In his turn, the British ambassador commented that to the Committee of Union and Progress 'Ottoman' evidently meant 'Turk' and that their present policy of 'Ottomanization' was one of pounding the non-Turkish elements in a Turkish mortar. In October 1911, the Congress of the Committee of Union and Progress resolved that 'the nationalities are a *quantité négligeable*'.[86]

Thus Ottomanism was abandoned and the regime was launched into Pan-Turanianism. This open movement was secretly favoured and pro-tected by the Union and Progress government.[87] Ziya Gok Alp, the out-standing figure in the Pan-Turanian movement, who gloried in Attila, was a member of the extremely influential Central Council of the Committee of Union and Progress and a close friend of Talaat. According to Tekin Alp, another of the protagonists of the movement, 'irredentism' had become a political and social 'necessity' for the Turks. Among the objects of Turkish irredentism there figured 'Siberia, the Caucasus, the Crimea, Afghanistan, etc., . . . directly or indirectly under Russian Rule.' Hence the conclusion followed:

> The Pan-Turkish aspirations cannot come to their full development and realisation until the Muscovite monster is crushed . . .

The apologists of political Pan-Turanianism also made use of Pan-Islamism for popular support. Islam might appeal to the reconquest by the Turks of Egypt and North Africa.[88] Evidently Pan-Turanianism could only be realised by national uniformity and at the expense of the Entente powers

85. Morgenthau, *Secrets of the Bosphorus*, p. 7.
86. *BDOW*, IX, I, pp. 208-9, Geary to Lowther, 28 Aug. 1910; ibid., p. 207, Lowther to Grey, 6 Sept. 1910; A.J. Toynbee, *Turkey: A Past and a Future* (London, 1917), p. 24.
87. Emin, *Turkey in the World War*, p. 193.
88. Tekin Alp, 'Thoughts on the Nature and Plan of a Greater Turkey' and 'The Turkish and Pan-Turkish Ideal . . .', quoted in Toynbee, *Past and Future*, pp. 28, 32-3; Lewis, *Emergence of Modern Turkey*, p. 344; Emin, *Turkey in the World War*, p. 195; Uriel Heyd, *Foundations of Turkish Nationalism* (London, 1950), pp. 31, 126; Ziya Gok Alp quoted in Toynbee, *Past and Future*, p. 18.

and especially the destruction of the 'Muscovite monster'.

It was therefore in an atmosphere of failure, frustration and humiliation on the one hand and of yearning for the restoration of national self-respect and prestige on the other that on 8 February 1914 the Ottoman government agreed, after prolonged negotiations, to the Armenian Reform Scheme. What Turkey finally accepted was only a compromise. But was the mood in Turkey receptive of such a Scheme?

During the discussions the Russian government had put forward the project of 1895[89] as the basis of the proposed Scheme. But if the powers did not take into consideration Turkey's own reform scheme, the men in power in Constantinople would sooner 'set all the Provinces ablaze' and go down fighting than submit, the British military attaché reported. In December 1913 Sir Louis Mallet, the ambassador, reported from Constantinople that 'strong' feeling was being shown against any European intervention in the matter of reforms. The Armenian Patriarch had received a threatening letter, an Armenian priest was twice stoned and an Armenian church was daubed red.[90]

Already after the Balkan wars the fear of coming further mischief was 'universal' among all Armenians. No one who knew the Near East could expect that the Turks would not revenge themselves on their Christian neighbours for the defeats they had suffered, the Chairman of one Armenian Association stated in London. Armenians were filled with gloomy anticipation of the fate that awaited them, the Balkan Committee reported.[91]

In December 1913 the Archibishop of Canterbury wrote to Grey, the Foreign Secretary, about the many letters he had been receiving which referred to the peril in which the Armenians believed themselves to lie and asked that all that was possible should be done.[92] Emily Robinson, well-informed,[93] had written to the Archbishop's Chaplain that Boghos Nubar had received threatening letters. The writers declared that if he continued to agitate on the Armenian question in Europe, they would 'destroy his life'. The Patriarch and the editors of *Azatamart,* an Armenian paper in Constantinople, had also been threatened. Earlier, Emily Robinson had again written to the Chaplain, stating in a terrified mood that '*very* serious news' had reached her from Constantinople. The brother of an Armenian doctor living there had said:

89. Proposed by the Great powers but not carried out. It sought to establish in the Eastern *vilayets* governors representative of the people.

90. *BDOW*, X, I, p. 449, Sazonov, circular, 24 May/6 June 1913; ibid., p. 483, Mallet, min. [July 1913]; ibid., p. 535, Mallet to Grey, 1 Dec. 1913.

91. FO 371/1520/68361: G. Hagopian, Arm. Patriotic Association, London, to Grey, 11 Nov. 1912; ibid., no. 51157, encl. in A.G. Symonds to Grey, 29 Nov. 1912.

92. Lambeth Palace Library, Davidson Papers, Box on Armenia, Archb. of Canterbury to Grey, copy, 10 Dec. 1913.

93. See below, p.41.

The Turkish papers unanimously declare that they will not accept European control & c & threaten to annihilate all the Armenians in Turkey if the 6 great powers dare to put pressure upon the Turkish government.

The Archbishop enclosed a copy of this sinister letter to Grey.[94]

The evidence given above and below clearly points to a mood of sheer Turkish hostility towards the Armenian people *before* 1914; and it goes a long way to refute the Turkish claim that the Armenian holocausts and deportations of 1915 (euphemistically called 'resettlements') were simply initiated as military measures to counter Armenian 'treachery' during the war. It appears that the war was only a pretext rather than the cause of these events.

It does not seem that the atmosphere in Turkey became clearer after 8 February 1914. Aneurin Williams,[95] wrote knowledgeably to the British Foreign Secretary about his information that all classes of Christians in Turkey were 'in great fear of a massacre' and that

. . . it is the settled policy of one, at least, of the highest placed Turkish Ministers to rid the country of the subject Christian races, . . .

whom he regarded as 'a weakness to the Empire'.[96] This disturbingly ominous letter was dated September 1914. Already on 2 and 6 August the Turkish government had concluded, on the initiative of a few of its members, a secret deal with Germany. If German assistance to Austria in the Serbian crisis led to war with Russia, Turkey would enter the conflict. In return, Germany pledged to protect any Ottoman territories threatened by Russia. She would, moreover, assist in the abolition of capitulations. Most significantly also:

Germany will secure for Turkey a small correction of her eastern border which shall place Turkey into direct contact with the Moslems of Russia.[97]

But separating Turkey and the 'Moslems of Russia' was a non-Turkish bloc, the mass of the Armenian people, an unassimilable ethnic minority, on whose behalf the continual protestations and admonitions of the European powers had been so irritating for so long. Their land and property might now be used to placate the thousands of discontented Moslems, who had become

94. Davidson Papers, Box on Armenia, E. Robinson to Macmillan (Chaplain), 8 Jan. 1914; ibid., 7 Dec. 1913, original emphasis; ibid., Archb. of Canterbury to Grey, copy, 10 Dec. 1913.
95. See below, p. 47.
96. FO 371/2116/51007, A. Williams to Grey, 18 Sept. 1914.
97. Ulrich Trumpener, *Germany and the Ottoman Empire 1914-1918*, (Princeton, 1968), pp. 15, 28.

refugees following the humiliating Balkan wars.

The uninterrupted decline of Ottoman power and prestige *vis-à-vis* Europe had profoundly shaken the national self-respect and self-confidence of Turkey. So to the men in government in 1914 the coming war seemed to be, according to Ahmed Emin, an exceptional chance to end the undignified role Turkey had so long played. To the nationalist leaders like Ziya Gok Alp it was a means of realising Pan-Turkish dreams.[98]

To the Armenian people it would bring the 'solution' of their 'question': the death of Turkish Armenia.

---

98. Heyd, *Foundations of Turkish Nationalism*, p. 170; Emin, *Turkey in the World War*, pp. 3, 195.

2   The Pro-Armenian Humanitarian Movement up to 1918

A. Concerned Individuals

The agitation over the Bulgarian atrocities in the 1870s had introduced, as never before in British politics, a moral issue. Turkish misgovernment had become a topic of public discussion. On the one hand Disraeli had advocated the 'traditional' policy of Britain — that of upholding the territorial integrity and independence of the Ottoman Empire. The security of India was the keynote of this attitude; in his zeal to protect and champion British interests and prestige in the Middle East, Disraeli had even asserted that 'in truth the whole of the Ottoman Empire is a British Interest'.[1] He had dismissed the atrocities as 'coffeehouse babble', and had maintained that the British government was forced to disapprove the scheme for establishing autonomous states in the Balkans, undoubtedly for fear of Russian influence over these areas. Finally, he had concluded that a deeper sentiment over and above the humanitarian and philanthropic considerations of the British people was 'the determination to maintain the Empire of England'.[2]

The argument between British interests and Turkish misgovernment and the traditional British point of view was given in a most comprehensive but in a more brutally frank way by Sir Henry Elliott, the British ambassador in Constantinople. He had explained his position by arguing that he was being guided by a firm determination 'to uphold the interests of Great Britain'; that those interests were deeply engaged in preventing the disruption of the Turkish Empire was a conviction which he shared in common with the most eminent British statesmen; and that the 'necessity . . . to prevent changes' from occuring in the Turkish Empire was 'not affected by the question whether it was 10,000 or 20,000 persons who perished in the suppression'.[3]

Mid-Victorian Britain, however, was a religious society. Two evangelical revivals and the Oxford movement had made at least one section of the public deeply conscious of moral principles, duties and moral responsibilities. Gladstone, a High Church Anglican, had given expression to popular feeling, when, raising the argument of the Bulgarian atrocities to a higher moral and humanitarian plane, he had asked about the consequence to

---

1. *Hansard*, 3rd Ser. 1877, CCXXXII, 717, 726; G. Buckle (ed.), *The Letters of Queen Victoria 1862-1878* (London, 1926), 2nd Ser., II, p. 572: Beaconsfield to Queen Victoria, 7 Nov. 1877.
2. *Hansard*, 3rd Ser. 1876, CCXXXI, 203; Ibid., 1877, CCXXXII, 721, 726.
3. PP, 1877, XC (Turkey no. 1), p. 197: Elliott to Derby, 4 Sept. 1876.

'civilization and humanity' if British national interests alone were to be the measure of right or wrong for British agents all over the world, and not moral principles also; he had asked about the consequence to 'public order' if such a 'national interests only' standard, set up for Britain, was asserted by every other nation for itself.[4] In his last public speech, pleading for the cause of the persecuted Armenians, Gladstone had once again taken up the humanitarian issue when he had reminded his 6,000-strong audience that the ground on which they all stood was not British, nor European, but human. With an intense earnestness he had pointed to the grave human and moral responsibility in the tragedy when he had added that the massacres of the Christians in the Ottoman Empire and the impudence of their denial would continue just as long as Europe was 'contented to bear it'. In Victorian minds, humanitarian interest and moral responsibility were contrasted to selfishness. Gladstone blamed selfish passions and especially selfish fears for keeping one section of the British people inaccessible to a knowledge of the real conditions in the Eastern countries.[5]

In his last years Gladstone had felt himself 'incessantly hammered' by the Armenian massacres of the 1890s and confessed that he could not keep his thoughts off the subject. His condemnation of the Turk as directly responsible for the mischief was outright: the Devil himself could not have shown more intense wickedness. But he was also tremendously aware of the moral and human responsibility of the European public and powers, and of their indirect share in the continuation of the massacres: an 'incredible and indelible disgrace' lay 'somewhere' — besides the indescribable odium, which lay on the Sultan whose infamy as the 'great wholesale murderer' was plain. Evasion of moral responsibility was a disgrace. In Gladstone's view, the British government had shrunk back from 'duty and honour'; and the attitude of Rosebery, his successor as Prime Minister, not to press coercive measures on Turkey had greatly helped the process to sever him from Liberalism as it stood.[6]

Another public figure, the Duke of Argyll, like Gladstone a survivor of the Crimean War Cabinet, had joined his voice to that of the latter by also decrying material things and emphasising that men had duties, as well as rights and interests, in the politics of Eastern Europe. The doctrine that the welfare of the subject populations of the Porte was quite a secondary consideration compared with the policy of maintaining and defending the government of the Sultan, was induced by motives of assumed 'self-interest of the narrowest kind' which were as 'short sighted as they were immoral'.[7]

To the argument of the general consideration of moral issues in politics,

4. *Hansard,* 3rd Ser. 1877, CCXXXIII, 605.
5. *The Times,* 25 Sept. 1896, p. 5, cols. 1-2; MS Bryce 10, f.13, Gladstone to Bryce, 6 Oct. 1877.
6. Ibid., ff. 147, 160 165-6, Gladstone to Bryce, 14 Apr. 1895, 5 Jan. 1896, 25 Nov. 1896 respectively.
7. Duke of Argyll, *The Eastern Question* (London, 1879), I, pref. xiv; ibid., II, pp. 203-4.

brought in mainly by the Bulgarian agitation, was added a sense of direct moral responsibility, 'indignation' and even of 'shame' by the Armenian massacres of 1894-6. The protagonists of this view argued that Britain, by substituting the Cyprus Convention and the Berlin Treaty for the Treaty of San Stefano, was under the 'heaviest national obligations'. Britain had choked off Russia, the 'only Power' which had the means and disposition to secure the fulfilment of any promises of reforms in the Eastern Provinces. She alone could give the protection which was possible under the 'inexorable conditions' of the physical geography of the country. Britain had, however, replaced the Treaty of San Stefano by the Cyprus Convention, without asking or offering any security for the execution of Turkey's promises to introduce reforms in Armenia. At Berlin, moreover, Britain had been instrumental in substituting for Turkey's promise to Russia, another promise, an 'absurd' one, to let all the powers superintend the application of reforms in a remote and very inaccessible country. The Turk with his sharp cunning must have concluded that while Britain was clearly excited in her opposition to Russia, she was comparatively careless about any changes in the Turkish system of government, and that practically the Christian population of Armenia were left entirely at his mercy.[8] The Duke of Argyll, a stern Protestant, had concluded that the massacres of the 1890s were the terrible consequences of all this selfish folly. That these holocausts were but the necessary price to be paid for a policy essential to British national interests was an 'abominable' and 'immoral' doctrine which had plunged this country into a great and conspicuous 'national humiliation'. Britain was under the heaviest national obligations arising out of her active and repeated interventions in favour of the Ottoman government. These obligations were 'patent and undeniable'.[9]

Thus, the Bulgarian atrocities of 1876 and the widespread Armenian massacres of 1894-6 had made the British public deeply aware of the misgovernment of the Turkish Empire and had aroused a genuine interest in the identity and the history of these oppressed peoples, who, to some sections of religious Victorians, also had the attraction of being Christian. In addition, they had introduced the moral issue into foreign policy and had also bred, at least among some groups, a strong sense of responsibility, obligation and even guilt.

It was a generation imbued with moral and humanitarian principles and inspired by Gladstonian Liberalism which took up the Armenian question in the early twentieth century. James Bryce (Viscount from 1914), Lady Frederick Cavendish, Noel and Harold Buxton, Aneurin Williams, T.P. O'Connor, Emily Robinson and their associates were all followers of such a tradition.

8. Duke of Argyll, *Our Responsibilities for Turkey* (London, 1896), pp. 1, 163; ibid., pp. 77, 71, 74, 72, 78, 76
9. Ibid., pp. 79, 147, 153-4, 163.

In 1877 Bryce had intended to beg from Gladstone the honour of being permitted to dedicate his book *Transcaucasia and Ararat* to him as a 'slight tribute of gratitude' for what he had done 'in awakening our callous national conscience'. But several friends had urged that this might give the book somewhat of a party character, and so injure whatever small usefulness it might have as an attempt to give an impartial account of Russian and Turkish rule in the countries he had visited. So Bryce had foregone the personal gratification of associating the book with Gladstone's name.[10] Likewise, many persons working for the cause of Armenia during and just after the First World War would proudly recall either their association with Gladstone or his views on that Question. Thus, Major Robert Peel, MP for Suffolk, Woodbridge Division, recalled that he had been to Hawarden in September 1896 on some other subject, but had found the great statesman entirely absorbed in the thought of Armenia. He had told him that just as when a young man his interests had been absorbed in the freedom of Italy, so in his old age he felt that his first obligation was towards the martyred people of Armenia. T.P. O'Connor, MP for Liverpool, Scotland Division, recalled that a friend of his was present at the last public meeting Gladstone had ever addressed. He had come to Liverpool 'a huddled-up figure' and had pleaded the cause of the Armenians.[11]

Bryce, the statesman and great man of letters, whose 'penetrating' eyes peering out from under 'bushy' eyebrows would remind Arnold Toynbee, the Oxford historian, of a Scottish terrier, and whose simplicity and perennial youthfulness would greatly impress him during the war years,[12] had been one of the few Englishmen to have had first-hand knowledge of the Armenian people and of one part of the Caucasus and the Ottoman Empire. He had gone to Transcaucasia in the autumn of 1876, had ascended to the summit of Mount Ararat where, according to the Scripture narrative of the Flood the ark had rested, and had returned along the Black Sea coast, from Poti to Constantinople. He had been led there by his wide political, historical and geographical interests, but as a practising Protestant, he could not have been unmindful of the biblical connections of the areas he visited.

A great traveller and mountaineer, Bryce had apparently been absolutely fascinated by the 'incomparable majesty' of Ararat. Once on its top he had viewed the plains below and around where seemed to lie the whole 'cradle of the human race', from Mesopotamia in the south to the great wall of the Caucasus in the north. he had also been able to distinguish at an abysmal depth below, the valley of the river Araxes which Armenian legend had selected as the seat of Paradise.

Bryce confessed that he knew nothing 'so sublime' as the general aspect of Ararat seen from the surrounding plains. There were but few other places in

10. MS Bryce 11, ff. 11-12, Bryce to Gladstone, 22 Sept. (1877).

11. *Hansard*, 5th Ser. 1918, vol. 110, col. 3257; ibid., 1922, vol. 150, col. 161.

12. A.J. Toynbee, *Acquaintances* (London, 1967), pp. 154-5.

the world where so lofty a peak, about 17,000 feet, soared so suddenly from a plain so low, 2,000-3,000 feet above the sea, and consequently few views equally grand. The great summits of the Himalayas, like those of the Alps and the Atlas, rose from behind high spurs and therefore lost to the eye a good deal of their real height. In the case of Ararat one's eye was not diverted by the variety of points of interest: all the lines led straight up to the towering, snowy summit. The very simplicity of both form and colour increased its majesty; no view filled the beholder with a profounder sense of grandeur. Certainly no one who had seen it rising in solitary majesty far above all its attendant peaks, and knowing the story of the Flood, could doubt that its summit must have first pierced the receding waves.[13]

Bryce described Ararat as being, to the Armenians, the ancient sanctuary of their faith, the centre of their once famous kingdom, 'hallowed by a thousand traditions'.[14]

Exploring the homelands of the Armenians, Bryce was aware of many biblical connections and religious legends and traditions. Erevan,[15] built of clay or plastered brick, claimed to have been founded by Noah, as its name in Armenian was said to mean 'the Apparent', as evidence that it was the first dry land the patriarch had seen. He had also visited the famous monastery of Etchmiadzin, which claimed to be the oldest monastic foundation in the world. It had been the ecclesiastical metropolis of the Armenian nation since the year 302, when, according to tradition, the first Christian church in Armenia was founded there by Saint Gregory the Illuminator, on the spot where the Saviour was said to have descended in a ray of light; and the word Etchmiadzin meant in Armenian, 'The only-begotten descended'. After the loss of their political independence in Armenia, and, as Bryce put it, through many centuries of oppression, the bulk of the race had turned to the sacred walls of Etchmiadzin as to an ark alone visible amid the rising flood of Mohammedan dominion. Doubtless, the neighbourhood of the holy mountain had added sensibly to the veneration which this oldest seat of their faith had commanded from all Armenians.[16]

Bryce had seen Armenians everywhere in Transcaucasia from Tiflis to Erevan. His impressions of them, given in his book *Transcaucasia and Ararat*, must have had considerable influence on public opinion in Britain. The book, described as one of the 'classics of travel', had had three editions within two years, 1877 and 1878. 'Everyone seems greatly struck with your great exploit on Mount Ararat', Gladstone had commented.[17] In 1896, Bryce had revised the book and had added a supplementary chapter on the

13. James Bryce, *Transcaucasia and Ararat*, 4th edn (London, 1896), pp. 190, 263, 329, 298, 293, 246, 247, 217.

14. Ibid., p. 249.

15. Successor to the Urartian Erebuni, see above, p. 1.

16. Bryce, *Transcaucasia and Ararat*, pp. 188, 191, 311, 314, 334, 329.

17. H.A.L. Fisher, *James Bryce* (London, 1927), I, p. 161; MS Bryce 10, f.17, Gladstone to Bryce, 29 Dec. 1877.

Armenian question for its fourth edition.

Bryce had found the Armenians usually strong and well-made, and the women 'often strikingly handsome', with fine dark eyes. He believed the Armenians to be the 'most vigorous and intelligent' of the Transcaucasian races and by far the most industrious. They were indeed an 'extraordinary people', tenaciously holding onto their national identity. A race that had endured so steadfastly must have 'bone and sinew' in it.[18] In the eastern provinces of Turkey their occupation was mainly agricultural and pastoral. In the Caucasus, although their vigorous life had chiefly expressed itself in practical directions, most of all in money-making, Bryce stressed that many Armenians had entered the civil or military service in Russia, and some had risen to posts of high dignity. He quoted the example of Loris Melikov, the commander of the invading Russian army in Asia in 1877. Melikov had been raised afterwards to be Chief Minister and was the prompter of the liberal policy of the latter years of Alexander II, but was overthrown by an intrigue.[19]

Yet the condition of these people in the Asiatic provinces of Turkey, Bryce commented, could not be more pitiable. On his return home, he had travelled along the Black Sea coast, and he despaired of conveying the impression of melancholy. A country blessed with every gift of nature, now was all 'silence, poverty, despair'. Everyone had the same answer as to its cause: 'misgovernment, or rather no government'. Bryce did not mince his words. He believed that the Turkish government 'deserves to die'. Yet in 1877 he did not think that the Armenians could have more than autonomy in Turkey.[20]

In the supplementary chapter to the fourth edition of his book published in 1896, the year which had seen, as he put it, the extinction of a large part of the Armenian people, Bryce reviewed their worsening condition and blamed the fatal inaction of the European powers. Before the Treaty of Berlin the Sultan had no special enmity towards the Armenians, nor had the Armenian nation any political aspirations. It was the stipulations then made for their protection that had marked them out for suspicion, and aroused in them hopes of deliverance. Under the Treaty of Berlin, the six powers had done 'nothing'. Britain, having undertaken a separate responsibility, had an 'uneasy conscience', and sought to quiet it by incessant remonstrances. But these remonstrances irritated the 'tiger' who decided to make the proposed reforms useless by killing those for whose benefit they were intended. Bryce was stern and unflinching in his judgement: a large part, and, in many districts, the best part, of the Armenians, a people who had maintained their nationality from time immemorial, 'before history began to be written', had

18. Bryce, *Transcaucasia and Ararat*, pp. 340, 463, 109, 430, 329, 345.
19. Ibid., pp. 463, 342, 342n.
20. Ibid., pp. 343, 400, 428; see also ibid., pp. 336, 344, 431-3.

been destroyed. This destruction 'might have been averted by the Powers of Europe'.[21]

Another Briton, H.F.B. Lynch, had also written on Armenia. His weighty two-volume book, *Armenia: Travels and Studies,* was an extensive account of two separate journeys lasting thirteen months altogether, which he had undertaken in 1893-4 and in 1898, in both Russian and Turkish Armenia. Like Bryce, he had ascended to the summit of Mount Ararat. He too had been fascinated by its 'majestic structure', the combination of grace with extraordinary solidity, upon which 'eye and mind dwell'.[22] He had visited and studied the ruined monuments of Ani, once the capital of the Armenian kingdom in the ninth and tenth centuries. He had commented on the 'love' and 'craft' of building of the ancient Armenians and on the 'excellent' and 'exquisite' masonry of some of the walls. He had particularly admired the cathedral of Ani, a momument to the 'conceptions of genius' of the Armenian people, completed, according to inscriptions, in 1010. Built in the early eleventh century, it had 'many of the characteristics of the Gothic style' — the pointed arch and the coupled piers — which became widespread in Europe only in the thirteenth century. Lynch was emphatic that the cathedral, a building of 'the highest artistic merit', denoted a standard 'which was far in advance of the contemporary standards in the West'.[23] He believed, however, that the development of the Armenians had been tragically arrested since the Seljuk conquest. Their genius had been exploited by the semi-barbarous peoples of Asia, while their abilities and character had progressively declined and become debased. If Lynch were asked what characteristics distinguished the Armenians from other Orientals, he would be disposed to stress their 'grit'. In this respect they were not surpassed by any European nation. Their intellectual capacities were supported by a solid foundation of character. But in order to estimate their true worth, they should be studied not in the Levant, with its widespread corruption, but in their homelands in Armenia.[24]

Sir Edwin Pears, a universally-recognised authority on Turkey, who had been the correspondent of the *Daily News* since the Bulgarian atrocities, and who would, in 1915, write about his *Forty Years in Constantinople,* had also his share in introducing the Armenians to the British public, in his work *Turkey and Its People,* published in 1911.

Pears, who had mostly lived in Constantinople, had known the Armenians as the 'most artistic' people in Turkey with a natural taste for art and a love for music and acting. They were an ancient Indo-European

21. Ibid., pp. 446, 523-5.

22. H.F.B. Lynch, *Armenia: Travels and Studies* (London, 1901), I, p. 150.

23. Ibid., I, pp. 127, 384, 372, 372n, 392, 373. According|to S. Der|Nersessian (*Armenian Art,* London, 1978), pp. 99, 101, the construction of the cathedral was completed in 1001 and its resemblance to Gothic churches is superficial.

24. Lynch, *Armenia: Travels and Studies,* I, pp. 391, 465-7.

people who had held their own against Persians, Arabs, Turks and Kurds. Stiff-necked, they had a toughness about them which prevented their being 'broken'. He believed that they had 'great mental capacity'. The Greeks might excel them in quickness of perception and vivacity but the Armenian had a 'steadiness, a thoughtfulness, and a canniness about him which was of value'.[25]

Yet this race, which under Turkish rule 'only asked' for the protection of life and property, was being fiercely persecuted. Discussing the Armenian massacres of the 1890s, Pears discerned four main causes, all of which had been in operation for years. He first blamed a traditional feeling among Moslem Turks that they had the right to plunder Christians. There also was the superior industry and thrift of the Armenians which had enabled them to become generally wealthier than their neighbours, who thus coveted their possessions. Then, their thirst for education had induced them to be less tolerant than they had formerly been of periodical robbery and outrages upon their women. Lastly, Pears blamed a series of petty persecutions by Turks and Kurds, the impossibility of obtaining redress, the resulting emigration of many Armenians to Russia and America and the formation of revolutionary committees outside Turkey. In despair of obtaining justice, a few Armenians within the Empire had joined these committees. These bodies had given Abdul Hamid the excuse for massacre. Pears insisted that the influence of the foreign revolutionary committees was greatly exaggerated. The massacres in Armenia in the 1890s and those in Cilicia in 1909, like those in Bulgaria in 1876 and in Chios in 1822, were 'cold-blooded' slaughters by 'inferior' races, perpetrated for the purpose of plunder and in the name of religion. The victims were 'not rebels'.[26]

The interest of Lady Frederick Cavendish, for long years the President of 'The Friends of Armenia', was mainly based on Christian piety and humanitarianism, her total admiration and devotion to Gladstone and the causes he championed, and in a general way, to Liberal views. But as the editor of her *Diary* points out, she was 'not' primarily a politician. She was 'primarily a Churchwoman'. As such she never ceased to feel a passionate sympathy for the 'unfortunate' Armenians. She was indefatigable in urging upon Prime Ministers and Foreign Secretaries the 'duty' and necessity of protecting these people.

Besides the obligation she felt as a Christian towards the Armenians, she was also attracted to them because of her personal links with the Liberal Party and Gladstone, both of whom were supporting the Christian subjects of the Sultan. Lady Frederick's husband had been an 'advanced Liberal'. He had been Private Secretary to Gladstone and was acting as Chief Secretary of Ireland when he was murdered. She herself was Gladstone's niece by marriage. She had entered enthusiastically into nearly all the crusades he

25. Edwin Pears, *Turkey and Its People* (London, 1911), pp. 274-5, 270-1, 276.
26. Ibid., pp. 276-7, 280, 294.

had embraced. It seems that she had adored Gladstone for his solid virtues: his face was 'like a prophet's in its look of faith and strength' and he gave her the impression of 'an oak' to lean against.[27]

Another champion of the Armenians, but one who had not been to Armenia, and had come to know about it only through Gladstone, was Miss Emily John Robinson. She herself has described how she had come to take up the cause of Armenia. Her father was Sir John R. Robinson, of the London *Daily News*, who was greatly interested in Armenia. She remembered well how in 1895-6 he had sent out special correspondents who had described the dreadful massacres in the columns of that paper. It was then that, she recalled, Gladstone had lifted up his strong voice on behalf of Armenia. A stern moralist, Miss Robinson believed that to know of a crime and to be a party to hushing it up was in itself a crime.[28] In 1913 she published a booklet, *The Truth About Armenia* and would also write *Armenia and the Armenians* in 1916.

The interest in Armenia of Noel Buxton, MP for North Norfolk from 1910, and of the Reverend Harold Buxton, had also a strongly Gladstonian and humanitarian basis. The great grandfather of the Buxton brothers, the first Sir Thomas Fowell Buxton, called 'Liberator', had been busy over poverty in the East End of London and later had taken up slavery at the request of Wilberforce. Their grandmother, Catherine Buxton, was one of the Quaker Gurneys. Both brothers had imbibed the Gladstonian tradition in the Buxton home, where Disraeli's pro-Turkish policy had been viewed with horror.[29] Both had been educated at Trinity College, Cambridge. The tall and humorous Harold Buxton, a truly humble person, deeply interested in people,[30] had entered the Church. Noel Buxton, in his turn, had helped to found the Balkan Committee in 1903 and had become its Chairman, while Bryce had occupied the position of President. After the latter's appointment as ambassador to the United States, Noel had become President. At the beginning of the First World War, Noel Buxton had been sent by the British Cabinet on a semi-official mission to the Balkan countries to try to bring them in on the side of the Entente. During this mission, while in Bucharest, he had been shot through the jaw by a Young Turk. In order to conceal the scar, he had henceforth worn a beard, which in later years would enhance his fine, elder-statesman-like appearance.[31]

In the autumn of 1913, the two brothers travelled together and 'explored'

27. John Bailey (ed.), *The Diary of Lady Frederick Cavendish* (London, 1927), I, Preface and Intro., xxiii, xxi, xx; ibid., II, pp. 318, 331.

28. *Ararat* (London), vol. I, no. 2 (Aug. 1913), 40-2. See a copy in FO 371/1773/39463, enc. by Miss Robinson.

29. N. Buxton Papers, private possession: N. Buxton, 'On our Ancestors', 4 June 1941; ibid., 'My Occupation', n.d. Mosa Anderson, *Noel Buxton: A Life* (London, 1952), pp. 57, 32.

30. I owe this information to Mrs Sarah Hogg, niece of the Rev. Harold Buxton, given on 3 Nov. 1979.

31. T.P. Conwell-Evans, *Foreign Policy from a Back Bench 1904-1918* (Oxford, 1932), pp. 88-90; Anderson, *Buxton*, pp. 33, 37, 66-7.

both Turkish and Russian Armenia and Persia. They published their impressions in 1914 in *Travel and Politics in Armenia*. Both, however, knew the working of the Turkish Empire quite well. The Reverend Harold Buxton had acted as an agent of relief funds in European Turkey, while Noel Buxton had been travelling in Turkey for the tenth time.

The Reverend Harold Buxton confessed that he had gone to Armenia considerably prejudiced against Armenians. They were known as expert and pushing traders in European towns and Anglo-Indians even credited them with being as 'smart' in a 'deal' as either Greeks or Jews. The Armenian was not, as a rule, able to get much sympathy from English travellers because he was not a sportsman, and he was 'apt to cringe'. Moreover, his heavy gold watch-chain did not add charm to the general impression. Yet after the surprises and discoveries of his journey Harold Buxton had come 'to revise' his former opinion, and to think that the real cause of jealousy of the Armenian was his success. To begin with, the commercial classes who settled abroad and became cosmopolitan should not be taken as typical of the nation. Not all Armenians were usurers or even men of business. They were really an agricultural race, and by far the larger part of them were peasants. Armenians were seen to the best advantage in their own country. The Armenian peasant, as the Buxtons had seen him in Turkish and Russian Armenia, was a fine stalwart fellow, virile and persistent and with an 'extraordinary love' of cultivating the soil. That they were cowardly as a race was a fiction, based on the evidence that unarmed men were unable to defend themselves against their oppressors. The best type of Armenian, and one not infrequently met in the country, was, as described by Harold Buxton, tall, square and dark, rather silent, slow and deliberate in speech. His sparkling black eyes bespoke resolution and intensity of purpose. A desperate man when his honour or that of his nation was at stake, he was made of the 'metal' which had produced warriors and fighters like the heroes of Zeitun, in Cilicia, who had 'never' surrendered to the Turkish yoke.[32]

With a profound humanity, Harold Buxton argued that it was recognised in the West that the uncertainties of industrial life could paralyse the force and will of a man. Uncertainty 'multiplied tenfold' obtained in Armenia. An Armenian peasant never knew when his home might be raided and all his savings carried off. His children might never grow up to inherit the fruit of his labour. Yet in the face of this the race survived; for Harold Buxton this was 'extraordinary'. He explained it by the 'persistent optimism' of the Armenian peasant who showed an astonishing power to believe that from a wreck there was always something saved, out of which to build anew.[33]

Noel Buxton, unlike his brother a politician, concluded, after this travel,

32. Noel Buxton and Harold Buxton, *Travel and Politics in Armenia* (London, 1914), pp. 64, 31, 30, 32.
33. Ibid., pp. 36, 37.

that with allowance for every fault, Armenians were a people most certainly fit for civilisation, who, however, were being artificially subjected to a system unfitted even for the government of 'savages'[34]

Both brothers had been aware in 1913 that a stream of Armenian refugees continually crossed the frontier from Turkish Armenia to Russian Armenia. At a frontier post they were actually told in October 1913 that more than 7,000 Armenian emigrants had arrived since January of that year. The great question of the lands seized by the Kurds in the massacre days, a 'vast robbery', was still unremedied even after five years of 'constitutional' rule. The more positive side of the Turkish evil was conspicuous in the policy of placing *mohajirun* — Moslem refugees from the Balkans — among Christians. This method was in force in 'numbers' of villages.[35]

The Buxtons concluded, most emphatically, that the solution, by Turkish reform from within, should be discarded, judiciously but absolutely. The evidence was final and damning. It was necessary to find the path towards 'actual European control'.[36]

Having also explored Russian Armenia, the Buxtons were aware of the 'amazing contrast' between Russian and Turkish Armenia. On a fine evening in September, Noel Buxton had taken a drive from Erevan, near Ararat in Russian Armenia, to see the Armenian villages in the Araxes valley. The plain, irrigated, looked like the rich land one saw in Belgium, but here growing vines, rice and cotton. In one of the villages he had stopped to see the priest, had sat on his balcony and had remarked on the prosperity of the priest's flock. He had agreed but had commented on the refugees from Turkey constantly arriving, driven out by violence. With a deep sense of guilt Buxton had been intensely aware that the 'tide of civilisation' had apparently 'paused' at the particular line of hills stretching to the east of Ararat: at the Russo-Turkish frontier only because the Great powers and in particular Britain had guaranteed it by the Cyprus Convention and the Berlin Treaty. He had, moreover, realised that had Russia not been baulked the great massacres would not have occurred.[37]

In order to be able more fully to consider the question of a Russian mandate to superintend reform in Armenia, the Buxton brothers had followed their visit by a stay in Poland. With no blindness to the inefficient cruelty of the Russian bureaucrats, and in spite of it, they had recorded their confirmed opinion that a Russian occupation of Armenia would unquestionably be to the good. Any evil would be preferable to the state of Turkish Armenia, where the Buxtons' concern had been for 'security of life, and property, and domestic honour'.[38]

34. Ibid., p. 121.
35. Ibid., pp. 44-5, 2, 8, 110-13, 116-17.
36. Ibid., pp. 122, 139.
37. Ibid., pp. 66-8, 140-4, 133.
38. Ibid., pp. 156, 157-8.

At the beginning of the twentieth century, therefore, there was quite a strong nucleus of people in British society who were deeply interested in Armenia. There were some who for humanitarian reasons felt Christian compassion for the sufferings of the Armenians. There were others who, following a Gladstonian tradition, believed that little peoples should not be allowed to be trampled by tyrannical and cruel governments. Some others felt a debt of honour arising out of the British obligations incurred by the Cyprus Convention and the Berlin Treaty. There were also a few others who actually knew about Armenia and the Armenians and believed that the natural development of this people was being unjustly baulked. With his high esteem of their merits, Bryce even believed that the regeneration of Asia Minor 'must devolve on the Armenians'.[39]

While exploring the views and activities of the more prominent pro-Armenian individuals and pressure groups at the beginning of the twentieth century, this chapter is not a discussion of pro-Armenian public opinion. If it were, it would include a detailed examination of the press: an indication of which papers were most interested in, gave most space to and were the best informed about, the Armenian question — that might be the subject of another study. Nor does it assess the degree of success in quality and quantity of these pressure groups in creating a pro-Armenian public opinion. That would be almost impossible to do because, as will be shown, the government, under war conditions, had an interest in, and also contributed to building up, such an opinion.

B. Pressure Groups

One of the earliest and oldest British societies conspicuous for sympathy with, and help for, Armenia in the twentieth century was the Friends of Armenia, founded in London in 1897. Lady Frederick Cavendish was the President,[40] and Miss E. Cantlow, the Secretary. Its General Committee included members from Belfast, Perth, Paisley and Edinburgh. Its organ, the *Friend of Armenia* — a quarterly — had started publication in February 1900. The Society described itself as one of the 'Relief Agencies', and its work as 'an effort at reconstruction' in Armenia.

Although it was a Relief Agency, it could not refrain from impinging on politics. It had to explain the need to organise relief. Thus, commenting on the death of the Duke of Argyll, who had been the President of the Scottish Armenian Association since its foundation in 1895, the *Friend of Armenia* stressed that the keynote of his book *Our Responsibilities for Turkey* was

39. Fisher, *Bryce*, I. p. 184.
40. The Hon. Mrs A.G. Fraser and Mrs Alfred Booth were the Vice-Presidents, E. Wright Brooks was the Chairman of the Committee and Hector Munro-Ferguson, the Treasurer. See *Friend of Armenia* no. 1 (Feb. 1900).

British *'national responsibility'* for what had taken place in Armenia. For three whole years, from 1905 to 1908, the organ of the Friends of Armenia quoted, on the top of the first page of every issue, the 61st Article of the Berlin Treaty and the 1st Article of the Cyprus Convention, under the heading of 'England's Treaty Obligations to Armenia'.[41] When hopes aroused in 1909 did not materialise and conditions went from bad to worse in the Eastern Provinces during and after the Balkan wars, Lady Frederick Cavendish wrote a 'private' letter to Grey pleading for help. What was to become of the Armenians, for whose protection England was *'doubly pledged'* by the Treaty of Berlin and by the Cyprus Convention? It seemed impossible to doubt, Lady Frederick maintained, that if no immediate measures were taken to protect them, extermination must be their fate, to the 'lasting shame' of Europe and, to a special degree, of England.[42]

Besides the Friends of Armenia there had also been an Anglo-Armenian Association, founded by Bryce in 1893. Francis S. Stevenson, MP was its first President. Its aim was to secure 'the execution' of Article 61 of the Treaty of Berlin. Edward Atkin was still its Honorary Secretary in 1912.[43]

In 1896 there had been organised the International Association of the Friends of Armenia with which was incorporated the Information (Armenia) Bureau. Its objects were (i) to furnish information upon the subject of Armenia, by means of a Central Depot for the publication and diffusion of literature; (ii) to supply the means of inter-communication between the various societies engaged in Armenian relief. The Bishop of Rochester was the President of the Association, and the Lady Henry Somerset, the Honorary Secretary. In 1897 its Information Bureau was established at No. 3 Bridge Street, Westminster, opposite the Houses of Parliament.[44]

The Armenians in Britain also had their own political societies. There had been an Armenian Patriotic Association in London, on whose behalf M. Sevasly had written letters to Bryce in 1888. In 1912 its Chairman was G. Hagopian.[45]

Another Armenian society was the Armenian United Association of London, founded in 1898 and reconstructed in 1913. Its Presidents during

41. Ibid., no. 1 (Feb. 1900), p. 16; ibid., no. 2 (June 1900), p. 1, original emphasis. See ibid., nos 23-35 (Autumn 1905-Autumn 1908).

42. FO 371/1773/6585: F. Cavendish to Grey, 16 Jan. 1913, original emphasis. For Grey's reply see above, pp.9-10.

43. See Bryce Papers, UB 66, Official Paper of Anglo-Armenian Association, 31 Jan. 1893; see also FO 371/1520/46286, Atkin to FO, 30 Oct. 1912.

44. See Bryce Papers, UB 66, Advance Proof of International Association of the Friends of Armenia.

45. Ibid., UB 63, Sevasly to Bryce, on Armenian Patriotic Association Paper, 23 May, 1 June 1888; FO 371/1520/48361, G. Hagopian to Grey, 11 Nov. 1912.

the First World War years were first Lieutenant-Colonel G.M. Gregory, and then James A. Malcolm, and the Honorary Secretary A. Yeretsian. It edited the periodical *Ararat: A Searchlight on Armenia.*[46]

In May 1918, the formation of an Armenian Bureau of Information was reported and pro-Armenian Britons welcomed its 'importance and value'. Its typescript papers on the various aspects of the Armenian question were written by Aram Raffi, the son of the well-known Armenian novelist. They contributed substantially to feeding information to interested groups. After Raffi's death in November 1919, the Armenian Bureau was placed under the direction of Arshak Safrastian.[47]

Even a British-Armenian Chamber of Commerce was inaugurated on 27 April 1920 in the hall of the Worshipful Company of Grocers. E.A. Brayley Hodgetts was the Chairman of the Council.[48]

But during 1915-23, the most active and influential political group was the British Armenia Committee, apparently an offshoot of the Balkan Committee of 1903 whose Chairman in 1912 was Noel Buxton, MP. With the victory of the Balkan nations over Turkey and the liberation of the Christian populations of the Empire in Europe, the Balkan Committee had now turned its attention to Armenia and a 'Special Committee' had just been formed to 'watch and promote the interests of Armenia' in the approaching settlement after the war. In a memorandum enclosed in a covering letter from Arthur G. Symonds, Secretary to the Balkan Committee, the (Balkan) Committee argued that thwarted in the Balkans, and filled with hatred and fury against the Christians who had defeated them, the Turks would be tempted to wreak their vengeance on the helpless Armenians unless it be prevented. To prevent it was the 'bounden duty' of all the powers, but especially of Great Britain. The practical remedy proposed was to apply the system of government established in the Lebanon by the statute of 1864. Under that statute the governor was appointed by the Sultan for five years but only after agreement with the ambassadors of the Great powers at Constantinople. What the Committee and the Armenians themselves simply asked for was good government, the memorandum added.[49]

Apparently, the British Armenia Committee was formed some time

46. *Ararat*, vol. 5, no. 55 (Jan. 1918), 290; also vol. 6, no. 59 (June-July 1918), cover.
47. Rhodes House Library, MSS British Empire S.22/G506, *British Armenia Committee* (hereafter *BAC*) *Minutes,* Oct. 1915-Feb. 1921; *BAC Propaganda Sub-Committee Minutes,* June-Nov. 1920. Bristol University Library, *BAC Minutes,* Feb. 1921-May 1924. Quoted in *BAC Minutes,* 2 May 1918. See Lambeth Palace Library, Canon J.A. Douglas Papers, vol. 61, ff.62-95, for Armenian Bureau Papers nos. 1-11; *Ararat*, vol. 6, no. 68 (Nov.-Dec. 1919), 538, 592-4.
48. Ibid., vol. 6, no. 69 (1920), 15.
49. FO 371/1520/51157, memo. by Balkan Comm., enc. in Symonds to Grey, 29 Nov. 1912.

between 29 November 1912 and 30 January 1913. On 30 January 1913, Symonds again wrote to Grey, but this time as Secretary to the British Armenia Committee.[50] The Chairman of the Committee was Aneurin Williams, JP. The son of a family with a business of ironworks in Middlesbrough, and himself a partner in Linthorpe Ironworks, Williams had been educated at London University and St John's College, Cambridge and had been called to the Bar but had never practised. A man of broad human sympathies, whose horizon knew no boundaries of colour, race or creed, he devoted his energies to the League of Nations Union, the International Cooperative Alliance, the Proportional Representation Society, the Land Nationalisation Society and the Balkan Committee.[51] He had been a Liberal MP for Plymouth in 1910 and was elected for North-west Durham in 1914. His excellent knowledge of the French language must have served him well in communicating with the Armenian leaders on the Continent.

As Chairman of the newly-formed British Armenia Committee, Aneurin Williams explained that the Committee was 'a small body of Englishmen', some of whom had 'first-hand' knowledge of Armenia and the East, all of whom had given special attention to the question, and had special means of coming in contact with the leaders of the Armenian people. At the time of the formation of the Committee one influential member of the Balkan Committee described Williams as a politician 'conspicuous for ability and self-effacement'.[52] Over the years, beginning from its formation in 1913 until its apparent dissolution in May 1924, a period during which both Britain and especially Armenia went through momentous oscillations, there necessarily were changes both in the aims of the Committee and its membership,[53] but Aneurin Williams remained, despite his repeated wishes to resign owing to his health, the 'self-sacrificing' Chairman, always showing a 'devoted and passionate' interest in the fate of Armenians.[54]

The British Armenia Committee was what its name expressed: a select Committee of Britons or rather Englishmen interested in, and devoted to, the cause of Armenia. It was not a society or a union with mass membership and apparently did not aim at becoming a mass movement. The members of the Committee were co-opted during Committee meetings. Thus Joseph

50. FO 371/1773/4961, Symonds to Grey, 30 Jan. 1913.

51. *Intern. Co-op Bull.* nos. 10, 11 (Oct.-Nov. 1920), 286-8; ibid., no. 2 (Feb 1924), 47; see also *DOD's Parl. Comp.* for 1915.

52. *The Times*, 12 July 1913, p. 7 col. 2; N. Buxton in Buxton, *Travel and Politics in Armenia*, p. 126.

53. See Bryce Papers, UB 64, Symonds to Bryce, 15 Jan. 1914. Early in 1914 the British Armenia Committee included the following MPs: J. Allen Baker, J. Annan Bryce, Noel Buxton, Sir W.P. Byles, G.G. Greenwood, Hugh Law, T.P. O'Connor, Arthur Ponsonby, A. Rowntree, A.F. Whyte and Penry Williams. Other members included Sir Edward Boyle, Bart., C. Roden Buxton, J.M. Dent, G.P. Gooch, Professor J. Rendel Harris, Canon Masterman and Canon C.H. Robinson.

54. *BAC Minutes*, 10 Oct. 1922, 4 Jan., 7 Mar., 29 May 1923; Motion, 29 May 1923; India Office Lib., Curzon Papers, MSS Eur F 112/232, f.46, Curzon to Williams, 6 Dec. 1921.

Bliss was unanimously elected a member on the motion of Noel Buxton. W.G.A. Ormsby-Gore and Sir Samuel Hoare expressed their willingness to join the Committee only when invited to do so by Aneurin Williams.[55] All three were Members of Parliament. It seems that the members of the Committee and their friends, by temperament or by conviction, did not much favour public agitation as a means of political activity. Thus, Lord Robert Cecil, formerly an Assistant Foreign Secretary and Minister of Blockade, advised in 1921 that an influential deputation to the Prime Minister would be more effective than a public meeting.[56] The Committee rather tried to influence by interviews, the submission of memoranda, by articles and letters in the papers and by statements in Parliament, those who were already politically influential and well-established. In 1918 alone, a deputation of the Committee and the Chairman had three interviews with Lord Robert Cecil at the Foreign Office. In 1919 Aneurin Williams, Lord Bryce and T.P. O'Connor had an interview with the Prime Minister. Later, Williams saw Lord Curzon, the Foreign Secretary, and other leading members of the government, as well as the Prime Minister. A deputation of the Committee twice had interviews with M. Krassin, of the Soviet Trade Delegation in London. In addition, memorials and numerous letters were written to both the Foreign Office and Lambeth Palace. In 1921, a memorandum was sent, under the names of the Chairman and Lord Robert Cecil, to all the members of the Imperial Conference.[57]

But public opinion was not disregarded. Thus, during the week ending 24 January 1921, C. Leonard Leese, the Organising Secretary, spoke at Walthamstow, Maidstone, Dorking and Doncaster.[58] Articles and letters were sent to the press more regularly. C.P. Scott, the editor of the *Manchester Guardian*, was a lifelong friend of Bryce, and published in his paper the appeals sent by the latter. G.P. Gooch, the historian, was a member of the British Armenia Committee, and the *Contemporary Review*, which he edited, apparently welcomed articles referring to Armenia. Thus, in 1921-2 alone this journal published articles by Bryce, Arnold Toynbee, Aneurin Williams and Harold Buxton.[59]

The British Armenia Committee did not have any arrangement for subscription from its members and had no funds until the end of 1919. Apparently expenses were met by individual members. Only on 18 December 1919, when it was suggested that a small meeting should be organised in

55. *BAC Minutes,* 15 Nov. 1917; ibid, 7 Mar. 1921.

56. See H.N. Fieldhouse, 'Noel Buxton and A.J.P. Taylor's "The Trouble Makers" ' in Martin Gilbert (ed.), *A Century of Conflict: Essays for A.J.P. Taylor* (London, 1966), pp. 186-7; *BAC Minutes,* 2 May 1921.

57. *BAC Minutes,* 12 Mar., 21 Oct. 1918. Ibid., 18 Dec. 1919, 27 May 1920. *BAC Propaganda Sub-Committee Minutes,* 2 Nov., 23 Nov. 1920; *BAC Minutes,* 20 Dec. 1920, 4 July 1921.

58. Ibid., 24 Jan. 1921.

59. See Bryce Papers, UB 25, Bryce to Scott, 28 Dec. 1921; ibid., 30 Nov. 1917. *Contemporary Review,* 119, (May 1921); 121 (Jan. 1922); 121 (Apr. 1922); 121 (May 1922).

Caxton Hall with 'powerful speakers', was finance first discussed and Noel Buxton was nominated Treasurer. By the end of March 1920 he had already collected £400, had secured an office at 96 Victoria Street and the services of C. Leonard Leese. In June 1920, the Armenian Refugees (Lord Mayor's) Fund bore the whole cost of printing the Committee's two memoranda and circulating them as pamphlets to their 5,000 subscribers.[60] According to the British Armenia Committee's list of receipts from 1 October 1920 to 31 December 1921, Aneurin Williams donated £280, Noel and Harold Buxton Trusts £250, and other members £105.18 towards the Committee's expenses. In the spring of 1920 Boghos Nubar contributed £2,000 and the Armenians in Manchester £1,900. In 1922 there were two donations amounting to £500 through James A. Malcolm, a representative in London of Boghos Nubar's Armenian National Delegation; as well as a donation of £150 by the Delegation, and £682 by Boghos Nubar himself. It was Noel Buxton however, with his character of 'rare' nobility, tender heart and ample means who provided most of the loans essential for the expenses of the Committee.[61]

Between 1 June 1920 and 23 November 1920 the British Armenia Committee also had an active 'Propaganda Sub-Committee'. It met once a week. According to its minutes, Noel Buxton, who was in the Chair, C. Leonard Leese, Arnold Toynbee, the Reverend Harold Buxton, the Reverend J.H. Harris and other members of the British Armenia Committee usually attended. The Sub-Committee drafted a National Memorial which was prepared by Toynbee and finally approved by Dr J. Holland Rose, the Cambridge historian. Toynbee had earlier urged that steps should be taken 'to pin down' the government to the statements made by Lord Curzon as a minimum of what the Committee would demand for Armenia.[62] Having worked during the war in the Intelligence Bureau of the Department of Information and in the Political Intelligence Department of the Foreign Office, and later in the Foreign Office section of the British Delegation to the Peace Conference,[63] Toynbee was a most suitable person for the task. The Sub-Committee also arranged that questions be put by the members of the British Armenia Committee on various aspects of the Armenian question in the House of Commons. In addition to these activities, the Organising Secretary provided the press with articles and letters about Armenia.

60. *BAC Minutes*, 18 Dec. 1919, 23 Mar. 1920; *BAC Propaganda Sub-Committee Minutes*, 15 June 1920.

61. See *BAC Minute-Book;* Archive Centre of Dashnaktsutiun, Boston, Mass., Republic of Armenia Archives, File 336/6, memo. by BAC in N. Buxton to Aharonian, 16 Oct. [1922]; Armenian General Benevolent Union, Saddle Brook, NJ, Armenian National Delegation Papers, microf. Reel 8C/14561, BAC receipts; G.P. Gooch, 'Foreword', in Anderson's *Buxton*, pp. 5, 9.

62. *BAC Propaganda Sub-Committee Minutes*, 1 June, 15 June, 29 Sept. 1920; ibid., 6 July, 20 July 1920; *BAC Minutes*, 18 Dec. 1919.

63. A.J. Toynbee, *The Western Question in Greece and Turkey* (London, 1922), Preface, p. ix.

During the week ending 23 September 1920, letters appeared in the *Eastern Daily Press, Yorkshire Herald, Scotsman, Birmingham Post, Sheffield Independent, Le Temps* (Paris), the *Manchester Guardian* and the *Westminster Gazette*. The Sub-Committee also sent its Secretary to Erevan and the Caucasus on a fact-finding trip, and gave him permission to obtain credentials as a correspondent to the *Manchester Guardian*.[64]

Lord Bryce, appropriately described by Boghos Nubar as the 'pre-eminent doyen' of the British friends of Armenia, carrying on 'the great Gladstone's traditions', was not a member of the British Armenia Committee.[65] The minutes of the Committee show, however, that he was always available for advice and guidance and unfailing in giving his time and experience without stint. Aneurin Williams was in communication also with both Lord Robert Cecil and the Archbishop of Canterbury. From time to time the British Armenia Committee meetings were attended, by special invitation, by Honorary Visitors, such as: the President of the Free Churches Council; Members of the American Mission who had lately visited the Caucasus; Boghos Nubar; Avetis Aharonian, the President of the Delegation of the Republic of Armenia; General Andranik (Ozanian); and A. Khatisian, a former Prime Minister of the Republic of Armenia.[66] Moreover, as Aneurin Williams and the Reverend Harold Buxton were involved in the Armenian Refugees (Lord Mayor's) Fund,[67] the British Armenia Committee could and did have access to the first-hand reports and information sent by the Fund's relief agents on the spot from all over the Middle East and the Caucasus. The Committee was, therefore, well informed on all aspects of the Armenian question.

What did the Armenians want before the war? They simply wanted good government in the Eastern Provinces — effective and not on paper; and this the newly-formed British Armenia Committee insisted upon. The Balkan peoples in the west of the Empire had been liberated from what was believed to be a wicked tyranny. Armenians could not have independence for ethnological and geographical reasons, but they should at least have physical

64. *BAC Propaganda Sub-Committee Minutes*, 10 Aug., 23 Sept., 5 Oct. 1920.

65. *Ararat*, vol. VI, no. 68 (Nov.-Dec. 1919), p. 531. In 1921 the British Armenia Committee included, besides the Officers, Aneurin Williams, Noel Buxton, Arthur G. Symonds and the two Organising Secretaries, C. Leonard Leese and T.P.C. Evans, the following MPs: Sir Stuart Coats, Bart., Capt. Colin R. Coote, Sir W. Howell Davies, Capt. W.E. Elliott, MC, Lt. Col. the Hon. Aubrey Herbert, Major J.W. Hills, Lt. Col. Sir Samual Hoare, Bart., Sir Robert Newman, Bart., T.P. O'Connor, Lord Eustace Percy and Col. Penry Williams. Among other members were Reverends J. Agar Beet, DD, J. Clifford, DD, A.E. Garvie, DD, J. Scott Lidgett, DD, F.B. Meyer, DD, the Right Rev. Charles Gore, DD. There also were the Rev. G.K.A. Bell, Chaplain to the Archbishop of Canterbury, Rev. Harold Buxton, Prof. J. Rendel Harris, Rev. Thos. Nightingale, Sec. Nat. Free Church Council and the historians G.P. Gooch and Arnold Toynbee. See list in BAC, *The Case for Armenia*, 1921, Bryce Papers, UB 65.

66. *BAC Minutes*, 4 Apr. 1921; 18 Aug., 25 Nov. 1919; 19 Feb. 1920; 21 Feb., 7 Mar., 8 Nov. 1921; ibid., 29 July 1920, 7 Mar. 1921.

67. See below, p. 64.

security and cultural autonomy. There were fears — soon to be substantiated — that, baulked in the west, Turkey's new rulers might resort to desperate action in the east. Turkey's near-bankrupt financial position and her need to raise her rate of customs duties, might, it was believed, be used as a means to enforce the necessary reforms in the Eastern Provinces.

Soon the newly-formed British Armenia Committee took part in an International Conference of delegates of Committees formed to watch over the interests of Armenia. The Conference was held in a Committee Room of the House of Commons in April 1913 and its Report was immediately forwarded to Grey. The French, German and Swiss Committees had sent their delegates. The Armenian National Delegation was represented by Boghos Nubar and H.N. Mosditchian; present also were representatives of the London and Manchester Armenian Committees. By far the strongest delegation was the British one.[68] The Conference unanimously agreed that the powers should be urged to make the solution of the Armenian problem an essential part of the general settlement which must follow the close of the war in the Balkans. It also recommended the appointment of a European High Commissioner to be nominated by the Sultan with the approval of the powers; a permanent Commission of supervision, to include representatives of the powers, and administrative, judicial and financial reforms. It was stressed that this proposal respected the 'integrity of the Turkish Empire' and demanded nothing but the most essential reforms[69] — a view shared by the vast majority of the Armenian people.

Aneurin Williams, as Chairman of the newly-formed Committee, stated in a letter he had written to *The Times,* that the Armenians earnestly desired to remain Ottoman subjects if tolerable government could be given them. But if reform was to be made 'real in Turkey' it could only be by European control. Turkey was once more proposing to reform and she would certainly need financial assistance. He urged, therefore, as an absolute condition of financial help, the acceptance of European control in the carrying out of the reforms. Later, the British Armenia Committee also presented a similarly-worded memorial to Grey. The deputation was led by two Members of Parliament, T.P. O'Connor and John Annan Bryce, brother of Lord Bryce. In its turn, *The Times* insisted, in a leading article, that the Armenians should obtain safety for their lives and for their homes. But 'honest reforms' as opposed to 'paper reforms' could be guaranteed only by the employment of Europeans with ample executive authority.[70]

It seems that pro-Armenian groups anxiously pressed for reforms at this

---

68. It comprised J. Annan Bryce, Noel Buxton, Sir Edward Boyle, T.P. O'Connor, Arthur Ponsonby, Dr V.H. Rutherford, Harold Spender, Aneurin Williams and Arthur G. Symonds.

69. FO 371/1773/19706: Report of Conf. on Question of Armenia held on 25 Apr. 1913, encl. in Symonds to Grey, 28 Apr. 1913.

70. *The Times,* 12 July 1913, p. 7, col. 2; ibid., 15 Aug. 1913, p. 5, col. 2; ibid., 31 Oct. 1913, p. 9, cols. 4-5.

time, as reports coming from official and unofficial sources depicted the increasing gravity of the position of the Armenians in the Eastern Provinces.[71] The British Armenia Committee sent Grey a copy of a strictly private letter received from one of the Principals of Robert College in Constantinople: the Turkish Cabinet had been forced to resign; Talaat Bey, a man 'deficient in self-control', had become Minister of the Interior; that the opportunity of the evil-doers had come and this was the hour of peril for the Armenians. The lives of thousands were at stake.

A member of the Foreign Office staff admitted that only a Russian occupation of Armenia could prevent massacres. But such an occupation was undesirable. It was 'quite useless' to make representations to the Turkish government on this subject. The minute went on:

> We might however as an *acquit de conscience* [to salve our conscience], instruct Sir G. Lowther to mention the matter in the form which he may consider the most suitable . . .[72]

The minute is extremely revealing and characteristic of the British government's attitude towards the Armenian question up to the eve of the war. Britain simply felt herself committed to the integrity of the Turkish dominions in Asia.

The British Armenia Committee or pro-Armenians did not need to provide the Foreign Office with the information about the conditions in Asiatic Turkey: the Foreign Office knew about them extremely well. It had already been reported that there was 'no public security' outside the towns. After a journey of over a thousand miles on horseback through Armenia and Kurdistan, W. Guinness, MP, similarly described the sad monotony in the stories of robbery and violence in the Christian villages. A 'horrible state of things'[73] was the impression left at the Foreign Office itself.

Yet, caught up in the conflict between the cause of humanity and alleged national interest, it had become expedient for the Foreign Office to hush things up in Turkey. Reference has already been made to the atmosphere of hostility in that country in 1913 and 1914.[74] When the Archbishop of Canterbury wrote to Grey about the peril in which the Armenians believed themselves to be, the latter coolly replied that he was 'glad to be able to say that this state of alarm' was 'not warranted'. Another instance of misinformation and an effort to show the state of affairs in Turkey in a rosier colour is provided by Grey's statement in September 1914 that the two European

71. See pp. 30-1.

72. FO 371/1773/4961: Symonds to Grey, 30 Jan. 1913, encl. letter from Dr Gates to Prof. R. Harris, 24 Jan. 1913; ibid., minute, initials unintelligible, 3 Feb. 1913.

73. Ibid., no. 5086, Col. Hawker to British ambass., 1 Nov. 1913; ibid., no. 16927, minute, [Apr. 1913].

74. See above, pp. 30-1.

Inspectors General 'have now proceeded' to the scene of their duties. Actually, according to the British ambassador in Turkey, Westenek had 'never' gone to Armenia, but he was in Constantinople and had been given leave on half pay. Hoff had gone but had been recalled by the Turkish government.[75]

Thus, in the pre-war period, while the humanitarians in Britain pressed for the effective amelioration of the condition of the Armenians by any and every means available, the Foreign Office would, for alleged national interests, do no more than make representations to the Ottoman government as an *acquit de conscience*.

When, however, Turkey entered the war on the side of the Central powers, this basic divergence between the humanitarians and the establishment, advocating national interests, ceased. It was even replaced by a convergence of attitudes. No longer did the government try to cover up and play down the condition of the subject nationalities in the Ottoman Empire. On the contrary, in order to stimulate the war effort, it found it to be in the national interest, and therefore expedient, to reveal and expose the state of affairs in that country which it had carefully and subtly tried to cover up for most of the nineteenth century. Thus, while for decades humanitarian public opinion had tried, sometimes effectively and more often in vain, to impress on the government the injustice the subject nationalities were suffering, now it was the weighty authority of the administration which collaborated closely with the humanitarians in order to rouse public opinion to the reality of misrule by the Turkish administration. Asquith, the Prime Minister, predicted in his annual speech at Guildhall that the Ottoman government had rung the death-knell of their dominions — not only in Europe but in Asia. With their disappearance would also disappear, he hoped and believed, 'the blight' which for generations past had 'withered some of the fairest regions of the earth'. The Turkish Empire had committed suicide, and dug with its own hand its grave. Lloyd George went further: he did not know what the Turks had contributed either to culture, to art, or to any aspect of human progress. They were 'a human cancer, a creeping agony in the flesh of the lands which they misgoverned, and rotting every fibre of life'. The hour had struck on the great clock of destiny for settling accounts with the Turk. Lloyd George was glad the Turk was to be called to a final account for his long record of infamy against humanity in this gigantic battle.[76]

Thus, quite a close collaboration grew up between the government and the pro-Armenian pressure groups when the Armenian people suffered the greatest of their hideous massacres and deportations in 1915. On the one hand, the government were anxious and able to show to the public that the

75. Davidson Papers, Box on Armenia, Grey to Archbishop of Canterbury 18 Dec. 1913; *Hansard*, 5th Ser. 1914, LXVI, 874. See also FO 371/2116/51007, Williams to Grey, 18 Sept. 1914; ibid., no. 56207, L. Mallet to Grey, 23 Sept. 1914.
76. *The Times*, 10 Nov. 1914, p. 10, col. 4.; ibid., 11 Nov. 1914, p. 10 col. 4.

war was against the forces of evil and wrong. In order to stimulate the war effort, the government stressed that only Allied 'victory' in the war would be the greatest possible protection for the Armenians.[77] The friends of Armenia, on the other hand, worked hard to put an end, if that was possible, to the massacres and deportations and to save by every means available the remnants of the race from total annihilation.

Aneurin Williams was first to enquire at the Foreign Office whether the United States government might be asked to instruct their ambassador in Constantinople to warn the Porte; or whether it was possible for the British authorities to let the Turks know that they would personally be held responsible for the outrages against the Armenians. It was Lord Bryce, however, who brought the question of the wholesale deportations of Armenians to the public notice abroad as well as at home. With the full responsibility and authority of his position as President of the British Academy, and as a former Cabinet Minister and ambassador to the United States, Lord Bryce told the House of Lords that information had reached him from Tiflis and Petrograd, from Constantinople, Switzerland and Paris, that 'terrible massacres' had been committed in Armenia. Later, in October 1915, he stated that the accounts given by the missionaries and by various Armenian sources of information showed that a total figure of 800,000 of those who had been destroyed during the five months since May last was quite a possible number. That was because the proceedings taken had been 'so absolutely premeditated and systematic'. The massacres were the result of 'a policy' which, as far as could be ascertained, had been entertained for some considerable time by the Turkish government. They had hesitated to put it into practice until they thought the favourable moment had come.[78]

There was not much the pro-Armenian pressure groups could do on the political side during the war. Their efforts were concentrated on the organisation of relief. The Foreign Office very willingly passed on to Aneurin Williams information received from the British Consul at Batum about the crazed flight and desperate plight of the hundreds of thousands of Armenian refugees — mostly women and children — in the Caucasus.[79] Both Williams and his associates and the Foreign Office were anxious to have these accounts made known to the public: the former in order to stimulate relief contributions; the latter in order to stimulate the war effort.

It will be seen below[80] that the co-operation between the administration and the Armenophiles culminated in the publication by the Foreign Office in

77. *Hansard*, 5th Ser. 1915, LXXV, 1775 (Robert Cecil).

78. FO 371/2488/54821/62512, Williams to Neil Primrose, 2 May, 17 May 1915. *Hansard*, 5th Ser. 1915, XIX, col. 777 (Archbishop of Canterbury); ibid., cols. 774, 1001; Fisher, *Bryce*, II, pp. 330-2.

79. FO 371/2488/51009/192671: G. Locock to Williams, encl. desp. from Consul Stevens, 21 Dec. 1915; FO 371/2768/1455/10980, Locock to Williams, encl. desps. from Stevens, 11 Jan. 1916 (FO wrongly had 1915), and 20 Jan. 1916.

80. See pp. 78-9.

1916 of a Blue Book: it was edited by Bryce and Arnold Toynbee.

Arnold Toynbee published, in addition, *Armenian Atrocities: The Murder of a Nation* and *The Murderous Tyranny of the Turks.* Apparently very strong public sympathy with the sufferings of the Armenians was also aroused by Aurora Mardiganian's story of her shocking personal experience during the deportations in Turkey. She had been rescued by Dr F.W. MacCallum, a missionary. Her book, *The Auction of Souls,* was 'interpreted' by H.L. Gates, who testified that one might read Aurora's story with entire confidence — 'every word is true'.[81] The book was first published in Britain by Odhams Limited in January 1920. In May of that year it went into its fifteenth impression.

On the political side, the British friends of Armenia tried, as much as they could, to be the exponent of the wishes, dreams and aspirations of the Armenian people and to seek from the British government a lasting and satisfactory settlement of the Armenian question. But the British government never committed itself to a definite settlement partly because of the shifting situations arising from the war, partly because it was only one of the members of the Entente and partly because it disparaged Armenia's importance, however much it had opposed Russia's presence there.

When the terrible news of the massacres and deportations came, Bryce advised the British Armenia Committee that while it should watch closely the course of events, it should both collectively and individually be very careful not to speak or publish anything which would inevitably reach the Turks, as that would undoubtedly lead to renewed acts on their part to continue and complete the extermination of the Armenian people.[82]

By the end of 1916, the broad lines of the secret Sykes-Picot Agreement, by which Britain, France and Russia had agreed on their territorial rewards for their war effort in the east, had leaked out. The dream of autonomy for a united Armenia under Russian and Allied protection[83] (mainly conceived after Turkey's abrogation of the Reform Scheme) was fast evaporating. Lord Bryce, well-informed about the Agreement, strongly urged that the Armenians should abstain from starting any propaganda attempts for autonomy for the whole of Armenia. He thought that after peace had been established, Armenians might secure, if not the whole of their desires, at all events peace and security of person and property such as they had not enjoyed for centuries. The Sykes-Picot Agreement had made clear that British interests lay in the south-eastern regions of the Turkish Empire — Mesopotamia and Palestine. It also made clear that northern Armenia would be Russian, and southern Armenia and Cilicia, French. Still, no part of it would remain under Turkish rule. So, the British Armenia Committee passed a resolution expressing its warm gratitude to Asquith, for his words

81. Aurora Mardiganian, *The Auction of Souls* (London, 1920), preface.
82. *BAC Minutes*, 9 Dec. 1915.
83. FO 371/2485/40247, Williams to Grey, 3 Apr. 1915.

of sympathy and hope to the Armenian people expressed in a speech at Guildhall. The Committee agreed that a copy of the resolution should be sent to the Prime Minister and also to the press. After referring to the 'wholesale massacre' of the Armenians which had 'shocked' the entire civilised and Christian world, Asquith had stated that the British government was 'resolved' that after the war there should be an era of 'liberty' for this ancient people.[84]

The British friends of Armenia saw the United States' involvement in the war and the Russian Revolution as likely to have beneficial effect. The old Tsarist government had entertained a secret plan simply to annex the 'six *vilayets*' and to colonise them by Cossacks to the exclusion of Armenians.[85] The Committee, therefore, sent telegrams of similar substance to P.N. Milyukov, the Foreign Minister, to the Catholicos at Etchmiadzin and to M. Papajanian, the Armenian member of the Duma, congratulating the Armenians in Russia on the declaration of recognition, by the Provisional Government, of the principles of nationality and Armenian autonomy. Moreover, it strongly urged the concentration of all efforts on the successful prosecution of the war.[86]

The Committee, however, was soon disappointed. In Russia, under the influence of revolutionary ideas, the Russian armies were fast being dissolved. Turkey, making use of this golden opportunity, began concentrating its armies on the Caucasian front. The condition of the Eastern Armenians now looked absolutely critical.

The secret Sykes-Picot Agreement made between Britain, France and Russia had covered Greater and Lesser Armenia. But the new Bolshevik government denounced the agreements and disclaimed annexations. In the Caucasus issues gradually became confused and prospects bleak with the advance of Turkish troops. Early in 1918 there was great uncertainty about conditions in Armenia. No telegrams were getting through, and the British Armenia Committee, similarly confused, wondered 'whether anything, and if something, what could be done'.[87]

However, in the south-east of the Ottoman Empire, in Mesopotamia, Syria and Palestine, the Turkish armies were being heavily defeated. When in October 1918 it was clear that Turkey would surrender, the Committee became active. In reply to a telegram sent by Aneurin Williams about the future, Balfour, the Foreign Secretary, referred to Lord Robert Cecil's letter published in the press on 3 October which 'reaffirmed' the government's 'intention to liberate Armenia'. Learning also that the Turkish government had applied to President Wilson to obtain an armistice, the

84. *BAC Minutes*, 14 Nov. 1916; *The Times*, 10 Nov. 1916, p. 10, col. 3.
85. Bryce Papers, UB 65, Boghos Nubar to Bryce, 27 Sept. 1916, encl. French transl. of Russian article in *Retsch*, 28 July/10 Aug. 1916.
86. *BAC Minutes*, 3 Apr. 1917. The telegrams were sent on 2 Aug. 1917.
87. Ibid., 12 Mar. 1918.

British Armenia Committee respectfully but earnestly asked him by cable that no conditions should be agreed to which did not entail the complete and final ending of Turkish rule and suzerainty over Armenia. The Committee also 'urgently' asked Balfour again, to demand, before granting an armistice to the Turks, 'the evacuation by them of all Armenian territory', namely the 'six *vilayets*' and the province of Cilicia. They requested, moreover, occupation by British and Allied military forces at such strategic points as they deemed desirable; the granting of all facilities for the immediate repatriation of the surviving refugees under British and Allied military auspices, and the liberation of the tens of thousands of Armenian women and children held in slavery in Turkish harems. This memorandum was sent on 22 October 1918. A few days later, Balfour acknowledged the receipt of the letter adding that the recommendations put forward would receive 'the most careful and sympathetic consideration'. Yet on 22 October, the Commander-in-Chief, Mediterranean, was sent in cable the draft of the Armistice terms. It advised him to obtain, as quickly as possible, the first four conditions — which mostly concerned secure access to the Black Sea.[88]

Thus, the terms of the Mudros Armistice, finally signed, left the six Armenian *vilayets* under the sovereignty of Turkey, and no provision at all was made for the repatriation of the refugees and deportees to their homes.[89]

One wonders, with hindsight, whether the numerous statements of the political leaders during the war about the liberation of Armenia and the close co-operation and collaboration between the government and the friends of Armenia, created some kind of deceptive self-satisfaction and false complacency among the latter; whether a more forceful demand and vigorous campaign might have resulted, in the terms of the armistice, at a time when Turkish resistance was at its lowest ebb, in provision for temporary British or Allied occupation of the strategic points in Armenia. It is now certain that the pro-Armenian groups were caught unaware and were deeply disappointed.

C. Relief Organisations

Pro-Armenian sentiments and interest among the humanitarian Britons were not confined only to statements and written words. Often they were also expressed in concrete forms such as the organisation of public meetings, relief groups and relief work.

As early as April 1880, when after the Russo-Turkish war the eastern provinces of Turkey had experienced famine, the Armenian Committees of

88. Ibid., 21 Oct. 1918, encl. copy of Balfour's tel., 8 Oct. 1918; FO 371/3404/177074, Williams and Symonds to Balfour, 22 Oct. 1918; FO to Williams, 28 Oct. 1918; FO 371/3448/178097, Admiralty to C.-in-C. Med., 46Z, 22 Oct. 1918.
89. FO 371/3449/181110, 593 Z, C.-in-C. Med. to Admiralty, 31 Oct. 1918.

London and Manchester, and their British friends headed by Bryce, had organised a meeting at the Mansion House on behalf of the people of Asia Minor and Armenia who were perishing in thousands. They had invited Gladstone to be present. In regretting that he could not be bodily present, he had sent £50 and expressed the hope that the public would make a liberal answer to the appeal. This would be alike conducive to the purposes of true charity, and to the good name of Britain in the East.[90]

Later, in 1895, during the massacres and atrocities in the Sasun district of Armenia, another public meeting was organised at St James's Hall, London, as a 'National Protest against the torture and massacre of Christians in Armenia'. It was chaired by the Duke of Argyll. The resolutions had recorded the meeting's intense indignation at the Porte's continued violation of the 'principles of humanity' in defiance of the solemn international treaty obligations it had incurred. The meeting had also called upon the British government to take immediate action for putting an end to the system of 'barbarous misrule' in Turkish Armenia. Among those who proposed and supported the resolutions were Canons M. MacColl and E.R. Wilberforce, the Bishops of Hereford and of St Asaph, the Moderator of the Church of Scotland, the Lord Mayor of Liverpool, the Lord Provost of Edinburgh and Members of Parliament.[91]

Considering the policy and commitment of the British government generally to bolster up Turkey, the organisation of pro-Armenian protest meetings and even of relief must have been the result of the undaunted determination and even sacrifice on the part of the organisers and of their unremitting belief in justice: for pressures from various directions there certainly were. Thus, with regard to the meeting in 1895, the Bishop of Manchester had declined to accept the presidency objecting that he was obliged to obtain first 'the agreement of the Foreign Office'. He had received from 'high circles' an indication that the government did not look favourably on these meetings and protests. Referring to the same meeting, Bryce informed Gladstone that the Sultan, through his envoy in London, was pressing the Archbishop of Canterbury and Cardinal Vaughan 'to forbid their clergy' to attend it. Moreover, the Sultan had besought 'us' [the government] 'to induce' Gladstone 'not to speak or write on the subject'. Bryce, amused, had concluded that the Sultan was 'in terror' of Gladstone's words.[92]

While pro-Armenian public meetings with political undertones were organised from time to time, relief organisations generally had an existence

90. MS Bryce 11, f.46, Bryce to Gladstone 22 Apr. (1880). MS Bryce 10, ff.26-7, Gladstone to Bryce, 26 Apr. 1880.

91. Bryce Papers, UB 63, poster about public meeting, 7 May 1895.

92. Ibid., Rev. Baronian, Armenian Rectory, Manchester, to Bryce, 20 Apr. 1895. MS Bryce, 12, f.167, Bryce to Gladstone, 3 May 1895.

lasting for years and aimed at directly helping the Armenian victims of Turkish misrule, oppression and atrocities. It seems that the motives of the various humanitarian groups for a contribution to, and the organisation of, relief were different but quite often related. Helping downtrodden and afflicted communities was a tradition among Quakers. The Church of England and the other religious denominations were equally concerned for the same philanthropic reasons and also probably because Armenia was the first state in the world to have adopted Christianity as its national religion. There was, moreover, some admiration for the moral courage of a people who, under Mohammedan domination for long centuries, had refused to renounce their faith. Some other groups, mainly of Liberal tradition, considered Europe and especially Britain morally responsible for Armenia's distress and suffering: had they not substituted the Treaty of Berlin for the Treaty of San Stefano, the Christian population would have been under the protection of Russia. Intellectuals and historians, on the other hand, were probably grieved that one of the oldest civilised races in western Asia, an historical nation important in the past, was suffering.[93]

The Religious Society of Friends, Armenian Mission, was apparently the first in Britain to take a humanitarian and educational interest in the Armenians of Turkey. In 1881, the Friends had established an Armenian Mission in one of the Armenian quarters at Constantinople, not far from the Armenian Patriarchate. Here Dr and Mrs Dobrashian had started medical work. In 1888 Ann Mary Burgess had joined them in their work. Under her guidance and responsibility, the Mission had soon organised an Armenian Sunday School, an Industrial Department and a Day School. By 1910 the number of children attending the Day School had risen to 150, those attending the Sunday School had averaged 400 and new school buildings had been acquired. On several occasions the Armenian Patriarch had expressed his gratitude to Miss Burgess. During the war of 1914-18, the work of the Mission had been severely curtailed, but under American protection it had been possible to keep over 500 women employed in industrial work. After the armistice the Mission had resumed its work, but in 1922 the armed conflict between Turkey and Greece had necessitated its transfer to Corfu. So, after thirty-four years in Constantinople, Miss Burgess had moved there to serve among the thousands of refugees.[94] In 1925 she had been able to write with apparent satisfaction that the Mission's women and girls in the

93. Lucy Violet Hodgkin, *George Lloyd Hodgkin 1880-1918* (Edinburgh, 1921), p. 50; A.J. Toynbee, *Armenian Atrocities: The Murder of a Nation* (London, 1915), pp. 17-18; see also Emily J. Robinson, *The Truth About Armenia* (London, 1913), pp. 3, 14-15; W. Llewellyn Williams, *Armenia's Tragic Story* (London, 1916), pp. 17-19.

94. Maud A. Rowntree, *In the City of the Sultan* (The Work of the Friends' Armenian Mission, Constantinople) (London, 1917), pp. 3-4, 63; Charles D. Terell, *Historical Sketch of the Friends' Armenian Mission from 1881 to 1926* (London, n.d.), pp. 7, 9–10, 12, 14.

Embroidery Department were as busy as ever and that during the previous year they had sold about £4,000-worth of hand-made goods.[95]

Besides this concrete humanitarian work, the reports sent by the Mission's field workers, being first-hand, are undoubtedly of historical value. The Friends' Armenian Mission in Constantinople reported for 1915 that their hearts were constantly saddened by the arrest of 'prominent Armenians, some of whom were hanged in the city, others exiled and murdered *en route*'. For 1918-19, the Report quoted a letter from Ann H. Harris in Constantinople, written in May 1919, where she had stated that the Mission's greatest trouble was, of course, 'the awful flood of cruelty which poured over the Armenian nation'. The unrest was still great, and in the interior 'terrible tragedies are still occurring'. For 1920-1, Miss Burgess had written from Constantinople what an American Missionary from Marsovan had told her: that the Turks had forbidden them to teach, on the grounds that their instruction was 'poisonous'. For 1921 she had reported that the Armenian people were 'very downcast, all kinds of sad news comes to us regarding their condition in the interior'.[96] The *Friend of Armenia* had also quoted a remarkable letter by Miss Burgess written in 1919 from Constantinople, in which she had discussed the sufferings of the Armenians during the war. She only wanted people at home to know that the crimes committed against women and children and aged people, too horrible to relate, were 'sorrowfully true'. A few of the deported Armenians were returning in 'a most deplorable state'. Some of the little orphans, the pretty ones, had been saved from death, and 'gathered as Turks, put into Moslem homes', but children with plain faces had suffered cruel deaths of a 'most painful nature'.[97]

When, after the Treaty of Lausanne in 1923, the settlement of the Armenian refugees in their homelands in north-eastern Turkey became impossible, the Quakers actively worked for the Syrian Settlement Scheme through their Armenia Committee as well as their Foreign Mission Association.

The Friends of Armenia,[98] founded in London in 1897 was another relief agency aiming at 'reconstruction' in Armenia. It was well organised from an office at 47 Victoria Street, Westminster, which also served as its London sales depot for Armenian lace, needlework and rugs. Usually the back cover of the quarterly issue of the *Friend of Armenia* carried an advertisement for these 'dainty articles' which could be seen in the showroom. According to these advertisements, all the goods were bought from the Mission Centres and sold for the benefit of widows and orphans. From 1 October to 31

95. Religious Soc. of Friends, 033.3, *Friends Armenian Mission Reports 1883-1925*, Friends Arm. Commit. Rep. 1924-5, quoting Burgess, 22 Apr. 1925.
96. Ibid., Friends' Arm. Mission in Constant., Reports for 1915, 1918-19, 1920-21.
97. *Friend of Armenia*, New Series, no. 73 (June 1919), p. 9.
98. See above, p. 44; and for Lady Frederick Cavendish, p. 40.

December 1899, it had been possible to collect, through the sales of work, over £172 from Manchester, £60 from Edinburgh, £60 from Paisley and £217 from Liverpool.[99]

By the summer of 1908, the Friends of Armenia had forwarded over £60,000 to the distressed districts of Armenia since they had begun work in 1897. These sums had been used to relieve the survivors of the 1890s massacres. When the Adana massacres occurred in early 1909, the *Friend of Armenia* devoted its summer issue, 'Massacre Number', to these atrocious events. Donations for 'Distress in Cilicia', included £500 from Miss Holt, £200 from Basil Orpin and a further £500 from him in memory of John Orpin, and £50 from Noel Buxton. In 1910, Basil Orpin contributed £550. Thus the Society was able to send, as it informed the Foreign Office, over £3,400 between 26 April and 9 June 1909 for the relief of distress in Cilicia.[100]

Although the chief aim of the Society of Friends, like other similar relief organisations, was to alleviate distress among the Armenians, they also touched, from time to time, on the political aspect of the Armenian question in order to be able to arouse interest among the public and induce them to contribute generously. As was mentioned earlier,[101] the *Friend of Armenia* often reminded its readers of Britain's obligations under the Cyprus Convention and the Treaty of Berlin. When Turkey entered the world war against Britain, and when the greatest massacres of Armenians occurred in 1915, British humanitarian circles felt vindicated in their views as to the government's mistaken policy towards Turkey. An article in the *Friend of Armenia* by the former editorial secretary, Miss E. Cantlow, argued that, had Britain, in mistaken self-interest, not bolstered up an empire she knew to be founded on cruelty and oppression, Turkey would have fallen to pieces long ago and the Armenian massacres of the 1890s, of 1909, and the 1915 deportations could never have taken place. Miss Cantlow asked what the British had gained by their policy. They had feared to have Russia paramount in Asia Minor, and now they wished her there. But even if the Russian armies advanced as quickly as the British now hoped, 'they come *too late,* for the dead return no more'.[102]

By March 1915, the Friends of Armenia had forwarded £98,000 to the distressed districts.[103] But the organisation of additional relief agencies, following the unprecedentedly desperate conditions of the Armenians during the war, diverted some of the appeal and interest that this society had commanded. It faithfully continued its work, but its hopes were not realised and the question of the refugees remained unsolved in the post-war period.

99. *Friend of Armenia*, no. 1 (Feb. 1900), back cover; ibid., no. 60 (Mar. 1915), back cover; no. 1 (Feb. 1900), p. 15.

100. Ibid., no. 34 (summer 1908), p. 112; no. 38 (summer 1909), pp. 18-24; no. 41 (spring 1910) p. 9. FO 371/773/21710, FO 371/771/16486, FO 371/772/20203, E. Cantlow to Grey, 9 June, 30 Apr., 28 May 1909 respectively.

101. See above, p. 45.

102. *Friend of Armenia*, no. 63 (April 1916), p. 16.

103. Ibid., no. 60 (March 1915).

All the relief agencies in Britain continued, often jointly, and in co-operation with the League of Nations, to devote their efforts to the settlement of the thousands of Armenian refugees in the Middle East.

The Armenian community of London also had its own relief agencies. The Armenian Ladies' Guild of London had been founded in 1913 by Mrs Nevric Gudenian, whose 'mother-heart bled' for orphans. After five years of strenuous work she had reluctantly relinquished her post as president. She was succeeded by Mrs Nevart Gulbenkian, a 'keen, energetic' and 'enthusiastic' worker of the Guild, who, in 1918 had formed a new committee.[104] Miss Chenor Mouradian was the Superintendent of the Workroom at 47a Redcliffe Square, London SW10. Early in 1918, in response to an urgent appeal for clothing from the Armenian General Benevolent Union in Cairo, the Guild despatched to that city seven bales of garments, kindly shipped by M. Bakirgian of Manchester. The Committee also organised sewing meetings to provide for the needs of the great numbers of Armenian refugees in the Near East. Four bales of goods were sent to the refugees in Baghdad, shipped free by Messrs. Lynch Brothers.[105]

The Armenian Refugees' Relief Fund was inaugurated in January 1915 and registered under the War Charities Act in 1916. It was controlled by the General Council of the Armenian United Association of London.[106] It collected and remitted 'substantial sums' to the various Armenian committees and organisations dealing directly with the refugees. The address of the offices of the Fund was the same as that of the workroom of the Armenian Ladies' Guild of London.[107]

It seems that the Armenian Red Cross and Refugee Fund was organised in January 1915 and that Bryce was the force behind it. It appealed to the 'generous heart' of the great British public for support to help the Armenian refugees by means of a letter in *The Times* which was signed by Lord Bryce, Lady Henry Somerset and Lady Frederick Cavendish.[108] Lady Bryce was the President of the Fund, Lieutenant-Colonel G.M. Gregory the Chairman of the Committee and Miss Emily Robinson the Honorary Secretary.[109] The aim of the Fund was to attempt to stem in some degree the torrent of misery

104. Miss Pauline Aganoor was Honorary Secretary, Miss Lily John, Honorary Treasurer and Mrs. Nevric Gudenian, Mrs. A.P. Hacobian, Mrs. Mosditchian and Mrs. Shahinian, Members.
105. *Ararat* (London), VI, no. 60 (Aug. 1918), pp. 126-7.
106. See above, pp. 45-6.
107. *Ararat*, VI, no. 59 (June-July 1918).
108. *The Times*, 12 Jan. 1915, p. 7, col. 3; among the Vice-Presidents were the three signatories to *The Times* letter cited here, the Right Honourable G.W.E. Russell, at one time a Private Secretary to Gladstone, the Hon. Mrs Alister Fraser, Sir Edwin Pears, Principal Whyte, DD of Edinburgh, Aneurin Williams, Noel Buxton and a few others.
109. For E. Robinson, see above p. 41.

caused by the war among the Armenian population of Turkey and Persia and to provide medical supplies for the Armenian volunteers fighting on behalf of Russia. The moving spirit of the Fund was certainly Emily Robinson who with her 'unfailing devotion and singleness of purpose' gave 'all' her time and energy to promote the cause of Armenia.[110]

The various relief societies and Funds organised up to 1915 and described above, had been very commendable but rather modest efforts by different groups to relieve certain aspects of distress in Armenia. Thus in 1908, the Friends of Armenia had been engaged in sending seed corn.[111] The Quakers were concerned with education and industrial work and other groups had despatched clothing. Over the years, although there had undoubtedly been oppression, massacres and consequent emigration of the people in the Armenian homelands, nevertheless, up to the beginning of 1915, the majority of the Armenian people had lived on their own lands, and relief had often helped them to rebuild their ruined homes or replenish their burnt hearths. What was singularly macabre about the 1915 massacres and deportations was that the whole native population was uprooted from its ancestral country and flung to the winds and sands as landless, roofless and jobless wretches.

The existing relief organisations could not possibly cope with this colossal task; hence the need for a *national* relief organisation; the Armenian Refugees (Lord Mayor's) Fund was set up in October 1915, after the 'terrible' nature of the reports from Turkish Armenia had leaked out. It was the best organised, and most active and influential of the relief agencies during 1915 to 1923. Some of the problems of the organisation were discussed in a special meeting at the House of Commons. Other problems were considered during British Armenia Committee meetings.[112] Even before the inaugural meeting, *The Times* stated that Bryce was taking a very active interest in this matter of raising a 'national' fund and that he would be one of the speakers. Cardinal Bourne would 'gladly' follow him. At the inaugural meeting on 15 October 1915 at the Mansion House, the Lord Mayor of London, the President of the Fund, recalled that during the massacres of the 1890s, Britain had raised the sum of £80,000 to relieve the victims. It was hoped that even in this time of war with so many claims on the country's means, a large sum might again be raised. For the present was probably 'the greatest massacre in any land or of any race which had ever been recorded'. Any money collected would be sent to the Caucasus through the British Consul-General in Moscow. In a letter of apology, A.J. Balfour, First Lord

110. Bryce Papers, UB 66, Statement by Arm. Red Cross and Ref. Fund, Aug. 1915; G.W.E. Russell, MP about E. Robinson, in *Ararat*, V. no. 49 (July 1917), p. 22.
111. FO 371/533/9622, E. Cantlow to Grey, 19 Mar. 1908.
112. Douglas Papers, vol. 61, f.117, 'Origin, Basis and Present Constit. of the Arm. Refugees (Lord Mayor's) Fund'; *BAC Minutes*, 13 Oct. 1915.

of the Admiralty and a former Prime Minister, also expressed the view that in the midst of all the horrors of this war, nothing was 'more horrible' than the treatment meted out to the Armenians by the Turkish government, which claimed to represent progress and reform. Bryce, Cardinal Bourne, the Bishop of Oxford, Sir Edwin Pears, Sir J. Compton-Rickett MP and T.P. O'Connor, MP also spoke. Lord Gladstone, Lord Kinnaird, Lord Beauchamp, Lord Robert Cecil and others expressed themselves in cordial sympathy with the appeal.[113]

The Vice-Presidents of the Armenian Refugees (Lord Mayor's) Fund included, among the notables, the Archbishops of Canterbury and York, Cardinal Bourne, Lord Bryce, Lord Curzon, the Bishops of London, Hereford, Ely, Oxford and Southwark, Lady Frederick Cavendish, the Reverend Doctors Lyttelton, Clifford and Meyer, George Cadbury, Arnold Rowntree and Basil Orpin. Aneurin Williams was the Chairman of the Fund and Joseph Bliss the Honorary Treasurer. Besides the Reverend Harold Buxton, who became its indefatigable Honorary Secretary, the Fund also had two working Secretaries, the Reverend Charles G.T. Colson and Miss Magda Coe. There were thirteen field directors headed by Harold Buxton.[114] In 1920 the Fund had about 5,000 subscribers. Its office was at 96 Victoria Street, London SW. Writing in *The Times* a few weeks after the formation of the Fund, the Chairman stated that it was also caring for Nestorian and Syrian Christians who had fled from the outrages in Turkey. Moreover, the Fund informed the public that the 'whole of the money' collected went to the refugees, all expense of administration being defrayed privately.[115]

The Churches in Britain closely co-operated with the Fund and many clergymen took a very active part in organising collections. The Archbishop of Canterbury himself described the massacre of Armenian and Assyrian Christians in the Turkish Empire as a crime which 'in scale and horror' had probably 'no parallel' in the history of the world. The sufferings baffled description. He therefore advised that to these people in their dire distress Christian aid should flow out ungrudgingly. In many churches, arrangements were made for collections on 6 February 1916, which would be observed throughout the country as 'Armenia Sunday'.[116]

Flag Days in aid of the Armenian Refugees (Lord Mayor's) Fund were also organised. In four months, since its formation, the Fund had collected over £37,000. But distress was also growing and the necessity for money was overwhelming. Early in 1916, the American Committee for relief reported

113 *The Times,* 5 Oct. 1915, p. 11, col. 3; Williams Papers, private possession, Card. Bourne to Williams, 8 Oct. 1915; *The Times,* 16 Oct. 1915, p. 5, col. 3; Douglas Papers, vol. 61, f.117, 'Origin, Basis and Present Const. of the Arm. Refugees (Lord Mayor's) Fund'.

114. Bryce Papers, UB 66, Official Statement, The Arm. Ref. (Lord Mayor's) Fund.

115. *BAC Propaganda Sub-Commit. Minutes,* 8, 15 June 1920; *The Times,* 8 Oct. 1915, p. 5, col. 3; ibid., 15 Nov. 1915, p. 9, col. 4; ibid., 18 Nov. 1915, p. 11, col. 2.

116. Ibid., 15 Dec. 1916, p. 7, col. 4; ibid., 3 Feb. 1916, p. 11, col. 2.

that the Russians were harbouring 'no fewer than 310,000 refugees', and that destitution and disease were widespread. Tolstoy's daughter, Vera, who had been working among them with the Russian Red Cross, had written: 'Never in my life have I seen such suffering'.[117]

The relief agencies had to care for hundreds of thousands of refugees, and the sheer numbers made relief an intractable problem. A problem made even more overwhelming by the mass movements among these refugees, consequent on the fluctuations of war and political oscillations. Those who had missed slaughter in 1915 had fled. When in 1916 the Russian armies had advanced deep into eastern Turkey, capturing Erzerum in February and Mush in August,[118] the refugees had started to return to their homelands. Under the auspices, therefore, of the Armenian Refugees (Lord Mayor's) Fund, a party of trained relief workers, headed by Harold Buxton and including Colonel Graham Aspland as medical officer, George Lloyd Hodgkin, Alfred Backhouse and a few nurses proceeded to the Caucasus and eastern Turkey in April 1916 to investigate distress and organise repatriation.[119] Visiting the Armenian hospitals and orphanages in Baku, the group were grieved to learn that many of the foundlings, starved and diseased, had been in such a state of shock at all they had gone through, that they had been 'perfectly dumb' during the first few weeks. In Tiflis they had called at six Armenian orphanages. Writing to his wife, George Hodgkin described the baby home as 'the saddest, with the look of intolerable strain stamped on the young mothers' faces'. In Turkish Armenia, in the exceedingly hot and dusty season of late June, they met hundreds of refugees going back on foot to the Van district: 'small children coming bravely along in the heat walking with animals' and still younger ones 'carried sleeping on the backs of their parents'.[120] In 1916 and 1917 the Fund arranged to supply the refugees with seed corn and oxen and set up cotton-spinning in and around the town of Igdir with a view to providing a livelihood for about 500 women.[121]

But the defection of Russia from the war and the subsequent reconquest of Turkish Armenia and even parts of Russian Armenia by Turkey in 1918, resulted afresh in the flight of thousands. The armistice naturally brought high expectations. Many of the refugees returned to the Kars district in the north-east, and to Cilicia in the south. However, the violent attacks of the resurgent Kemalists in 1920 and 1921 and the abandonment of the

117. Ibid., 24 May 1917, p. 3, col. 6; ibid., 17 Feb. 1916, p. 9, col. 4. Alice Stone Blackwell, 'Help the Armenians' in *New Armenia* (New York), VIII, no. 2 (15 Dec. 1915), p. 31.

118. *The Times*, 17 Feb. 1916, p. 8, col. 3; ibid., 25 Aug., 1916, p. 6, col. 3.

119. Harold Buxton, *Trans-Caucasia* (London, 1926), preface; Hodgkin, *Hodgkin*, p. 49; *The Times*, 6 Apr. 1916, p. 4, col. 6.

120. Hodgkin Papers, private possession, *Journal*, f.12, Hodgkin to Robin, 24 Apr. 1916; f.20, Hodgkin to Mary, 28 Apr. 1916; Hodgkin Papers, Hodgkin to Mary, 30 June 1916; ibid., 2 July 1916.

121. Arm. Ref. (Lord Mayor's) Fund, *Armenians: Saving the Remnant* (London, 1917), p. 4; *The Times*, 8 June 1916, p. 6, col. 3.

Armenians by the Allied powers cruelly dashed the hopes of resettlement, resulting, yet once again, in the panicky exodus of numberless people.

Thus, under the exigency of circumstances, the pro-Armenian groups and relief agencies had not only to provide aid and to cope with political oscillations, but they had also to press the policy-making and decision-taking bodies, especially after 1918, for a just settlement of the Armenian question.

However, during the war the Armenian question in general and the Armenian massacres in particular had served a purpose for the government — to show the people that they were fighting for justice and against evil, and to encourage the war effort. By 1918 the Armenian question had fulfilled its function and apparently was of no further use. There still exists a precious paper in the collection of Randall Davidson, the Archbishop of Canterbury. Apparently he had jotted down the main points of a major speech he was to make in the House of Lords about the Armenian horrors, together with two of the war-time statements made by Lloyd George, the Prime Minister, as to the liberation of the Armenian homelands. One sentence of the Archbishop's notes reads:

My fear is that the story of these horrors and OUR PROMISES may be forgotten in resettlement.

Significantly, the words 'our promises' are underlined twice.[122] It seems that with the end of the war the views of those professing the advocacy of national interests and of those who really cared for the Armenians would fatally diverge.

122. Davidson Papers, Box on Armenia, 'House of Lords' Paper, 17 Dec. 1919; See also *Hansard*, 5th Ser. 1919, XXXVIII, 279-88.

3 British Interests and the Armenian Question During the War

Concern for her interests and prestige in the Middle East had induced Britain to bolster up Turkey during the greater part of the nineteenth century. With her singular position, Turkey was considered an effective buffer against Russian expansion and influence. Her misrule was a secondary consideration — the occupation of humanitarians. Even at the beginning of the twentieth century, the British leaders were not prepared to see the delicate balance of power disturbed in this sensitive area. They vigorously supported, therefore, the integrity of the Ottoman Empire despite significant political changes taking place in the Near East.

Germany, rather behind in her unification, industrialisation and the development of her capitalism, and bidding for markets, political influence and prestige, had made approaches to Turkey since 1883. She alone of all the Great powers was free from the taint of protest against massacres and greed for Ottoman territory. Germany's attitude was not unwelcome to Turkey who needed her for economic and, especially, diplomatic support. But equally Germany needed Turkey. According to Djemal Pasha, the Turkish statesman, whereas the Entente governments wanted to 'dismember' Turkey, Germany was the *'only'* power which desired to see her strong: the only way in which Germany could escape 'encirclement' and the pressure of the 'iron ring' was by preventing the 'dismemberment of Turkey'.[1] Turkey's gradual but clear drift to the German camp was a significant development for both Britain and Russia. Another was the expulsion of Turkey from Europe following her disastrous defeat in the Balkan wars. Asquith, the Prime Minister, had 'a strong opinion' that it was only a question of time before the instability and 'rottenness' of the Turkish Empire would bring about her downfall in Asia as well. Britain, he maintained, ought to face these probabilities.[2]

Notwithstanding these developments and British misgivings about Turkey's future, the British government's 'one constant and consistent desire', up to the First World War, was to see Turkey 'strengthened and reinvigorated' by reform and the 'integrity' of her Asiatic dominions preserved. In 1913 Grey and the Cabinet were of the opinion that for the time being the 'only safe policy' was to maintain Ottoman rule in Asia. This course was regarded as 'the only alternative to anarchy and confusion'.[3]

1. Djemal Pasha, *Memories of a Turkish Statesman 1913-1919* (London, 1922), p. 113.
2. Bodleian Library, MS Asquith 7, f.54, Cab. Meeting, 9 July 1913.
3. *Hansard*, 5th Ser. 1909, I, col. 41; ibid., 1914, LIX, 2191; MS Asquith 7, f.54, Cab. Meeting, 9 July 1913; Grey of Fallodon, *Twenty-Five Years 1892-1916* (London, 1925), I, p. 185, Grey to A. Nicolson, 14 Oct. 1908.

After the declaration of war between Germany, Austria-Hungary and the Entente powers, the 'most pressing question' for the British Cabinet was Turkey's attitude. Both Lord Kitchener, the Secretary of State for War, and Lord Crewe, the Secretary of State for India, stressed their anxiety about Moslem susceptibilities in India and Egypt. Likewise, Grey pointed out to the French and Russian ambassadors that it would be very embarrassing to Britain 'both in India and in Egypt' if Turkey came in against the Allies. Kitchener insisted that Turkey must be kept neutral, or, if this was impossible, her entry into the war should be delayed at all costs until the Indian troops got through the Suez Canal on their way to France.[4] The Cabinet even approved a telegram from Churchill, the First Lord of the Admiralty, to Enver, the Minister of War, agreeing to deliver up to the Turks, at the end of the war, the two battleships the *Reshadie* and the *Sultan Osman,* requisitioned in Britain, and to pay '£1000 a day' for their use from the time that the German crews of the *Goeben* and the *Breslau* left Turkish territory.[5] Indeed, one cannot stress sufficiently the sensitivity of the British government to Moslem feelings. They were almost apologetic about their going to war with Turkey: ' . . . in spite of repeated and continuous provocations, I strove to preserve, in regard to Turkey, a friendly neutrality', the King stated in Parliament, expressing the views of his Ministers, and added:

> My Mussulman subjects know well that a rupture with Turkey has been forced upon Me against My will . . .[6]

The entry of Turkey into the war was completely unprovoked. The Entente powers tried hard to ensure her neutrality. Like Britain, France also was anxious not to provoke Moslem sentiment in her overseas territories. Undoubtedly, both countries needed their complete strength to fight Germany. Moreover, they feared a military threat to the Suez Canal — it was important for the fast passage of Indian troops to France. Then, the closing of the Dardanelles by Turkey might dry up the westward flow of Russia's grain and might obstruct the eastward flow of arms to her. The Balkan states might be intimidated. Russia also favoured Turkish neutrality because it would free her from the need to keep troops on the Caucasian frontier. Moreover, if Turkey was a belligerent, Greek and Bulgarian aspirations regarding Constantinople might be inflamed. The war with Turkey was 'in spite of our hopes and efforts, and against our wills', Asquith stated.[7] The ambassadors of the three Allied powers jointly made a 'written' declaration that the 'independence and integrity' of Turkey would be

4. MS Asquith 7, f. 170, Cab. Meeting, 17 Aug. 1914; Grey, ibid., II. pp. 167, 165.
5. MS Asquith 7, f.174, Cab. Meeting, 19 Aug. 1914.
6. *Hansard,* 5th Ser. 1914, LXVIII, 4. Also in MS Asquith 85, f.270.
7. *The Times,* 10 Nov. 1914, p. 10, col. 4, Guildhall speech.

respected during and after the war, in return for her neutrality. Nothing was asked from Turkey, Grey would recall later, no help, no facilities for the Allies open or covert, nothing except that she should remain neutral.[8]

But the leaders of Turkey committed her to Germany. In late September Constantinople was placed under German control. The British Cabinet was 'grievously dissatisfied'. It took the momentous decision that henceforward Britain 'must finally abandon the formula of "Ottoman integrity", whether in Europe or in Asia'.[9] By October Turkey had chosen to fight on the German side against Britain.

The die was now cast. The overriding consideration of the British government was to win the war. To defeat her enemies Britain had to mobilise not only all the material resources under her command but also her moral forces. The peoples of the British Empire should be fully aware of, and know, the kind of enemies they were being asked to fight. Only the prospect of the destruction of evil forces and the creation of a better world would inspire the fighting millions. Thus, Lloyd George predicted that in this battle between 'right and wrong' the downfall of the 'ravagers' of Armenia and the desolators of Flanders, the Turk of the East and the Turk of the West, would bring peace and gladness to a world which for generations had been oppressed and darkened by their grim presence.[10]

The British government had to stimulate the war effort by demonstrating that the sacrifices demanded at home were justified and worthwhile. It had also to sustain the loyalty of the Moslem subjects of the Empire who were fighting the Ottoman armies, and to quieten their conscience by showing that the war was not against Islam but against the cruelty and oppression of the Turkish government. They had to try to influence, in addition, some of the neutral countries, especially those in the Balkans who were sitting on the fence. In the United States of America there were sections, headed by Theodore Roosevelt, the former President, who did not favour the passivity of their country. So, Britain had to make every possible effort to win over public opinion in the neutral countries and especially in the greatest of them, the United States. In this connection the blockade of Germany, considered as 'essential' to the victory of the Allies, was a difficult problem. Britain had to counter the arguments against blockade and face the very delicate question of the contraband of the neutral countries. According to Grey, Germany and Austria were self-supporting in the huge supply of munitions. But the countries of the Entente had soon become dependent on the United States. It was essential, therefore, that the allies

8. Grey, *Twenty-Five Years*, II, pp. 167, 176: Grey to Mallet, 22 Aug. 1914, Mallet to Grey, 6 Sept. 1914; ibid., II, p. 166, See also, W.S. Churchill, *The World Crisis — The Aftermath* (London, 1929), p. 130.

9. MS Asquith 7, f.206, Cab. Meeting, 23 Sept. 1914; ibid., ff.210-11, Cab. Meeting, 2 Oct. 1914.

10. *The Times*, 11 Nov. 1914, p. 10, col. 4 (at the City Temple).

and especially Britain should not lose the good-will of the neutral powers. Above all, Britain had to counter the propaganda of the German agents who were representing Britain as the cause of the war. The German ambassador in the United States had actually stated in the press that Britain had declared her intention of 'fighting to a finish' — for 'selfish purposes'.[11] Thus, it was vital for the wartime British leaders to impress upon their own people in the Empire and upon public opinion in the neutral countries and especially in the United States that Britain was only fighting for worthwhile causes against the injustice, cruelty, oppression and the use of brutal force of her enemies.

It seems that the large-scale Armenian massacres of 1915 provided the British government with this opportunity. In October 1916 Grey would state at the luncheon of the Foreign Press Association that there was taking place in Turkey horrors on an 'unprecedented' scale in an attempt to 'exterminate' the Christian population; horrors which Germany could have prevented, and which could only have gone on with her toleration. At the Guildhall, Asquith also spoke about the 'wholesale massacre' and 'incredible' sufferings of the Armenian people. Germany, 'the master of Turkey', he added, could have arrested this organised campaign of outrage and massacre, but had looked on 'unmoved, quiescent, for all we know complacent'.[12]

Yet at the beginning of the massacres, the British government itself was very cautious in expressing its views. Since Britain had no direct contact with Turkey they did not know whether the news leaking out was authentic. Moreover, they had always to act in consultation with France and Russia. Above all, they could never disregard Moslem susceptibilities.

The first official intimation of these happenings in Turkey reached the British Foreign Office through two 'notes' both forwarded by the Russian ambassador in London on 27 April 1915. According to the first note, the Catholicos of the Armenians had addressed to the King of Italy and the President of the United States — both neutral countries — a request to intervene with the Sublime Porte to stop the Armenians being massacred 'in all of Turkish Armenia'. The Russian ambassadors in Rome and in Washington had been instructed by Sergei D. Sazonov, the Foreign Minister, 'to support in the name of the Imperial Government the request of the Catholicos'. According to the second note, Sazonov proposed that together with the Russian government, the British and French governments should issue a message to the Porte which would hold the members of the Council of Ministers of Turkey, as well as those Turkish military and civilian officials directly involved in this disaster, 'personally responsible'.[13]

The Foreign Office reaction was initially hesitant. Grey thought it advis-

11. Grey, *Twenty-Five Years,* II, pp. 103, 108, 114; ibid., p. 116, Spring-Rice to Grey, 17 Sept. 1914.
12. *The Times,* 24 Oct. 1916, p. 10, col. 2; ibid., 10 Nov. 1916, p. 10, col. 3.
13. FO 371/2488/51009/51010, 27 Apr. 1915.

able to await the result of the appeal of the Armenian Catholicos to the governments of the United States and Italy. Very soon, however, he was informed that the American, Italian and Bulgarian representatives at Constantinople had made representations to the Porte.[14]

On 4 May 1915, Gevorg V, the Catholicos of all Armenians, appealing to the high philanthropic sentiments of King George V, asked him if orders might be given to the British diplomatic representatives to the neutral governments so that by the influence of the latter an end could be put

> . . . to the frightful persecution of my people in Turkey abandoned to the fury of Turkish fanaticism.

Temporising, Grey replied that the position of Armenians in Turkey was 'engaging the attention' of the British government.[15] On 11 May the British ambassador in Petrograd cabled that the Russian Foreign Minister still thought that the three Allied governments should make a declaration about Turkey's responsibility for the massacres of Armenians. Grey, however, was, as before, slow to respond because the government did not possess 'sufficiently trustworthy data' on which to base such a message. It also seemed that such a pronouncement instead of having a moderating effect, might, on the contrary, 'instigate' the Turkish authorities to be still 'more vindictive' towards the Christians.[16]

It seems that Grey was totally missing or ignoring the value of such a statement as a deterrent to the Turks.

It was only when the Russian ambassador in London represented to him that for military reasons it was 'very important' for his government to make a public declaration 'in order to satisfy Armenian opinion in Russia', that Grey concurred and expressed his willingness to publish such a statement in London as soon as the French government agreed to do likewise.[17] Over 150,000 Russian-Armenians were fighting in the Russian armies, and thousands more from the Armenian diaspora had joined the Allied forces. Apparently both the Russian government and presently Grey agreed to condemn the Turkish authorities solely from military considerations, in order not to lose Armenian support in the war. The proposed declaration was handed in to the Foreign Office by Benckendorff, the Russian ambas-

14. Ibid., no. 51010, cypher tels, to Spring-Rice, R. Rodd and Buchanan, 29 Apr. 1915; ibid., File 51009, nos. 53073, 53153, Rodd to Grey and Spring-Rice to Grey, 1 May 1915.

15. Ibid., no 55449, Catholicos, Etchmiadzin, to King, 4 May 1915; Grey to Catholicos, draft of tel., 12 May 1915.

16. Ibid., no 58387, Buchanan to Grey, 11 May 1915; ibid., nos. 58350, 58387, Grey to Bertie, 11, 12 May 1915.

17. J.S. Kirakosian (ed.), *Hayastane Mijazcayin Divanacitutyan ev Sovetakan Artakin Kaghakakanutyan Pastateghterum, 1828-1923* (Armenia in the Documents of International Diplomacy and Soviet Foreign Policy, 1828-1923) (Erevan, 1972), p. 376, Benckendorff to Sazonov, 20/7 May 1915; FO 371/2488/51009/59097, Grey to Bertie, 18 May 1915.

sador in London. The reference, in the original draft, to these crimes being committed 'against Christendom', was omitted on the suggestion of Sir F. Bertie, the British amabassador in Paris. Both Grey and the French Foreign Minister agreed:[18] they could not disregard the religious sensitivity of the non-Christian populations in the British and French Empires.

Finally, on 24 May 1915, the British government, in common with the governments of France and Russia, made a public declaration that from about the middle of April, Kurds and the Turkish population of Armenia had been engaged in massacring Armenians with the connivance and often with the help of the Ottoman authorities. Such massacres had taken place at Erzerum, Bitlis, Sasun, Mush, Zeitun and in all Cilicia. Inhabitants of about 100 villages near Van had all been assassinated. At the same time the Ottoman government in Constantinople was raging against the inoffensive Armenian population. The statement concluded that

> In face of these fresh crimes committed by Turkey the Allied Governments announce publicly to the Sublime Porte that they will hold all the members of the Ottoman Government, as well as such of their agents as are implicated, personally responsible for such massacres.[19]

The Foreign Office soon had ample evidence that happenings in Turkey, which at first had seemed to be unbelievable, were very real indeed. Communications sent independently by the British representatives in the various Middle Eastern countries confirmed the complete authenticity of the reports. In Sofia the Armenian community had observed 17 August as a day of mourning on account of the massacres in Turkey. The British Vice-Consul in Philippopolis reported that it was difficult to find room in that town for all the refugees, 90 per cent of whom were women and children. The men had been sent to an 'unknown destination'.[20] Philip P. Graves of the Intelligence Department of the War Office, who in 1913 had been the correspondent of *The Times* in Constantinople, writing personally to Lloyd George from Cairo, also referred to the Armenian massacres. About 5,000 refugees, mostly women and children, picked up by the French, had arrived in Egypt and were under the care of the British. Blaming the pretentious Pan-Turkism of the Turkish rulers and their 'narrowly violent' ideas, Graves grimly added:

> Making all allowance for exaggeration there can be no doubt that there has been a carnival of murder and rape in many parts of the interior and that if this continues, TALAAT's threat 'I will make any idea of

18. FO 371/2488/51009/59205/63095/63903, note by Benckendorff, 12 May 1915; Bertie to Grey, 19, 21 May 1915; minutes by Grey under nos. 63095, 63903.
19. Ibid., no. 63095, 23 May 1915, 10.50 pm for pub. in Monday's papers (24 May).
20. Ibid., no 115852, O'Beirne to Grey, 19 Aug. 1915.

Armenian autonomy impossible for 50 years' will be fulfilled . . . In my experience and that of all who know Turkey at all, no massacre ever takes place in Turkey save when the Government lets it be known that it desires a massacre.[21]

In his turn, Lord Bryce had written to Asquith, the Prime Minister, about the events in Turkey:

Terrible accounts reach me through various channels, each confirming the others, of the sufferings of the Armenian population of the region round Van and between that city and the Russian frontier. The Turks and Kurds have been massacring the whole Christian population of these regions.

It seems that by early September 1915, the British government had no doubt whatsoever about the scale of the massacres and deportations committed in Turkey.[22]

It also seems that by September 1915 it had become part of the policy of the British government to use the Armenian massacres as one of the means available to influence public opinion in the United States of America. They used any available means in their desperate military need. Perhaps they also felt, rightly, that Americans might be more sensitive to Armenian suffering and more sentimentally involved than any other people in the neutral countries, as over the years US missionaries had done more for the education and the relief of that people than any other humanitarian or educational organisation in the world.

The first intimation of a decision by the British government to use the Armenian sufferings to influence American opinion, is a remarkable minute by Lord Robert Cecil, the Parliamentary Under-Secretary for Foreign Affairs, on 9 September. It followed a minute by Harold Nicolson, then of the War Department of the Foreign Office:

We know that this account of the persecution of Armenians is not as exaggerated as it first appears.

Lord Robert Cecil added: 'This should be published — for U.S.' Both minutes were in a despatch by Sir Henry McMahon, the British High Commissioner in Egypt. A few days later, the Foreign Office sent the copy of McMahon's despatch and the enclosure (a letter from an Armenian in Constantinople respecting the state of affairs in Armenia), to G.H. Mair of

21. House of Lords Record Office, Lloyd George Papers, D/20/2/18. Graves to Lloyd George, 15 Sept. 1915. Lloyd George minuted 'I am in agreement with the views he expresses about the Turk' (1 Oct. 1915).

22. FO 371/2488/51009/123491, Bryce to Asquith, 28 Aug. 1915. See minute initialled by E.P., 2 Sept. 1915: 'There is no doubt, I fear, about the facts'.

the News Department, for perusal and return. The Foreign Office letter went on to say:

> Lord Robert Cecil thinks that it would be desirable to arrange for the letter of the 13th July to the Archbishop Tourian to be made known to the American Press. As we cannot vouch for all the particulars given I am a little chary of giving it officially to the Americans here, but perhaps you could arrange to put it into the right hands.[23]

In the meantime, Patrick Stevens, the British Consul in Batum, had been despatching to the Foreign Office detailed information taken from the Tiflis press, about the deplorable condition of the Armenian and Chaldean refugees in the Caucasus. According to these reports Turkish regulars had 'completely ravaged' Sasun. Great masses of refugees had arrived from the Melazkert and Archesh districts and from Van. Most of them had found shelter in the villages situated in the province of Erevan, while about 35,000 had remained at Etchmiadzin. The pitiful condition of this starved and emaciated mass of human beings was 'beyond all description'. Not long after, the Foreign Office sent a particularly revealing cable in cypher to the British ambassador in Petrograd:

> It has been suggested to us that if any photographs of Armenian atrocities or Armenian refugees exist good use might be made of them in America.

The Foreign Office asked if it would be worthwhile to enquire of the Russian authorities or of the British Consul in Batum whether any photographs were available.[24]

Again, when on one occasion Consul Stevens in Batum had enclosed a translation of an article published in the *Kavkazskoe Slovo* of 14/27 November 1915, describing instances of Turkish treachery used to exterminate the Armenian population, 'this might be shown to some of the American correspondents', was the Foreign Office minute. The article described how the Turkish authorities in Bitlis and Erzerum had given notice that all Armenians in hiding would be allowed perfect freedom if they returned. Many had believed in and had responded to the call and then had been slaughtered. 'I have given a copy of the enclosure to Mr. Bathurst' minuted G.H. Locock, Lord Robert Cecil's private secretary. The report was handed over with Lord Robert's concurrence.[25]

23. Ibid., no. 125295, McMahon to Grey, 26 Aug. 1915; minutes by H. Nicolson and R. Cecil, 6, 9 Sept. 1915; G.H. Locock to Mair, copy, 14 Sept. 1915.
24. Ibid., no. 140259, Stevens to Grey, 10 Sept. 1915; no. 148680, FO to Buchanan, 11 Oct. 1915.
25. Ibid., no. 192672, Stevens to Grey, 29 Nov. 1915; minutes by H. Nicolson, R. Cecil and Locock, 18, 19, 20 Dec. 1915, respectively.

A. Harvey Bathurst, stationed in London, was the European editor of the influential *Christian Science Monitor* of Boston. It seems that fairly close co-operation existed between the British Foreign Office and the *Christian Science Monitor,* whose chief editor, Frederick Dixon, was an Englishman. 'He has given us much useful information', Locock had minuted. Significantly, it had even been arranged that Dixon should cable his confidential reports to Locock through the British Consul General in Boston.

Neither Bathurst nor Dixon refrained from exposing the Armenian atrocities and from pointing to the responsibility of the Turkish and German authorities. Bathurst sent to the Foreign Office cuttings of the lead and special articles published in the *Christian Science Monitor* on 15 September 1915. The special article, written by a special correspondent of the paper in Constantinople, referred to a riot of crime and carnival of fatalities aimed at the 'annihilation' of the Armenian and Greek races. The lead article regarded this despatch from Constantinople as not only sorry but shameful reading.[26] It is clear that the Foreign Office was keenly interested in the feeling the Armenian massacres, and the responsibility for them, was arousing in the United States. Bathurst wrote to Locock again next day, this time enclosing a copy of the cable on the Armenian situation which he had sent through to Boston for publication that morning. 'It will, I think, interest you', he added. The cable considered whether neutral nations might be successful, as London hoped, in assisting the Armenians by representations to Germany. But as the *Monitor* European Bureau had learnt, in many cases German consuls had 'encouraged and even directed [the] proceedings'. Proof of their 'complicity' was available.[27]

Whether Germany was innocent or guilty, the British government saw its interest in exposing the direct or indirect responsibility of each one of the Central powers for what was regarded as the greatest crime of the war. This was thought to be valuable in order to win over opinion in the neutral countries and especially in the United States. There were already some groups in that country who thought neutrality was morally unjustifiable when the issue was the use of brute force. It seems that the British Foreign Office was not only benevolently interested in such groups but was even encouraging and patronising them. Sir Cecil Spring-Rice, the British ambassador, had transmitted to London a cutting of a remarkably forceful letter by Theodore Roosevelt, published in the *New York Times* on 1 December 1915. Roosevelt believed that even to nerves dulled and jaded by the heaped-up horrors of the previous year and a half, the news of the terrible fate that had befallen the Armenians must give a fresh shock of sympathy and indignation. But he had emphatically pointed out that sympathy and

26. Ibid., no. 148432, minute by Locock, 12 Oct. 1915; ibid., no 143444, Bathurst to Locock, 1 Oct. 1915, cuttings *Ch. Sc. Mon.,* 15 Sept. 1915.
27. Ibid., no. 143477, Bathurst to Locock, 2 Oct. 1915. See also ibid., nos 148432, 151442, 171151.

indignation were useless if they exhausted themselves in mere words. All the terrible iniquities of the previous year and a half, including 'the crowning iniquity of the wholesale slaughter of the Armenians', could be traced directly to the 'initial' wrong committed by the German invasion of Belgium. Roosevelt insisted, however, that

> . . . the criminal responsibility of Germany must be shared by the neutral powers, headed by the United States, for their failure to protest when this initial wrong was committed . . . We have refused to do our duty by Belgium; we refuse to do our duty by Armenia, because we have deified peace at any price . . . Wrongdoing will only be stopped by men who are brave as well as just, who put honor above safety, . . . and who shrink from no hazard, not even the final hazard of war, if necessary, in order to serve the great cause of righteousness.[28]

Ambassador Spring-Rice assessed, of course, the extent of the existing indignation the American people felt at the Armenian massacres and deportations. What the British government tried to do was to build on this indignation and to tip the scales of public opinion against the Central powers. In a long despatch, Spring-Rice informed Grey that the American Committee on the Armenian Atrocities, consisting of prominent Americans interested in Turkish affairs, had issued a report according to which the crimes being perpetrated upon the Armenian people surpassed in cruelty anything that history had recorded during the past thousand years. The Committee had been engaged for months in investigation. It vouched for the truth of the statements published. Its report had been supplemented by the personal experience of missionaries arriving from Van. In the last few weeks, the State Department had received 'innumerable' reports of wholesale massacres and atrocities in Asia Minor. The German ambassador had at once stated that they 'appear to be pure invention'. He was also said, however, to have defended the Turks' action as a necessary wartime measure. Spring-Rice added that the State Department, according to the press accounts, had made representations to the Turkish government for the second time in the last two months. However, it was generally believed in Washington that no official action would be taken unless American missionaries or American property had suffered wrong.[29]

If the German embassy in Washington was making statements that the reports of the atrocities were exaggerated and that the action taken by the Turkish government was simply a military measure, the Foreign Office on its part apparently felt fully justified in publishing the information which it was receiving from its own representatives abroad. Consul Stevens was con-

28. Ibid., no 191832, cutting from the *New York Times,* 1 Dec. 1915.
29. Ibid., no. 153862, Spring-Rice to Grey, 8 Oct. 1915.

tinually sending long reports describing the crushing misery of the hundreds of thousands of refugees in the Caucasus.[30] Evelyn Grant Duff, the British Minister in Berne, had transmitted to Grey an 'Appeal' by the Swiss 'Committee for Help to Armenians' signed by prominent Swiss citizens which the Committee had asked to be brought to the notice of the British government. The Appeal referred to the 'systematic annihilation of a people, the Armenians'.[31] J.D. Bourchier, the veteran Middle Eastern correspondent of *The Times* and a contributor to the *Encyclopaedia Britannica,* had sent to his paper, through the British Minister in Bucharest, a grim telegram about the fate of the bulk of the Armenian population in Turkey:

> Memorial previously addressed Bulgarian Government . . . gives frightful picture sufferings Armenian prisoners Asia Minor hands Turkish authorities document furnishes list twenty nine districts whole Armenian population numbering some eight hundred and thirty five thousand persons either killed exiled or forcibly converted Islam one ecclesiastic burnt alive.[32]

It was perfectly natural that Britain, as one of the major belligerents, should make use of the information reaching her from various independent sources, about the inhuman doings by one of her enemies; doings which apparently had the tacit approval of her other enemies. When John Moffat from New York, the Chairman of the 'Publicity Committee' of a Society for Armenian Relief cabled Grey that his committee, presided over by Senator Elihu Root, was inaugurating a great national campaign in aid of Armenian sufferers, the Foreign Office responded immediately. It was very willing to put its whole weight behind this American pressure group. Moffat had said that he would be grateful if Grey would 'endorse same' by cable. The Foreign Office 'most warmly' approved and supported the 'great national campaign' in aid of the Armenian sufferers. Its cable went on:

> Much fresh information makes clear that the facts stated in Arnold Toynbee's book Armenian Atrocities embodying speech and letter by Lord Bryce are extremely moderate and conservative . . . High and skilled ability plans the scheme and low brutality carries it out. The world is aghast at these hellish incidents.

Arnold Toynbee's book *Armenian Atrocities: The Murder of a Nation,* published in 1915, was, as its title implies, a lashing indictment of the attempt on the part of the Turkish rulers 'to exterminate' the Armenian race 'once and for all'. In addition, the Foreign Office reference to Lord Bryce's

30. Ibid., nos. 140259/143153/192671/192672/198351/200063.
31. Ibid., no 156771, Duff to Grey, 18 Oct. 1915.
32. Ibid., no. 196244, G. Barclay, Bucharest, to A. Nicolson, 18 Dec. 1915.

speech and letter in the telegram just quoted, was indeed extremely expedient and politic. Spring-Rice had earlier notified that the statement published on the authority of Bryce had attracted 'very great attention' in the United States.[33]

Grey was well aware of Bryce's popularity in America.[34] Asquith had repeatedly stated that 'no one else' could have served as ambassador there equally well. It seems that at the beginning of the war, with a view to influencing American public opinion, he had appointed Bryce (a former Regius Professor of Civil Law at Oxford as well as Cabinet Minister) to act as Chairman of a Royal Commission on German atrocities in Belgium. Spring-Rice had cabled in May 1915 that the Report, just published, was having 'an immense effect' much increased by Bryce's authority. The *New York Tribune* had commented that for all who knew Bryce, his name was 'as final as that of the highest Court'. 'Your report has *swept* America', Charles F.G. Masterman, head of the Department of Information wrote.[35] Apparently the view of influencing American opinion through Bryce had succeeded well.

Throughout 1915-16, Bryce had been receiving 'first-hand' reports from the American missionaries in Turkey about the deportations and massacres of the Ottoman Armenians. The Foreign Office, therefore, asked him to collect these documents for publication in a Blue Book and also provided him with the assistance of the Oxford historian, Arnold Toynbee. A copy of this Blue Book, *Miscellaneous, No. 31, 1916,* a collection of documents relating to the treatment of Armenians in the Ottoman Empire 1915-16, was presented by Bryce to Grey in the House of Commons, on 23 November 1916. A few months earlier, Lord Robert Cecil had stated that 'a valuable Report' consisting chiefly of a collection of documentary evidence, had been prepared 'at the suggestion' of Bryce by Toynbee and would be laid before Parliament in due course. Writing half a century later, Toynbee recalled that Bryce had agreed to 'a request' from the British government to collect these documents for publication.[36] Whether the collection of these documents was made 'at the suggestion' of Bryce, as Lord Robert had stated, or by Bryce at the 'request' of the government, as Toynbee stated — a course which seems more probable — is, it seems, immaterial. The fundamental fact is that these documents were issued as a Blue Book by the Foreign Office and the

33. FO 371/2768/1455/12592, Moffat to Grey, 20 Jan. 1916. See draft of reply, ibid., n.d.; A.J. Toynbee, *Armenian Atrocities: The Murder of a Nation* (London, 1915), p. 17; FO 371/2488/51009/153862, Spring-Rice to Grey, 8 Oct. 1915.

34. Grey, *Twenty-Five Years*, II, p. 86

35. Bryce Papers, UB 1, Asquith to Bryce, 28 Apr. 1908, 19 Dec. 1912; ibid., UB 57, Spring-Rice to N. Primrose, copy, n.d., rec'd 14 May 1915; ibid., UB 54, 'American Press Resumé', for Cab., prepared in Dept. Inform., 27 May 1915, quot. *New York Tribune*, 13 May 1915; same also in UB 57; ibid., Masterman to Bryce, 7 June 1915.

36. A.J. Toynbee, *Acquaintances* (London, 1967), p. 149; PP, 1916, vol. XXXIII, *The Treatment of Armenians in the Ottoman Empire 1915-16. Hansard*, 5th Ser. 1916, LXXXVII, 1547; ibid., LXXXV, 2650.

editor — Bryce — was probably the most trusted Briton in the United States. One has also to add, however, that this must have been a labour both of loving duty and of grief for Bryce: a self-imposed 'duty' to collect 'in the interest of historic truth' all the available data for an 'authentic record', as he put it, of what had occurred in 1915;[37] a 'grief' because of his life-long distress at the fate of the Armenian people in that year.

In February 1916 Spring-Rice informed Grey about the press announcement that the US government had now made a 'formal' protest against the continuation of the Armenian atrocities. Apparently the protest was to the effect that the American government could 'no longer doubt' that 'authorities of the Turkish Government were responsible for hitherto unparalleled' atrocities. The formal protest to Turkey had been made despite German Ambassador Bernstorff's two statements, made 'on official authority' and published in the same week; one, that there were no atrocities; two, that the Armenians by their rebellious behaviour had merited and received the severest punishment.[38] This information from Spring-Rice pointed to clear evidence that the United States was now definitely at variance with both Turkey and Germany. Referring to this communication, Laurence Collier of the War Department of the Foreign Office minuted:

> I suppose we are already making use of the Armenian question for propaganda in the U.S.[39]

Thus, the propagation of information about the Armenian massacres and deportations became, under war conditions, one aspect of British policy and a means, in the hands of the sophisticated Foreign Office, for diminishing American sympathies for the Central powers.

Also in February 1916 the Russian ambassador in London communicated a memorandum enquiring on behalf of Sazonov if the British government would be disposed to contribute a half share in a joint subsidy of one million francs for the relief of Turkish Armenians evacuated by the Turkish government in the region of Aleppo-Mosul railway and farther towards Baghdad. The sum might be put at the disposal of the Armenian Patriarch and the Armenian Catholicos through the United States, or it might be distributed among Armenians by American agents. The memorandum ended by advising that the source of the fund should be kept secret 'to avert the danger of fresh violence against the Armenians'. The minutes written in the Foreign Office are extremely revealing:

> From one point of view the whole object of such a donation would be the

---

37. PP, 1916, vol. XXXIII (Misc. No. 31, *The Treatment of Armenians in the Ottoman Empire 1915-16)*, pp. xvi, xxi.
38. FO 371/2768/1455/45923, Spring-Rice to Grey, 26 Feb. 1916.
39. Ibid., 10 Mar. 1916.

effect in the U.S.A. etc. & it would be valueless if it were kept secret,

wrote Harold Nicolson. A more senior official added:

> I should be disinclined to make any donation for the benefit of Armenians
> in Turkey without publicly stating that we were doing it.[40]

The Treasury was consulted about the ambassador's memorandum. But it
expressed the view that a voluntary private fund was the only appropriate
means of raising money for the Armenians. Accordingly, the Foreign Office
replied to Benckendorff that the object in view did not appear to affect
British 'national interests' in such a way as to justify a grant from the public
funds.[41] The British half-share in the joint subsidy of one million francs
would have been about £20,000. But Harold Nicholson had indeed aptly
expressed the Foreign Office view that the 'whole' object of a donation
would be its effect in the United States, and it would be 'valueless' if it were
kept secret. Statements and reports passed on to American journalists and a
Blue Book describing the Turkish cruelties were certainly more useful to the
Foreign Office *vis-à-vis* the view of British national interests than a secret
contribution to Armenian relief.

The Treasury had, once before, in August-September 1915, refused to
contribute towards Armenian relief. Asquith and Grey had not insisted.
This was at the time when 'terrible accounts' of the massacres and deportations were reaching Bryce. He had written an informal and unaffected, but
deeply impassioned, letter to Asquith asking if it would be possible for the
British government, and that of France, to make a grant towards the relief of
Armenian misery. A vast host of refugees, he had claimed, had been
pouring, homeless and helpless, into Russian Transcaucasia. Private
benevolence could not cope with the appalling situation:

> Even £20,000 or £30,000 would do much, and the moral effect would be
> great in giving some sort of cheer to a people which has suffered more
> than any other during this war, for they have lost everything . . .

But no payment came from the Treasury.[42]

It is difficult to assess the extent of influence the Armenian massacres and
deportations had on American public opinion. But, that these events were
used by the British Foreign Office to arouse antipathy against the Central

40. Ibid., no. 20335, memo by Russian ambassador, 1 Feb. 1916; minutes by H. Nicolson, 2
Feb. 1916 and by HOB? n.d.

41. Ibid., FO to Treasury, draft, 7 Feb. 1916; ibid., no. 35658, Treasury to FO, 23 Feb. 1916;
ibid., FO to Benckendorff, copy, 3 Mar. 1916.

42. FO 371/2488/51009/123491, Bryce to Asquith, 28 Aug. 1915. Minutes by A. Nicolson,
Lord Crewe and Eustace Percy, 3 Sept. 1915. Draft of letter, Crewe to McKenna, 6 Sept. 1915.

powers, there is no doubt. Half a century after these events, Toynbee claimed that the British government had issued the Blue Book for a special purpose, of which he was unaware at the time, and, he believed, Bryce was also unaware. According to Toynbee, the Russian armies, when retreating across the Polish-Lithuanian frontier in the spring of 1915, had committed barbarities against the Jewish diaspora there, and the advancing German armies had tried to exploit them. Jewish-American journalists, invited to the German-occupied Russian territories, had sent 'lurid' despatches to American papers, and the British government in London had been seriously perturbed. Thus in February 1916, the New York *American* had advised the whole American people to demand that 'Christian England and Christian France' restrain the 'savagery' of their barbarous allies.[43] Toynbee believed the government was worried lest American Jewry might retaliate against the Allies by throwing its weight into the anti-British scales in the debate in the United States. The 'considerably worse' barbarities committed against the Armenians had provided the British government, according to Toynbee, with 'counter-propaganda' material against the Central powers.[44]

Noel Buxton, as well as Asquith and Stanley Baldwin, asserted that the British government did make use of the Armenian tragedy to win over American support during the war. They ascribed, however, to the Foreign Office less specific but definitely much more important and broader motives than Toynbee. Noel Buxton, who had 'a close and lasting' relationship with Colonel E.M. House, President Wilson's confidential adviser on foreign affairs, 'believed' according to his biographer, that the account of the sufferings of the Armenians had 'a great influence' upon American opinion. The description of their expulsions and massacres, as documented in Bryce's Blue Book, had been 'one of the moving factors' in President Wilson's 'decision to enter the war'. Asquith, who was Prime Minister when the Blue Book was issued in 1916, and Stanley Baldwin, Prime Minister in the 1920s, also held similar views. In their remarkable joint memorial presented in 1924 to the then Prime Minister, Ramsay MacDonald, they stated in no uncertain terms that Bryce's Blue Book was

. . . widely used for Allied propaganda in 1916-17 and had an important influence upon American opinion and upon the ultimate decision of President Wilson to enter the war.[45]

The Armenian sufferings were also used by the British leaders to influence opinion both in other neutral countries, especially Bulgaria, and among the

43. Toynbee, *Acquaintances,* pp. 149-52; Bryce Papers, UB 57, cutting, New York *American,* 2 Feb. 1916.
44. Toynbee, *Acquaintances,* pp. 149-52.
45. Mosa Anderson, *Noel Buxton: A Life* (London, 1952), pp. 81, 110; Bodleian Library, Toynbee Papers, Box on Armenia, 'Memorial', 26 Sept. 1924.

Moslem subjects of Britain.

There were about 70 million Moslems in the British Empire and, as Lord Cromer pointed out, they might naturally have a certain amount of sympathy with their co-religionists, the Turks. They would be unwilling to believe ill of them unless they had positive proof. On the other hand, the British authorities were very anxious to retain their unswerving loyalty and uninterrupted flow of manpower. The Armenian tragedy, therefore, could serve as evidence of the true nature of the Turkish government; Britain was fighting not Islam but a criminal government.

Sending beforehand a copy of the questions he intended to ask about the Armenian massacres in Parliament, Lord Cromer assured Lord Crewe, the Lord President of the Council, that his principal reason for raising this subject was to give the utmost publicity to the Turkish proceedings, and bring home to the 'educated Mahommedans in India' what the nature of the Turkish government was. So, knowing in advance the direction the debate in the House of Lords would take, the Foreign Office decided to take additional 'steps to draw the attention of neutrals' to it.[46] There were deep fears that Bulgaria might join the Central powers.

According to his intentions, Cromer began his statement by saying that Britain had been 'shocked' by the renewed accounts of Armenian massacres. His own belief was that all the educated Mohammedans in India would look with as great 'a horror' as the British did upon the proceedings of the Turkish government. When once fully informed, they would see that it would be an 'insult' to the Mohammedan religion if they in any way identified the cause of Islam with the cause of the existing government in Constantinople. He urged publicity for the Armenian massacres for yet another reason. Bulgaria was apparently about to commit not only 'a grave political error' but also one of the blackest acts of political ingratitude. He reminded the Bulgarians that they themselves had suffered in the past so severely from Turkish rule that it was inconceivable that they should not extend some sympathy to these 'poor Armenians'. Cromer concluded with his crucial message: Britain could warn all other races, whether Christian, Mohammedan or Hindu, that by associating themselves or sympathising with the Germans and the Turks, they would in the eyes of posterity acquire 'a taint and a stain which can never be removed'. Lord Crewe, for the government, was happy to give all the information about the Armenian atrocities which the British Consul in Batum had been transmitting. These were 'terrible facts' and, of course, in no way authorised by the precepts of Islam.[47]

---

46. FO 371/2488/51009/143621, Cromer to Crewe, 2 Oct. 1915; ibid., no. 148483, minute by Locock, 'We have taken steps to draw the attention of neutrals to this Debate', n.d. but Oct. 1915.

47. *Hansard*, 5th Ser. 1915, XIX, cols. 994-1000.

It seems that the British government also made use of the Armenian massacres at home to stimulate the war effort against the enemy. The Foreign Office very willingly passed all the information about the massacres and the deportations, gathered through its embassies and consulates, both to the British papers and to the humanitarian groups. The latter were particularly anxious to have such information in order to be able to organise relief. Consul Stevens had been transmitting detailed information about the Nestorian and especially Armenian refugees, who had been pouring into the Caucasus. The treatment of these Christians by Turkish hordes had been characterised, he wrote, by exceptionally distressing conditions, painful cruelty and a series of dastardly acts. G. Locock minuted:

> . . . we might send the whole of this despatch to Mr. Aneurin Williams, informing him, at the same time, that it may be published if considered necessary . . .

Lord Robert Cecil approved: 'Yes, send it at once.' In further despatches Consul Stevens reported that sickness of every kind was prevalent among the orphans of massacred Armenians. The children were so emaciated that they looked more like skeletons than human beings.[48] Many of the refugees had settled in and about the town of Etchmiadzin, where they had to be accommodated without cover in yards and open spaces in the neighbourhood of the monastery. Telegrams from Etchmiadzin reported that from 350 to 400 deaths were daily taking place owing to destitution, starvation and epidemics. The Russian government had contributed important sums and latterly funds had been flowing in from the United Kingdom and the United States.[49]

The substance of all such information was invariably passed on to Aneurin Williams with a hint that there was 'no objection' to his making these facts 'public' if he so desired.[50]

Two reports by Moslem eyewitnesses, Lieutenant Sayied Ahmed Moukhtar Baas and Lieutenant Hassan Maaroue, about the Armenian massacres, had been communicated to the Foreign Office by Sir Mark Sykes, the Middle Eastern expert. Both reports were circulated to the King and the War Cabinet. The first eyewitness had been a member of the Court Martial in Trebizond. Orders for the deportations of the Armenians to the interior had come from Constantinople. But 'I knew that deportations meant massacres'. The Armenian Bishops of both Trebizond and Erzerum were murdered at Gumush-Khana. All able-bodied men were taken out of

48. FO 371/2488/51009/192671, Stevens to Grey, 27 Nov. 1915; minutes by Locock, 17 Dec. 1915 and R. Cecil, 19 Dec. 1915; ibid., nos. 198351, 8098, Stevens to Grey, 9, 29 Dec. 1915.

49. FO 371/2768/10980, Stevens to Grey, 3 Jan. 1916.

50. Ibid., no. 1455, FO to Williams, 11 Jan. 1916 (wrongly written 1915); ibid., no. 10980, 20 Jan. 1916; FO 371/2488/51009/200063, 'Substance to . . . A. Williams and the Archb. of Canterb.', H. Nicolson, 29 Dec. 1915.

town in batches of 15 or 20, lined up on the edge of ditches prepared beforehand, shot and thrown into the ditches. The women and children on their way to Mosul were attacked by the 'Shotas', the armed bands who committed the most dastardly outrages. The military escorts had 'strict orders not to interfere with the "Shotas" '. The infants in Trebizond were stabbed, put in sacks and thrown into the sea.[51] The report of the second eyewitness, Lieutenant Hassan Maaroue, is a chilling description of atrocities committed at Bitlis, Zaart, Erzinjan and Mamakhatun. In August 1915 he had seen large numbers of dead bodies of Armenians in the fields around Mush, most of them 'horribly mutilated'. Sir Ronald Graham, an Assistant Under-Secretary of State for Foreign Affairs, and Sir Mark Sykes thought that these reports 'ought to be published' but no clue should be given as to the identity of the officers because their relatives might suffer. It was to these reports that Robert Cecil referred in December 1916 when he gave to the House of Commons further information, about 'systematic' outrages, received from a 'reliable source'.[52]

Likewise, the communication about a meeting of protest against the Armenian atrocities held in the 'largest' hall in Stockholm, transmitted by the British Minister, was sent to *The Near East* by Stephen Gaselee of the News Department of the Foreign Office. It was Stephen Gaselee again who arranged that a copy of a painfully disturbing article in the April issue of the Swiss *Orient-Mission,* and a translation of it, transmitted to the Foreign Office by Sir Cecil Hertslet, the British Consul General in Zurich, should be sent 'to Mr. Arnold Toynbee at Wellington House for Lord Bryce'. It might be noted that Toynbee was at this time working in the Intelligence Bureau of the Department of Information, on Turkish affairs.[53] Sir Cecil Hertslet had pointed out that the article signed by Dr Ed. Graeter, late teacher at the German 'Realschule', Aleppo, was written by a Swiss citizen who did 'not hesitate to give his name'. The writer was answering a correspondent of the *Neue Winterthurer Tagblatt* of 28 February, who had asked 'where is the truth to be found?' Graeter, who claimed to have been a witness of the Armenian persecution in all its phases, replied that there could be 'no doubt' for any thinking person as to the facts. In spite of the dreadful accusations made by the German professor Dr Niepage, and in spite of the reports published in the German missionary paper *Vor Sonnenaufgang,* no official German *dementi* (denial) had ever appeared. This for the simple reason, Graeter claimed, that the German government itself possessed in the detailed reports of its Consuls the most compromising documents. These reports would not be published during the war because the German-Turkish

---

51. FO 371/2768/1455/261608, communic. by M. Sykes, FO stamp, 26 Dec. 1916.
52. Ibid., no. 261609, communic, by Sykes, FO stamp, 26 Dec. 1916; minute by R. Graham, n.d.; *Hansard,* 5th Ser. 1916, LXXXVIII, 1636.
53. FO 371/3052/74082, Sir E. Howard to Balfour, 29 Mar. 1917. Minute by Gaselee, n.d.
A. J. Toynbee, *The Western Question in Greece and Turkey* (London, 1922), preface ix.

'friendship would hardly benefit by it'. Neither could new witnesses be found because of the great difficulties in sending letters from Turkey or leaving the country. But Graeter as a witness would complete Dr Niepage's statement, as during some journeys into the interior of the country he had seen even more than Dr Niepage:

It would be impossible for me to picture, or for anybody to imagine, what I have suffered for a whole year when I had to witness, inactive, the death-rattles of a dying nation, which has not deserved such a destiny. Even at present, at a time when these events have been effaced by new impressions, I almost long never to have seen the Armenian corpses in the Euphrates, the Syrian steppes, or to have heard the insane mothers and the whimpering children, when I counted the days until I was allowed to go to a country where people are not tortured to death in the open street. If, however, my experiences enable me to break a lance for a good cause, then I have not made such experiences in vain.

There is 'absolutely no doubt' as to these horrors having taken place, minuted Lord Hardinge of Penshurst, the Permanent Under-Secretary at the Foreign Office.[54] When Major-General Sir George Macdonogh, the Director of Military Intelligence, asked the Foreign Office if Dr Graeter's article could be published in the Blue Summary of the Foreign Press issued by M.I.7.b., War Office, Hardinge replied that there was no objection to making public the 'responsibility of German officials' for recent atrocities perpetrated against the Armenians.[55]

It is worth noticing that Hardinge pointed, strangely, to the responsibility not of the Turks, but of the Germans. Without having actual evidence of the complicity of the latter, he was certainly stretching the case against Germany and trying to discredit her. But, after all, Germany and not Turkey, was Britain's major enemy in the war, and previous to it the great threat to her political and economic position. It was expedient, therefore, to stress at least her moral responsibility. As referred to above, Grey and Asquith assumed that Germany, the master of Turkey, could have stopped the massacres had she wished to do so.[56] *The Times* also referred to Germany's role in two leading articles, besides publishing reports under such disparaging headings as 'Trail of death in Asia Minor: German callousness' and 'German aid to murder: participation in Armenian massacres'. In one of the leaders it emphasised that the 'ultimate guilt' for the attempt to obliterate the Armenians must rest with Germany because one word from Berlin would

54. FO 371/3052/74082/88066, transl. and copy of article in Swiss *Orient-Mission*, April (1917), transmitted by Hertslet to Balfour, 26 Apr. 1917. Minutes by Hardinge, n.d.; by S. Gaselee, 4 May 1917.
55. Ibid., no. 97911, Director of Military Intelligence (hereafter DMI) to FO 14 May 1917. Ibid., FO to DMI, copy, 18 May 1917.
56. See above p. 70.

have stopped the 'orgy of murder'. In the other article it implied that
Germany 'condones massacre'.[57]

Having read the German Foreign Office documents, Ulrich Trumpener
has concluded that Germany 'neither instigated nor welcomed' the wartime
persecution of the Ottoman Armenians. However, under war conditions she
was much too concerned with keeping the Turkish armies on the field to risk
alienating the Porte. On the other hand, the latter vigorously and effectively
resisted German attempts to meddle in the internal affairs of the Ottoman
Empire.[58]

In Britain, it is clear that the Armenian massacres were freely used by the
government to discredit Turkey directly and Germany indirectly. The
authorities aimed at stimulating the war effort at home and among the
Moslem subjects of the Empire in order to inflict military defeat on the
Central powers and especially Germany. The massacres were also used to
win over public opinion in neutral countries and draw it away from the
enemies of Britain.

During the last years of the war, the Armenian atrocities committed by
Turkey together with Allied statements about the liberation of Armenia
were further used by the British government to counter successfully the
growing charges that Britain was fighting an imperialistic war with a view to
annexations.

During the middle of 1917 both Italy and France were exhausted and
war-weary. In Britain there was growing doubt as to whether military victory
was possible. As the war wore on, people asked if the sacrifices which were
being demanded of them were justified. The Union of Democratic Control
for the first time became a force with which the government had to reckon.[59]
It was known that the United States had always advocated a negotiated
peace settlement. Now with the March Revolution in Russia, the principle
of 'no annexations and no indemnity' became fashionable. There already
were suspicions that the Allies designed the partition of the Turkish Empire.
H.B. Lees-Smith, MP, actually asked Balfour, the Foreign Secretary,
whether the whole of Asia Minor was to be 'carved up'. In the House of
Commons the pacifist minority moved a resolution calling for peace prelimi-
naries, provided satisfactory guarantees could be obtained with regard to
the independence and restoration of Belgium and 'the evacuation of other
occupied territory'.[60] But Britain 'intended to stick' to both Mesopotamia

59. V.H. Rothwell, *British War Aims and Peace Diplomacy 1914-1918* (Oxford, 1971), p. 96;
Marvin Swartz, *The Union of Democratic Control in British Politics During the First World War*
(Oxford, 1971), pp. 194-8.

57. *The Times,* 4 Jan. 1916, p. 7, col. 5; ibid., 8 Feb. 1916, p. 7, col. 5; ibid., 30 Sept. 1915, p.7,
col. 2; ibid., 8 Oct. 1915, p. 7, cols. 2-3.

58. Ulrich Trumpener, *Germany and the Ottoman Empire 1914-1918* (Princeton, 1968), pp.
204-5; see also, pp. 221, 370, 232, 266.

60. *Hansard,* 5th Ser. 1917, XCVIII, cols. 2007-8.

and Palestine, as a member of the War Cabinet indicated.[61] British statesmen, therefore, had to devise war aims which would show that British policy was not completely based on imperialist greed. The Russian cry for a peace settlement without annexations and based on self-determination provided the British statesmen with a ready-made formula for explaining away the projected dismemberment of the non-Turkish areas in the Ottoman Empire. The principle of self-determination had a strong attraction both for the political left in Britain and for President Wilson in the United States.[62] In addition, the British leaders forcefully stressed Turkish misrule and Armenian suffering — such statements thereby giving an air of idealism to their arguments. Britain should not appear to aim at undisguised annexations in the Middle East.

Balfour's answer to the resolution from the pacifists asking for 'the evacuation' of territory occupied since the beginning of the war, was masterly. He blamed the mover and the seconder of the resolution for extreme narrowness of interpretation. Was there no interest in those elements in the Turkish Empire which were suffering under the most brutal and barbarous tyranny? Was it to be a matter of indifference that Armenia should be put back under Turkish rule? The government, he claimed, did not want to destroy any true Turkish community; but they should not put altogether out of sight one of the objects which they ought to aim at — the possibility, the duty of taking away from under Turkish rule people who were not Turks, and whose development had been stopped by the Turks. What was 'imperialistic' he asked, in wishing to see Armenia freed from Turkey?[63] Balfour in his statement had also referred to the liberation of Poland and other non-Turkish territories but Armenia was 'a particularly shrewd stroke in the Gladstonian tradition'. Lloyd George, the Prime Minister, could be more emotive and rhetorical: an 'idealistic wind' was blowing from Russia. He had to compete in idealism both with the Russians and with President Wilson.[64] Speaking in the House of Commons in December 1917, he chose to repeat one part of the statement he himself had made about Mesopotamia and Armenia in Glasgow on 29 June 1917. He had then said that what should happen to Mesopotamia must be left to the Peace Congress, but there was one thing which would 'never' happen. It would 'never be restored to the blasting tyranny of the Turk', who had been false to his trust. The trusteeship should be given over to more competent and more equitable hands, chosen by the Congress. That same observation applied to Armenia, 'the land soaked with the blood of innocence, and massacred by

61. G.A. Barnes in CAB 23/13, War Cab. 308A, minute 3, 31 Dec. 1917.
62. Rothwell, *British War Aims*, pp. 131, 288.
63. *Hansard*, 5th Ser. 1917, XCVIII (98), 2038, 2041-3.
64. A.J.P. Taylor, 'The War Aims of the Allies in the First World War' in R. Pares and A.J.P. Taylor (eds.), *Essays Presented to Sir Lewis Namier* (London, 1956), pp. 499, 497.

the people who were bound to protect them'. Lloyd George then went on to dismiss the view that all territory occupied by military power, to whichever side it belonged, should be restored to its original owner. Was it suggested, he asked, that to the Armenians, who had gone through 'terror and massacre', Britain should say, 'in the interest of international morality . . . go back?'[65]

Thus, bringing in the liberation of Armenia, a desolated country where Britain had no territorial interests whatsoever, and tying it in with the liberation of strategically important, oil-rich and fertile Mesopotamia, where Britain did have distinct ambitions of her own, the British leaders could confuse the issues, silence those critics who were accusing them of waging an imperialistic war, and could even give notions of idealism and humanity to their war aims.

During the war, the British Foreign Office rightly tried to show that the measures taken by the Turkish authorities against the Armenians went much further than military requirements warranted. It also repudiated the charges of British responsibility for 'provocations'.

In 1915, the Turkish Embassy in Gulahak (Tehran) issued a statement accusing the Armenians of having 'helped the Russians in their plans' from the beginning of the war. In order to put a stop to Armenian agitation, the Ottoman government had been 'obliged' to remove the frontier Armenians into the interior of the country. In Washington, the German ambassador likewise characterised the Turkish policy towards the Armenians as a necessary wartime measure. A statement by Dr M.M. Rifat, editor of *La Patrie Egyptienne,* issued in Denmark, a neutral country, held Britain responsible for the severe reprisals against insurgent Armenians. She had been organising a conspiracy, and a rebellion was to break out as soon as the Allies had got through the Dardanelles. The Foreign Office considered Rifat a 'notorious' agitator whose statement was a 'lie' and asked Reuters to issue a refutation.[66] But the 'first official defence' by the Turkish government against the charges of the Armenian massacres laid by the American ambassador, was made, according to the New York *Sun,* in February 1916. Under the headings of:

> Killed Armenians, Turks now admit. 'Deplorable excesses' are acknowledged — Blame laid on Allies,

the *Sun* gave the statement by the Turkish government which laid the blame

65. *Hansard,* 5th Ser. 1917, X, 2219-21.

66. FO 371/2488/51009/127223, notice by Turkish embassy, n.d. encl. in Marling to Grey, 13 Aug. 1915. Ibid., no. 153862, Spring-Rice to Grey, 8 Oct. 1915. Ibid, no. 149875, H. Lowther to Grey and min. by George Russell Clerk, both 13 Oct. 1915.

for the bloodshed on revolutionary uprisings among the Armenians and asserted that the disturbances were incited by the British, French and Russian governments. According to the statement, the removal of Armenians from certain regions to others was a measure 'dictated by imperative military necessity'; no coercive measures were taken by the Imperial government against the Armenians 'until June, 1915', by which time they had risen in arms at Van and in other military zones. This was 'after' they had joined hands with the enemy.[67]

It is worth pointing out that the reference by the Turkish government to the absence of coercive measures before 'June 1915'[68] shows a time lag. As seen above, the Russian ambassador had informed the British Foreign Office of these massacres on 27 April. Was it the case, then, that the repressive measures were taken much earlier, and that at a few places the Armenians were forced to consequent resistance?

Besides the denial of Turkish charges issued through Reuters and telegraphed to the neutral countries, including the United States, Grey asked the British Minister in the Vatican if he considered it advisable to give 'the most formal' assurances on behalf of the British government that they had 'never' provoked or encouraged any Armenian rising against the Turks. This was in reply to the Minister's report that the Vatican's efforts with the Ottoman government, since July 1915, to stop the massacres, had been unavailing. On 10 September 1915 the Pope himself had addressed an autograph letter to the Sultan, but no answer had been received.[69]

In a masterly argument based on evidence, Bryce and Toynbee refuted the Turkish charges point by point in their 'Summary' of Armenian history in the Blue Book. They indicated that the Armenian volunteers organised in the Caucasus were, generally, not Armenians resident in Turkey, but rather Russian Armenians — citizens of the Russian Empire. In addition they stressed that there was no organised revolt in Van; Armenians had defended their quarter only after it had been beleaguered and attacked by Turkish troops. Sazonov, the Russian Foreign Minister, was also of this view and had 'no doubt' about it. He argued in early May 1915 that it would have been 'senseless' for the Armenians to start a rebellion against superior Kurdish and Turkish forces before the arrival of Russian troops. Bryce and Toynbee, moreover, referred to the evidence of the unity of design and the fundamental uniformity of procedure in the deportations and concluded that 'the war was merely an opportunity and not a cause' and that the deportation

67. *Sun* (New York), 16 Feb. 1916, extr. transmitted by Spring-Rice to Grey, 18 Feb. 1916, in FO 371/2768/1455/39517.

68. [Turkey], *Verité sur le mouvement revolutionnaire Arménien et les mesures gouvernementales* (Constantinople, 1916), pp. 13, 15.

69. FO 371/2488/51009/152040, mins, by Grey n.d. [Oct. 1915], and H. Montgomery?, 19 Oct. 1915; ibid., Grey to Gregory, copy, 21 Oct. 1915; ibid., Gregory to Grey, 16 Oct. 1915.

scheme had flowed inevitably from the 'policy' of the Turkish government.[70]

In any event, no one would argue against the necessity of 'counter-measures' in answer to the 'provocations'[71] of individuals or even of certain groups, if these were well-founded. But military considerations can never justify deportations and suffering on a *mass* scale. Moreover, it seems that in 1915 military considerations were only the pretext for essentially political decisions aiming at the 'clearance' of the race: the one word used by Winston Churchill three times on one page, to describe the actions of the Turkish government.[72] Djemal Pasha, as Commander of the Fourth Army, was himself 'furious' that the deportees were sent to far-away Mesopotamia, thus hindering the movement of Ottoman troops, instead of being resettled in central Anatolia.[73] Hans von Wangenheim, the German ambassador, reported in June 1915 that the deportations were obviously no longer based on 'military considerations alone'. In July he was convinced that the Porte was 'actually' trying to exterminate 'the Armenian race' in the Turkish Empire. On 10 August 1915 Enver told Dr Johannes Lepsius that the Porte was out to 'make an end of the Armenians now'. Earlier, in May 1915, Consul Scheubner-Richter wired from Erzerum about the 'senseless' expulsions and the 'terrible' misery of thousands of women and children camping outside the city without food.[74] The separation of families, the suffering inflicted on women and children and the attempt at mass extermination surely made no sense as 'military' measures. The policy behind all these proceedings would be aptly called 'biological genocide' by one historian.[75] Another would point to it as an example of the 'classic simplicity of genocide' which resolved the complex political problem of a troublesome minority people by eradicating the people itself.[76]

70. PP, 1916, XXXIII (*Miscellaneous no. 31*), pp. 627-32, 637, 633; Kirakosian (ed.), *Hayastane Pastateghterum*, p. 374, Sazonov to Russian ambassador London, tel. no. 2247, 15/2 May 1915. See also Naim Bey, *The Memoirs of Naim Bey: Turkish Official Documents Relating to the Deportations and Massacres of Armenians* (London, 1920); Mevlanzade Rifat, *Turkiye Inkilabinin Icyuzu* (The Inner Aspects of the Turkish Revolution) (Aleppo, 1929), parts of which are quoted in E.K. Sarkisian and R.G. Sahakian, *Vital Issues in Modern Armenian History* (trans. E.B. Chrakian) (Watertown, Mass., 1965), pp. 22, 29, 33-6; *Daily Telegraph*, 29 May 1922, p. 11, cols. 5-6

71. This is the line usually taken by Turkish historians. See Yusuf Hikmet Bayur, *Türk Inkilabi Tarihi* (History of the Turkish Revolution), (Ankara, 1957), III, pt. 3, pp. 6-10, 35-49; Esat Uras, *Tarihte Ermeniler ve Ermeni Meselesi* (The Armenians in History and the Armenian Question) (Ankara, 1950), pp. 618-25; Ahmed Rustem, *La Guerre Mondiale et la Question Turco-Arménienne* (Berne, 1918), pp. 63-4, 133-4.

72. Churchill, *The Aftermath*, p. 405.

73. Djemal Pasha, *Memories*, p. 277.

74. Trumpener, *Germany and the Ottoman Empire*, p. 212, quot. Wangenheim to Bethmann Hollweg, 17 June 1915; ibid., p. 213, Wangenheim to Hollweg, 7 July 1915; ibid., p. 218, quot. from Johannes Lepsius (ed.), *Deutschland und Armenien 1914-1918. Sammlung Diplomatischer Aktenstücke* (Postdam 1919), no. 131. Trumpener, ibid., p. 209.

75. J.S. Kirakosian, *Arajin Hamashkharhayin Paterazme yev Arevmtahayutyune* (The First World War and the People of Western Armenia) (Erevan, 1965), p. 349.

76. Howard M. Sachar, *The Emergence of the Middle East 1914-1924* (New York, 1969), pp. 114-15.

In 1915, Lord Robert Cecil repeated in the House of Commons over and over again that the crimes were premeditated and there was no provocation whatever. There was no insurrection and no riot. It had been suggested in the United States that British agents had instigated Armenians to rebellion. He assured the House that this was not so. Even if there had been instigation, it could not excuse, or even palliate the crimes committed. They were a deliberate act 'not to punish insurrection but to destroy the Armenian race'.[77]

In fact the military authorities in Britain consistently and persistently refused in 1915 to provide arms and training to the Armenian volunteers in the diaspora, and especially in the United States. Both Kitchener, the Secretary of State for War, and the Army Council did not consider the use of 'untrained and unarmed' irregulars a 'feasible' project.[78] When the Armenian community in Egypt learnt, through the personal descriptions of the Italian Consul at Aleppo and the American missionaries from Cilicia, about the mass deportations in Turkey, they wrote to Lieutenant General Sir John Maxwell, the Commander-in-Chief of the British Forces in Egypt, about their strong feelings that the time had come to rush to the help of their brothers in danger and that it would be simply criminal on their part to wait any longer and to procrastinate. Volunteers in Egypt would be joined by volunteers from the Armenian communities in America, Bulgaria, Romania and Greece. But they asked for the active support of the British government. A landing in Cilicia, they stressed, could also help the Allied war effort. It could completely isolate Syria, Mesopotamia and Arabia and could deprive the Turkish government of its important reservoirs of military forces.[79] A little later, a delegation of the Armenian National Defence Committee, calling on General Maxwell in Cairo, personally appealed for help. They were daily receiving the most alarming news on the massacres and deportations in Cilicia. They could not be 'indifferent and inactive'. They would have no difficulty in holding the Taurus, Anti-Taurus and Amanus Mountains especially now that the Turks were fully occupied with the Russians on the Caucasus and the Anglo-French in Gallipoli. But they needed the authorisation of the British government, arms that could be spared, permission to congregate in Cyprus, assistance in transport and a small Allied contingent. The movement should be under the direction of British military authorities. In Buenos Aires, 300 Armenian volunteers asked the British Consul-General for acceptance as fighting units with the

77. *Hansard*, 5th Ser. 1915, LXXV, col. 1774.

78. Bryce Papers, UB 55, Kitchener to Bryce, 10 Apr. 1915; FO 371/2485/30439, min. by A. Nicolson to Grey, 9 Mar. 1915; see also ibid., no. 51438, WO to FO, 28 Apr. 1915.

79. Ibid., nos. 30439/106762, Moutafoff and A. Gamsaragan, Arm. Commit. of Nat. Defence, Alexandria, to Maxwell, 3 July 1915, in McMahon to Grey, 15 July 1915.

British and French forces operating in Turkey.[80]

Grey and the Foreign Office, however, out of consideration for Moslem feeling, were against the use of Egypt as a base for Armenian volunteers. Moreover, whenever proposals by Armenian volunteers in the diaspora to help their compatriots in Turkey were referred to the War Office, the reply of the Army Council was invariably a short refusal. They were against the use of Armenian irregulars for a landing and a rising in Cilicia.[81] Geographical, strategic and other reasons would render it impossible for the Allied troops to give assistance, they claimed.[82] It was felt that an Armenian volunteer force would not be helpful to the British war effort.

Throughout the war and especially during the first years, the War Office was, it seems, obsessed with the Western front. It always deprecated the opening up of new fronts on the East. Both the General Staff at home and the British High Command in France supported the view that the war could only be won on the Western front, and that all the military resources of the Empire should be concentrated there except when it was essential to defend such imperial interests as the Suez Canal.[83] It seems that trusting a proposed new front to an untrained irregular force was out of the question. However, General Sir John Maxwell, in contact with the Armenian community in Egypt, apparently did not share the rigid outlook of the War Office in London. He cabled Kitchener in no uncertain terms: 'everything should be done, I think, to help the [Armenian] movement'.[84] But his was a lone voice. Both the War Office and the Foreign Office believed that an Armenian movement in Cilicia might result in complications and become an additional liability. Thus the zeal and the enthusiasm of the Armenian communities in the diaspora, to take part in the great war effort and rescue their compatriots in Turkey, were wasted. A landing in Cilicia, were it successful, might have also provided the Allies, bogged down in Gallipoli, with some relief from Turkish pressure.

On 7 September 1915, the French Admiral on the Syrian coast cabled the High Commissioner in Cyprus that 6,000 Armenians were 'bravely' fighting against the Turks at Jebel Musa near the bay of Antioch. On request the Admiral had supplied them with munitions and provisions, but they had asked for the removal of their 5,000 old men, women and children to Cyprus. The Admiral asked the High Commissioner of Cyprus what he should reply. The latter thought that it was 'quite impossible' to receive

80. Ibid., no. 106769, Commit. Arm. Nat. Def., 20 July, 24 July 1915, Notes to Maxwell, encl. in McMahon to Grey, 27 July 1915; ibid., no. 196024, Br. Consul-Gen. Buenos Aires, to Grey, 23 Nov. 1915.

81. Ibid., no 30439/106769, FO to Army Council, copy, 11 Aug. 1915; ibid., no. 106762, minute by H. Nicolson, 4 Aug. 1915; ibid., nos. 113148, 136059, WO to FO, 15 Aug., 21 Sept. 1915; ibid., no. 196024, FO to Consul-Gen. Buenos Aires, 23 Dec. 1915.

82. FO 371/2488/51009/172811, Nicolson, Note, 15 Nov. 1915.

83. Rothwell, *British War Aims*, p. 7.

84. FO 371/2490/130257, Maxwell to Kitchener, copy, 10 Sept. 1915.

them. There was very limited accommodation on the island and politically it was inadvisable. General Maxwell, however, asked the Minister of War to do everything to help the movement; if either Cyprus or Rhodes took their women and children, the Armenians could make 'an important diversion from the Dardanelles'. Maxwell advised pressure on Cyprus. Grey, however, did not favour the acceptance of these refugees either in Egypt or Cyprus which had Moslem communities. The government 'cannot agree to receive the refugees in either country' Grey said in his 'urgent' cable to Ambassador Bertie in Paris. It was the French Admiral who had undertaken to embark these refugees, and it was therefore

> . . . for the French Government to arrange either for their temporary accommodation at Rhodes or their transport to Algeria.[85]

However, Grey's cable was delayed and the French Admiral landed the 5,000 Armenian refugees in Egypt. The Egyptian authorities had to make temporary arrangements for their accommodation at Port Said. 'They are a severe strain', Sir Henry McMahon, the High Commissioner reported from Alexandria. Grey did not despair. He instructed Bertie to urge the French government to transport the refugees 'elsewhere as soon as possible'. A few weeks later they were recruited by the French military agent in Egypt 'for service at Gallipoli'.[86]

Thus in 1915 all proposals to form Armenian volunteer groups under British direction were rejected. Even refuge to the families of those 'bravely' fighting at Jebel Musa was grudgingly given. One tends to ponder whether a landing in Cilicia would have ended in failure, or whether the fate of the bulk of Armenians in Turkey and of the British in Gallipoli might have been different had the proposals for volunteer groups from the Armenian diaspora not been rejected in 1915.

In 1917, however, it was the British authorities who tried hard to recruit Armenian manpower in the Caucasus.

During the middle of 1917, Britain was faced, in the international and military fields, by a truly bleak prospect. What most disturbed the British authorities and inspired real dread was the German submarine offensive. The Western front was still at stalemate. The principal European combatants were almost exhausted. 'Italy [had] never been wholeheartedly in the war.'[87] The Nivelle offensive launched in April on the main operational

---

85. Ibid., nos. 129419, 130257, McMahon to Grey, Maxwell to Kitchener, both 10 Sept. 1915; ibid., no. 131046, Grey to Bertie, 14 Sept. 1915.
86. Ibid., no 131502, McMahon to Grey, 14 Sept. 1915; Grey to Bertie, 15 Sept. 1915; ibid., no. 148384, Bertie to Grey, 11 Oct. 1915.
87. Rothwell, *British War Aims*, p. 99; Paul Guinn, *British Strategy and Politics 1914-1918* (Oxford, 1965), pp. 225, 235. WO 106/1516, f.16, Note by DMI, 17 Nov. 1917.

front had failed to effect any tactical gains. The French reserve of manpower was becoming depleted. In Palestine, the frontal assault made by the Egyptian Expeditionary Force, the 'Second Gaza', in mid-April ended in unmistakeable defeat. General Sir Archibald Murray, the Commander, again asked London for two additional infantry divisions.

In the general gloom the entry of the British and Indian troops into the fabled city of Baghdad on 11 March 1917 had been the first striking British success. For the first time in the history of the war, the British government viewed the forces under the Egyptian and Mesopotamian Commands and the Russian army in the Caucasus as armies engaged in a common task. Their object was to be the conquest of the outlying territories of the Ottoman Empire. They should force Turkey to accept defeat, which in turn would lead to the defeat of Bulgaria.[88] In considering their plans after the capture of Baghdad, the British had relied on Russian co-operation by an advance on Mosul and a vigorous offensive by their main Caucasus army.[89]

However, after the 1917 Revolution, it soon became evident that the Russians in the Caucasus were neither sufficiently organised nor in a fit condition to carry out effective operations against the Turks. The Russian armies were losing their will to fight. In April 1917, Consul Stevens reported from the Caucasus that desertion had become very rife: 400 deserters had taken refuge in the town gardens of Tiflis. On 6 August the men of the 21st Caucasus Rifles Regiment and the 6th Caucasus Rifles Division had thrashed their Colonel and seven other officers.[90]

With such apathy among the Russians and the probable disintegration of the Eastern front, the prospects of war for the Allied statesmen were not encouraging. It was feared that the Germans might be able to transfer their troops to the Western front. More immediately, the disintegration of the Caucasian front threatened to remove one of the principal strategic bases for the general offensive against the Ottoman Empire. Sir William Robertson, the CIGS, believed that should the Russian pressure in the Caucasus entirely cease, the Turks might concentrate on the Tigris as many as 200,000 men and then try to recover Baghdad. Such a step could endanger the security and the tranquillity of the North-West Frontier, India and Western Persia. Germany too might be interested in encouraging an offensive against Baghdad, because she had not yet surrendered her eastern ambitions embodied in the Baghdad railway project. The collapse of the Russian Caucasian front might, moreover, open the valuable oil resources of Baku to the Central powers at a time when the shortage of oil was tending to weaken

88. Guinn, ibid., pp. 224, 222, 217; WO 106/1516, f.16, note by DMI, 17 Nov. 1917.

89. F.J. Moberly (comp.), *The Campaign in Mesopotamia 1914-1918* (based on official documents) (London, 1923-7), vol. III, p. 298. L. Woodward, *Great Britain and the War of 1914–1918* (London, 1967), p. 110.

90. FO 438/10/4, Stevens to Balfour, 7 Apr. 1917; CAB 24/22, GT 1605, Caucasus Milit. Agent to DMI, 1 Aug. 1917; ibid., GT 1671, Caucas. Milit. Agent to DMI, 7 Aug. 1917.

their war machine in Europe. It might also encourage the Pan-Turanian ambitions of the Turks.[91] The military balance in the Middle East might easily be tipped against Britain. However, the foremost concern of the British was the provision of military support for their troops in North Persia and Mesopotamia.

On 15 October 1917, General Barter, Head of the British Mission at the Russian General Headquarters, informed the CIGS that perhaps the 'whole difficulty' of getting proper military support for General Maude in Mesopotamia might be solved. His Staff Officer, Lieutenant-Colonel Maitland-Edwards, had just returned from the Caucasus, where after having made exhaustive enquiries he had come to the conclusion that the only really loyal troops in the Caucasus were the Armenians. It was not surprising that the Armenians were loyal. Being surrounded by Moslem races their only hope for survival was in the success of the Russian troops. Edwards had been assured by influential members of the Armenian Committee that their countrymen were only too willing to fight, as they would be doing so for their very existence. It was unfortunate that the Russians themselves had not grasped the importance of having all their available Armenian soldiers on the Caucasus front. Of about 150,000 Armenians in the Russian armies, less than 35,000 were there. The Committee had begged the British through Edwards to procure, if possible, the transfer of the 100,000 odd Armenians on the other fronts to the Caucasus. Elated with the prospect of having discovered a valuable source of manpower for north Persia and Mesopotamia, General Barter concluded:

I feel strongly that this is a question we should insist on, and one on which we should not hesitate to bring diplomatic pressure if necessary. It is obvious that 150,000 Armenian infantry anxious to fight, and moreover having fullest confidence in us would prove an invaluable asset to the general strategical situation in the Caucasus. I propose to suggest to Russian G[eneral] S[taff] that as many reinforcements as possible for Caucasus Army should in future consist of Armenians . . . I shall propose that this plan . . . shall be adapted first of all to troops in north Persia, i.e. those who are likely first to [?come] into contact with Maude. It would perhaps be good to offer to take Armenian infantry into our Mesopotamian forces? Might it not also be possible to obtain the consent of the Americans to allow Armenians in America to be enrolled for service in Mesopotamia with Maude?

91. Moberly, *Campaign in Mesopotamia,* III, pp. 299, 302; ibid., IV, pp. 9, 102; Woodward, *Great Britain and the War of 1914-1918,* p. 111. W.E.D. Allen and P. Muratoff, *Caucasian Battlefields: A History of the Wars on the Turco-Caucasian Border 1828-1921* (Cambridge 1953), p. 457.

The CIGS fully concurred. The Turks were taking advantage of the dis-integration of the Russian forces. As a result there were indications of instability among all the Mohammedan races from the Caucasus to the borders of Chinese Turkestan. Accordingly, he wrote immediately to the Secretary of the War Cabinet suggesting that 'all in our power' should be done to secure the early inclusion of as great an Armenian element as possible in the Russian forces in the Caucasus and in North Persia.[92] The War Cabinet discussed the question on 23 October 1917 on the suggestion of the CIGS. They authorised:

> The Secretary of State for Foreign Affairs to concert with the United States Government in bringing diplomatic pressure to bear on the Russian Government:-
> (a) To get the Armenian troops now serving on the Eastern Front sent to the Caucasus.
> (b) to allow of the recruitment and formation of Armenian units for service on the Caucasian Front.[93]

Such views to make use of Armenian manpower were reinforced by a despatch from Consul Stevens in Tiflis. He reported that a scheme for the 'nationalisation' of the military forces in the Caucasus was being put forward. It was hoped that the Armenian forces at the front, reported to be the most loyal and reliable troops, would reach the numbers needed to offer effective resistance to an advance of the Turk. The Mohammedan troops in the Caucasus were to be variously employed, but they were not considered sufficiently reliable, Stevens added, to be sent to fight the Turk.[94]

In the meantime, in Russia itself, discipline broke down and fighting stopped. Henceforth, the British military authorities had to depend in the Caucasus only on the Armenians and the Georgians. In late October 1917, General Offley Shore cabled the DMI:

> If by any chance general defection of Russian Infantry were to result, nothing stands between anarchy and order in this province but Armenian and Georgian troops.

However, six Armenian battalions, just formed in the Caucasus, refused for 'political reasons', to be sent to the Persian front in October. The Armenian Committee in Petrograd also decided 'not to press' for the formation of Armenian military units until the future political status of Armenia was

---

92. CAB 24/29, GT 2347, Barter to CIGS, 15 Oct. 1917, CIGS to Barter, 19 Oct. 1917; CIGS to Secretary, War Cab. 20 Oct. 1917. Moberly, *Campaign in Mesopotamia*, IV, p. 102.
93. CAB 23/4, War Cab. 255, min. 7, 23 Oct. 1917.
94. FO 438/10/169, Stevens to Buchanan, 31 Oct. 1917.

decided upon.[95]

It is evident that while the War Cabinet and the British military authorities, uneasy at the dissolution of the Russian armies, wanted the Caucasian Armenians to fight in northern Persia, Mesopotamia and the Caucasus, these Armenians were naturally anxious to safeguard above all the prospects of their own homeland. During the war, the Caucasian armies, including Armenian volunteers, had crossed the Turkish frontier and had occupied three of the six Armenian *vilayets*. Now with the disintegration of the Caucasian front, not only these provinces but also that of Erevan in the Russian Caucasus were in danger. Who would defend them against the Turks?

Moreover, Armenians did not know what objectives they were being asked to fight for. They were uncertain and worried about their future. About 150,000 Caucasian Armenians had loyally fought in the Tsarist armies. But they had been disillusioned with Russia. It was reported that they were 'very disgusted' with, and suspicious of, the Russian authorities. In the Caucasus the Armenian troops had been forced to do all the fighting and had sustained heavy casualties. But in the reconquered portions of Armenia, Armenian landowners had been evicted and Tatar and Cossack settlers put in their place.[96] Apparently even Kerensky, the new Russian leader, had objected to the formation of 'anything like an Armenian Corps'. At the Foreign Office it was the view, both of Lord Robert Cecil and Sir Ronald Graham, that in these circumstances there was little prospect of inducing the Armenians to make any further efforts unless the future of Armenia was guaranteed by the Western powers.[97]

Thus, it was mainly in order to stimulate further the war efforts of the Armenians on the fast-disintegrating Caucasian front that the British leaders found themselves necessarily having to make generously sympathetic statements about the liberation of Armenia.

On instructions from the Foreign Office, Lord Bertie, in Paris, discussed with Boghos Nubar the refusal of the six Armenian battalions to go to the Persian and Mesopotamian fronts, and the decision of the Petrograd Armenian Committee to wait for the settlement of the future of Armenia before organising the recruitment of new volunteers. Lord Bertie pointed out to Boghos Nubar that the Persian, Mesopotamian and Caucasian fronts were all parts of one campaign on which the future of Armenia depended. He asked him to intervene with the Catholicos at Etchmiadzin and the Petrograd Committee.

95. FO 371/3016/209437/208687, Shore to DMI, 28 Oct. 1917; Barter to CIGS, 24 Oct. 1917.

96. Ibid., Graham to Hardinge, min. on conv. with Malcolm of Arm. Nat. Deleg., 8 Nov. 1917; Bryce Papers, UB 65, transl. of article in *Retsch* of 28 July/10 Aug. 1916, encl. in Boghos Nubar to Bryce, 27 Sept. 1916.

97. FO 371/3016/209437, Shore to DMI, 28 Oct. 1917; FO 371/3062/219742, R. Cecil, note, FO stamp 17 Nov. 1917; FO 371/3016. Graham to Hardinge, min., 8 Nov. 1917.

Boghos Nubar, however, 'strongly' insisted on the feeling among Armenians that they should only fight on the Armenian front. There was a fear that the Russian troops might abandon the three conquered *vilayets* to Turkey on the principle of 'no annexations'. In such a case, the hopes for liberation of the Armenians would fade away. Moreover, the Armenians in the Caucasus feared that the advancing Turks and Kurds would join hands with the Moslems of the Caucasus in the extermination of the Armenian population, both native and refugee. But, Boghos Nubar believed, army units composed of Armenian soldiers, having their native land to defend, would hinder the Turkish army from reconquering the provinces and would succeed in preventing massacres. Boghos Nubar asked, therefore, for help to organise on the Caucasian front a strong army composed of Armenians. There were then 35,000 on this front and it was desired that this total should be increased to 150,000, by reuniting all the Armenian soldiers from other fronts. Later on, it might even be possible to send detachments to Mesopotamia by pushing through Diarbekir.

Sir Ronald Graham, an Assistant Foreign Under-Secretary, believed there was 'force' in these arguments, and Balfour, the Foreign Secretary, minuted 'Yes'.[98]

By this time, Kerensky's government had fallen. It now became the main consideration of the British government to resist by every means possible any move by Russia to sign a separate peace with Germany. It was essential to keep, in one way or other, the Eastern front open, otherwise the expected transfer of German troops from the Eastern to the Western front might have calamitous effects. Moreover, the coal and corn of the Ukraine and the oil of the Caucasus might fall into German hands. The Allies, and especially Britain, tried to come to an understanding with the Bolsheviks that a separate peace with Germany would be 'neither democratic nor durable nor Russian'.[99] When their efforts failed, they decided to support any group which was prepared to fight the Central powers.

On 3 December 1917, the War Cabinet discussed Russia. They believed that their only hope of preventing her 'from making a separate peace' with Germany was to strengthen by every means in their power those groups who were genuinely friendly to the Entente. If a southern block could be formed consisting of the Caucasians, the Cossacks, the Ukrainians and the Romanians, it would probably be able to set up a reasonably stable government and would, in any case, through its command of oil, coal and corn, control the whole of Russia. The War Cabinet decided that the policy of the British government was to support any reasonable body in Russia that would

98. Ibid., FO to Bertie, 10 Nov. 1917; ibid., no. 218746, Bertie to FO, 15 Nov. 1917; ibid., no 221496, Boghos Nubar to G.D. Grahame, Br. Embassy, Paris, 17 Nov. 1917 and minutes, 20 Nov. 1917.

99. Richard H. Ullman, *Anglo-Soviet Relations, 1917-1921, Vol. I, Intervention and the War* (Princeton, 1961), p. 28, quot. Balfour to Buchanan, ?3 Dec. 1917.

'actively oppose the Maximalist movement' (Bolshevism), and at the same time to give money freely, within reason, to such bodies as were prepared to help the Allied cause. Accordingly, Lord Robert Cecil cabled Sir George Buchanan, the British ambassador in Petrograd, adding that 'no regard should be had to expense'.[100]

A few days later, the War Cabinet specifically discussed Armenia and 'authorised' the Secretary for Foreign Affairs to render suitable financial help, through channels to be chosen by himself in consultation with General Macdonogh, the DMI, 'to the Armenians'.[101] In Paris, Balfour, General Macdonogh and Lord Milner (a member of the War Cabinet and Minister without Portfolio) all had conversations with Boghos Nubar, 'as to making use of Armenian forces'. Boghos Nubar drafted a telegram to the Armenian leaders in the Caucasus, to be transmitted by the British authorities through the Catholicos at Etchmiadzin. It was indispensable, he stated, to increase the number of Armenian soldiers in the Caucasus and to raise volunteers in order to resist a Turkish offensive on the liberated Armenian provinces and eventually join hands with the British army in Mesopotamia. He had obtained for this purpose full material and financial assistance from the British and French governments. To the British leaders, on the other hand, Boghos Nubar stressed that the great needs were organisation and funds. It was 'essential' that the British government should send 'the strongest possible' Mission, headed by a General who must not only be a good soldier but also a diplomat.[102]

In his turn, the CIGS informed General Shore that he could authorise the Armenian and Georgian chief authorities to buy arms and equipment from the Russians for such a force as they were likely to put in the field. 'British officers will be sent' to help organise the Armenian and Georgian forces, he added. This was in response to Shore's earnest appeal for British troops, army or marine. *'I cannot emphasize this too strongly'*, he had cabled. It would locally give confidence and restore order.[103]

Such a project to fill by native forces the vacuum created in the Caucasus by the dissolution of the Russian armies was also considered desirable by the French government. A memorandum, prepared by Lord Milner and Lord Robert Cecil, specified that the Allies were bound to protect if possible the remnant of the Armenians, not only in order to safeguard the flank of the British-Mesopotamian forces in Persia and the Caucasus, but also because an Armenian autonomous or independent state, 'united if possible' with a

100. CAB 23/4, War Cab. 289, min. 10, 3 Dec. 1917. FO 371/3018/229192/232002, Cecil to Buchanan, 3 Dec. 1917.

101. CAB 23/4, War Cab. 294, min. 14, 7 Dec. 1917.

102. Bodleian Library, Milner Papers, Box 88, Diary, 2 Dec., 6 Dec. 1917; FO 371/3016/230983, Balfour to FO, copy, stamp, 5 Dec. 1917; FO 371/3062/244368, DMI, note of convers. with Boghos Nubar, 23 Dec. 1917.

103. FO 371/3018/236815, CIGS to Shore, repeated by FO to Marling, 16 Dec. 1917. MS Milner, dep. 369, Box GI, Marling, quot. Shore, 8 Dec. 1917.

Georgian state, was the 'only barrier' against the development of a Turanian movement that would extend from Constantinople to China. The memorandum was accepted by G. Clemenceau, the French Prime Minister, and S. Pichon, the Foreign Minister, on 23 December 1917.[104] When the French government expressed its willingness to undertake the responsibility for financing and organising the Ukraine and Bessarabia, General Macdonogh suggested that in that case the organisation and financing of the Cossacks, Armenians and Georgians should be left to the British government. Indeed, 'division of responsibility' was considered to be most desirable.[105] The agreement was finalised on 23 December 1917. Help to the Armenians, therefore, would be a British duty.

All the above-mentioned consultations, despatches and memoranda pointed to the desirability, from both the British and Armenian points of view, of continuing the war in the Caucasus and defending it against the Turks, and even the Germans, by native forces and especially by the Armenians. Boghos Nubar hoped that with the assistance of Allied officers it might be possible to hold Armenia against 'the reduced Turkish troops on that front'. The CIGS had also expressed the view that since Russian pressure in the Caucasus was ceasing, the Turks might withdraw some divisions and concentrate on Mesopotamia in order to try to retake Baghdad.[106]

However, the expectation that Turkey would reduce her Caucasian commitment was falsified: the Turks did not withdraw any divisions. Similarly, the assumption that Britain would be able to finance and organise native forces was not realised. Moreover, close co-operation never developed between the various peoples in the Caucasus. Thus the British plan to fill by native forces the vacuum in the Caucasus, created by the Russian collapse, did not succeed.

In December 1917 the Turks lost Jerusalem. General Ludendorff, the Deputy Chief of the German General Staff, had repeatedly pointed out to Enver, the Minister of War, that his task was in the first place to fight Britain on the Palestine front. But for the Turkish government the revolution in Russia and the consequent political and military vacuum created in the Caucasus had come as 'the predestined moment' for the realisation of all their ambitious schemes of Pan-Turanian expansion.[107] Liman von Sanders, the Chief of the German military mission, argued in vain that Turkey was no longer menaced on the Caucasian front. But a decree issued by Enver promised to officers on the southern fronts of the Empire the advantages of

---

104. FO 371/3018/245628, memo., 'Suggested Policy in Russia', n.d.
105. FO 371/3062/240614, Spiers to WO, copy, 17 Dec., 18 Dec. 1917; DMI to Hardinge, 20 Dec. 1917; min. by H. Nicolson, 21 Dec. 1917.
106. FO 371/3016/230983, Balfour, Paris, to FO, stamp, 5 Dec. 1917. Moberly, *Campaign in Mesopotamia*, III, p. 299.
107. General Ludendorff, *My War Memories 1914-1918,* 2nd edn (London, n.d.), II, p. 620; Allen and Muratoff, *Caucasian Battlefields,* p. 459.

'promotion and double pay' if they would volunteer for service in the Caucasus. It will ever remain unique in military history, mused von Sanders, that promotion and increased pay were offered to officers for transfer from a severe battle-front — the Palestinian — to service in a theatre where no fighting was in prospect for some time. Such a policy was difficult to understand from a purely military point of view. It could only be explained as an attempt in favour of Pan-Turanian projects which aimed at territorial expansion in the Caucasus and Persia. Despite the lull on the Russian front in 1917 and the urgent need for reinforcement on their southern fronts, the Turks had kept their Third Army under Vehib Pasha earmarked for the Caucasus. In the early summer of 1918 they had 'something between 55,000 and 60,000 seasoned infantry divisions' with the addition of several thousand irregulars. According to Allen and Muratoff, the military historians, such a force would be more than sufficient to overcome any resistance by Georgians and Armenians.[108] Through the 'bottomless advance into Trans-Caucasia' the Turks are going 'to lose all of Arabia, Palestine and Syria', Liman von Sanders wrote in June 1918.[109] And indeed these provinces they lost. On the other hand they recovered in the north not only the 1914 Russo-Turkish frontier, but even the 1878 frontier. Moreover, joining hands with the Tatars in Azerbaijan, they occupied Baku on the Caspian Sea.

Britain proved unable either to organise Armenian and Georgian forces or to finance them. Major-General L.C. Dunsterville, who would later write *The Adventures of Dunsterforce,* was appointed by the CIGS British repre-sentative at Tiflis and Chief of the British Mission to the Caucasus on 14 January 1918. Yet he only reached Baku, with 'less than 1000 rifles', on 17 August 1918.[110] By then all the Caucasus was under Turko-German domi-nation. Baku fell to the Turks on 16 September. 'Dunsterforce' had come 'too late and proved too small'.[111]

This failure was caused first of all by physical difficulties which compli-cated the question of sending a military mission to the Caucasus: the Dardanelles and the Bosphorus were closed to the Allies; parts of the Caspian Sea were in Bolshevik hands. The advantage of assisting the Cossacks to the north of the Caucasus and the Armenians to the south was obvious. But the difficulty was 'how to do it'. The British could reach them effectively neither by the Baltic nor the Black Sea, nor through Persia and the south. There was but one remaining line of communication possible: the Siberian railway, Balfour believed.[112] However impractical the suggestion

108. Liman von Sanders, *Five Years in Turkey* (Annapolis, 1927), pp. 268, 254. Moberly, *Campaign in Mesopotamia*, IV, preface, pp. ii, iii. Allen and Muratoff, *Caucasian Battlefields*, pp. 459-60, 470; see also Sanders, ibid., p. 256.

109. Saunders, ibid., p. 244.

110. Moberly, *Campaign in Mesopotamia*, IV, pp. 105, 246, 216; Ronald G. Suny, *The Baku Commune 1917-1918* (Princeton, 1972), p. 335.

111. Allen and Muratoff, *Caucasian Battlefields*, p. 485.

112. British Library, Balfour MSS 49699, ff.53-4, Balfour to Bertie, to Rodd, to Barclay, copy, 26 Jan. 1918.

seems today, it points to the tremendous difficulties involved. Thus General Dunsterville arrived at Baghdad from India on 18 January 1918. He was stranded in north-west Persia and his mission 'entirely failed' to reach Tiflis, its original object. Winter storms, road difficulties, the problem of the supply of food and petrol, the hostility of the Kurds and the Jangalis, Persian neutrality, the possible enmity of revolutionary Russians and the indispensability of only 'light vehicles' for motor transport had all to be faced. Along with such difficulties there was also the fact that events in the Caucasus were changing with kaleidoscopic suddenness, as the British Vice-Consul at Baku would recall.[113]

But the Foreign Office view that the question of military intervention in Armenia was one which had been before the authorities 'for the last three months' and that its solution depended on military considerations over which the Foreign Office itself had no control,[114] points to a rather confused state of affairs. Apparently for three months the military authorities could not decide whether there should be effective help for Armenia or not. 'I am very uneasy about the direction of our military affairs in the Middle East' Lord Robert Cecil wrote to Balfour. Giving examples, he pointed to the confusion of authority and to the necessity of having unity of military direction. To continue this state of affairs was to court disaster.[115] It seems that there also was a lack of inter-departmental co-operation. Thus, the War Office, which usually had the most comprehensive intelligence reports from its agents on the spot, once refused to allow two members of the Foreign Office access to telegrams from the Caucasus. Under war conditions the military authorities were felt to have additional importance. Moreover, the clash of personalities in various positions did not contribute to effective action in the Caucasus. Lord Curzon strongly held to the Persia Committee and to the Middle East Committee, both of which Robert Cecil attempted 'to smother decorously'. On the spot, in the Caucasus, General Shore insisted on having, for financial assurances, the authority of only the War Office, instead of Sir Charles Marling, a diplomat, the Minister in Tehran responsible for the Headquarters of the British Financial Mission.[116]

The objects of Dunsterville's mission, according to the instructions of the CIGS, were to be the raising, training and equipping of the military forces of the Caucasian peoples with a view to enabling them to protect the occupied

113. L.C. Dunsterville, *The Adventures of Dunsterforce* (London, 1920), pp 3, 13-14, PRO, Robert Cecil Papers, FO 800/198, f.175, encl. in CIGS to R. Cecil, 29 Aug. 1918. Ranald MacDonell, ' . . . *And Nothing Long'* (London, 1938), p. 202.

114. FO 371/3404/109357, min. by H. Nicolson, 20 June 1918 and draft of letter, cancelled, 'in the sense' of which Balfour wrote to G. Barnes.

115. WO 106/64, EC 1564, R. Cecil to Balfour, copy, 15 Sept. 1918.

116. Milner MSS, Box G.1, memo., signature illegible, 18 Jan. 1918. Balfour Papers, Add. MS. 49738, ff.200-1, Cecil to Balfour, priv. 8 Jan. 1918. FO 371/3018/235977, Marling to FO, 13 Dec. 1917; CAB 24/34, GT 2852, Shore to DMI, 2 Dec. 1917; MacDonell, ' . . . *And Nothing Long'*, pp. 179, 185.

portions of Turkish Armenia; to prevent the realisation of Pan-Turanian designs; and to assist indirectly the British forces in Mesopotamia by covering the Persian frontier.[117] The mission's failure was partly a reflection of the muddled state of affairs in the War Office. It had appointed as head of such an important mission someone about whom it had misgivings itself and expressed its intention of relieving him of his command even when he was in the Caucasus. This extract from a despatch sent by the War Office to the Command in Mesopotamia is self-explanatory:

. . . we doubted whether Dunsterville was the most suitable man for his appointment in which Mesopotamia did not agree. We fully realise the difficult and hazardous nature of the task which Dunsterville was called to execute. It was with full knowledge of these difficulties that, in view of the immense importance of the results to be achieved, we took the risk involved and for any failure of the Baku expedition we accept full responsibility. As to Dunsterville's suitability for his present post we have had misgivings for some time past . . . should you deem it advisable, you are at full liberty as soon as the situation permits to relieve General Dunsterville from his command.[118]

Thus, Britain could neither organise the Caucasian — including the Armenian — forces, nor give them effective help.

The other assumption of the British leaders, that 'a southern block' consisting of the Caucasians, the Cossacks, the Ukrainians and the Romanians might be formed to continue the war, and that an Armenian autonomous, or independent, state 'united if possible' with a Georgian state, might act as a barrier against the Turanian movement,[119] also fell flat. There was neither co-operation nor unity among these peoples.

Following the Bolshevik seizure of power at Petrograd, a temporary administration, the Transcaucasian Commissariat, with Georgian, Azerbaijanian, Armenian and Russian representatives, had been formed in November 1917. Soon the Transcaucasian Commissariat found itself at a loss when Vehib Pasha asked to send a delegation to Tiflis in order to negotiate a peace. All such vital questions, as those of peace and of the relationships between the central government of Russia and the border provinces, were supposed to be answered by the All-Russian Constituent Assembly. But the latter was dissolved by the Bolsheviks on 19 January 1918. The Commisariat therefore invited the governments of the Ukraine and of South Russia for consultations about Vehib Pasha's proposal. No

117. Moberly, *Campaign in Mesopotamia,* IV, p. 105.
118. FO 371/3411/154943, WO to GOC, Mesopotamia, 65999 cypher, 9 Sept. 1918; Artin H. Arslanian 'Dunsterville's Adventures: A Reappraisal', *Internat. Journal of Middle East Studies,* vol. 12 (1980b), pp. 199-216.
119. FO 371/3018/229192/232002/245628, Cecil to Buchanan, 3 Dec. 1917; memo. by Cecil and Milner, n.d. [1917].

delegates arrived.[120]

Neither were relations between the three main Caucasian peoples, the Georgians, the Tatars and the Armenians more cordial. A Transcaucasian Federation was formed in April 1918 mainly to deal with the emergency created by the Treaty of Brest-Litovsk[121] (forced on Bolshevik Russia by Germany) and the relentless advance of the Turkish troops into the Caucasus. But the tendencies and the interests of the three national groups constituting the Federation were totally divergent. The Tatars of Azerbaijan could base their hopes for the future on Turkish friendship. The Georgians were hesitant while the Armenians remained strongly pro-Ally. From a Turkish advance the latter had most to lose. The Armenians tried to develop a national army and hoped to secure support from Britain. By early 1918 the Armenian Corps consisted of two divisions of Armenian rifles, three brigades of Armenian volunteers, a cavalry brigade and some battalions of militia. But the formation of such groups depended on long and disorganised lines of communication which were 'infested by bands of hostile and angry' Moslems. Several thousands of able-bodied men remained in the Erevan, Elisavetpol and Baku provinces. The Armenians accused the Tatars of Transcaucasia of sabotage and of destroying the railway to the front lines.[122]

According to one historian, the Azerbaijani members of the Caucasian delegation looked upon the Turks as 'relatives' at the peace talks in Batum in May 1918. During the 'entire length' of the conference they had been keeping the Turks 'informed' of the deliberations of the Transcaucasian delegation.[123] On the other hand the volatile Georgians, without informing either the Armenians or the Tatars, asked for and secured German protection, in order to save their country from the Turkish onslaught. Yet all this time the Armenians were 'shedding blood' for their existence around Erevan. 'How can you abandon us?' Alexander Khatisian (the Head of the Armenian Delegation in Batum, and later, a Prime Minister) asked Noi Zhordania, the Georgian Menshevik leader. 'We cannot be drowned with you' the latter had replied.[124] But only if Georgia was independent could she invite German protection. Thus the Transcaucasian Federation had to be dissolved during the last days of May 1918 and the independent republics of the Caucasus were born. Georgia was anxious to have the protection of

120. R.G. Hovannisian, *Armenia on the Road to Independence, 1918* (Berkeley/Los Angeles, 1967), pp. 107, 119-21; F. Kazemzadeh, *The Struggle for Transcaucasia*, (New York/Oxford, 1951), pp. 57, 84, 86; Richard Pipes, *The Formation of the Soviet Union*, revised edn, (Harvard, 1964), p. 103.

121. Article IV related to Armenia and the Caucasus. See John W. Wheeler-Bennett, *Brest-Litovsk: The Forgotten Peace, March 1918* (London, 1938), pp. 405-6.

122. Allen and Muratoff, *Caucasian Battlefields*, pp. 458-9; Khatisian, *Hayastani Hanrapetutian Dsagumm U Zargatsume* (The Creation and Development of the Republic of Armenia), 2nd edn (Beirut, 1968), pp. 29, 32; Hovannisian, *Independence*, p. 115.

123. Kazemzadeh, *Struggle*, pp. 111, 114.

124. Khatisian, *Hanrapetutian Zargatsume*, p. 82.

Germany, while Azerbaijan solicited the friendship of Turkey. With no help from anywhere, Armenia could only be at the mercy of the latter.

Thus, in a way, independence was thrust upon Armenia following the political collapse of the Transcaucasian Federation.[125] Still, independence was also due, under the existing circumstances, to the boldness of decision of a handful of Armenian leaders: 'Had we wavered, had we delayed our declaration, Armenia might have remained *res nullius'* (unclaimed territory), and as such she might have been shared between her neighbours, Hovhannes Kajaznuni, the distinguished-looking first Prime Minister of the republic and the last President of its Parliament would comment.[126] But the decision was not easy. True, autonomy had been a dream for generations. Yet Simon Vratsian, the last Prime Minister of the republic, likened the birth of Armenia in 1918 to that of a 'sick child'.[127]

The Treaty of Batum, by which the fighting stopped, was signed between the 'Republic of Armenia' and Turkey on 4 June 1918. It stipulated that Armenia would only have an area[28] of 10,000 square kilometres; Ottoman troops and material would be transported unhindered over Armenian territory; and the Ottoman army would reserve the right to use its own forces if the Armenians proved incapable of maintaining order and facilitating transportation. Turkish cannons were installed four miles from Etchmiadzin and four miles from Erevan.[129]

It was under such harsh conditions that the republic was born. Still, there was at least an Armenia in a small corner on the map of the world.

Enver would later tell Khatisian with a strange boast that it was he and his friends who had 'created Armenia', well outside Turkish territory.[130] It was true that the British hope for the co-operation and unanimous resistance of the Caucasus against the Central powers was not realised. Left alone, isolated and with no external help, the Armenians lost not only the three Armenian provinces in Turkey, but also some territory in the Caucasus. Armenia succumbed, but not wholly. Turkey could not trample on her and virtually walk over her. During the last desperate days of May 1918, when Erevan and Etchmiadzin — the very heartland of Russian Armenia —were threatened, the Armenians were able not only to stop the advance of the Turks at the battles of Sardarabad, Bash-Abaran and Karakilisa, but even to repulse them. The Turkish leaders, now competing with the Germans, the British and the Soviets for the control of Baku,[131] had to prefer to make

125. Christopher J. Walker, *Armenia: The Survival of a Nation* (London, 1980), p. 257.

126. H. Kajaznuni, *H. H. Dashnaktsutiune Anelik Chuni Aylevs* (Dashnaktsutiun Has Nothing To Do any More) (Vienna, 1923), p. 30.

127. S. Vratsian, *Hayastani Hanrapetutiun* (The Republic of Armenia) (Paris, 1928), p. 155.

128. About one-third of Soviet Armenia, Khatisian, *Hanrapetutian Zargatsume*, pp. 86-7; Vratsian, *Hayastani Hanrapetutian*, p. 155, gives 12,000 square kilometres.

129. A certified copy of the Treaty obtained by Br. Milit. Intelligence from the Porte after the Armistice is in FO 371/9158/E5523; Hovannisian, *Independence*, pp. 196-8, 201.

130. Khatisian, *Hanrapetutian*, pp. 89, 102.

131. Jacques Kayaloff, *The Battle of Sardarabad* (The Hague/Paris, 1973). See also Vratsian,

peace with Armenia in order to reserve their forces for the dash forward to the oil-city.

Furthermore, various Armenian groups outside the republic's frontiers, went on fighting the Turks even after the Treaty of Batum. Thus General Andranik (Ozanian) the 'quiet, dignified and soldierly' hero of the Turkish-Armenians, the officer for whom the British War Office had 'a good deal' of respect, had been fighting the Turks the whole way back from Erzerum to Karabagh. He 'absolutely refused' to make peace with the Turks, minuted a member of the Foreign Office staff. Denouncing both the signatories and the Treaty of Batum for handing over the Armenian Plateau to Turkey, Andranik continued his fight in Zangezur.[132] Likewise, in Baku, it was the nationalist Armenians, in an unholy alliance with the local Soviet, which to a large extent kept the Turks out of the oil centre until 16 September 1918, that is only about a month before the Armistice of Mudros was signed.

Thus, in their own way, the Armenians made a small but significant contribution to the Allied war effort, despite a host of difficulties. For Caucasian Armenia there was first of all the immense human burden of the thousands of refugees, the remnants of the decimated population of Turkish Armenia. There was also, initially, the necessity to defend the long Erzinjan-Van front, a distance of nearly 250 miles. Other difficulties in poor communication, lack of experience as a regular army, suspicion between Russian Armenians and Turkish Armenians and especially inability to maintain lasting discipline, dissipated their strength. In addition, as Allen and Muratoff have pointed out, the Armenian military leaders manoeuvred according to the classic rules of 'regular war', while the Armenian terrain favoured a partisan strategy.[133] But despite these inauspicious conditions and mistakes, the Armenian forces took over the Caucasian front after the breakdown of the Russian army and, as Lord Robert Cecil acknowledged, 'for five months', from February to June 1918, 'delayed the advance of the Turks', thus rendering 'an important service to the British army in Mesopotamia'.[134]

The British authorities were aware that their promises to organise and finance the Caucasian and Armenian forces were not realised. Boghos

Hayastani Hanrapetutian, pp. 97, 118-21; Khatisian, *Hanrapetutian Zargatsume*, p. 80; Kajaznuni, *H.H. Dashnaktsutiune*, pp. 30-1; Suny, *Baku Commune*, pp. 280-7.

132. FO 371/3659/95969, G. Kidston, min., 27 June 1919. Hovannisian, *Independence,* p. 194. M. Philips Price, the *Manchester Guardian* correspondent, has described Andranik as 'thick-set and hardy', 'a simple child of the mountains' with 'a kind, almost benevolent face', in *War and Revolution in Asiatic Russia* (London, 1918), p. 136. D.S. Northcote, resid. Erevan, 1922-5, has referred to the legends about Andranik's invulnerability among the Armenian peasantry: British Library, Northcote Papers, Add. MS, 57560, 'Armenia', p. 26.

133. See Hovannisian, *Independence,* pp. 114-15; Khatisian, *Hanrapetutian Zargatsume,* p. 32. Allen and Muratoff, *Caucasian Battlefields,* pp. 470-1.

134. Bryce Papers, UB 55, R. Cecil to Bryce, 3 Oct. 1918; copy in FO 371/3404/164847. See also, ibid., no. 162647, Toynbee, min., 24 Sept. 1918.

Nubar's and General Shore's special requests for strong military missions[135] were particularly unfulfilled. Yet all this time, the British leaders were anxious to stimulate the war effort in the Caucasus. This they could only do by sympathetic statements. Thus, idealistic statements concerning British war aims, including the liberation of Armenia, became a substitute for effective help.

In their turn, the Armenians themselves were anxious for some clear assurances about their future. They wanted to know what they were fighting for especially after their traumatic experience at the hands of Turkey and their bitter disillusionment as regards Allied intentions in the first half of the war. The Bolsheviks had publicised the Allied agreements to the partitioning of historic Armenia between Tsarist Russia and France. Disappointed, the Armenians asked for assurances. These the British leaders readily gave under war conditions.

For over a century, the conflicting policies of Britain and Russia in the Middle East were considered the main cause of the misfortunes of the Armenians in Turkey. When, however, Britain and Russia entered the war on the same side, it had seemed that a new era would dawn for the Armenian people. Not only had Russian Armenians, as citizens of the Russian Empire, enlisted in the Russian army, but they had also formed volunteer forces mainly composed of Armenians from the diaspora (the Balkans, France and the United States), and had borne the brunt of some of the heaviest fighting in the Caucasus. M. Philips Price, the special correspondent of the *Manchester Guardian,* has captured in his diary the mood of these volunteers in the basin of Van at the beginning of the war. While in a Russian regiment orders from officers would be followed by the simple reply of '*Tak tochna, vashy blagorody'* (Exactly so, your honour), things would be done among the Armenians by the general consent of everyone after 'endless talking' around camp-fires. Every one felt the presence of the spirit of Armenia, for which they were all fighting.[136]

Across the border, in Turkey, the general Congress of Dashnaktsutiun, sitting in Erzerum in the autumn of 1914, had been offered autonomy by Turkish emissaries, if it would actually assist Turkey in the war. The Congress had replied that the Armenians, as Ottoman subjects, would faithfully do their duty individually, but as a nation they could not provoke revolts in the Russian Empire. It was following this refusal, described as 'courageous' by Robert Cecil, that the Ottoman Armenians had been systematically murdered by the Turkish government in 1915.[137]

At the beginning of the war about 150,000 Russian-Armenians were

135. See p. 99.
136. Price, *War and Revolution,* p. 139.
137. FO 371/3404/164439, Cecil to Bryce, 3 Oct. 1918; Hovannisian, *Independence,* pp. 41-2.

enlisted in the Russian armies. In addition, seven groups of volunteers operated on the Caucasian front.[138] Besides these, Boghos Nubar had been instrumental in the formation of the *Légion d'Orient,* at the 'request' of the French government and with the agreement of the British government in late 1916.[139] It was composed mainly of his own compatriots from the Armenian diaspora. Moreover, as seen above, the British strongly pressed through Boghos Nubar and the Catholicos, in late 1917, for the formation and concentration of Armenian troops and volunteers on the Caucasian front following the Russian defection.

Throughout the war, the Armenians were sustained in their war effort by the statements of sympathy of the Allied statesmen. It seems that in the beginning they were even satisfied by vague generalisations. During his tour of inspection of the Caucasian front, soon after the declaration of war, Tsar Nicholas II had told Catholicos Gevorg V 'Tell your flock, Holy Father, that a most brilliant future awaits the Armenians', in response to the Catholicos' appeal to liberate the Turkish Armenians and take them under Russian protection.[140] Sazonov, the Foreign Minister, in his turn had formally stated that the Russian government had 'disinterestedly' endeavoured to alleviate the lot of the Armenians. By the Russo-Turkish Reform Scheme of 26 January 1914, Turkey had recognised the privileged position of Russia in the Armenian question. When the war ended, Sazonov had added, this exclusive position would be employed by the Imperial government in a direction 'favourable to the Armenian population'.[141] Of course, Armenians did not know then that the Tsar was 'not at all keen to incorporate' the Armenian *vilayets* and did not wish to have much to do with Armenians, as the Russian ambassador had told Sir Arthur Nicolson, the Under-Secretary for Foreign Affairs, during a conversation in 1915. Nor did they know that during the Sykes-Picot negotiations, Russia had insisted that Sivas and Lesser Armenia should go to France and in return she should get Kurdish populated Hakkiari-Mush in the east. The reason had been Tsarist Russia's desire to have 'as few Armenians as possible' in the Russian territory and to be relieved of Armenian 'nationalist responsibilities'.[142]

British statements relating to Turkey during the first two years of the war

138. Churchill, *The Aftermath,* pp. 404-5; CAB 24/29, GT 2347, Barter to CIGS, 15 Oct. 1917; Hovannisian, ibid., pp. 44, 47.

139. Agreement between Georges Picot, Sir Mark Sykes and Boghos Nubar at French Embassy, London, 27 Oct. 1916, quot. in Arm. Nat. Deleg. Papers, microf., reel 13C/005234-7; Bryce Papers, UB67, Boghos Nubar to Bryce, 9 Feb. 1917.

140. Ts.P.Aghayan, *Hay Zhoghoverdi Azatagrakan Paykari Patmutyunits* (From the History of the Liberation Struggle of the Armenian People) (Erevan, 1976), p. 383; Hovannisian, *Independence,* p. 45; Kazemzadeh, *Struggle,* p. 25.

141. *The Times,* 11 Feb. 1915, p. 7, col. 2. See also FO 371/2481/24821.

142. FO 371/2485/30439/32321, min., A. Nicolson to Grey, 18 Mar. 1915. FO 371/2768/938/68431, draft tel., Mark Sykes to Clayton, 10 Apr. 1916; ibid., no. 70889, Grey to McMahon, 14 Apr. 1916. 'Russia does *NOT* wish to have Armenia under her suzerainty', Lancelot Oliphant minuted on 24 Apr. 1916 in FO 371/2768/938/77075.

did not include the liberation of the peoples under her rule as war aims. But the idea that Turkey would have to pay the penalty for her unprovoked entry into the war was accepted by the Cabinet even before the actual declaration. As seen above, the Cabinet had agreed, on 2 October 1914, to abandon the formula of 'Ottoman integrity'. After the actual declaration of war, the British leaders were unsparing in their condemnation of the successive Turkish governments as forces of evil. As already mentioned, Asquith had referred to the 'blight' of Turkish rule and Lloyd George predicted that the day had come when the Turk would be called to account for his long record of infamy against humanity.[143]

Such statements from great leaders — all vague and made in general terms — apparently elated the Armenians, a people hitherto without a state and therefore without the experience of statecraft. It was probably owing to their political weakness that they attached such 'great faith' to any 'word' spoken by the Allied powers, a political leaflet correctly diagnosed.[144] Writing to Lloyd George, A. Tchobanian, the Armenian intellectual and Secretary to the Armenian Committee in Paris, expressed the view that his speech was the magnificent prelude to the implementation of 'justice' which England had at last decided to pursue. Later, he also pleaded for an autonomous state under the protection of the three great Allied powers — a state where the Armenian people would do everything to be worthy once again of the words of the immortal Gladstone: 'To serve Armenia is to serve civilisation'.[145] Boghos Nubar expressed the conviction that the British government which was then fighting for 'civilisation, for [fundamental] rights as well as for the principle of nationality', would support the reconstitution of national unity of the Armenian people. They had placed 'all [our] hopes on the Allied Powers', he wrote to Bryce.[146]

In fact, the Allies made no statement at all at the beginning of the war as to their aims with regard to the peoples in the Ottoman Empire. But then none of the Great powers had entered the war with defined war aims; each had taken up arms for an ostensibly defensive reason. A purely defensive war, however, would lack inspiration, as A.J.P. Taylor has pointed out.[147] Public declarations were made, therefore, from time to time. The statements about the Ottoman Empire had been general expressions of repugnance against Turkish rule and of sympathy with the sufferings of Armenia. Only in November 1916 did Asquith at Guildhall, as already mentioned, tell his

143. See above, pp. 69, 53.

144. Douglas Papers, vol. 61, f.79, The Armenian Bureau (London), leaflet no. 6, 'France and Armenia', 29 July 1920.

145. Lloyd George Papers, C/11/2/72, Tchobanian to Lloyd George, 20 Nov. 1914. FO 371/2485/56472, Tchobanian to Grey, memo. 5 May 1915.

146. FO 371/2488/96760, Boghos Nubar to A. Nicolson, memo, 13 July 1915. Bryce Papers, UB 67, 9 Feb. 1917.

147. Taylor, 'War Aims', pp. 475-6.

audience, amid cheers, that the British government

> . . . are resolved that after the war there shall be an era of liberty and redemption for this ancient people.[148]

On 18 December 1916, President Wilson invited the belligerents to announce the terms on which they believed the war might be ended. Replying on 10 January 1917, the Allies listed among the aims

> . . . the enfranchisement of populations subject to the bloody tyranny of the Turks.[149]

In late 1916, when the Allies decided to organise a *Légion d'Orient* in view of an eventual landing in Asia Minor or Syria, they appealed to the Armenians, and, in return, promised an autonomous Cilicia under the protection of France. Boghos Nubar's telegram to Arakel Nubar, his son in Cairo, asking him to encourage the enrolment of Armenian volunteers, was sent in cipher by the French Ministry of Foreign Affairs. In it Boghos Nubar repeated that he had received a 'formal assurance' that after the victory of the Allies the Armenian 'national aspirations would be satisfied'.[150] In early 1917 he also wrote to Bryce an extremely significant letter where he used the word 'formal', to characterise the assurances given, no less than three times. He was worried about the deportees, still exposed to the vengeance of Turks, in the deserts of Mesopotamia. It was, however, impossible for the Armenians, he claimed, to reply to the Allies by a refusal. Boghos Nubar knew that the three Armenian *vilayets* of Erzerum, Van and Bitlis would probably be annexed by Russia, but that the other *vilayets*, reunited with Cilicia, would devolve to France. It was for this Armenia, having an access to the Mediterranean, that he had asked for an autonomy of the largest kind, and for which he had obtained 'a formal promise'. The Armenian volunteers for the *Légion d'Orient* would come from Egypt, Europe and America. But all publicity would be avoided.[151]

The Russian Revolution of 1917 had considerable impact on the definition of British war aims. The new phrase of a peace with no annexations and based on self-determination forced Western statesmen into a competition in idealism. In June 1917, the War Cabinet considered the Russian formula, and agreed that it should be pointed out that Mesopotamia had never been Turkish in nationality. Moreover, Turkey had grossly abused its trust. The

148. *The Times*, 10 Nov. 1916, p. 10, col. 3.
149. Taylor, 'War Aims', p. 491.
150. Arm. Nat. Deleg. Papers, microf., reel 13C/005234-7, Agreement between Georges Picot, Sir Mark Sykes and Boghos Nubar at French Embassy, London, 27 Oct. 1916; ibid., B. Nubar to Arakel Nubar, copy, 27 Oct. 1916.
151. Bryce Papers, UB 67, Boghos Nubar to Bryce, 9 Feb. 1917.

case was the same in Armenia.[152] By the middle of 1917, the Allied and British statesmen had already agreed on the allocation of special spheres in Turkey-in-Asia and therefore it was simply expedient to talk of the high principles of self-determination, nationality and the 'liberation' of the non-Turkish regions in the Ottoman Empire — Arabia, Mesopotamia, Syria, Palestine and Armenia. Moreover, the statement of such principles might encourage the war effort of the subject peoples. The Allied leaders had simply to make use of any possible source of manpower.

The new Russian concept advocating no annexation but self-determination should have been universally welcomed by the Armenians had the Armenian provinces in eastern Turkey not been completely depopulated. Some prudent Armenians were, therefore, greatly apprehensive about their future. Discussing with Arnold Toynbee, of the Political Intelligence Department of the Foreign Office, the effect of the Russian Revolution on the Armenian question, Boghos Nubar had expressed the view that his 'sole fear' was lest Russia's renunciation of annexations might lead 'to the abandonment of Armenia' to the Turks.[153] A few days later the Bolshevik Revolution had occurred resulting in armistice, the withdrawal of Russian forces from occupied Turkish territory, a separate peace, and the creation of an enormous vacuum in the balance of power in eastern Turkey and the Caucasus. Harold Nicolson minuted: 'The Russian Revolution has changed the whole aspect of the Armenian question'. Originally it was understood that Russia would exercise a Protectorate over Greater Armenia, and France occupy Lesser Armenia (Cilicia).[154] Certainly, the problem of the liberation and protection of the Armenian provinces became extremely difficult after the Russian Revolution. Henceforth, British statements about the actual liberation of Armenia simply became unrealisable utterances.

The reaction of the British government to the effects of the Bolshevik Revolution on the Caucasian front had involved, as seen above, efforts to recruit manpower and organise the native forces. Exposed to fatal danger, the reaction of the Armenian people was to seek clear assurances as to their future.

As already mentioned, six Armenian battalions had refused to go to the Persian front for 'political reasons', and the Armenian Committee in Petrograd had decided not to press for the formation of military units until the 'future political status' of Armenia had been decided upon. There was indeed 'little prospect' of inducing the Armenians to make any further efforts unless the future of Armenia was guaranteed by the Western powers.[155] Boghos Nubar's Armenian National Delegation was convinced

---

152. CAB 23/3, War Cab. 171, 27 June 1917.
153. Toynbee Papers, Box on Armenia, note of convers. between Boghos Nubar and Toynbee, by latter, 6 Nov. 1917.
154. FO 371/3062/227539, H. Nicolson, min., 17 Nov. 1917.
155. See above pp. 96-7.

that Armenian volunteers would respond to its appeal, especially if the Allied governments gave the Armenians the assurance that 'the liberation of Armenia is one of their war aims'.[156]

In early December 1917, not only was armistice between Bolshevik Russia and Turkey becoming a reality, but rumours were also flying around that the other Allies too were contemplating peace with Turkey. The Armenian Military Defence Committee in the Caucasus, evidently in a panic, told the British Consulate at Tiflis that were armistice with the Turks to be concluded, Armenia would be in danger of 'returning under Turkish rule'. The Committee urged the interference of Russia, Britain, France and the United States with a view to securing 'the immediate autonomy of [the] country under their protection'. A few days later it was the British ambassador in Petrograd who cabled that Armenians were 'most anxious' that some statement 'more definite' than any yet made by any responsible Allied statesman should be published indicating

> . . . what the Allies are prepared to do for Armenia after the war. They are not satisfied with such generalities as have hitherto been pronounced on the subject of Armenia and wish to know whether they are to be autonomous, to have Home Rule, to be annexed, or protected by Russia or what.

The telegram was circulated to the King and the War Cabinet.[157]

It was against this background and mainly to stimulate the Armenian war effort that the British leaders made their 'pledges' to the Armenians from December 1917 onwards.

The answers of the sophisticated Foreign Office to both the above telegrams were very subtly drafted. They were designed on the one hand to induce the Armenians to go on fighting on the tottering Caucasian front and, on the other hand to avoid too much commitment. The telegram to Consul Stevens asked him to assure the Armenian Military Defence Committee that the British government were prepared to assist the Armenians 'to the best of their ability' in their efforts to remain free from the Turkish yoke. Lord Hardinge, experienced and hard, minuted: 'I think this tel. is all right and does not commit us too far'. To the second telegram it was again Lord Hardinge who found the equivocal solution:

> 'Liberation from the Turkish yoke' implies either annexation by another Power or some form of self-government. I think a discreet use of some such term might be made in reply to a friendly question in the H. of Commons.

156 FO 371/3016/221496, Boghos Nubar to G.D. Grahame, embassy in Paris, 17 Nov. 1917.
157. FO 371/3062/234125, Consul Stevens to FO, 10 Dec. 1917; ibid., no. 237702, Buchanan to FO, 14 Dec. 1917.

Balfour minuted: 'If I speak on Wed., I might bring Armenia in'.[158]

It was however Lloyd George who spoke instead, and as referred to above, emphasised that Mesopotamia would 'never' be restored to the blasting tyranny of the Turk. That same observation applied to Armenia.[159] Thus Lloyd George showed himself superbly adept in dismissing the accusations of British imperialistic designs of annexation, in assuring his pacifists at home and in encouraging the Armenians in the Caucasus — all at the same time. In a major speech on war aims, discussed beforehand in the War Cabinet, and given at a Conference of Trade Union Delegates on 5 January 1918, he touched on Armenia again when he stated:

> Arabia, Armenia, Mesopotamia, Syria, and Palestine are in our judgment entitled to a recognition of their national conditions . . .

and 'it would be impossible to restore' these territories to their former sovereign — Turkey.[160]

Such public declarations, beyond promising Armenia freedom from Ottoman rule, did not define her future political status. They were deliberately equivocal, vague and ambiguous. Perhaps Britain could not go far in her commitments. The Armenian *vilayets*, now forcibly depopulated, had never appeared among her territorial desiderata. Moreover, secret agreements had been made between the Allies as regards the Ottoman Empire, and Russia had renounced her claims. Therefore, there were problems which needed clarification before Britain could fully commit herself.

The statements made were meant to maintain the morale of the Armenians combating the Turks. Yet, at the same time, Britain seriously contemplated, in the dreary winter of 1917-18, making a separate peace with Turkey. The European powers were quite exhausted; the United States of America could not as yet give much military assistance; the Russian Revolution had weakened the Entente and had, moreover, removed the initial stumbling block to a peace with Turkey — the issue of Constantinople. Detaching Turkey from the Central powers looked viable: it would leave Bulgaria and the south-eastern flanks of Austria and Germany to some extent at the mercy of the Allied powers. It was the military defeat of Germany at which Britain above all aimed. Moreover, peace with Turkey might free Britain from a heavy military, naval and financial drain. After all, by the beginning of 1918, British arms had successfully conquered those territories in the Ottoman Empire where she had distinct ambitions. In December 1917 the King was recommending that 'every inducement' should

---

158. Ibid., 234125, FO to Stevens, 13 Dec. 1917; Hardinge, min., n.d. stamp, 11 Dec. 1917; ibid., no. 237702, Hardinge, min., 16 Dec. 1917; ibid., Balfour min.
159. See above, p. 87.
160. CAB 23/5 War Cab. 314, append., 4 Jan. 1918.

be made to Turkey to break with Germany.[161] Aware of the growing conflict in the Caucasus between Turkey and Germany, Lloyd George, the great improviser, dubbed 'the Wizard of Wales' by some of his colleagues, and 'the Goat', by others, significantly asked his War Cabinet in June 1918, whether advantage could not be taken of this situation:

> He pointed out that the Turks were more anxious to acquire this rich country than they were to regain Mesopotamia or Palestine, and suggested that some peace arrangement might be arrived at with the Turkish Government by which the Turanian territory might be given to them . . . [162]

Thus, in order to come to an 'arrangement' with Turkey and entice her away from her south-eastern territories, Lloyd George was prepared very easily to abandon the Caucasus, including Armenia, the land he had twice described in public as 'soaked with the blood of innocence'.[163] On yet another level, while Armenians were being urged by sympathetic statements to fight the Turks on the Caucasian front, Ranald MacDonell, the Vice-Consul in Baku, was financing from June 1918, according to his own memoirs, not so much groups fighting the Central powers, but anti-Bolshevik plots. Using the two million rubles hidden in his apartment, he supplied Russian priests, old officers and aviation cadets with funds for counter-revolutionary activity. Captain Reginald Teague Jones, Intelligence Officer in Persia, had told MacDonell in Baku that

> . . . the new policy of the British and French Governments was to support the anti-Bolshevik forces which were rallying at various points on the outposts of the Russian Empire. It mattered little whether they were Tsarist or Social Revolutionary as long as they were prepared to oust the Bolsheviks.[164]

But there was nothing contradictory in all these aspects of policy: encouraging the Armenian war effort against the Turks, considering at the same time peace with Turkey, and helping to oust the Bolsheviks. They all aimed at winning the war or serving British national interests.

Only a fortnight after Lloyd George's contemplation of a deal with Turkey in the Caucasus, the British government went, probably, farthest in its 'pledges' to the Armenians. In July 1918, Ramsey MacDonald, the

161. Rothwell, *British War Aims*, pp. 131, 2. Lloyd George Papers, F/29/1/52, King George V to Lloyd George, 25 Dec. 1917.
162. CAB 23/6, War Cab. 435, min. 8, 24 June 1918; Lord Beaverbrook, *Men and Power 1917-1918* (London, 1956), p. 344.
163. See above, p. 87.
164. MacDonell, ' . . . *And Nothing Long'*, pp. 225-9, 223; Suny, *Baku Commune*, p. 305.

Leader of the Opposition Labour Party, asked if the Secretary of State for Foreign Affairs was following the resistance which the Armenians were offering to the Turkish army, and whether the Allied governments would 'pledge' themselves to do everything so that after the war the future of Armenia could be decided upon the principle of self-determination. Balfour answered:

> Yes, Sir; His Majesty's Government are following with earnest sympathy and admiration the gallant resistance of the Armenians in defence of their liberties and honour, and are doing everything they can to come to their assistance. As regards the future of Armenia, I will refer the hon. Member to the public statements made by leading statesmen among the Allied Powers in favour of a settlement upon the principle he indicates.[165]

Lloyd George himself was not far behind. Replying to the address of Manchester Armenians, he solemnly asked them 'to believe', that

> . . . those responsible for the government of this country are not unmindful of their responsibilities to your martyred race.[166]

Finally, writing to Bryce when the end of war was already in sight, Lord Robert Cecil, now Assistant Foreign Secretary, mentioned four points which the Armenians might regard 'as the charter of their rights to liberation at the hands of the Allies', including their services to the Allied cause and their suffering. He also referred to the Armenian soldiers 'still fighting' in the ranks of the British, French and American armies, and to the part they had borne in General Allenby's great victory in Palestine.[167] Concluding his letter, he added 'for the British Government':

> I am quite ready to reaffirm our determination that wrongs such as Armenia has suffered shall be brought to an end and their recurrence made impossible.[168]

A few days later Balfour repeated to Boghos Nubar 'personally the

---

165. *Hansard*, 5th Ser. 1918, vol. 108, col. 473.

166. Bodleian Library, Fisher Papers, Box 11, Arm. Nat. Deleg., *Memorandum on the Arm. Question* (Paris, 1918), p. 4, quot. Lloyd George on 11 Sept. 1918; also in Toynbee Papers, Box on Armenia, *Armenia's Charter* (London, 1918), p. 9.

167. Allenby himself was 'proud' to have had, under his command, an Armenian contingent which had fought 'brilliantly': see Arm. Nat. Deleg. Papers, microf., reel 3C/004136-7, quot. Allenby to Boghos Nubar, 12 Oct. 1918 and ibid., reel 4C/006830, Allenby to Lt. Shishmanian, 29 Dec. 1919.

168. Bryce Papers, UB 55, R. Cecil to Bryce, 3 Oct. 1918. Copy in FO 371/3404/164439; Arm. Nat. Deleg. Papers, microf., reel 4C/006834 in Fr. see also *The Times*, 4 Oct. 1918, p. 8, col. 4.

assurance that the liberation of Armenia is one of the war-aims of the Allies'.[169]

One is inclined to agree with V.H. Rothwell about the 'genuine repugnance' felt by most British leaders towards the Turks *vis-à-vis* their attempt to exterminate the Armenian population and their ill-treatment of prisoners. Thus, when Aubrey Herbert, a Turkophile Member of Parliament, asked permission to send a letter to Talaat appealing for better treatment of British prisoners, the Foreign Office refused. George Russell Clerk remarked that if Talaat could be caught he 'should be tried and hanged for his Armenian massacres'. Robert Cecil minuted, 'If Captain Herbert had heard the account given to me by Mr. Jackson, late United States consul at Aleppo, of the Armenian massacres he would not desire to send this letter'. Certainly, sympathy with the Armenian suffering was also genuine: ' . . .we could not acquiesce in the betrayal of the Armenians', Balfour stated in the privacy of the War Cabinet, when it was known that by the peace conditions forced on the Bolsheviks at Brest-Litovsk, the Germans had handed over 'the whole of Russian as well as of Turkish Armenia to the Turks'.[170]

On the other hand it seems that most leaders did not feel bound by their public declarations. According to Lloyd George, declarations about liberating nationalities inside the enemy Empires were 'intended to have a propagandist effect'. They would help to break up the solidarity of the enemy countries. On his part Robert Cecil argued in a different context that in order 'to weaken' Austria by 'stirring up internal trouble', Britain had felt 'compelled' to endorse the claims to independence of the various nationalities. Thus the statements about 'liberation' were aimed at bringing about a disruption within enemy countries rather than at fulfilling the principle of nationality and satisfying the aspirations of subject peoples. Further, Lloyd George had maintained during a Supreme War Council Meeting that 'Nobody was bound by a speech'.[171] It appears that the public declarations about the liberation of the non-Turkish territories in the Ottoman Empire and the expressions of sympathy with Armenia were assurances intended mainly to encourage the war effort rather than pledges to be fulfilled. They were pronounced as war aims; and war aims were in fact 'weapons of war',[172] to be set aside, perhaps, at the end of the conflict, if they no longer responded to new interests.

Pro-Armenian humanitarians could not share such an attitude. A few weeks before his death, Lord Bryce wrote about the threat of extinction of

169. FO 371/3404/162745, Balfour to Boghos Nubar, copy, 12 Oct. 1918.

170. Rothwell, *British War Aims,* p. 138; FO 371/3060/169535, Herbert to Lord Newton, with Minutes by Clerk and Cecil, 23 Aug. 1917, quot. in Rothwell, p. 138. CAB 23/16 War Cab. 362a, 8 Mar. 1918.

171. D. Lloyd George. *The Truth About the Peace Treaties* (London, 1938), p.. 1118; British Library, Robert Cecil Add MS 51105 f.144, memo., initialled R.C., 7 Aug. 1918. CAB 25/120/80, Supreme War Council Minutes, 2 Feb. 1918, quot. in Rothwell, ibid., p. 285.

172. Taylor, 'War Aims', p. 491.

the Armenians, of

> . . . the nation which the Allied [sic] [caused] to fight for them and have now deserted . . .[173]

The view was a heavy indictment, expressing in his habitual restrained way, the grief of a person who would not accept that the Great powers should use a small people and then break their pledged word.

The major difficulty for Britain, which would also become an impasse for her politicians, was the disproportion between her wartime interest in the Armenian people and the total lack of it in their lands.

Having abandoned the formula of Ottoman integrity, Britain had willingly agreed, under war conditions, to the territorial demands first of Russia and then of France and Italy, her major allies, in the Ottoman Empire.[174] When considering the counter-claims of the British government, Lord Kitchener and the naval authorities had pointed to Alexandretta for its military and naval importance; Lloyd George had suggested Palestine for prestige; and Lord Crewe had stressed that all shades of opinion in the India Office agreed on the Basra *vilayet* forming part of the British Empire.[175] The Prime Minister had next appointed an inter-departmental Committee under Sir Maurice de Bunsen, including Sir Mark Sykes and representatives from the Foreign, War and India Offices, the Admiralty, and the Board of Trade, to consider the nature of British desiderata in Turkey. The Bunsen Committee, its thirteen meetings and its final report, clearly point to the overwhelming importance given to the Persian Gulf. The report stressed that one of the 'cardinal' principles of British policy in the East was the consideration of Britain's 'special and supreme position in the Persian Gulf'.[176]

It is of vital importance, for the purposes of this study, to recognise that never, not even once, were the Armenian provinces mentioned as a region of British territorial interest. Indeed, the numerous maps attached to the report most clearly bear witness to the fact that the British territorial desiderata were south of Anatolia. In the nineteenth century Britain had strongly resented Russian presence in Armenia as a threat to her position in the Persian Gulf.[177] But the importance of Armenia would simply become superfluous for Britain once she had gained control of Lower Mesopotamia.

Considerations of national interest had induced Britain before the war to support Turkey staunchly as a buffer against Russia. In this respect she had considered it essential that the Armenian territories should remain under

173. Bryce Papers, UB 25, Bryce to C.P. Scott, 28 Dec. 1921.
174. MS Asquith 8, ff.17-18, 23-4, Cab. Meetings 9 Mar., 23 Mar. 1915; Grey, *Twenty-Five Years*, II, pp. 177-82; CAB 42/2/3/5/14, War Council Meetings, 3 Mar. 10 Mar., 19 Mar. 1915.
175. CAB 42/2/5/14, War Council Meetings, 10 Mar., 19 Mar. 1915.
176. CAB 27/1, paras. 11, 12, 32, 100; Aaron S. Klieman, 'Britain's War Aims in the Middle East in 1915', *Journal of Contemporary History*, vol. III, no. 3 (July 1968), pp. 237-73.
177. See above p. 5.

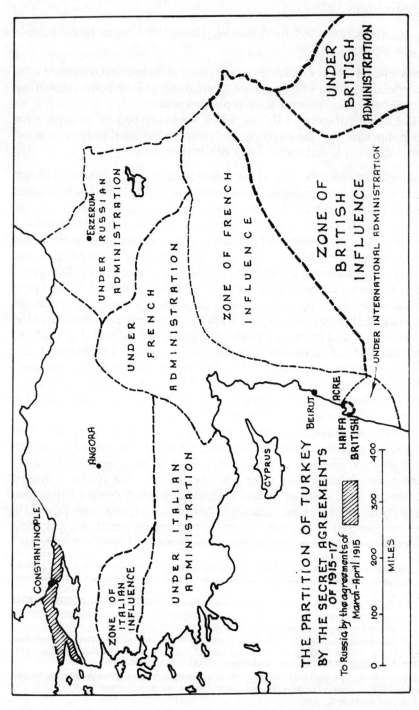

Map 5: British Territorial Interests During the War: South of Anatolia

the sovereignty of Turkey. The misrule of the Armenian people was considered of secondary importance. During 1914-18 Britain was likewise guided by considerations of national interest. In the greatest war of her history she sought to use all her resources, both material and moral, to defeat her enemies. So, she extensively made use of the Armenian holocausts of 1915 to discredit her enemies, Turkey directly and Germany indirectly. She publicised the massacres as part of her policy of winning the sympathy of the United States of America and of the other neutral countries away from the Central powers and of keeping the loyalty of her Moslem subjects. In 1917 she relentlessly pressed for the organisation of Armenian forces when the Caucasian front was disintegrating. Compassion for the Armenian people and their suffering was genuine, but the numerous public statements of sympathy and the 'pledges' for the liberation of Armenia were also motivated by interest. They aimed at stimulating the war effort both among the Armenians in the Caucasus and among the peoples in the Allied countries; they were, moreover, meant to silence the pacifists at home and prove that Britain was not waging an imperialistic war of greed. In the later part of the war the British government seriously contemplated also making peace with Turkey[178] in order to detach her from Germany once the British armies had won their victories in the south-eastern territories of the Ottoman Empire; the concessions to Turkey might come in the north.

Thus Britain was guided by her considerations of national interest. However, the war radically changed the focus of her interests in Armenia. It turned from the lands to the people. Britain's nineteenth-century commitment to Ottoman integrity became meaningless and consequently she lost her interest in Armenian territory. In order to satisfy her allies, she even agreed to, and approved of, the partition of historic Armenia[179] between Russia and France. Her interest in these lands further declined when her desiderata over the Persian Gulf region were recognised and her armies occupied southern Mesopotamia. On the other hand, the war brought a dramatic growth of sympathy with the Armenian people. This disproportion, however, between the decline of interest in Armenian territory and the increase of concern with the Armenian people was inauspicious for the future. Moreover, as interest in the Armenians and sympathy with their suffering had flowed out of the conditions of the war, they were bound to subside after 1918.

Thus, compassion and considerations of national interest had necessitated during the war sympathetic British statements about the liberation of Armenia. After the war, however, national interests would no longer warrant concern for Armenia.

178. See above p. 113.
179. The Armenian National Delegation asked for an autonomous state including the 'six *vilayets*' and Cilicia under protection of Allied powers, one acting as mandatory. Memo, June 1918, in Fisher Papers, Box 11. For other Armenian memoranda, see FO 371/2485/43561/48572/56472; also, FO 371/2488/96760; FO 371/3404/183916.

4   British Dilemmas: From Mudros to Sèvres

The British government and informed public opinion had been unanimous during the war about the desirability of liberating the Armenian provinces from Turkish rule. The government itself had contributed to building up public opinion which anticipated that Armenia would not be returned to Turkey after the war. The assertion that Armenia, like Mesopotamia, could 'never' be returned to Turkey, had been included, at a War Cabinet meeting, as one of the items in the 'considered policy of the Government'. The War Cabinet had, at a later date, again agreed that it would be 'impossible' to restore Armenia, any more than Arabia, Mesopotamia, Syria and Palestine, to their former sovereign — Turkey.[1] Thus the liberation of Armenia had been one of Britain's aims.

Neither the British government nor the pro-Armenian humanitarian groups, however, had any clear and positive plans as to the future rule and protection of Armenia. In 1917 revolutionary Russia had disclaimed annexations in the Armenian provinces. At one time it was thought, according to Lord Bryce, that France had also dropped her idea of obtaining Cilicia. So, when the United States entered the war, the Armenian organisations in France had hoped that she might be induced, by philanthropic motives and by the interest of her missionaries, to take it in hand for a time. Bryce thought this was very unlikely, but his old friends of the influential American Mission Board in Boston believed the scheme not impossible. Communicating this information to the Foreign Office, Bryce had added that the problem had always been difficult, and was even more so now because of the depopulation caused by the massacres. Answering for the government, Balfour had expressed the view that as far as he personally was concerned, he desired nothing better than that such an autonomous state should be placed under the sole protection of the United States, if the United States government would consent to assume such a responsibility. But before any decision was reached, Britain's Allies would have to be consulted and Russia might raise objections.[2]

In the War Cabinet, George Barnes had also suggested an American Protectorate over Armenia. But apparently, doubting the possibility of American involvement in the Old World, the same Cabinet meeting had

1. CAB 23/3, War Cab. 171, 27 June 1917. CAB 23/5, War Cab. 314, 4 Jan. 1918.
2. FO 371/3062/231416/24251, Bryce to R. Cecil, 28 Nov. 1917; extr. of letter from American Mission Board to Bryce, 5 Nov. 1917; Bryce to Balfour, 20 Dec. 1917; Balfour to Bryce, copy, 18 Dec. 1917.

reached a general conclusion favouring the creation of an autonomous Armenia 'perhaps' as part of a Russian Federation. Thus, it is clear that besides a sympathetic desire for her liberation from Turkish sovereignty, the War Cabinet had neither a comprehensive plan nor a tangible interest in the future of Armenia. At this same meeting in contrast, Barnes had suggested that, as regards Palestine and Mesopotamia, it should be said in 'diplomatic language', that the British intended to 'stick' to them.[3]

During the war the British government had sympathised, mainly in its own interests, with the suffering of the Armenian people and with their future. After the war, therefore, it was faced by a number of dilemmas, all arising from the basic dilemma: how to reconcile public statements with its reluctance to assume responsibility for Armenia. It resorted to various expedients: efforts to throw the responsibility of aid on to other countries; awkward arguments to justify its reluctance to help; half-hearted measures instead of effective action. Britain was not willing to spend money or men in a far-away and inaccessible country which was of no interest to her either on strategic or on economic grounds; a desolate country which was only rich in misery. Thus at the end of the war, the Armenian question looked like an additional liability for British statesmen.

The Armistice of Mudros was the first blow to Armenian aspirations. It both left the Armenian homelands under Turkish rule and failed to provide in a precise way for Turkey's disarmament. Yet, is it not possible that at the time, an exhausted Turkey might not have been pressed, albeit unwillingly, into making concrete concessions towards the Armenians? Even before the war many Turkish troops had been in the most wretched condition. In 1916 some were fighting with 'no overcoats and no boots' and thousands were deserting. By 1918 Turkey was in the grip of war-weariness and bankruptcy. Prices had risen by nearly 2,000 per cent.[4]

During the war it was reported that the Party of Prince Sabah-ed-Din, opposed to the existing government of Turkey, would be prepared to discuss terms of peace which also included an

. . . autonomous ARMENIA (Vilayets of ERZEROUM, BITLIS, VAN, TREBIZOND (Parts of ?) under Russian suzerainty.[5]

By mid-1918, the Caucasus had caused the Turco-German alliance to become strained. Apparently, relations were also strained within the Turkish army and within the Committee of Union and Progress. Secret agents reported that Turkish insurgents in the army had sent an ultimatum to the government demanding the immediate resignation of the Cabinet. One

3. CAB 23/13, War Cab. 308A, 31 Dec. 1917.
4. Liman von Sanders, *Five Years in Turkey* (Annapolis, 1927), pp. 9, 130-1, 260. Robert Cecil Papers, Add. MS 51094, ff.28, 29, memo by H. Nicolson on *Turkey,* 11 Aug. 1918.
5. FO 371/2768/87999, McMahon to Grey, 25 Apr. 1916.

faction of the Committee of Union and Progress had decided to propose a separate peace to Britain. Enver, the Minister of War, was hostile to the whole scheme of peace proposals, but the majority of the Committee did not trust him.[6]

Soundings for a separate peace were made by various Turkish authorities: each had its own plan. A certain Ruchdi Bey was sent directly by the Sultan as his personal emissary. His proposals, presented to Sir H. Rumbold, the British Minister in Berne, emanated from a group opposed to the Committee of Union and Progress. They promised autonomy to the Hejaz, Syria, Palestine and Mesopotamia under Ottoman suzerainty after the model of Egypt before the war. The remaining 'provinces essentially Turkish', should be organised by reforms to be carried out under British control. There was no reference to Armenia at all.[7] On the other hand, Rahmy Bey, the *Vali* of Smyrna, claimed, in a communication to Lord Granville, the British Minister in Athens, that he had at last been able to make the necessary arrangements to overthrow the Turkish government and assume power himself. He proposed that Constantinople and the Straits should remain under Turkish control but with guaranteed complete freedom of passage for ships of all nations; there should be completely free governments for Syria, Arabia, Mesopotamia and Armenia but with retention of nominal Turkish sovereignty.[8] In late October, the Turkish government underwent a change. Halil, the Turkish military attaché asked, with direct authority from the new Grand Vizier, that the British Legation in Berne should make known to Turkey Britain's minimum conditions. Turkey on her part perfectly realised the necessity of recognising the autonomy of Armenia, Mesopotamia, Palestine, Syria and Arabia. She hoped, however, that some arrangement could be reached to spare the susceptibilities of the Ottoman people and avoid any suggestions of actual dismemberment.[9]

Thus, three of the four proposals for peace — those from Sabah-ed-din, the *Vali* of Smyrna and the new Vizier — agreed to Armenian autonomy; while the fourth, the Sultan's, apparently considered Armenia among the 'provinces essentially Turkish'. At this time in Constantinople, Raouf Bey, the Minister of Marine and the chief Turkish delegate to negotiate the armistice, asked Alexander Khatisian, one of the Members of the Armenian Republic's Delegation to Turkey, to accompany him to Mudros to show to the British that the Turks and the Armenians had become 'reconciled' and had 'no quarrels' any longer. In return, the Turkish government would be willing to re-establish the 1914 international boundary, thus ceding the provinces of Kars and Ardahan, and would also give up part of the Alashkert

6. FO 371/3411/166047, Rumbold, Berne, to FO, 20 Sept. 1918. FO 371/3448/167085, Misc. Military, from Agent B.15, Berne, 1 Oct. 1918. Ibid., no. 165602, Rumbold to FO, 1 Oct. 1918.
7. Ibid., nos. 167085/170727, Rumbold to FO, 4 Oct., 5 Oct. 1918.
8. Ibid., no. 167738, Granville to FO, 6 Oct. 1918.
9. Ibid., no. 177193, Acton to FO, 22 Oct 1918.

Valley in Turkey.[10]

On the whole, then, it is evident that at least some of the various Turkish authorities were reconciled to the idea of making concessions to Armenians. It seems that the British government could certainly have bargained on this point, had it wished to do so. An official report, written in December 1918, also stated that the Moslems in India admitted the fact that Turkey had foolishly been dragged into the war. So, the report went on, they would accept, sorrowfully but without lasting rancour, the severance of Arabia and Armenia from the Turkish Empire as part of the penalty due.[11]

In the Foreign Office, the determination was final to detach completely the Arab provinces from the Ottoman Empire. But there was also a clear inclination not to have Armenia returned to Turkish rule. Thus, Sir. H. Rumbold told the Sultan's emissary that he was 'struck' by the ommission of all reference to Armenia whose fate must occupy a 'prominent' place in any future settlement. Sir Mark Sykes, the Middle Eastern expert at the Foreign Office, also found the absence of any reference to the Armenian question significant, and categorically rejected the Sultan's proposal of mere administrative reforms:

> 120 years of this should have taught us what reforms are worth. The legislation since the TANZIMAT would fill a library; the butcher's bill runs into millions.[12]

On 3 October 1918, Balfour told the War Cabinet that the Turkish armies were no longer a formidable force anywhere and that Turkey was throwing out feelers in Switzerland.[13] To be ready for any eventual offer of armistice, the War Office and the Admiralty prepared a set of draft conditions and submitted it to the Foreign Office in early October. These conditions were naturally based on military and naval considerations alone. Foremost among them were the opening of the Bosphorus and the Dardanelles, access to the Black Sea and the occupation of the Dardanelles forts. A dominant influence over this waterway was a traditional British consideration, particularly important now when Russia was no longer a friendly power. In the prevailing war situation, the detachment of Turkey from the Central Alliance and control of the Dardanelles would not only expose the eastern flank of both Germany and Austria, but might also prevent their control and exploitation of the wealth of southern Russia and the Caucasus. Other terms asked for the occupation of Baku; occupation of the Taurus tunnel system;

---

10. A. Khatisian, *Hayastani Hanrapetutian Dsagumn u Zargatsume* (The Creation and Development of the Republic of Armenia), 2nd edn (Beirut, 1968), p. 113. The Armenians did not agree.

11. House of Lords Record Office, Bonar Law Papers, 94/20, memo. by Sir Hamilton Grant, For. Secr., to Govt. of India, 20 Dec. 1918.

12. FO 371/3448/167085, Rumbold to FO, 4 Oct. 1918 and minute by Sykes.

13. CAB 23/14, War Cabinet 482A, min. 6, 3 Oct. 1918.

immediate withdrawal of Turkish troops from north-west Persia and Trans-Caucasia to behind the pre-war frontier; the surrender of all garrisons in the Arab provinces; compliance with such orders as might be conveyed for the disposition of the Turkish army and its equipment; and handing over of all Allied prisoners of war unconditionally to the Allies.[14]

In the Foreign Office, Sir Eyre Crowe, an Assistant Under-Secretary, conceded that it would of course be desirable to let any armistice deal exclusively with military and naval conditions. 'But', he minuted, 'I do feel that some guarantees against further Armenian massacres will be called for.' Lord Robert Cecil insisted that some provision 'must be inserted to protect Armenians'; Sir Mark Sykes advised the occupation of Cilicia by the Allies. Arnold Toynbee, from the Political Intelligence Department, suggested that police control in the 'six *vilayets*' might be inserted in the clause concerning the Allied prisoners, as another humanitarian desideratum. In a further minute, Sir Mark suggested that not only should the towns of Sis, Hajin, Zeitun and Aintab in Cilicia be occupied, but also that the Allies should have the power to repatriate the deportees and should afford them the necessary military protection.[15] Major W. Ormsby-Gore pointed out that the importance of Armenian rights in Cilicia lay in the separation thereby recreated between the Turk and the Arab. Toynbee supported these views as regards Cilicia; the advantage of a Mediterranean seaboard was obvious. But he insisted that some stipulation with regard to the 'six *vilayets*' was also essential in view of the British 'commitments' since 1878 and the repeated Turkish atrocities.[16]

However, safeguarding Armenia in the terms of an armistice with Turkey as effectively as Syria and Mesopotamia could be safeguarded, presented difficulties on 'geographical and military grounds'. In the Arab regions of Palestine and Mesopotamia the British had decisively defeated the Turks and had occupied large areas. The case was completely different in the Armenian provinces where the Russian defection had given the Turks their opportunity. Exhausted and defeated on other fronts, Turkey was victorious in the Caucasus and master in the 'six Armenian *vilayets*' and Cilicia. Who would undertake the protection of the Armenians were provision made for the detachment of these regions? The problem was further complicated by the fact that the native Armenian population had either been massacred or become refugees in the Caucasus. Moreover, the British apparently did not have much trust in the ability of the 'new-born or still-born' Caucasian republics — including Armenia — to control further territories. They

14. FO 371/3448/166382/168408, Oct. 1918 and 7 Oct. 1918.
15. FO 371/3404/55708/166169, Crowe, min., 3 Oct. 1918; FO 371/3448/166382/168408, mins. n.d. [Oct. 1918].
16. Ibid., nos. 169045/168408/169045, Ormsby-Gore, memo., 7 Oct. 1918; Toynbee mins., 8, 10 Oct. 1918.

themselves needed protection.[17] Besides these difficulties, Sir Mark Sykes perceived some latent Turcophilism lingering in Britain and suggested that the *Saturday Review*, the *Yorkshire Post* and the *Morning Post* were all newspapers still affected by 'financial and sentimental pro-Turkism'. Major Ormsby-Gore regarded the prevalent sentimentality about the 'clean-fighting' Turk as 'sickly'.[18]

On the whole, then, the Foreign Office staff clearly wished to provide protection for the Armenian *vilayets* in the armistice terms. Lord Robert Cecil agreed with Toynbee that policing by Americans would do very well. Lieutenant-Colonel W.H. Gribbon of the War Office pointed out that the government could hardly insist on military grounds on immediate evacuation, but he also agreed that a stipulation might be inserted providing for the immediate despatch of British or American officials, to ensure security for the Armenians. Indeed, the 'six *vilayets*' did not occupy a strategic position on the way to vital water and land routes: policing and administrative responsibilities could be justified only on humanitarian grounds. But it seems that the Foreign Office staff was unanimous that Armenia should be specifically brought under Allied occupation. Sir James Headlam-Morley, the Assistant Director of the Political Intelligence Department, believed that policing the Armenian *vilayets* would be possible without probably requiring as many troops as were engaged in Palestine and Mesopotamia, if the fleet were in the Black Sea and the British held the Caucasian railways.[19]

Thus, quite a few members of the Foreign Office definitely did not think that providing some kind of security in these areas during the interim period between armistice and peace was beyond the reach of the British government, had it wished to do so. However, the preoccupations of the War Cabinet were totally unconcerned with the Armenians in the autumn of 1918. With the stalemate on the Western front, it was vital to detach Turkey from Germany. The success of the British forces on the Mesopotamian and Palestinian fronts might make this possible and might result in the Allied, or rather British, mastery of the Dardanelles straits. Such military success might also be used to consolidate the British position in the Near East and thus tip the scales in this area against France, Britain's major rival. Apparently, the ever-active brain of Lloyd George had turned to the possibility of scoring victories simultaneously over the Germans, the French and even the Russians. If the Straits, Palestine and Mesopotamia could be secured, concessions to Turkey might be made in the Caucasus or the Eastern Provinces. After all, neither the Caucasus nor the Eastern Provinces had

17. Ibid., no. 178219, note, Toynbee to Kidston, 26 Oct. 1918. FO 371/3411/166030, Toynbee, *Desiderata for a Possible Armistice with Turkey: Position in Caucasus*, 2 Oct. 1918.
18. FO 371/3448/167085, M. Sykes, mins., n.d. [Oct. 1918]; FO 371/3400/182320, Ormsby-Gore, min., 5 Nov. 1918.
19. FO 371/3448/166382, R. Cecil and Toynbee, mins., 3 Oct. 1918. FO 371/3404/166169, Kidston, min., 3 Oct. 1918. FO 371/3411/167860, Headlam-Morley, min., 1 Oct. 1918.

ever weighed so heavily as the Dardanelles, the Mediterranean or the Persian Gulf among British interests. If Enver had made use of the disintegration of the Caucasian front, following the Russian Revolution, for pushing ahead his Pan-Turanian schemes in the north, Lloyd George, a greater improviser, could similarly make use, in his turn, of the vacuum in the south, created by the detachment and defeat of the Turkish troops. As referred to above, during a meeting of the War Cabinet in June 1918, he had made the point that some 'arrangement' might be arrived at with the Turkish government by which the Turanian territory — in the north — might be given to them. A little later, he had expressed most significantly the opinion that

> . . . it would be better for us for the Turks to hold Baku, as it was not probable they would ever be dangerous to our interests in the East, whilst, on the other hand, Russia, if in the future she became regenerated, might be so.[20]

Thus, the north-east might be conceded to Turkey, at least temporarily, in exchange for areas in the south. She might also be used, as in the past, as a buffer against a regenerated Russia in the future.

In the autumn of 1918, then, considerations about the Caucasus and especially Armenia were pushed to the background. All-important for the War Cabinet, and especially for Lloyd George, was the use of British military success in the Middle East for gaining advantage over Germany, France and Russia abroad and prestige at home.

The Sykes-Picot Agreement of 1916 had allocated large areas in the Ottoman Empire to France. But during 1917 and 1918, almost all the fighting in these areas had been done by the British. It seemed vital to Lloyd George, therefore, that the British themselves should hold the reins of the armistice negotiations and exploit to the full their military success by acting as swiftly as possible. When the collapse of Turkey was imminent, the French reminded Balfour that General Allenby's armies had entered the French sphere of influence as defined in the Sykes-Picot Agreement, and that appropriate arrangements should be made as regards administration. British efforts to procure modification of this Agreement had been entirely unavailing, Lord Curzon reported to the War Cabinet. But the Prime Minister, who seemed determined to make use of British victories in the east, now told his Cabinet colleagues that refreshing his memory about this Agreement, he had come to the conclusion that it was altogether 'most undesirable' from the British point of view and 'quite inapplicable' to the new circumstances. Having been concluded more than two years before, it was inappropriate to the new British position in Turkey, which had been won by very large British forces with very little Allied help.[21]

20. CAB 23/6, War Cab. 435, min. 8, 24 June 1918.
21. CAB 23/14, War Cab. 482A, min. 8, 3 Oct. 1918.

Strongly pressed by the Admiralty and the military authorities, the War Cabinet and especially Lloyd George were poised to score as many points as possible over both Germany and France during the period of Turkish armistice. The draft terms of the armistice were discussed during six War Cabinet meetings. Top priority was naturally given to the condition of obtaining a free and secure passage through the Dardanelles. Balfour, the Foreign Secretary, regarded such a condition as of 'great importance' for the British. Bonar Law, the Chancellor of the Exchequer and Leader of the Conservative Party, always practical, totally agreed, suggesting that to accord an armistice on this condition 'alone' was enough since it would really give the British 'all' they required. Lord Milner, the Minister of War, concurred. Balfour in addition stressed that no hope should be held out to the Turks that they might be permitted to keep sovereignty over occupied territory. This clearly showed that Britain was determined not to make concessions over Palestine and south Mesopotamia. The Prime Minister, concerned as usual with his own and British power and prestige, insisted that it was 'very important' to take action 'at once'. Moreover, he insisted, the action should, if possible, be taken by the British and not by the French.[22]

The British priorities were thus set. There was no mention of Armenia at all.

During the next Cabinet meeting, it was revealed that Clemenceau, the French Prime Minister, was objecting to a British admiral's commanding the Fleet which it was intended to send to Constantinople if the Turks surrendered, as it was to the French that the supreme naval command of the Mediterranean had been handed early in the war. He did not accept the argument that the British had taken by far the larger part of the burden of the war against Turkey. Clemenceau had retorted by pointing to France's contribution on the Western front as a reason for the negligible amount of French troops in the Near East, and had declared that as France was Turkey's principal creditor, the French had the greatest interest there. Accordingly, the French Admiral Gauchet had been authorised to proceed to Mudros if he considered it expedient, possibly with a view to proceeding up the Straits in command of the Allied Squadron.[23]

But the Admiralty would not allow this. Vice-Admiral Sir S.A. Gough Calthorpe, the British Commander-in-Chief, Mediterranean, had cabled his conviction that nothing would be more 'disastrous' to British prestige throughout the east than the prospect of an Allied force going up the Dardanelles under any but a British admiral.[24] In the War Cabinet, Admiral Sir R. Wemyss, the First Sea Lord and Chief of Naval Staff, also

22. Ibid., War Cab. 489A, min. 3, 21 Oct. 1918.
23. Ibid., War Cab. 489B, min. 4, 22 Oct. 1918. D. Lloyd George, *War Memoirs* (London, 1936), VI, pp. 3310-11, Lloyd George to Clemenceau, 15 Oct. 1918 and Clemenceau to Lloyd George, 21 Oct. 1918. CAB 23/14, War Cab. 490A, min. 1, 24 Oct. 1918.
24. FO 371/3448/175953, Calthorpe to Admiralty, copy, 21 Oct. 1918.

insisted that handing over to the French the command of the fleet which entered Constantinople was most undesirable. In vain did George Barnes advise 'to carry the French with us'. Lloyd George supported his Chiefs of Staff. Accordingly, a telegram was sent to Admiral Calthorpe instructing him not to hand over the control of any negotiations with the emissary from Turkey. The War Cabinet also approved the paper on the conditions of the armistice jointly prepared by Sir Henry Wilson, the CIGS, and Sir R. Wemyss. These two had taken the conditions as agreed to by the French and the Italians and had arranged them 'in order of importance'. According to Sir Henry Wilson, if the first four of the 24 terms were secured, the remaining twenty 'could be cut out' without serious loss. After the Prime Minister had once again urged that 'delay was the one thing to be avoided', the War Cabinet instructed the Admiralty to telegraph the draft armistice terms to the British Admiral Commanding-in-Chief at Mudros. The crucial cable stressed the 'paramount importance' of the first four conditions which if carried out would

> . . . so inevitably make us master of the situation, that we do not wish you to jeopardise obtaining them . . . by insisting unduly on all or any of the rest . . .[25]

Of the 24 terms arranged 'in order of importance' the first three were about the opening of the Dardanelles and secure access to the Black Sea. The fourth concerned the handing over of Allied prisoners and Armenian interned persons. Only the twenty-fourth term referred to Armenia.

On the advice of Sir Henry Wilson, the War Cabinet also decided that General Allenby should be informed of the probable armistice negotations with Turkey, and should be instructed that 'consequently' it was of the 'greatest' importance that he should occupy Aleppo 'as soon as possible' and should also press on 'towards Mosul'.[26]

Thus, the War Cabinet had deliberated under the powerful influence of the Service Chiefs. Lord Curzon, a member of the War Cabinet, had strong misgivings about the terms of the armistice being based only on military considerations. He privately wrote to Lloyd George, but rather late in the day, after the guidelines for the armistice had been cabled to Admiral Calthorpe on 22 October.[27] He believed they were 'jettisoning' practically the whole of the armistice terms *vis-à-vis* Turkey for the sake of getting through the Dardanelles; that Britain was contemplating the cessation of war before Mosul or Aleppo or Alexandretta was recovered, while Turkey was still in the Caucasus and 'before any attempt' had been made 'to settle

25. CAB 23/14, War Cab. 489B, mins. 4 and 6, 22 Oct. 1918; War Cab. 490A, min. 1, 24 Oct. 1918.

26. Ibid., min. 2, 24 Oct. 1918.

27. FO 371/3448/178097, Admiralty to C.-in-C. Medit., no. 46Z, 22 Oct. 1918.

the Armenian question'. It would not be easy to get the Turk out of any territory which was not already in military occupation. The Turk was 'a first-rate and astute bargainer'. He would 'flatter' with his assurances of conversion and all the while would be 'laughing' behind the backs of the British at his skill in escaping the penalty of his misdeeds and in getting the better of the stupid Englishman . . . Curzon feared that a great chance in settling all these affairs might be jeopardised in an eagerness to grasp the plums which must in any case soon fall from the tree.[28] A few days later, in the War Cabinet also, Curzon questioned the wisdom of the decision that the admiral at Mudros, if unable to obtain all the terms of the armistice drawn up in Paris, should be authorised to be content with agreement on the first four. At the next meeting he pointed out that all reference to Armenia was omitted from these, and that a telegram had been circulated by the Foreign Office on that very morning in which some Armenian authority had urged that Armenia should not be overlooked. The Prime Minister, apparently straining his powers of argument for glossing over this question, replied that as far as Armenia was concerned, the view was that if the Allies were in Constantinople, they could do what they liked as regards Armenia. This was of course a wishful view. In a country the size of Turkey, with poor communications, control over Constantinople did not entail control over Armenia. Two years later Sir Henry Wilson would scribble in his diary that the 'writ' of the Allies had 'never' run in Turkey in Asia,[29] and that it was not possible to detach the Eastern Provinces on behalf of Armenia.

During this same Cabinet meeting, Balfour, always philosophical and balancing, supported, it appears, both Curzon and Lloyd George. He agreed with the former that, in the last resort, it was 'absolutely essential' to get security for the Armenians and the Caucasus. He also agreed with the latter that if the British were in Constantinople, Turkey would not be in a position to resist British demands.

> The great danger was that during the period of the armistice the Turks might do something foolish in Armenia or the Caucasus. Surely, however, we might assume that they would not be so foolish . . .

Balfour argued, viewing events which might happen with his usual detachment.[30] Apparently no one asked him how it was possible to sense the 'great danger' of the Turks acting in a foolish way in Armenia, and, at the same time, 'surely . . . assume' that they would not be foolish.

Balfour's argument was characteristic of his personal inclination to

28. Lloyd George Papers, F/11/9/19, Curzon to Lloyd George, 23 Oct. 1918.
29. CAB 23/14, War Cab. 491A, min. 7, 25 Oct. 1918, War Cab. 491B, min. 12, 26 Oct. 1918. C.E. Callwell, *Field-Marshal Sir Henry Wilson: His Life and Diaries* (London, 1927), II, p. 229, entry for 3 Mar. 1920.
30. CAB 23/14, War Cab. 491B, min. 12, 26 Oct. 1918. About Balfour's detachment, see Lord Vansittart, *The Mist Procession* (London, 1958), pp. 58, 218, 232.

indulge in analytical exercises. But it was also characteristic of the general attitude of the British government which was sympathetic towards Armenian suffering, and genuinely considered it 'absolutely essential' that security should be provided for the Armenians, but also wished to 'assume' that the responsibility for gaining it would not fall upon Britain. The British government could not reconcile its interest in the Armenian people — aroused, as seen in the last Chapter, under war conditions — and its indifference to their lands in eastern Anatolia.

The Prime Minister was decisively consistent during the Cabinet meetings before the armistice: if Admiral Calthorpe reached Constantinople, 'nothing else really mattered'. He opposed Austen Chamberlain's suggestion that a fresh telegram might be sent to Calthorpe advising him to try, if possible, to secure from among the remaining twenty points certain items to be designated. Altering terms, the Prime Minister pointed out, would involve the British in difficulties with the French and the Italians. The War Cabinet agreed with the Prime Minister. Curzon's protest against this decision was, at his own request, recorded. Neither did the concern for the 'security' of the Armenians, expressed by both G. Barnes and Lord Robert Cecil at a later War Cabinet meeting, result in fresh instructions to Mudros. Thus the last telegram sent to Calthorpe was the one stressing the 'paramount importance' of the first four terms and instructing him not to jeopardise obtaining them quickly by insisting 'unduly' on any of the rest.[31]

The War Cabinet was extremely pleased with the armistice and 'very strongly' expressed the opinion that Calthorpe should be 'heartily congratulated' on carrying the negotiations to a successful conclusion.[32] The first four terms, considered as vital to British interests, had been accepted by the Turks without any alteration. Calthorpe had made it absolutely clear that otherwise the negotiations would be broken off. The clauses amended were those about demobilisation, Trans-Caucasia and Cilicia — indeed, those mostly affecting the Armenians. Curzon, who usually gave the impression that his views were 'rigid and inflexible', but who, according to Lord Beaverbrook actually had a talent for being on 'both sides of every controversy', now joined the Cabinet in its expression of satisfaction.[33]

It is true that the 'six *vilayets*', the homeland of the Armenian people, were not well provided for in the final draft. Only in the case of disorder could the Allies have the right to occupy them. Still, had all the clauses concerning the Armenians been carried out, security to a great extent might have prevailed in Anatolia. This did not happen. Almost all the concessions made at Mudros were at the expense of the Armenians. The amendment to

31. CAB 23/14, War Cab. 491B, min. 12, 26 Oct. 1918. CAB 23/8, War Cab. 492, min. 9, 29 Oct. 1918. CAB 23/14, War Cab. 489B, min. 6, 22 Oct. 1918.

32. Ibid., 494A, min. 1, 31 Oct. 1918.

33. Lord Beaverbrook, *Men and Power 1917-1918* (London, 1956), p. 309. CAB 23/14, War Cab. 494A, min. 1, 31 Oct. 1918.

the clause relating to demobilisation and the lack of precision defining its terms would prove especially fatal. The clauses important for the Armenians and the changes brought about therein included:

5. Immediate demobilization of the Turkish Army except for such troops as are required for the surveillance of the frontiers and for the maintenance of internal order (effectives to be determined later by the Allies).

5. The significant phrase was added: 'after consultation with the Turkish Government'.

7. Occupation by Allied troops of important strategical points.

7. Accepted

10. Allied occupation of the Taurus tunnel system.

10. Accepted

11. Immediate withdrawal of Turkish troops from North-West Persia and Trans-Caucasia to behind the pre-war frontier.

11. Amended as follows: 'Part of Trans-Caucasia has already been ordered to be evacuated by Turkish troops, the remainder to be evacuated if required by the Allies after they have studied the situation there.'

16. The surrender of all garrisons in the Hejaz, Assir, Yemen, Syria, Cilicia and Mesopotamia to the nearest Allied Commander or Arab Representative.

16. From this list of garrisons, only the name of 'Cilicia' was significantly omitted; instead the Clause read: 'and the withdrawal of troops from Cilicia, except those necessary to maintain order . . .'

24. It should be made clear:
a) That in case of disorder in the six Armenian vilayets the Allies reserve to themselves the right to occupy any part of them;

24.
(a) was kept as it was.

b)	That in connection with Clauses (7), (15), and (10) the towns of Sis, Hajin, Zeitun and Aintab should be occupied.[34]	(b) was removed altogether.[35]

Sir Mark Sykes was quick to react. In an outspoken telegram to Lord Robert Cecil, circulated to the King and the War Cabinet, he maintained that the published terms of the armistice were 'worse', from the Armenian point of view, than he ever anticipated and could not fail to confirm the Armenians' fear that 'some betrayal' was contemplated. Article 24 allowed Allied intervention in Armenia only in the event of fresh massacres — as if 'actual million already massacred [was] not . . . sufficient justification for immediate action'. The Turks had managed to strike out the part of the clause about the occupation of Sis, Zeitun and Hajin by the Allies. Article 16, while ensuring absolute evacuation of certain specified areas of 'economic and political interest' to certain Allied powers, even left Turkish forces to maintain order in Cilicia, an area where some of the worst massacres had taken place.[36]

Apparently, the War Cabinet itself was aware how unsatisfactory the armistice was from the Armenian point of view. Sir George Cave, the Home Secretary, undertook to make the announcement in Parliament about the signing of the armistice, but asked what 'steps' he should take if questions were put to him on points 'such as the protection which was to be given to the Armenians'. The War Cabinet authorised him 'to satisfy' the House 'on that point'.[37]

It is worth asking whether there was ground for the lingering suspicion that the British government had made a deal: concessions to Turkey over Armenia in return for the liberation of its Arab provinces. The British authorities were well aware of Turkey's Pan-Turanian ambitions in the Caucasus and Persia. Both in 1917 and 1918 the Turks had concentrated their forces primarily on the northern front to the neglect of the Mesopotamian and Palestinian fronts. In the summer of 1918, Harold Nicolson, discussing the arguments for a separate peace with Turkey, had said that the British government could scarcely induce the Ottoman government to give way with regards to Arabia and Syria without some concession to the Pan-Turanian idea, which 'inevitably' entailed 'some sacrifice' of the Armenians. Nicolson, however, had rejected this solution because it would give immense impetus to the Pan-Turanian movement and thereby react dangerously on India. On his part, Toynbee had disclosed that a certain

34. FO 371/3448/178097, Admiralty to C.-in-C. Medit., 46Z, 22 Oct. 1918
35. FO 371/3449/181110, C.-in-C. Medit. to Admiralty, 593Z, 31 Oct. 1918.
36. FO 371/3404/183152, M. Sykes to R. Cecil in R. Rodd to FO, 3 Nov. 1918.
37. CAB 23/14, War Cab. 494A, min. 2, 31 Oct. 1918.

group in the Committee of Union and Progress, men such as Dr Nazim, were known to have contemplated a proposal to the British government that it should keep the Arab provinces in return for giving the Turks a free hand in the Caucasus. Toynbee, writing about this in early October 1918, had strongly urged that some provision should be made in the armistice for the 'six *vilayets*', otherwise turning the Turks out of all non-Turkish territory except Armenia would be regarded as one form of such a 'deal'.[38]

Reference has already been made to Lloyd George's actual suggestion of arriving at 'some arrangement' with Turkey on these lines in the summer of 1918.[39]

Thus, when the terms of the armistice were announced and it was known that Turkish garrisons would surrender in the Hejaz, the Yemen, Syria and Mesopotamia, but that Turkish troops were to be allowed to remain in the Armenian provinces, suspicions were aroused. Joseph Bliss, Liberal MP for Cumberland (Cockermouth) and member of the British Armenia Committee, asked Balfour whether 'a secret understanding' had been arrived at with Turkey relating to the retention of Armenia and of Constantinople. Likewise, Sir G. Toulmin asked whether at the Peace Conference Britain would be free to advocate terms securing the full liberty of Armenia. In reply, Balfour told the House that 'no understanding' of any kind had been entered into with Turkey, other than the terms of the armistice as published, and that at the Peace Conference Britain would be free to advocate terms securing the full liberty of Armenia.[40]

One is inclined to come to the conclusion, from the evidence above, that although no such bargain — of concessions to Turkey over Armenia in return for the liberation of its Arab provinces — was explicitly made, yet it was implicit in the removal of Turkish power in Mesopotamia, Palestine and Syria on the one hand and the postponement of the Armenian settlement until the Peace Conference, on the other. From the British point of view, it seems that as long as the great waterway of the Dardanelles was open and free, and Turkish power was crushed in the Arab provinces where the Allies had specific ambitions, nothing else much mattered. The conclusion by the British of the armistice negotiations and the British command of the Allied fleet proceeding up the Straits would ensure British prestige and power. For the rest, responsibility for the Armenian provinces might be deferred to the Peace Conference.

Even before the armistice, Armenians had been alarmed at the rumours of abandonment. James A. Malcolm, a representative in London of Boghos Nubar's Delegation, had called 'hot-foot' at the Foreign Office to plead for a clear provision for the Armenian provinces. George Kidston, Chief Clerk at

38. Robert Cecil Papers, Add. MS. 51094, ff.30-1, 36, memo. on *Turkey* by H. Nicolson, 11 Aug. 1918. FO 371/3404/166169, 3 Oct. 1918.
39. See p. 114 above. CAB 23/6, War Cab. 435, 24 June 1918.
40. *Hansard,* 5th Ser. 1918, vol. 110, col. 2087.

the Eastern Department of the Foreign Office, had reassured him by 'generalities', pointing out that the protection of the Armenians was one of the 'leading principles' of the policy of the British government. He had also suggested to his Foreign Office colleagues, as he himself minuted, to send some 'soothing' message to Boghos Nubar in 'general' terms. Arnold Toynbee was disturbed: 'we are drifting into a false position towards the Armenians', he remarked.[41]

The protection of the Armenians might be one of the 'principles' of British policy but it never became a British interest.

The French press on the whole welcomed the armistice. In *Victoire, Matin* and *Homme Libre* satisfaction was expressed that the opening of the Dardanelles would above all enable the Allies to instigate an active and efficient policy against the Bolsheviks, who had 'stolen' twenty milliards of francs' worth of French savings. *Temps* declared that France could not forget that her material interests in the Ottoman Empire were, before the war, estimated at about three milliard francs; and *Journal* observed that the road was now clear for taking up again the traditional policy which for centuries made Turkey the best 'moral colony' of France.[42]

The skill in diplomacy shown by the Turks, their cunning and their persuasive ability, had been remarkable just before and during the negotiations. The Foreign Office was, initially, placed in an unwelcome position of uncertainty and suspense by its awareness that the Turks might turn for peace negotiations not only to the French but to the Americans as well.[43] Later, a combination of professions of friendship and admiration for Britain on the one hand, displeasure towards other nationalities and threats of the probable fall of the Turkish government on the other, were freely used by Raouf Bey during the actual negotiations with Calthorpe at Mudros. Thus, he told Calthorpe that Turkish public opinion was 'looking forward to a square deal' from the British; that 'frankly' speaking the British could come up and secure the guns in the Dardanelles forts, but if the Greeks also came in to occupy the forts, it would mean 'a revolution' in Turkey. Moreover, the surrender of garrisons in the Arab provinces should only be to a British Commander, because if the Turks surrendered to the Arabs they would be 'badly treated'. Raouf Bey also objected strongly to the surrender of garrisons in Cilicia. He had a 'special' request that the clause about the Allied occupation of the towns of Sis, Hajin, Zeitun and Aintab in Cilicia should be cancelled; otherwise 'on this' the 'Government may fall'.[44] At the conclusion of the negotiations, Calthorpe assured Raouf Bey of his ardent desire to promote by all means in his power the most friendly relations between

41. FO 371/3448/165564/18219, mins., Kidston and Toynbee, 26 Oct. 1918.
42. FO 371/3449/182464, Lord Derby to Balfour, 1 Nov. 1918.
43. FO 371/3448/165602/172713/173330, min. R. Graham, 2 Oct. 1918; Sir A. Hardinge, 15 Oct. 1918; Barclay, 15 Oct. 1918.
44. FO 371/5259/E5732, copy of actual negotiations concerning the Armistice of Murdros.

Britain and Turkey. In the Foreign Office Lord Robert Cecil was afraid that he had been 'completely taken in by the Turks'[45] and was much disturbed.

The armistice was, for Lloyd George, a gratifying victory not only over Germany and Russia but also over France. Besides exposing the eastern flanks of Germany, it assured the strategic access of the Allies and especially of Britain to Russia:[46] no longer would Germany have exclusive control of the mineral and agricultural wealth of southern Russia. Moreover, the armistice established Britain as the dominant power in the Near East. It seems that during October 1918, Lloyd George was obsessed by the prospect that other nations, such as the Italians and especially the French, might gain advantages in the Near East, basing their claims on previous agreements, while it was the British who were mainly doing the fighting in this area and consequently should maintain superiority. Although Balfour and Bonar Law had pointed to the original idea that any territories acquired by the Allies should be pooled,[47] Lloyd George, undeterred, had done his utmost in Paris to renege on the Sykes-Picot Agreement and to secure Palestine and Mosul for Britain.

Arguing vehemently with Clemenceau in a 'very *exalte*' frame of mind, he had pressed — 'his plan was to pretend' — that both Syria and Palestine should be given to the United States, hoping that 'in fear' of losing Syria, Clemenceau would agree to Palestine being given to Britain. Lloyd George had also quarrelled with Clemenceau when he had suspected that the projected attack on Constantinople would be reserved for the French. At the Conference, the two leaders had 'spat at one another like angry cats'.[48] This was indeed personal diplomacy, overriding the Foreign Office; diplomacy at its worst. But there had been another 'fearful row' in Paris when Calthorpe had excluded the French from the armistice negotiations at Mudros. Lloyd George 'gave more than he got', Sir M.P.A. Hankey, the Secretary to the War Cabinet, wrote in his diary. When the armistice was actually signed, a communiqué had been immediately telephoned to London to be read out in the House of Commons, 'explaining clearly that the *British* Admiral had made the armistice'.[49] In the end, the French smarted, sulked and almost sabotaged the peace with Turkey.

The Armistice of Mudros, drafted and concluded in great haste in an atmosphere of rivalry and mistrust, was, as Harold Nicolson has pointed out, 'not a scientific document'. Its clauses were haphazard and optimistic and they contained no precise stipulations regarding the disarmament of

45. FO 371/3449/186944, Calthorpe to Raouf Bey, copy, 30 Oct. 1918. Minutes n.d. [Nov. 1918].
46. Arno J. Mayer, *Politics and Diplomacy of Peacemaking* (London, 1968), p. 95.
47. CAB 23/14, War Cab. 482A, min. 8, 3 Oct. 1918.
48. FO 800/201, R. Cecil, Paris, to Balfour, priv., 7 Oct. 1918.
49. Churchill College Library, Hankey Papers, HNKY 1/6, diary, Paris, entries for 30, 31 Oct. 1918.

Turkey.[50] The War Cabinet, prompted by Lloyd George and the Service Chiefs, had rushed into it. The armistice temporarily brought power and prestige to the British. But it was an ominous event for the Armenians because it failed to provide for the liberation of the Armenian homelands on the one hand, and for the proper disarmament of the Turkish troops on the other. Its inauspicious consequences became worse with the fatal delay in the peace settlement, since it perpetuated the domination of Turkey over the Armenian provinces in Anatolia. The Armenian refugees and deportees could not return to their homes and remained as a crushing burden on the tiny Republic of Erevan. It gave the opportunity to the Turks to re-arm themselves, and it was in these very provinces that the Turkish nationalist movement started to grow. The armistice not only failed to prepare the basic ground for the implementation of the Treaty of Sèvres, but it even made possible its defiance. The recommendations of the Foreign Office Staff, from Robert Cecil, Eyre Crowe, Headlam-Morley, Ormsby-Gore, Mark Sykes to Toynbee,[51] to provide for protection over the Armenian provinces, were disregarded. The improvisation by Lloyd George that once the Allies were in Constantinople they could do what they liked as regards Armenia, remained merely a statement; and Balfour's assumption that during the period of the armistice 'surely' the Turks would not do something foolish,[52] proved to be a philosophic speculation. In February 1920, even before the peace, the Kemalists massacred thousands of Armenians in Cilicia;[53] and in October 1920 they trampled on the Treaty of Sèvres by invading the Republic of Erevan.

Sir Mark Sykes, who himself had a hand in drafting the clauses relating to Armenia, described the armistice as 'ridiculous'. On his last active day before his death, he blamed Lloyd George, 'the little man' who had suddenly gone off at 'half-cock', and wired the admiral to negotiate immediately in such a way as to be first into Constantinople. The Turks had knocked out every term that he had personally inserted, including the occupation by the Allies of the Fortress of Zeitun.[54] In Parliament also the terms of the armistice were strongly criticised. Aneurin Williams thought it would have been wiser to have occupied certain 'strategic points' in the eastern provinces until a lasting settlement was reached. Joseph Bliss shared these views. Lord Bryce, likewise, expressed his concern about the lack of security in these provinces. The Turkish troops, just demobilised, would rob and murder, especially during the prevailing very great scarcity of food. The refugees would not be able to return to their homes. The thousands of young

50. Harold Nicolson, *Curzon: The Last Phase 1919-1925* (London, 1934), pp. 116-17.
51. See above, pp. 124-5.
52. See above, p. 129.
53. *Documents on British Foreign Policy 1919-1939* (hereafter DBFP) (London, 1947-), vol. VII, p. 298. (All volumes referred to in this book are in the first series.)
54. Diary of E. Sandars, 10 Feb. 1919, quot. in Shane Leslie, *Mark Sykes: His Life and Letters* (London, 1923), p. 291; R. Adelson, *Mark Sykes: Portrait of an Amateur* (London, 1975), p. 294.

women, seized and consigned to the 'most odious kind of slavery' in the Turkish harems and the large number of boys carried away to be brought up as Moslems, could not be released except under the authority and by the action of European officers. Lastly, the American Relief Committee, who were preparing to send out ample funds for the refugees, would not traverse the country unless they could have protection. Lord Bryce considered the armistice, whose provisions were made with 'little consideration and no foresight', as a 'capital error'.[55]

The British were careful, however, to protect their own interests. Under the threat of the use of force the War Cabinet compelled — in early November — the surrender of Alexandretta on the Mediterranean and of Mosul in Mesopotamia even after the Armistice of Mudros was signed.[56] Moreover, writing to Calthorpe, now British High Commissioner in Constantinople, Balfour asserted — prior to any Peace Conference:

> . . . it is a fixed part of our policy that the territory at present occupied by us in Mesopotamia, Syria and Arabia should not revert in the future to Ottoman sovereignty or administration . . .[57]

Thus, where British interests were involved, the Cabinet took decisions independent of the armistice or the Peace Conference. As regards the general question of Armenia, Balfour emphasised that the future of that country could only be decided at the Peace Congress. He had himself little doubt that the Congress would, at the very least, decide upon its 'complete administrative severance' from the Ottoman Empire. Balfour in no uncertain terms warned Calthorpe that

> . . . public opinion in this country and the United States of America would not for one moment forgive any outbreak in Armenia which might lead to further massacres and to belated intervention on our part . . .

and advised that it might well be desirable that 'strategic points in Armenia should be occupied without delay' as a precautionary measure.[58]

This was not done. During the interim period before the peace settlement, the strategic points in Armenia were never properly and effectively occupied.

The Turks very successfully exploited the loopholes in the armistice, ensuring that they were not demobilised or disarmed. If the politicians had

55. *Hansard,* 5th Ser. 1918, vol. 110, cols. 3245-6, 3249; ibid., XXXII (Lords), 35-41; ibid., 1919, XXXIII (Lords), 255-8; ibid., 1920, vol. 39 (Lords), col. 395; Bryce, 'The Revision of the Turkish Treaty: Armenia', *Contemporary Review,* vol. 119 (May 1921), p. 578.

56. CAB 23/8, War Cab. 499, mins. 3 and 5, 7 Nov. 1918.

57. WO 106/1571, no. 28, Balfour to Calthorpe, 9 Nov. 1918.

58. Ibid.

failed to draw up a precise document, the military authorities, it seems, failed equally dismally to implement its terms. Tragic and sometimes farcical situations of utter failure were confessed to and tolerated, without arousing, strangely, an acute sense of responsibility. In March 1920, the Military and Naval Representatives of the Allied powers reported that, as the Armenian provinces in Turkey were occupied by four Turkish infantry divisions with 'large stocks of military materials', the Erevan republic was not in a position to establish her sovereignty there. By describing such a situation the military authorities themselves were surely, if unconsciously, passing judgement on their own efficiency, skills and performance. Sir Henry Wilson, the CIGS, confessed that the British had 'never', even directly after the armistice, 'attempted' to go into the backward parts of Turkey. From depots which were under the strict control of the British and French, Turkish officers of position managed to take out arms, ammunition and other military equipment, a Turkish contemporary recorded.[59] During one raid on Gallipoli, presumably organised by the Nationalists, 8,500 rifles, 33 machine guns and 500,000 rounds of ammunition were carried off. A military intelligence report stated in October 1919 that although the Turkish army might be considered as disarmed, some hundreds of machine guns and a number of field guns were known to be at Trebizond and Erzerum. The civil population could set up a troublesome warfare owing to the 'large quantities of rifles and S.A.A.' (small arms ammunition), known to be in their possession.[60]

Lieutenant-Colonel A. Rawlinson, specially sent to Anatolia to supervise the demobilisation, was defiantly informed by Kiazim Pasha in Erzerum that the munitions in Turkish possession could not be permitted 'to cross the frontier'. It was a situation whereby the General of a defeated country was giving orders to the representative of the mightiest victorious power. Rawlinson thereupon pointed out that such action must automatically bring the armistice to an end. When he asked for instructions, the British Commander-in-Chief, Constantinople, merely ordered him to get all his men out of the country at once. Later, in March 1920, Rawlinson and his men were detained and imprisoned by the Kemalists in Erzerum as a retaliation for the occupation by the Allies of Constantinople. The British flag was hauled down at their headquarters. They were all but starved to death and were 'hardly able to crawl'. No wonder the heading of a chapter in Rawlinson's book reads: 'The Turkish Armistice a Fiasco — Foundation of the Nationalist Party'.[61]

It was indeed the failure of the armistice that would make the Kemalist

59. CAB 24/103, C.P. 1035, Annex II, section 1, no. 6, enc. in letter of Foch to Lloyd George, 30 Mar. 1920. Callwell, *Wilson*, II, p. 229, entry for 3 Mar. 1920. Halidé Edib, *The Turkish Ordeal* (London, 1928), p. 21n.

60. WO 106/330, Gen. Staff no. 189, Feb. 1920. WO 106/349, Summary of Intell., 22nd Series no. 37, 27 Oct. 1919.

61. A. Rawlinson, *Adventures in the Near East 1918-1922* (London, 1923), pp. 225-6, 231, 288, 290, 299.

attack on the Republic of Erevan possible in the autumn of 1920. Oliver Baldwin, the Prime Minister's son, who served in the Armenian army at Erevan in late 1920 and early 1921, maintained that the 1920 Turkish-Armenian war was the continuation of the 1914 war, broken out afresh as a result of Britain's weakness in her dealings with Turkey. Yet, at the time of the armistice, the Turks were, according to 'universal testimony', as docile as lambs, L.P. Chambers, the Harvard-educated son of a Canadian missionary, who had lived almost all his life in Turkey, wrote from Constantinople. Bryce could not blame enough the 'initial blunder' of a weak and improvident armistice, and the 'want of foresight and of energy' in neglecting to see it enforced at a time when the Turks 'lay at the mercy of the Allies'.[62]

Perhaps there was some mishandling of certain aspects of diplomacy by Lloyd George; and probably the military authorities chose to be negligent as regards Turkey. But whatever the case, it seems that it was the Foreign Office who lacked a firm grip over policy, decision and execution.

Despite the change of government in Constantinople just before the armistice, the Committee of Union and Progress still controlled the important offices of the new administration[63] and was far from inactive. With the connivance of the Turkish government, they stimulated Kurdish activity to establish Kurdish majorities in certain districts of the 'six *vilayets*', especially Van, and to prevent the return of Armenian refugees from the Caucasus and Persia. These activities had been reported in the Armenian Delegation memorandum of 15 May 1919. When questioned, the General Officer Commanding Mesopotamia commented that the memorandum was 'probably based on facts'; and that 'further measures to decrease [the] number of Armenians are certainly threatened'. 'Tchete' bands (irregulars) were being reorganised in Asia Minor.[64]

Cilicia was gradually occupied by the British after the armistice; nevertheless, the Turks endeavoured to keep up their activities. After a personal visit, Sir Mark Sykes reported that 'encouraged by the [local] authorities', agitators were stirring up the Turkish population by spreading fear of Arab and Armenian massacre. The Moslems in Aintab had stated that 4,000 to 5,000 rifles had been distributed during the past weeks. In Adana, demobilisation was being circumvented by increasing the gendarmerie beyond all necessary requirements or by issuing surplus rifles to villagers nominally for self-defence against imaginary enemies.[65]

Not only were the Turkish authorities able to arm the local population and

62. Oliver Baldwin, *Six Prisons and Two Revolutions* (London, 1924), p. 9. Bryce Papers, UB 67, Chambers to Bryce, 6 Apr. 1921, 14 Oct. 1919. Bryce, 'The Revision of the Turkish Treaty: Armenia', pp. 578-80.

63. CAB 23/8, War Cab. 492, min. 9, 29 Oct. 1918.

64. FO 371/3659/89585/86314, Baghdad, 5 June 1919. FO 371/3411/184497, Lord Acton to FO, 5 Nov. 1918.

65. FO 371/3400/211505/213559, Sykes nos. 50 and 54 in Gen. Clayton, 23, 29 Dec. 1918; see also ibid, no. 209471, in Clayton, 19 Dec. 1918.

thus prevent the return of Turkish Armenians to their homes in the eastern *vilayets*, but they also systematically and effectively tried to hamper, across the border, the Erevan republic. They used every pretext and the utmost cunning for delaying the withdrawal of their troops from the pre-war Russo-Turkish frontier; and apparently they succeeded in keeping some of their forces as native Tatar troops. The DMI was himself aware of the new Grand Vizier's order to the General Officer Commanding the Islam Army on 31 October that the Turkish troops holding the Caucasus and such of the Caucasus Islam Army *'as does not wish to remain'* should complete the evacuation of these districts.[66] (The Islam Army was composed of Turkish volunteers and Tatars and was organised in the spring of 1918 by Nuri, Enver's brother, with the purpose of occupying Baku.') Under the guise of indigenous troops, the Turks intended to retain some of their forces in the Caucasus. The DMI had received 'very reliable' information to the effect that a division, presumably the 5th Caucasian Division of the Turkish army, had been distributed among Azerbaijani formations in accordance with orders previously received from the Turkish Supreme Command, and that this division no longer really existed as such. On 1 November 1918, Naim Javad Bey, the Chief Political Officer of the Caucasus Islam Army, had declared that the Porte would spare no pains to organise a strong friendly Azerbaijani army. All ranks of the Turkish army in Azerbaijan would be considered as in the service of the Azerbaijan republic where they would stay as long as their help was required.[67]

It seems, then, that the Turks were determined to hold their own not only in Anatolia but indirectly also in the Caucasus. To this end they used every means in their power — direct and indirect. Even when forced to withdraw from the Caucasus, they apparently took meticulous care that they should leave behind a desolate country, and make the recuperation of the Armenians still surviving in the Caucasus impossible. Thus, on 4 and 5 December 1918, an American officer had seen Turkish regulars at Alexandropol, in the Erevan republic, removing large quantities of household goods, railway engines and trucks, building material, cotton and foodstuffs which Turkish officers had told him were going into Turkey. These officers had stated that they would be dealing a final blow to the Armenians and had taken from this district 7,000,000 *poods* of wheat and 200,000,000 *poods* of cotton. At every station there were large quantities of wheat being ruined by rain but the people were forbidden to touch it under penalty of death.[68]

If the armistice with Turkey was concluded hastily under war conditions, surely the peace settlement would be better deliberated. Armenians all over

66. FO 371/3449/183785, 4 Nov. 1918.
67. FO 371/3416/194789, DMI to FO, 25 Nov. 1918. WO 106/1571, *Execution of the Armistice with Turkey*, p. 11. Report of General Marshall, 13 Nov. 1918.
68. FO 371/3657/10607, GOC in C. Mesop. to WO, 21 Dec. 1918.

the world were hopeful. In Winston Churchill's distinctive words:

> Their persecutors and tyrants had been laid low by war or revolution. The greatest nations in the hour of their victory were their friends, and would see them righted.

Boghos Nubar, the President of the Armenian National Delegation in Paris, who had 'assiduously' worked in the cause of Armenia, warmly congratulated Great Britain — Champion of 'justice': the day was 11 November 1918,

> . . . one of the most memorable days in history which will determine the destiny of nations by bringing them liberty and justice . . .

In reply, Balfour expressed his deep sympathy for the terrible sufferings 'so bravely' endured by the Armenian people, and his 'firm confidence' in their future.[69] A few days later, at a meeting in the House of Lords to celebrate the victory, Lord Curzon stated:

> Never did our voice count for more in the councils of nations; or in determining the future destinies of mankind.

The mightiest country in the world and the other victorious powers were sympathetic towards Armenia; and the Turkish government 'if not cowed, was subservient'.[70]

That the Armenian territories should somehow be liberated from Turkish rule was the genuine wish of the British leaders without exception, according to all available evidence. The Ottoman government had shown itself unable and unwilling to fulfil the duties of a government in the 'six *vilayets*' and Cilicia, read the statement of British policy prepared by the British Delegation to the Peace Conference.[71] In November 1918, Balfour told the House of Commons:

> . . . we have always regarded the freeing of the Armenians from Turkish misrule as an important part of our Middle Eastern policy, and that we confidently look forward to its accomplishment.

In answer to the warm statements made by Aneurin Williams, Joseph Bliss, Sir George Greenwood, Major Robert Peel, Sir John Spear, Hugh Law and

---

69. Winston S. Churchill, *The World Crisis — The Aftermath* (London, 1929), p. 407. FO 371/3404/131379, Balfour to Boghos Nubar, 2 Aug. 1918. FO 371/3416/187270, Boghos Nubar to Balfour, 11 Nov. 1918; Balfour to Boghos Nubar, draft, 14 Nov. 1918.

70. Nicolson, *Curzon*, p. 2 (18 Nov. 1918). Curzon, quot. in Churchill, *The Aftermath*, p. 361.

71. FO 608/83/7442, Paris, 18 Feb. 1919.

Arthur Ponsonby in the House on 18 November 1918, Lord Robert Cecil expressed 'on behalf of the Government' the profound agreement with which he had heard the expression of sympathy with the Armenian people, and added:

> As far as I am concerned — and I believe in this matter I am speaking for the Government — I should be deeply disappointed if any shred or shadow of Turkish government were left in Armenia.[72]

Even the traditionally pro-Turkish War Office[73] and the pro-Moslem India Office clearly envisaged just after the war the liberation of the Armenian territories. Colonel F.R. Maunsell of the War Office recommended the creation of both a separate state of Armenia and a separate state of Kurdistan, Armenia occupying the country round Mount Ararat and Lake Van and including Erzerum and the Black Sea ports of Trebizond and Kerasund. The belt of country to the south should form Kurdistan. Edwin Montagu, the Secretary of State for India, suggested 'a large Armenia'. He hoped that the Armenian republic to which the Turkish Delegation assented, would be delimited, not by the Turks but by the Allies.[74] Most importantly, the Foreign Office recommended, as will be seen, a Great Armenia including Cilicia and the 'six *vilayets*' as well as Caucasian Armenia.

On the other hand, it seems those in power were convinced that the Armenians, like the other Caucasian peoples, would not be able to 'stand alone at first'.[75] In 1915 and 1918, Boghos Nubar himself, and a memorandum by his National Delegation, had asked for an Armenia under the protection of the Allied powers, 'one of them acting as mandatory . . . for the organisation and administration of the New State for a term of years'. Avetis Aharonian, the President of the Republic of Armenia's Delegation in Paris, likewise implored for a mandatory and offered to put the Armenian army under Allied supervision. Later, both he and Boghos Nubar pleaded that Armenia should be placed under the protection of the League of Nations.[76] The 'Statement of British Policy . . .', prepared by the British Delegation in Paris, also recommended that the Peace Conference should

72. *Hansard*, 5th Ser. 1918, vol. 110, cols. 2088, 3239-69, 3264, 3268.
73. Churchill, *The Aftermath*, p. 367.
74. WO 106/64, Maunsell, 'Kurdistan', 1 Dec. 1918. CAB 27/24, War Cab. Eastern Commit. 40.2 Dec. 1918 (hereafter War Cab. E.C.). Trinity Coll., Cambridge, Montagu Papers AS-IV-6, 846 (4), note by S.S. for India, 25 June 1919.
75. CAB 27/24 War Cab. E.C., 42, R. Cecil, 9 Dec. 1918.
76. FO 371/2488/51009/96760, 'Note sur la Question Armenienne' in Boghos Nubar to Sir A. Nicolson, 15 July 1915; FO 371/3404/183916, Boghos Nubar to Balfour, 4 Nov. 1918; Fisher Papers Box 11, Arm. Nat. Deleg. memo on Arm. question (Paris, June 1918), p. 12. Rep. of Arm. Archives, File 337/7, Aharonian to Williams (no. 4330), copy, 27 Aug. 1921; ibid., File 333/3, Aharonian to Lloyd George (no. 462), copy, 7 Aug. 1919; ibid., File 334/4, Nubar and Aharonian to Presid., Peace Conf., copy, 20 Mar. 1920.

give a mandate over Armenia to one of its members. But not even one British statesman ever contemplated a British protectorate, although it was believed that were the Armenian population, both at home and in the diaspora polled, in all probability they would opt for Britain — as Lord Curzon put it. The British had no tangible interests of their own in the Armenian territories. Even staunch Armenophiles did not think of the possibility of such an arrangement.[77]

A protectorate over Armenia might mean involvement in the Caucasus. Long before the armistice with Turkey, Toynbee had strongly argued that for the sake of future relations with Russia, it was 'most undesirable' for Britain to assume such a responsibility. She should avoid it. Moreover, he added, with extended interests in the Arab region and Persia, Britain could not afford further dispersal of strength. Sir Eyre Crowe also believed that it would be dangerous from the point of view of future relations with Russia, if Britain accepted the mandate. Curzon, in his turn, emphatically opposed such an obligation for financial reasons. Britain already had far too much upon her own hands to be able to undertake 'so colossal' a responsibility. British interests would best be served were the task of a mandatory power entrusted to some other 'friendly' Great power, Crowe maintained.[78]

But what would happen if the other friendly Great powers also put forward, like Britain, similar objections to assuming responsibility for Armenia? How would British statesmen reconcile their hope of seeing Armenia liberated with their unwillingness to give her practical and effective help? Without a policy, the British government could not solve this dilemma. It resorted to various expedients, all of which in the end failed.

Among the various government departments, the Foreign Office, anxious to follow the principle of self-determination and national governments, and sensitive to humanitarian public opinion, was the most sympathetic towards Armenia. In a memorandum[79] by its Political Intelligence Department, it claimed, as referred to above, that Britain was 'bound, perhaps juridically and certainly morally' by article 61 of the Berlin Treaty, which was substituted, at Britain's instance, for article 16 of the superseded Treaty of San Stefano. Turkey had omitted to carry out her pledge and the result had been the massacres of 1895-7, 1909 and of 1915. It was 'clearly incumbent' upon Britain to put an end to these wrongs to humanity and violations of a treaty to which she was a party, now that it lay within her power to do so. It would be expedient, the Foreign Office memorandum stated, to extend the areas

77. FO 608/83/7442, Br. Deleg. Paris, 'Statement of Br. Policy . . .', 18 Feb. 1919. CAB 27/24, War Cab. E.C. 40, Curzon, 2 Dec. 1918. H.A.L. Fisher, *James Bryce* (London, 1927), II, p. 211, quot. Bryce to Storey, 20 Feb. 1919.

78. FO 371/3411/166030, Toynbee, *Desiderata . . .*, 2 Oct. 1918. CAB 27/36, E.C. 2359, Eyre Crowe, *Memorandum on a Possible Territorial Policy in the Caucasus Regions*, 7 Nov. 1918. CAB 27/24, War Cab. E.C. 40, 2 Dec. 1918.

79. Circulated to the Eastern Committee of the War Cabinet 'provisionally only' since Balfour had not had time to give his 'full consideration'. See above, p. 11.

of Armenia 'as widely as possible'. Such a settlement would be an effective barrier against Pan-Turanianism, and also against the aggression of foreign powers in the direction of the Arab countries. Since the population was mixed, the principle of equal rights for all nationalities should be applied. On the other hand, in settling the proportional claims of these various elements to a voice in the government of the country, it should be laid down in Armenia that 'the dead and the exiles should be taken into account' and Armenian immigrants from other parts of the world should be given facilities for settling down in their 'ancestral homes'. If France were chosen as the mandatory, this should make her more ready to forego her claims in Syria, in case these claims were not confirmed by the Syrians themselves. Britain was already committed to France's establishment of a direct or indirect administration in the south-western half of Armenia, the memorandum maintained.[80] If it was urged that a US mandate would suit Britain better, Sir Eyre Crowe pointed out that there was, unfortunately, little hope that the Americans would be ready to accept it. He believed the best hope for a 'practical solution' lay in a French mandate for Armenia and the South Caucasian territories. It would probably be welcomed by the Armenians, and secondly, it would square with the Anglo-French agreement of 1916. It might even be possible, by including in the mandate the four Caucasian states, to induce France to make concessions as regards her claims in Syria, Mesopotamia and Palestine.[81]

Armenia was specificially discussed, among other subjects, by the Eastern Committee of the War Cabinet, in a number of meetings in December 1918. The object was to help shape the policy to be followed by the British Delegation at the Peace Conference. In a long, lecture-like introduction to the subject, Lord Curzon, the Chairman of the Committee, referred to Britain's special interest in Armenia since the Treaty of Berlin. Britain wanted to have an independent Armenia, he added, which at some time in the future should be a self-governing community. His reasons were, in the first place,

> . . . to provide a national home for the scattered peoples of the Armenian race. As long as they are diffused in helpless and hopeless minorities, . . . any chance of settled life or autonomous existence cannot be said to exist. Secondly, we want to set up an Armenian State as a palisade . . . against the Pan-Turanian ambitions of the Turks, which may overflow the Caucasian regions and carry great peril to the countries of the Middle East and East. Thirdly, we want to constitute something like an effective barrier against the aggression — . . . in the future — of

80. CAB 27/37, E.C. 2525, memo. Respecting the Settlement of Turkey and the Arabian Peninsula, FO, 21 Nov. 1918.
81. CAB 27/36, E.C. 2359, Crowe, memo., 7 Nov. 1918.

any foreign Powers, impelled by ambition or by other motives to press forward in that direction.

But Curzon opposed the Foreign Office view of a large Armenia where the Armenians would be in a decided minority. Presenting the Foreign Office view to the Eastern Committee, Lord Robert Cecil, the Assistant Foreign Secretary, advocated an Armenia which should include the 'six *vilayets*' and Cilicia. In the 'six *vilayets*' before the war, the population was 35 per cent Armenian, 25 per cent Turk, 20 per cent Kurd and 20 per cent minorities — including other Christians and 'Pagan'.[82] These figures showed, what he supposed was true, that before the war, throughout the 'six *vilayets*', the Armenians were singly 'the most numerous body'. He was inclined to favour a large Armenia:

> Historically, there is a good deal to be said for it. Then, what else are you going to do if you do not do that? Are you going to give back a portion of Armenia to the Turks? That would be a most objectionable thing to do, surely, as a result of their massacres; and what portion of it, because the Armenians are scattered all over it.

If there were not a large Armenian state, the Turks would have a direct connection between Anatolia and the Turkish population in the Caucasus, which was exactly what the British wished to avoid, so far as Pan-Turanianism was concerned. Robert Cecil agreed with Curzon that it would be very difficult to have one mandatory for Armenia and another for the Caucasus Republics. He admitted that the Americans did have a sentimental interest in Armenia, but he was convinced that they would never go to the Caucasus. They would 'never be there permanently, they cannot'. So it was proposed to recommend the creation of Armenia 'under the aegis of the French'. Montagu, the Secretary of State for India, agreed. It was 'difficult' to get the Americans to undertake the Armenian mandate. On the other hand the French, with their railway enterprises in eastern Anatolia, were the natural power to undertake it. Robert Cecil remarked that this was the way his own mind moved.[83]

The Foreign Office was of the view, therefore, that a French mandate over Armenia and the Caucasus would provide the best practical solution.

On 5 December 1918, however, the General Staff of the War Office issued a paper concerning the government's view that it might be necessary to grant a mandate to a Great power to ensure the stability of Transcaucasia and that this power 'would probably be France'. It specifically referred to Sir Eyre

82. It is not clear to whom Lord Robert refers. For different population statistics in the 'six *Vilayets*' see FO 371/1773/16927; FO 371/2137/56940; FO 371/2116/4947. See also above, pp. 3, 5.

83. CAB 27/24, War Cab. E.C. 40, pp. 4-6, 14, 17, 22, 2 Dec. 1918. ibid., 38, min. 5, 21 Nov. 1918. Ibid., 40, p. 19, 2 Dec. 1918.

Crowe's memorandum.[84] The paper, apparently prepared by Sir Henry Wilson,[85] the CIGS, explained that from the military point of view it would be 'most undesirable' for the approaches to India from South Russia, the Black Sea and Turkey-in-Asia, which converged at Baku, to be placed at the disposal of an ambitious military power, which was Britain's 'historic world rival'. The situation of France in virtual possession of the six Armenian *vilayets* would bring her into close contact with the 'recruiting fields' of Anatolia which would provide valuable military material for the French instructors. Then Britain would be compelled on her part to maintain abnormally large garrisons in Egypt and Mesopotamia for all time. A 'still greater danger' would be a potential alliance between a reconstructed Russia and France, the General Staff paper added.

Having conjured up a frightening picture, the General Staff were emphatic: British policy 'should be directed' to maintaining a self-contained block between the French sphere of influence and the Caspian. It appeared to the General Staff that no other power 'except herself can be permitted by Great Britain' to function in the Caucasus. From the military point of view, therefore, the first essential in Trans-Caucasia was that the British position in Georgia and in Russian Armenia should be firmly established. This made it necessary, the General Staff went on, that Russian Armenia should be kept separate from Turkish Armenia. In other words, the French influence should cease on the pre-war Russo-Turkish frontier. The maintenance of the 'separate' entities of Armenia 'should form the keynote' of Britain's Caucasian policy according to the General Staff paper.[86]

The generals were emphatic and unanimous: Britain should go to the Caucasus. Lieutenant-General Sir G.M.W. Macdonogh, the Adjutant-General to the Forces, agreed. Major-General W. Thwaites, the DMI, also indicated that Britain 'ought' to be on the important line of communications in the Caucasus: 'we ought to be sitting there ourselves, and nobody else'.[87]

Curzon found Sir Henry Wilson's paper 'very powerful and valuable'. 'I almost shudder' at the possibility of putting France in such a position, he told his colleagues referring to the Caucasus. She might become a political and military danger were she to exercise control from the eastern corner of the Levant right up to the Caucasus.[88]

The Eastern Committee finally agreed as regards the Caucasus that if, at the Peace Conference, it was decided that the services of a Great power were required for a period to protect international interests,

. . .the selection of America would be preferable to that of France, but is

84. See p. 144.
85. CAB 27/24, War. Cab. E.C. 42, p. 5, 9 Dec. 1918.
86. CAB 27/36, E.C. 2243, Future Settlement of Trans-Caucasia, Gen. Staff, 5 Dec. 1918. Also in CAB 27/38 E.C. 2632.
87. CAB 27/24, War Cab. E.C. 41, p. 5, 5 Dec. 1918. Ibid., 40, p. 24, 2 Dec. 1918.
88. Ibid., p. 22, 2 Dec. 1918; ibid., 42, p. 5, 9 Dec. 1918.

not in itself desirable. The selection of France would on broad grounds of policy and strategy be undesirable. Only in the last resort, and reluctantly if pressed to do so, might Great Britain provisionally accept the task.[89]

This decision, which implied that the presence of France in the Caucasus should definitely not be encouraged, meant a change in the policy previously advocated by the Foreign Office: by Lord Robert Cecil and especially Sir Eyre Crowe.[90] They had argued that a French mandate over Armenia and the Caucasus would be the best practical solution, since it was virtually certain that Britian would not accept a mandate over Armenia. Yet there was little hope of the United States accepting it either. Such an arrangement on the other hand would square with the Sykes-Picot Agreement. In addition, in return for the Caucasian states, France might be induced to make concessions in Syria and Mesopotamia. However, the General Staff unyieldingly insisted on an exclusively British presence in the Caucasus. When Sir Henry Wilson was asked about his choice of alternatives, of either accepting the Sykes-Picot Agreement and letting France remain in the south and arranging for Britain to go to the Caucasus, or clearing France out of the south and letting her go to the north, his answer was simply evasive:

GENERAL WILSON: Cannot we bribe France in some other way?

LORD ROBERT CECIL: How?

GENERAL WILSON: I do not know; that is not my part of the business . . . That is a Foreign Office affair.[91]

So, according to the military view, France should have neither the Caucasus, nor Mesopotamia, Palestine, nor even Syria. Such an inflexible and unstatesmanlike attitude towards France, superseding the judicious views of the Foreign Office — of give and take — could hardly promote a feasible arrangement about Armenia. In a few months' time however, the General Staff would change their own views and would press for the evacuation of British troops from the Caucasus. All that would be left unchanged would be their mode of relentlessly arguing in favour of their adopted views.

    C.R.M.F. Cruttwell has rightly observed that during the war the dividing line between politics and strategy was often obliterated for the benefit of the soldiers. Their successes were exaggerated by the civilian leaders themselves who used every means of publicity on behalf of the military in order to sustain public confidence. Universal service also contributed to exalt the prestige of the military leaders,[92] with the result that they came out of the

89. Ibid., 43, 16 Dec. 1918.
90. See pp. 144-5 above.
91. CAB 27/24, E.C. 42, p. 18, 9 Dec. 1918.
92. C.R.M.F. Cruttwell, *A History of the Great War 1914-1918*, 2nd edn (Oxford, 1936), p. 625.

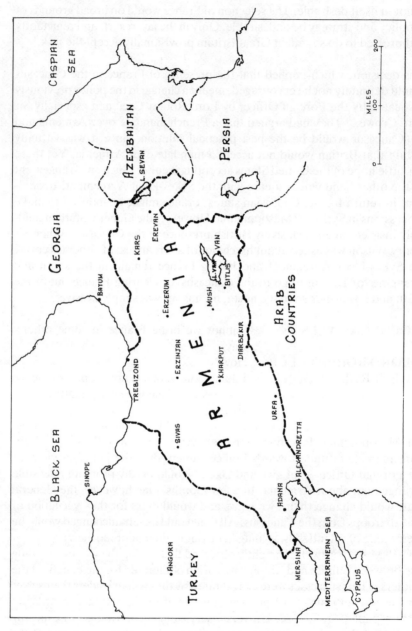

Map 6: The Boundaries of Armenia as Proposed by the British Delegation, 1919

war with heightened influence and often insisted on, and succeeded in, imposing their views on the politicians.

The remarkable 'Statement of British Policy' as regards Armenia, prepared by the British Delegation for submission to the Peace Conference clearly favoured a large state, which should include the 'six *vilayets*' and Cilicia. It argued that:

> His Majesty's Government consider that the Ottoman Government has shown itself unable and unwilling to fulfil the duties of a government in the territories (roughly corresponding to the district of Cilicia and the 'Six Vilayets' of the Treaty of San Stefano) . . . , which are inhabited by a mixed population of Turks, Kurds, Armenians, Greeks and other elements, and that these territories ought to be entirely detached from Turkey and formed into a separate State.

The southern boundary of this state should follow approximately a line from the Mediterranean coast at Alexandretta to the Euphrates by Birejik. The northern boundary should start from the Black Sea 'between Trebizond and Surmene'.

> For the rest, it would depend on whether the Trans-Caucasian Armenians opted to join the new State or to form an independent Republic. In the former alternative (which is believed to be the more probable) the northern frontier would follow the boundary between Trans-Caucasian Armenia on the one hand and Georgia and Azerbaijan on the other, within limits which would include Olti, Kars, Alexandropol, Erivan and Julfa, and would touch the Persian frontier near Ordubad.

> Whether or not Trans-Caucasian Armenia opts for inclusion, the new State formed out of the north-eastern territories of the former Ottoman Empire should be called Armenia. That has been its historical name in the past; the Armenians are at present the most progressive and prolific element in the population; there will be an immigration of Armenians from abroad and they are likely to play the leading part in the future.

On the other hand, the statement went on, the country could not be handed over to the Armenian element and organised as an Armenian national state, as the Armenians would be found to form 'a considerably smaller fraction' of the total population. The Conference would, therefore, have to intervene to keep the peace between the nationalities and to reconstruct the country materially after the depopulation and devastation of the war. The British government recommended that the Conference should give a mandate for this purpose to one of its members. The population was too much divided to opt for assistance with a united voice, and the Armenians, who were the only articulate element, were believed to be content that the Conference should select the power which was 'to afford it'.[93]

So, it was official British 'policy' to see Cilicia and the 'six *vilayets*' 'entirely detached' from Turkey and formed into an 'independent' republic. Had this 'statement of British policy' been realised Armenians might have thought that justice had at last come their way.

This 'policy' however, was actually a statement of sympathy only, perhaps designed to satisfy pro-Armenian public opinion, and did not envisage any responsibility. British interests in Armenia were merely sentimental and humanitarian. This was made absolutely clear by the resolution adopted by the Eastern Committee of the War Cabinet in December 1918:

> If an independent Armenian State be constituted . . . and if a Great Power be called upon either by the League of Nations, or by the people themselves, to act as protector to the new State, Great Britain should refrain from advancing any claims, and should support the case either of America or France preferably, in the interests of a revision of the Sykes-Picot agreement of 1916, of France.[94]

Thus, Britain had no positive policy at all as regards Armenia. She would refrain from assuming responsibility. She would like to see a large Armenia under the protection of the United States — for which there was little hope — or under the protection of France. If the latter, however, she should not be permitted to go to the Caucasus, and should also be cleared out of the rich Ottoman lands in the south, if possible.

Britain, therefore, found herself in the dilemma between her general desire for the liberation of Armenia on the one hand and her unwillingness to assume any practical responsibility or to give any effective help for the realisation of her pledges, on the other. In the end, the British government neither provided protection for Armenia nor could it induce the United States or France to assume a mandate. It could not arrange a collective protection either. Britain failed completely to solve the dilemma.

But while Britain was unwilling to go to the new State of Armenia, she was quite prepared, at least on a temporary basis, to protect 'international interests' in the Caucasus, where she considered the presence of the United States preferable to that of France but not in itself desirable, and that of France undesirable.[95]

On 17 November 1918, a British force from north Persia accompanied by a

93. FO 608/83/7442, 'Statement of British Policy in the Middle East for Submission to the Peace Conference', prep. by Br. Delegation, Paris, 18 Feb. 1919.
94. CAB 27/24 War Cab. E.C. 43, 16 Dec. 1918.
95. Ibid..

pro-Entente force of Russian troops, occupied Baku, acting on behalf of the Allies. They would ensure the execution of the armistice terms, as both the Armistice of Mudros and the German armistice provided for the evacuation of Trans-Caucasian territory by Turkish and German troops respectively.[96]

The decision to exercise some measure of military and political control over the Caucasus was taken by the Eastern Committee of the War Cabinet in December 1918, when the question was discussed during a number of meetings. The reasons given were the security of India, the fear that the possession of this region by a hostile force might turn the flank of the British position in Asia, and the necessity of protecting Persia and the countries lying to the east of it from 'anarchy, disorder, or Bolshevism'. Other reasons stressed the commercial and material importance of the region: Batum would become the emporium for the central part of Asia; it was impossible to allow the 'great oil resources' of Baku to fall into the hands of a tiny mountain republic like Daghestan, or into the hands of a 'very doubtful' element like Turkish Azerbaijan. In addition, British presence in the Caucasus would help to ensure British control of the Caspian Sea, to maintain order in the Caucasus, to 'protect' the Batum-Baku pipeline and railway and to back up General Malleson who was supporting the Trans-caspian government.[97]

The despatch of British troops to the Caucasus was certainly a major post-war decision; yet Balfour claimed that he 'was never consulted about it'.[98] A further example of how the Foreign Office was sometimes superseded, or allowed itself to be superseded.

In the Caucasus, Britain was faced by another dilemma. Her forces were already helping the pro-Entente Russian armies. Would she support their claim to represent an indivisible and pro-Allied Russia into which the Caucasus should be reintegrated? In 1918 the four Republics of Georgia, Azerbaijan, Armenia and Daghestan had come into existence when Russian power had collapsed in the Caucasus. They were now claiming the right of self-determination and clamouring for recognition as independent states. Should Britain recognise them? Sir Eyre Crowe argued that it would appear safe to begin by recognising effective national governments in those areas, in which they had been established, in such a form as not to prejudge the question of their permanent independence or reintegration with Russia. If the anarchy in Russia lasted, their separation from her would probably be permanent. If Russia recovered rapidly, they might rejoin her in some federal relation. It would be prudent, added Eyre Crowe, to follow a course which might be calculated to leave a reconstituted Russia no ground for considering that the Allies had taken advantage of her temporary weakness.

96. FO 371/7729/E8378, W.J. Childs and A.E.R. McDonnell, 'Outline of Events in Transcaucasia from 1917 to 1921', p. 10, 31 May 1922.
97. CAB 27/24, War Cab. E.C. 40, 42, 43, held on 2, 9, 16 Dec. 1918 respectively.
98. Ibid., 42, p. 12, 9 Dec. 1918.

Curzon agreed. But, he maintained, these rising republics were 'furiously anti-Russian and furiously anti-Bolshevik' and they should not be led to suppose that Britian was ignoring their claims to independence.[99] Evidently Curzon was thinking of these Caucasian states as an eastern barrier against Russian expansion, Bolshevik or otherwise. From the General Staff point of view, these Caucasian states, with their national aspirations, might also maintain a self-contained block between Russia and a French sphere on the one hand and between the latter two countries and the British-dominated Caspian on the other. So it was expedient for the British to encourage the spirit of independence among these states. It was especially in the Allied interest, according to a Foreign Office memorandum, to give what support they could to a population of seven or eight million who were 'resolved to bar to the utmost the advance of Bolshevism'.[100]

With all these considerations in mind, therefore, the Eastern Committee of the War Cabinet formulated their view:

> We desire to see strong independent States — offshoots of the former Russian Empire — in the Caucasus . . .

> Whether the independent States of the Caucasus combine hereafter in a Federation, or prefer to remain separate is a matter for their own determination.

> Similarly, their relations to the present or future Government or Governments of Russia is a matter that in the main concerns themselves.[101]

But the Allies also backed up by 'lavish' and 'almost limitless' supplies of arms the anti-Bolshevik movement in Cis-Caucasia, north of the Caucasus Mountains. They saw in this movement, led by General Denikin, 'the chief hope' for the overthrow of Bolshevism by Russian effort. In early 1919, however, after his victories over the Bolsheviks, Denikin directed his troops to Baku, as he had always strongly urged that its possession was of vital importance to Russia, and he came to the borders of both Georgia and Azerbaijan.[102]

Thus Britain found herself protector of two camps which were both hostile to Bolshevism, but more hostile to each other. There seemed little doubt that Denikin intended 'to crush Georgia', Curzon believed. To Churchill, the Secretary of State for War, there also seemed 'no doubt' that Russia would recover and would reconquer the Caucasian republics. He pressed for

99. CAB 27/36, E.C. 2359, memo. 7 Nov. 1918; CAB 27/24, War Cab. E.C. 40, 2 Dec. 1918.
100. CAB 27/38, E.C. 2632, Gen. Staff, 5 Dec. 1918. FO 371/7729/E8378, Childs and McDonnell, 'Outline of Events in Transcaucasia', p. 13, 31 May 1922.
101. CAB 27/24, War Cab. E.C. 43, 16 Dec. 1918.
102. FO 371/7729/E8378, Childs and McDonnell, 'Outline of Events in Transcaucasia', pp. 13-16, 31 May 1922.

definite support for Denikin in his struggle against the Bolsheviks and was indifferent to the independence of the Caucasus. Yet British statesmen had said from the beginning of the war that their intentions were to support ideals of nationality and self-determination in relation to the little nations, as Professor J.Y. Simpson of the Political Intelligence Department of the Foreign Office reminded the Inter-Departmental Conference on the Middle East. He urged that the British should keep Denikin out of the Caucasus till the Peace Conference had settled the question. He asked:

> Are we preserving order in the Caucasus in the ultimate interest of a united, undivided Russia, or of these new, self-created States?

This was a dilemma which the British government could not solve. Both the Caucasian peoples and the Russians alike were 'frankly puzzled' by the attitudes of the British and regarded them with complete mistrust.[103]

The Caucasian republics were not recognised as independent states either by Britain or the Allies and so they could not raise the loans they sorely needed. In vain did Avetis Aharonian[104] repeatedly implore that the official recognition of the Armenian republic would be the salvation of the country. The British dilemma was finally solved for them only when the White Russian armies collapsed at the end of 1919. Early in January 1920, Lloyd George heard the 'very disturbing news' that the Bolsheviks, having entirely defeated Denikin's army, were advancing upon the Caspian. Only now did the British government suggest, and the Allied powers agree on, the *de facto* recognition of the Caucasian republics and on the principle of sending them material help — arms and ammunition — 'on the express condition' that they would resist the Bolsheviks.[105] The recognition came too late and the help was too little.

Besides London's apparently contradictory attitudes towards the Caucasus, there also was a lag between policy and decision making at home and actions taken on the spot, which further added to the confusion. Thus, the Eastern Committee discussed the Caucasus only in December 1918, and resolved that they desired to see 'strong independent States' in that part of the world. But the British troops had already been there for a month; and early in November when Major-General W.M. Thomson had entered Baku, he had made a proclamation disregarding the independence of the Caucasus and implied that he had come to one part of Russia proper:

> . . . we are not unmindful of the great services . . . rendered by the

103. Curzon Papers. MSS. Eur. F112/275, Inter-Departmental Conference on Middle East (IDCE) 11 mins., 6 March 1919.

104. Presid. of Deleg. of Repub. of Armenia at Paris.

105. Rep. of Arm. Archives, Files 333/3, 332/2, Aharonian to FO., copies, 14 Nov., 10 May 1919, respectively; DBFP, vol. II, pp. 725, 796-7, 924-5, 10 Jan., 19 Jan. 1920.

Russian peoples in the earlier part of the War. The Allies cannot return to their homes without restoring order in RUSSIA . . .

Unrest still exists in the Caucasus. It is my duty to remove this from the Baku area . . . There is no question of the Allies retaining possession of one foot of RUSSIA.[106]

Again, the British government had been disinclined to give formal recognition to these republics, hoping that the Russian situation might clarify. But the newly-born republics, infected by morbid nationalism, had jumped at each other's throats over territorial disputes, immediately after the withdrawal of the Turkish and German troops. As these issues could not wait for the deliberations of the policy makers in Paris, the generals on the spot had often to take decisive actions of far-reaching political importance. Besides this confusing time lag, contradiction was also created by the opposing sympathies of the British troops involved. According to a Foreign Office memorandum, General Thomson's Mesopotamian division, mainly officered from the Indian army, had the 'traditional' Anglo-Indian suspicion of Russian imperialism and was said to 'adore' Moslems. On the other hand, Major-General G.T. Forestier-Walker's British force, detached from the Salonika army, which had occupied Batum on 23 December and had its headquarters at Tiflis, disliked Moslems and sympathised with every 're-actionary' Russian party — to which the Georgians were opposed. Thus, between these two opposing lines of sympathy, the peoples of the Caucasus could discover 'no definite British policy'.[107]

When forced to intervene between the Caucasian nationalities over territorial disputes, the British authorities on the spot could only resort to expedients. It was assumed that all settlements were on a temporary basis because it was the Peace Conference which would resolve such conflicts. The British in the Caucasus had 'no desire to encroach into inter-State quarrels', Curzon stressed.[108] But at times the British generals could not help getting involved.

It seems that British mediation in the Caucasus often disregarded Armenian aspirations. The insufficiency of troops may have been one consideration for the British authorities favouring the stronger of the states contesting disputed territories.[109] Another consideration may have been the well-publicised view that Armenia would expand in the direction of Turkey-in-Asia. So her territorial ambitions in the Caucasus might be limited in

106. FO 371/3667/11067/11067, Gen. Staff Norperforce, Copy of Proclamation to be issued on occupation of Baku, 9 Nov. 1918.

107. FO 371/7729/E8378, Childs and McDonnell, 'Outline of Events in Transcaucasia' 31 May 1922.

108. Curzon Papers. MSS Eur F. 112/275, IDCE 6th mins., 13 Feb. 1919.

109. Bodleian Library, Wardrop Papers, MS Wardr. d.38/9/8, Eric Forbes Adam to Wardrop, 9 Dec. [1919].

favour of Georgia and Azerbaijan. There also were the pro-Moslem sympathies of Thomson and his Mesopotamian division; and perhaps the necessity of keeping the Azerbaijanis in good humour when the British were taking very large quantities of oil from Baku (they had obtained almost half a million metric tons by August 1919).[110]

Armenia was the least important state in the Caucasus in terms of strategic position and natural resources and therefore could not be of much use to British imperial interests. Probably it was for this reason that the British favoured Azerbaijani ambitions in Karabagh and also sent great quantities of armaments from the fortress of Kars not to Erevan — but to Baku and to Denikin's Russia. It was the protection of the Batum-Baku railway from 'any Bolshevik incursion' from the north that was of primary importance in the Caucasus for the War Office. The Armenians would often feel frustrated by British decisions. Yet they had welcomed the British in the Caucasus with open arms. During the war they had fought the Turks and defied the Germans while both the Tatars of Azerbaijan and the Georgians had welcomed them.[111]

On his arrival in Batum, General Forestier-Walker found the Armenians and the Georgians in armed conflict over the Akhalkalak and the southern region of the Borchalu counties of Tiflis province. The Armenians, claiming to be the majority of the population, based their arguments on the principle of national self-determination. Georgia, on the other hand, put forward historical, economic and strategic reasons. When the British arbitrated it was rather in favour of the Georgians, whose detachments would remain in Akhalkalak. Borchalu would be neutral under British control.[112]

Of all the territorial disputes in the Caucasus the most serious was the Armeno-Azerbaijani conflict over Mountainous Karabagh in the province of Elisavetpol. The Moslem Azerbaijanis outnumbered Armenians two to one in the province, but the Armenians constituted the absolute majority of the population of Mountainous Karabagh. Avetis Aharonian claimed 72 per cent; and Professor Simpson confirmed that this figure differed by only '1% or 2%' from the Russian statistics of some years before.[113] In the first half of 1918 Mountainous Karabagh was virtually autonomous. Following the declaration of Azerbaijani independence in May 1918 the Azerbaijani government tried to bring the disputed territories of Mountainous Karabagh

110. R.G. Hovannisian, *The Republic of Armenia, Vol. I. The First Year 1918-1919* (California, 1971), p. 158fn.

111. See Rep. of Arm. Archives, File 334/4, *L'Angleterre et L'Arménie* by 'Observateur', Dec. 1920; FO 371/3661/1015/31192, WO to Gen. Milne, copy, 15 Feb. 1919; FO 371/7729/ E8378, Childs and McDonnell, 'Outline of Events in Transcaucasia', p. 10, 31 May 1922; Firuz Kazemzadeh, *The Struggle for Transcaucasia* (New York/Oxford, 1951), pp. 172-3, 176.

112. Rep. of Arm. Archives, File 107/6, 'La Répub. Armén. et ses Voisins: Questions territs.', 1919, pp. 19-23; Kazemzadeh, ibid., pp. 155, 181; FO 371/7729/E8378, p. 12.

113. FO 371/3659/97452, 17 June 1919; see also Rep. of Arm. Archives, File 107/6, 'La Répub. Armén. et ses Voisins: Questions territs.', 1919, pp. 3, 7, 11.

and the Zangezur county of Elisavetpol under its jurisdiction with the help of Ottoman armies. But while the Turco-Tatar forces first concentrated on subjugating Baku, the Turkish-Armenian leader General Andranik and his partisans entered Zangezur in July, destroyed a number of Moslem settlements, and brought the central region of the county under Armenian control. On 2 December 1918 Andranik and his volunteers crossed the Karabagh border. Within a few days the Karabagh Armenians might have come under the jurisdiction of the Republic of Armenia. General Thomson, however, commanding at Baku, sent instructions to Andranik to stop all military operations and return to Zangezur. The war had ended and all disputes were to be settled by the Paris Peace Conference. Andranik who was poised for victory, complied and was back in Zangezur on 4 December. He even disbanded his following.[114]

In mid-January 1919, Thomson made his decision public: both Zangezur and Mountainous Karabagh would be administered by Azerbaijan pending the final verdict of the Paris Peace Conference. But the Peace Conference never settled the conflict of Karabagh. To this day it remains an autonomous region in Soviet Azerbaijan. Moreover, Thomson approved the Azerbaijani government's choice of Dr Khosrov Bek Sultanov, a notorious Armenophobe, as the Governor General of the two regions.

If in the Mountainous Karabagh the Armenians formed the absolute majority of the population, in the Nakhichevan, Sharur-Daralagiaz and the Surmalu counties of the Erevan province they were outnumbered by Moslems who wanted to secede and live under Azerbaijani jurisdiction. The Moslems based their arguments on the principle of self-determination. In their turn, the Armenian government claimed that these counties were part of the province of Erevan where the Armenian Christians outnumbered the Moslems two to one. Moreover, these regions had been part of historic Armenia and were the most fertile area of the republic. Their loss would greatly harm the country's economy. At the end of 1918 the Armenian government had expelled a number of Moslems from Daralagiaz and re-populated their villages with Armenian refugees. But the Tatars of Sharur and Nakhichevan would not allow the resettlement of Armenians in their counties and were prepared to fight. The British authorities again intervened. Finally, General Forestier-Walker turned both Sharur and Nakhichevan into a British military governorship in late January 1919. When in the spring of 1919 the British became aware of intense Pan-Turanian activity along the Armenian border, they arranged for the addition of Nakhichevan to the Republic of Armenia, which was achieved in the middle of May.

A supplementary clause to the Armistice of Mudros had required the

114. Artin H. Arslanian, 'Britain and the Question of Mountainous Karabagh', *Middle Eastern Studies*, vol. 16, no. 1 (Jan. 1980), p. 93. Rep of Arm. Archives, File 333/3, Aharonian to Presidents of Italian, French, British and American Delegs., copy, 15 May 1919; Kazemzadeh, *Struggle*, p. 215.

evacuation of the Turkish armies from Kars, a province beyond the pre-war Russo-Turkish frontier. But Yakub Shevki Pasha, commander of the Ottoman Ninth Army, managed to delay the abandonment of this province for a further two months. This delay enabled the defeated Turks to set up the South Western Caucasian Republic, in an attempt to preserve their foothold in Transcaucasia. It seems that at first the British Command sanctioned the activities of the republic's Moslem National Council at Kars: they mustered some 8,000 men, armed them from the abandoned Russian dumps, claimed authority from Batum to Nakhichevan and actively supported the local Turco-Tatar bands fighting the troops of Armenia along the border.[115] The National Council was apparently determined to keep the province under Turkish influence and to block the repatriation of over 100,000 Armenian refugees who had escaped to the Tiflis and Erevan provinces during the Ottoman offensive of early 1918. On 7 January 1919 Forestier-Walker personally informed the commander of the Turkish troops in Kars that the Ottoman troops should evacuate the province by the end of the month. Kars, he added, would provisionally become a British military governorship. Its civil administration would be provided by the Republic of Armenia. The following day Forestier-Walker concluded an agreement with the Armenian Minister of Foreign Affairs to this effect. The Moslem National Council of Kars, however, rejected these arrangements. When Captain Clive Temperley attempted to enter Kars with a company of British infantry and a number of Armenian officials to assume his duties as military Governor General of the province, armed Moslems warned him that his party would be fired upon unless the Armenian officials returned. The National Council thus openly defied the British authorities. Only in mid-April 1919 did the British move in and, after expelling the National Council, transfer the power over the southern part of the Kars district to Armenia.[116]

The government of Erevan must have been well pleased that by the middle of May 1919 its jurisdiction extended over Kars and Nakhichevan in the pre-war Russian Caucasus. Alexander Khatisian would later tell a British Armenia Committee meeting in London that from the United States of America they had received much assistance of a material kind, but 'political help only from Gt. Britain'.[117] But Armenia, like the other Caucasian states, still grievously lacked recognition of her independence. Moreover, pending the decisions of the Peace Conference, these territorial arrangements were said to be temporary — prolonging overall uncertainty. Thus, the Armenian jurisdiction still looked nominal. It was not yet established and it faced strong opposition from the Moslem Turco-Tatars both

115. W.E.D. Allen and P Muratoff, *Caucasian Battlefields: A History of the Wars on The Turco-Caucasian Border 1828-1921* (Cambridge, 1953), pp. 497-8; Kazemzadeh, ibid., pp. 199-200.

116. Rep. of Arm. Archives, File 333/3, Forestier-Walker to Shevki Pasha, 7 Jan. 1919; and Agreement with S. Tigranian, copies, 8 Jan. 1919. Hovannisian, *Republic*, I, pp. 202-24.

117. *BAC Minutes*, 29 July 1920.

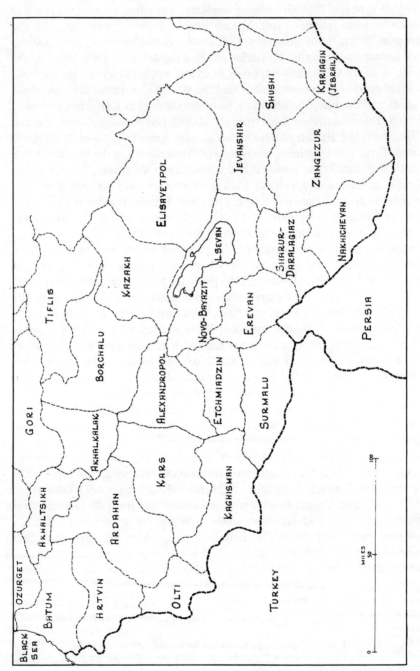

Map 7: The Counties of Western Transcaucasia

within and outside the provinces. Above all, there hung over them the disquieting and disturbing prospect of the British withdrawal from the Caucasus.[118]

Less than three months after the despatch of British troops to the Caucasus, Lloyd George's Cabinet decided on their withdrawal. The British Command in the Caucasus, caught up in the local territorial disputes, had made demands for more and more troops. Involvement had grown. Yet the Cabinet was not prepared to incur these additional responsibilities. On 30 January 1919, Lloyd George formally asked the Supreme Council in Paris that the military representatives of the Allied powers should meet 'at once' and present a report as to the most equitable and economical distribution among the powers of the 'burden' of supplying military forces for maintaining order in the Turkish Empire and Transcaucasia pending the decisions of the Peace Conference. On 5 February, the military representatives agreed that Italian troops should replace the British in Transcaucasia and Konia.[119]

The decision of the British to withdraw reflected yet another of the dilemmas of the post-war Cabinet: the need for reconciling worldwide British liabilities, at their apogee by the end of the war, with the necessity for retrenchment, and with the demands of an electorate in the background which was parsimonious and pacific and resolved that 'Never Again' should there be wars. It was in order to catch the war-weary public mood that Lloyd George had apparently promised, during the 1918 elections, an immediate demoblisation and return to a peace footing, and Sir Henry Wilson accused him of conducting a 'cursed campaign' for 'vote-catching'.[120] A quick demobilisation would satisfy an electorate which was fatigued and pacific and a Treasury urging the necessity for retrenchment.

Even from the earliest stage, Balfour had opposed the policy of assuming responsibilities in the Caucasus. He was 'really frightened' at the responsibilities which the British were taking upon themselves:

Who has to bear those responsibilities? . . . The War Office and the Treasury are mainly concerned. Where are they going to find the men or the money for these things? I do not know. Those matters are never considered.[121]

In a number of memoranda the Treasury stressed that the country expected

118. Wardrop Papers, MS Wardr. d. 29/11/2, American Commit. for Relief in Nr. East, memo [1919].
119. Curzon Papers, MSS Eur F. 112/275, IDCE, 6th mins., 13 Feb. 1919; CAB 25/118, I.C. 128, secr. Supreme War Council, 30 Jan. 1919, S.W.C. 365, A Report, Supreme War Council Military Representatives, 5 Feb. 1919.
120. Michael Howard, *The Continental Commitment* (London, 1972), pp. 74, 79. Callwell, *Wilson*, II, pp. 160–1, entries for 4 and 6 Jan. 1919.
121. CAB 27/24, War Cab. E.C. 43, 16 Dec. 1918.

and the situation demanded 'the severest economy'. As debt charges, war pensions, superannuation, education grants, old-age pensions and insurance caused irreducible expenditure, the Treasury argued that it was difficult to see where economies could be made except on the expenditure of the army, navy and air force. Great reductions could 'only be obtained by reductions in *men*'.[122]

So the British armies melted fast. On the day of the general Armistice the total strength of the army was 3,615,900; on 16 September 1919 it had dropped to 904,164.[123] A disproportion was emerging between policy and strength. Hence, policy should be tailored to fit strength.

Lloyd George himself was also keen on drastic economy. Reading history he had found that after the Napoleonic Wars, a strong government like his had been knocked out by Parliament on expenditure.[124] One of the major considerations of the British Cabinet in deciding the withdrawal of troops from the Caucasus was the financial burden incurred by keeping them there. Perhaps there also was the Labour Party's pressure against intervention in Russia generally. But Lloyd George blamed, for withdrawal, 'national expenditure', which was otherwise, under the prevailing conditions, 'very crushing'.[125]

The prospect of Denikin's victories must have been another major consideration justifying withdrawal. In the spring of 1919, the White armies had registered a series of successes against the Bolsheviks. In the end they would also take possession of the Caucasus as they had never kept secret their determination to do. From Britain's point of view, therefore, there was no necessity for her to fill the vacuum created in the Caucasus by the collapse of Imperial Russia. The Caucasus now became 'a secondary theatre of operations' as Lord Curzon put it. Churchill urged the 'quickest possible evacuation' since the British had 'no interests there' any longer.[126] In his turn, the CIGS, who, a few months earlier, had insisted that no other power except Britain should be in the Caucasus, also believed that this was a territory in which the Empire was now 'not vitally interested'. Yet another reason for the withdrawal was Lloyd George's wish, as recorded by Sir Henry Wilson in his diary, to force the pace in the settlement of Asia Minor: to force President Wilson to take his share in garrisoning or in naming the mandatory.[127] There was also his view that the British troops in the Caucasus should reinforce those in Constantinople and Asia Minor, ready to counter any possible move by the Italians (who were basing their territorial claims on

122. MS Milner dep. 136, f.286, F.C. 13, Memo., by Chancellor of Excheq., 17 Oct. 1919. Ibid., f.212, Treasury memo., 20 Sept. 1919; ibid., f.161, G. 257, memo. by Treasury, 18 July 1919.
123. Ibid., ff.245-6, memo by Treasury, Appendix K, 20 Sept. 1919.
124. Hankey Papers, HNKY 1/5, diary entry for 4 Dec. 1920.
125. Lloyd George Papers F/27/3/37, Lloyd George to A. Henderson, copy, 14 Aug. 1919.
126. Curzon Papers, MSS, Eur. F. 112/275, IDCE, 11th mins., 6 Mar. 1919.
127. Callwell, *Wilson*, II, p. 164; ibid., II, pp. 167–8, entry for 1 Feb. 1919.

the wartime Treaty of London, of April 1915).[128]

It seems, however, that for British politicians withdrawal was not a cut and dried formula: in fact a British detachment remained in Batum until June 1920. The British government and especially the Foreign Office were only anxious to alert the Allies, and especially the United States, and secure a fairer distribution of the financial burden for keeping order in such areas of the former Russian and Turkish Empires, where, the British now felt, they had no vital stake.

The military authorities, however, having made up their mind that the British line of defence in South Asia should be neither the line Constantinople-Batum-Baku-Krasnovodsk-Merv, nor the line Constantinople-Batum-Enzeli-Tehran-Meshed, but should be the railheads of the systems of Palestine, Mesopotamia and India, that is, Palestine-Mosul-Khanikin-Burujird,[129] as relentlessly and singlemindedly pressed for withdrawal as they had pressed for the despatch of British troops into the Caucasus in November and December 1918.

It seems that the War Office, and especially Sir Henry Wilson, were equally contemptuous of both the politicians at home and their professions of interest in the emerging nationalities and new states abroad. Sir Henry Wilson found the 'Frock[coat] mind' simply amazing, and did not refrain from making 'most contemptuous' remarks about the 'Frocks'. He considered the Foreign Office to be both badly organised and incompetent, and those 'academic fools', who wanted to back the Greek against the Turk, 'dangerous'.[130] Equally, he had no regard whatsoever for the principle of nationality: as seen above[131] he had recommended the creation of two separate Armenias. He was generally impatient with the budding national states. Like Marshal F. Foch, the supreme military adviser to the Allied powers, he had the 'lowest opinion' of the Caucasian states and characterised the representatives of Georgia and Azerbaijan in Paris as 'dagos' who told ridiculous cock-and-bull stories.[132]

The War Office generally did not think that the former subject nationalities were fit to govern themselves. In the past, Imperial Russia and Imperial Turkey had provided stable governments, and Denikin's Russia would have now been the best security for India and Central Asia against Bolshevism.

128. Briton Cooper Busch, *Mudros to Lausanne: Britain's Frontier in West Asia, 1918–1923* (New York, 1976), p. 155; Hovannisian, *Republic*, I, p. 307.

129. CAB 23/21, Cab. 30 (20), min. 3, 21 May 1920; Callwell, *Wilson*, II, pp. 221–2, entry for 12 Jan. 1920.

130. Callwell, ibid., p. 227, entry for 15 Feb. 1920. Lord Riddell, *Intimate Diary of the Peace Conference and After 1918–1923* (London, 1933), p. 204, entry for 20 June 1920; p. 270, entry for 25 Jan. 1921. Imperial War Museum, Wilson Papers, 73/1/8, 12 E/7, Wilson to Sackville-West, copy, 11 Oct. 1919.

131. See above, p. 146.

132. Hankey Papers, HNKY 1/5, diary, entry for 24 Jan. 1920. Callwell, *Wilson*, II, p. 224, entry for 19 Jan. 1920.

When, however, Denikin's armies collapsed, it seems that the traditionally pro-Turkish sympathies of the War Office[133] were completely transferred to the support of Turkey. Without much consideration for past Turkish misrule or the widely professed principle of nationality for subject peoples, the War Office strongly and sometimes effectively pressed their pro-Turkish views on the government. They even made attempts to define and interpret policy. While the Foreign Office and particularly its junior staff was more sensitive to public opinion and conscious of the various pledges given for the liberation of Armenia, the War Office showed no interest whatsoever in that quarter.

It appears, therefore, that while withdrawal was considered by the Foreign Office to be the intended policy of the government, the War Office tried to make it the only policy of the government. But pending the decisions to be taken at Paris, Britain could not escape from responsibility in the Caucasus, which she herself had willingly assumed. Likewise, during the interim period, Britain held the major share of responsibility for the security and order in the Asiatic provinces of Turkey since, excluding all other powers from negotiations, she alone had conducted the surrender.

The declared withdrawal of the British troops from the Caucasus and Anatolia led to a deterioration of the situation. It definitely encouraged the Turks and led in the latter territory to a policy of 'open defiance' against the Allies.[134] General George F. Milne, the Officer Commanding the Army of the Black Sea, with jurisdiction over an extensive area including Anatolia and the Caucasus, was himself apprehensive of disorder. The Turkish National defence movement which was growing in Turkish Armenia and the hostility of the Tatars towards the Armenians provided the material for a serious conflagration. On the southern frontier of the Armenian republic the situation was very disturbed, Milne reported. In the districts of Shardissi and Nakhichevan the Tatars were being guided by 'Turkish officers', — a breach in the terms of armistice. The Armenians considered their chance of retaking these districts as nil, owing to 'scarcity of ammunition'. The general opinion was that massacres would ensue in these two districts, General Milne warned.[135]

Referring to the above two despatches, the Military Representative of the British Delegation in Paris — apparently under public pressure — asked the War Office whether in view of the Armenian shortage of ammunition, it would be possible for the British troops, on commencing their evacuation on 15 August, to leave with the Armenians a proportion of their munitions of war. The Army Council, however, 'strongly' opposed such action because it

133. Churchill, *The Aftermath*, p. 367; Hankey Papers, HNKY, 1/5, diary, entry for 27 Mar. 1920.

134. Rawlinson, 'Adventures', p. 250.

135. FO 371/3659/121298, GOC-in-C. Const. to CIGS and to WO, 27 and 28 July 1919 respectively.

would tend to aggravate the existing dangerous situation in Transcaucasian Armenia.[136]

The inability of the Allied powers either to recognise the independence of the Caucasian republics with well-defined frontiers, or to consider the region as part of a reconstituted future Russia, the delay in the peace with Turkey and the evacuation of British troops threatened to create perilous conditions in the Caucasus especially for Armenians. As British withdrawal would remove the only stabilising and restraining factor in the area, various groups in the disputed territories, often supported covertly by their respective states, hastened to create their own territorial *faits accomplis*. In this respect the oft-repeated Allied pledges marked the Erevan republic as an object of all-round hostility. As seen above, Erevan had already been given jurisdiction over Kars and Nakhichevan in pre-war Russian territory. But it had not been provided with the proper means for effective control; nor was the local Moslem population disarmed. The British withdrawal presented, therefore, an opportunity for the Kurds, Tatars and Turks of these disputed territories, to try to sabotage and invalidate, with the active help of Turkish officers and arms,[137] any territorial arrangement which might favour Armenia.

In their turn Armenian bands in Kars, 'without discipline and not under effective control', apparently pillaged insurgent Moslem villages and committed atrocities. They argued to Lieutenant-Colonel Rawlinson that in order to take control of the region it was necessary that they should disarm the population. This sometimes led to forcible measures. Such actions certainly could not be conducive to friendly relations between peoples who were bound to live together. But the authorities in Erevan had not yet had the time or the money to organise a properly disciplined army. Moreover, it seems that Armenians felt themselves separated from the Turkic peoples by the blood of hundreds of thousands of their kinsmen systematically murdered during the war. These mutual relations were apparently widely discussed in Paris. On 4 March 1919, Stephen Bonsal, the distinguished American journalist serving as secretary to President Wilson, referred in his diary to the 'blood-curdling' atrocities committed against Armenians by the Turks which he had seen with his 'own eyes' in Turkey. Now,

. . . I do not close my eyes to the crimes which the Armenians have since committed . . . from time to time when the rare occasion presented against the diabolical Kurds and the Turkish irregulars . . . Indeed, I approve of them.[138]

136. Ibid., Br. Milit. Rep., Paris to WO, n.d.; ibid., Army Council to FO, 26 Aug. 1919.
137. FO 608/78/5936, Aharonian to Sir L. Mallet, 31 Mar. 1919; Rawlinson, *Adventures*, p. 157.
138. Rawlinson, ibid., pp. 227, 196. Stephen Bonsal, *Suitors and Suppliants: The Little Nations at Versailles* (New York, 1946), p. 186.

Meanwhile, in the Caucasus the state of affairs became worse. The General Headquarters, Constantinople, reported that Kurds had now cut the Kaghisman-Kulp road and had captured most of the surrounding villages. Lieutenant Colonel J.C. Plowden, the British Military Representative in Erevan, had met Khan Tekinskii, the Moslem leader, in Nakhichevan but could not improve matters. He had been insulted by Khan and on his return journey to Erevan had been 'imprisoned for several hours'. At all important villages he had found 'Turkish officers and soldiers'. The Tatars were well-organised and well-armed and were 'hungering' for violence.[139]

The Foreign Office sharply reacted to these reports. M.D. Peterson of the Eastern Department considered the presence of Turkish soldiers across the old Russian frontier a 'clear breach' of the armistice conditions. The situation was certainly alarming, he thought, because the Tatars and Turks were now threatening the capital and heart of the Armenian republic itself. Peterson commented on the 'absurdity' of the War Office plea that to give arms to the Armenians would be to encourage disturbances.[140]

In Paris, the Armenian representatives desperately requested that the British, before withdrawal, should arm their republic against the imminent danger from Turkish and Tatar armies. The arms in possession of the Armenian army — 14,380 rifles, 158 machine guns, 42 field and mountain guns — were all in bad condition and spare parts were lacking. Robert Vansittart, a member of the British Delegation, found the request 'eminently reasonable'. He apparently fumed at the War Office reply that it did not favour the idea. '*They* are not going to get their throats cut' he minuted. The minimum the British could do was to put the Armenians in a position to defend themselves before their forces were withdrawn, Vansittart maintained. 'The matter has been handled in a manner that is not creditable' he concluded.[141]

The War Office was unmoved.

Earlier, Admiral Calthorpe, now the British High Commissioner in Constantinople, submitted that as withdrawal from the Caucasus would set free a large body of British Indian troops, some of these be transferred to Asia Minor for enforcing the armistice, for pacifying the country and for enabling the repatriation of Armenians to go forward 'without molestation'. The response of the Army Council was negative. The pacification of Asia Minor and the repatriation of Armenians 'must be left to the Mandatory Power'[142] they replied, pointing to policy.

139. FO 371/3659/121849, GHQ Constant. to WO enc. I.6871 and I.6880, copy, 23 and 25 Aug. 1919, respectively.

140. Ibid., nos. 121849/121298, minutes, 28 Aug. 1919.

141. Rep. of Arm. Archives, File 333/3, Aharonian to Lloyd George, copy, 7 Aug. 1919; ibid., Milit. Adviser, Deleg. Arm. Rep. to DMI, copy, 2 Sept. 1919; FO 608/78/18333, minutes by Vansittart, 26 and 27 Aug. 1919; and by Milit. Sect., 27 Aug. 1919.

142. FO 371/3667/11067/61966, Calthorpe to FO 20 Apr. 1919; ibid., FO to Army Council, 26 Apr. 1919; ibid., no. 70160, WO to FO, 7 May 1919.

In mid-August, after receiving information from Colonel Rawlinson and other sources that the Turkish troops and the Moslem tribesmen, all well-armed, were gathering around Armenia and that the withdrawal of the British forces would be the signal for the massacre of the entire Armenian population, Lord Curzon spoke to Sir Henry Wilson. A few days later, Sir Ronald Graham, too, spoke in the same vein asking the CIGS to postpone or delay the departure of the British troops. Whatever the obligations of the other powers in the matter might be, he argued, the British alone had troops on the spot, and they alone could, by retaining them there, at least mitigate the disaster. When Balfour also wrote to Lloyd George a few days before the British withdrawal that the consequence would be massacres, Sir Henry even went to tell Curzon that 'if we did not remove A.J.B. [Arthur James Balfour] we would never make peace or end anything'.[143] It seems that with their remarkable singlemindedness the men in the War Office could often have their way over a hesitant Foreign Office. The evacuation began on schedule.

In addition, the Army Council persistently rejected requests for assisting the Armenians with arms and equipment even after the bulk of the British troops were withdrawn. The Council argued that they had neither arms nor equipment available. Moreover, the provision of arms would lead to 'provocative action' on the part of Armenians and would further complicate the situation. In the neighbouring states, jealousy would be created, and the hostility of Mohammedans in Turkey both to the Armenians and towards the Entente powers might be increased. It would be 'well to abandon the idea of a Greater Armenia' for the present. The Armenians should be induced to believe that the best prospects for their future lay in the creation of 'two small states', one in the Caucasus and one in Cilicia, the Army Council advised the Foreign Office.

The War Office was again dabbling in policy problems.

Eric Graham Forbes Adam of the British Delegation in Paris could not clearly understand why the jealousy of Georgia and Azerbaijan and especially an increase of hostility on the part of Turks and Tatars should preclude the British helping the Armenians. He hoped, in any case, that

> . . . the apparent desire of the War Office to take every and any opportunity of influencing the Conference in favour of leaving an independent Turkey as large as possible . . . will not play any large part in the final decisions of H.M.G. [His Majesty's Government] and the Conference.

Sir Eyre Crowe, now Head of the British Delegation in Paris agreed. There was surely more danger of the Armenians being attacked by Turks and

---

143. FO 371/3668/11067/122957, R. Graham to Wilson, 29 Aug. 1919 and minute; Imperial War Museum, Wilson Diary, microfilm, DS/MISC/80, reel no. 8, entry for 11 Aug. 1919.

Tatars rather than of the latter being attacked by Armenians, he maintained. The War Office generally, and the India Office too, appeared to be so obsessed by the pan-Islamic bogey that they were really afraid to tackle the Turkish settlement on national lines. The idea of winning the Turks from pan-Islamism by 'truckling' to them was 'insane'. He personally still hoped that the Peace Conference might find means of imposing on Turkey terms according to the spirit and the letter of the Supreme Council's reply to the Turks in July 1919 in the matter of the subject races. Crowe believed that a lasting settlement on 'national' lines could be imposed in Turkey, 'if we can only keep the will alive'.[144]

With his deep faith in Britain and the power of human will, Sir Eyre Crowe sounded a lone prophet standing up against the forces of appeasement which were now gradually setting in.

For appeasement there certainly was. It was the 'inaction' of the powers which emboldened the Turks to disregard completely the terms of the armistice in eastern Anatolia, and they found they did so with impunity.[145] The power and prestige of the Turkish Nationalists rest only upon the 'abstention of the Allies to intervene', L.P. Chambers wrote from Constantinople. In his turn, referring to the Turks, Bryce concluded:

> . . . the maddening part of the whole Near East business is that it could have been settled with little trouble had it been taken up immediately [after] the war. There would have been no Angora rebellion, no pernicious Khalifate agitation in India . . .[146]

Certainly, Turkey and Armenia were not exclusively British problems. But Britain was by far the most influential power in the whole Near East. So, if there was a lack of foresight and of energy in neglecting to create the requisite conditions in eastern Anatolia and Armenia for the implementation of the Peace Treaty, it is perhaps worthwhile, at this stage, looking a little more closely at the personalities and Departments chiefly responsible for decisions and the execution of policy as regards Turkey.

The Supreme Council's masterly reply to the Turkish Delegation,[147] referred to by Sir Eyre Crowe, was written by Balfour. It was one of the most 'arresting and incisive' documents ever to emanate from his pen in which he had characterised the 'calculated atrocity' of the wartime Turkish massacres as equalling or exceeding 'anything in recorded history'; and he had indicted Turkish rule over alien races as one causing in all cases the diminution of

---

144. FO 608/78/20367, Creedy, WO to FO copy, 23 Oct. 1919; minute E.G.F. Adam, 13 Nov. 1919. Ibid., nos. 20367 and 20832, Crowe to Kidston, 17 Nov. and 1 Dec. 1919.
    145. Bryce, 'The Revision of the Turkish Treaty: Armenia', p. 578.
    146. Bryce Papers, UB 67, Chambers, Report on 'National Forces' in a letter to Bryce, 14 Oct. 1919; ibid., UB 25, Bryce to Scott, 28 Dec. 1921.
    147. See DBFP vol. IV, pp. 645–7.

material prosperity and the fall in the level of culture. On his part, Lord Curzon (Foreign Secretary from October 1919) also argued strongly that Turkish rule over the various subject races had been a record of misrule, oppression, intrigue and massacre 'almost unparalleled' in the history of the eastern world.[148] The two successive Foreign Secretaries firmly believed that Turkish rule over subject races should, definitely, not be allowed any more. However, both looked like being unable to impose their authority effectively on a War Office which attempted to follow a propitiatory policy of its own towards Turkey, at the expense of the subject peoples. Moreover, they could not prevent the authority of their own country from being defied, from the very beginning, by a defeated Turkey.

At the end of the war both felt exhausted under the strain and stress of the past five years. 'A holiday I *must* have' wrote Balfour in August 1919, asking Curzon to replace him as Foreign Secretary. In his turn, Curzon replied that on more than one occasion he had 'broken down' and that for the next month it would be a physical impossibility for him to undertake a fresh task.[149] More important, these two successive Foreign Secretaries were not, in their own different ways, men of action.

A philosophic doubter, Balfour with his extraordinary analytical powers and his inevitable 'but on the other hand' phrases and mentality, saw both sides of a question too clearly to be able to come readily to a conclusion. In 1918 at one of the meetings of the Supreme Council he had spoken about a difficult question for ten minutes, and when he had finished, old Clemenceau turning his twinkling eyes on him had abruptly enquired, 'For or against?'.[150]

On the other hand, Curzon, majestic in speech, appearance and demeanour, was too much concerned with statements about things, and too little about getting things done. Moreover, he was a person who often domineered, but never dominated and led, and was 'grievously unstable'.[151]

Thus, the men at the top in the Foreign Office lacked the qualities of decisive action. The resignation of Lord Robert Cecil from the government after the election of 1918 must also have weakened the cause of Armenia.

In the War Office, on the other hand, Sir Henry Wilson, who, as he himself put it, was 'determined to make love to the Turk',[152] was not only a

---

148. Lloyd George, *The Truth About the Peace Treaties* (London, 1938), II, pp. 1009-15.

149. Balfour Papers, Add MSS 49734, ff.153–4, Balfour to Curzon, copy, 16 Aug. 1919; Curzon to Balfour, 20 Aug. 1919.

150. Lloyd George, *Peace Treaties*, I, p. 261; Lloyd George, *War Memoirs*, II, pp. 1014–16. W.S. Churchill, *Great Contemporaries* (London, 1937), p. 254; ibid., pp. 239–40, 251. See also Vansittart, *The Mist Procession*, pp. 218, 232; Harold Nicolson, *People and Things* (London, 1931), pp. 12–13.

151. Churchill, ibid., pp. 278, 281; Churchill, *The Aftermath*, p. 413, K. Young, *Arthur James Balfour* (London, 1963), pp. 243, 428. See also Beaverbrook, *Men and Power*, pp. 304, 309; Thomas Jones, *Whitehall Diary* (K. Middlemas, ed.) (London, 1969), I, p. 220; Vansittart, ibid., p. 272.

152. Wilson Papers, 73/1/8, 12E/7, Wilson to Sackville West, 11 Oct. 1919.

shrewd person of remarkable intellectual gifts but also 'a schemer and intriguer'. Under his responsibility, the General Staff somehow did not deal effectively with the disarmament of Turkey. In addition, the Army Council, under his guidance, consistently and persistently refused — as seen above — to provide the necessary arms and ammunition to the Republic of Armenia. The military authorities in Batum even held up for some time two aeroplanes 'privately' purchased in Paris by the republic — to the indignation of the Acting British High Commissioner. Yet later Sir Henry Wilson victoriously argued that the republic was not capable of taking possession of the ancient homelands of Armenia as earmarked by the Foreign Office experts of the British Delegation in Paris:

> How do you expect Armenia to hold her own against a fully armed Turkey and a rearmed Azerbaijan, herself being unarmed?

he asked.[153] But one is inclined to enquire why Turkey was allowed, in his own words, to be 'fully armed' even before peace was made (when she should have been disarmed); why Azerbaijan was rearmed and why Armenia was left 'unarmed'?

Having said this, one comes back to the point that it seems the Foreign Office somehow failed to hold its overall responsibility for foreign affairs and allowed itself to be superseded.

Having made up his mind that Turkey should become the major power in the Near East, once Denikin had collapsed, Sir Henry Wilson continued to press his views resolutely. When President Wilson asked him how many troops he required for the Armenian mandate, Sir Henry replied 'up to five' divisions and this 'terrified' the President.[154] It seems that Sir Henry persistently tried to frustrate any encouragement which might be given to Armenian independence. He-distrusted emerging nationalities and new states.

Pressing the government to make concessions to Turkey, the General Staff saw in the Turkish Nationalist movement a patriotic organisation, the main object of which was to oppose the dismemberment of the Ottoman Empire. The General Staff argued that if Britain opposed the ends it had in view, she should be prepared for a spread of Pan-Islamic feeling, allied perhaps to Bolshevism from Trans-Caspia to India and for unrest in the Middle East. Antagonising the 'patriotic elements' in Turkey would preclude the possibility of reducing British garrisons in Egypt, Palestine and Mesopotamia, and would cost the British taxpayer unnecessary millions.[155]

153. Lord Beaverbrook, *Politicians and the War 1914–1916* (London, 1960), pp. 191-2; Beaverbrook, *Men and Power*, 'Biographies', p. xxvi; Lloyd George, *War Memoirs*, VI, p. 3377. DBFP, vol. XII, p. 609; Harry C. Luke, *Cities and Men* (London, 1953), II, p. 176. Callwell, *Wilson*, II, p. 234, entry for 20 Apr. 1920.
    154. Callwell, ibid., II, p. 188, entry for 5 May 1919.
    155. CAB 24/89, G.T. 8292, Military Policy in Asia Minor, by Gen. Staff, 9 Oct. 1919.

The government also came under strong pressure from the India Office for a pro-Turkish policy. Edwin Montagu, the Secretary of State for India, was, as the representative in Britain of 80 million Moslem fellow subjects, extremely sensitive to their feelings. Apparently Montagu and Sir Henry Wilson closely co-operated on the issue of concessions to Turkey[156] at the former's request. Hankey, the Secretary to the War Cabinet, believed that by expressing some 'extraordinary' military views, Wilson could, on occasions, influence the government Ministers; and that Montagu allowed, through his 'cowardice', Indian opinion to become seriously moved in favour of Turkey.[157]

The War Office and the India Office successfully used the double levers of strategic requirements and opinion in India to press their pro-Turkish views on the government.

Montagu warned Lloyd George as regards the treaty contemplated with Turkey, that the peace of the east would be seriously jeopardised unless the government's Eastern policy was altered. The 'soldiers and sailors' and the Assistant High Commissioner in Constantinople, Rear Admiral Richard Webb, were all 'in agreement' with him. Next, he quoted from a telegram sent by the Viceroy in India, pointing to the real danger of the 'unusual fraternisation' between Hindus and Moslems fostered by the discontent of the latter over the Turkish peace.[158] Montagu continually circulated selective notes to his colleagues or the Cabinet using the bogey of unity among the population of India and unrest among the Moslems which might complicate British rule there. Thus, Sir George Roos-Keppel, lately Chief Commissioner of the North-West Frontier Province, believed the Hindus were hoping that a decision adverse to the claims of Turkey would throw the Indian Moslems into their arms in Indian politics. Sir Hamilton Grant, Foreign Secretary to the government of India, likewise predicted that were the Turks to be expelled from Constantinople, the Moslems would unite with the Hindus and the 'cleavage' which made British administration there comparatively simple, might give place to a 'formidable union'.[159]

Concessions to Turkey were urged, therefore, in order to appease the Moslems in India and to keep them divided from the Hindus.

Montagu viewed the proposed peace with Turkey as disastrous and incredible. The Allies did not have the military strength to enforce it, he argued. Moreover, it was wholly opposed to the interests of the British Empire. The British should try to get the Turks to help them against the Bolsheviks. A 'friendly' Turkey would profit Britain; an 'incensed' Turkey would never

156. Callwell, *Wilson*, II, p. 218, entry for 30 Dec. 1919.
157. Hankey Papers, HNKY 1/5 diary, entry for 24 Jan. 1920.
158. Montagu Papers, AS-IV-3, 697 (1–5) and 698, Montagu to Lloyd George, copy, 15, 16 Apr. 1919.
159. Bonar Law Papers, 94/20, Note by Roos-Keppel, Jan. 1920, and memo. by Grant, 20 Dec. 1918, both circul. 5 Jan. 1920.

cease to foment trouble in India, he maintained.[160] 'I know that you agree with me he wrote to Bonar Law,[161] the Leader of the House of Commons and of the Conservative Party.

Not so with Lloyd George. He did not agree with all Montagu's views nor with his claim that his memorandum on the draft Peace Treaty with Turkey be submitted to the Peace Conference. Moreover, he wrote a particularly biting letter concerning his 'constant stream' of arguments urging concessions in favour of the Turks. Montagu's attitude often struck him as that of 'a successor on the throne of Aurangzeb'. His memorandum did not pay sufficient regard to the rights of the 'nationalities' oppressed and massacred by the Turks in the past. During the war alone it was estimated that the Turkish government had massacred 800,000 of its subjects and drove 200,000 more from their homes. 'Nationality', Lloyd George's Private Secretary, Philip Kerr, explained a few days later, represented the fundamental view as seen by the Prime Minister.[162]

But Britain could not solve the dilemma of reconciling her international obligations with her determination for economic retrenchment. The abstract principle of nationality alone could not provide the answer to Armenia's problems. The Prime Minister himself was specific about a country which did not impinge on vital British interests: 'with every desire to assist, we really cannot police the whole world', he told the House of Commons. Only a few seconds later, however, he pressed that Britain should not abandon Mosul which was a province with great possibilities: it had 'rich oil deposits'. Asquith, the Leader of the Liberal Party, agreed about Armenia. Although his sympathy with that country was deep and heartfelt, he certainly could not advocate — 'it would be madness to do it' — that Britain should undertake a mandate there. He was indeed alarmed at the extent of the mandates which Britain had already undertaken,[163] Asquith concluded.

The British government would only be too pleased were responsibility for Armenia assumed by other Allied powers. In February 1919 Italy had agreed to send two divisions of troops to the Caucasus and one battalion to Konia in Anatolia for the supervision of law and order pending the peace settlement. But she soon retracted her agreement. Tommaso Tittoni, the Foreign Minister, told Balfour that holding the Caucasus would need about 40,000 men and this was more than Italy could afford. Coal and raw materials were Italy's real need and not fresh territorial responsibilities, he

160. Lloyd George Papers, F/40/3/1, paper by Montagu, 1 Jan. 1920; ibid., F/40/3/2 Montagu to Lloyd George, 20 Jan. 1920. CAB 24/103, C.P. 1046, memo., 9 Apr. 1920.

161. Bonar Law Papers, 98/7/5, Montagu to Bonar Law, 9 Feb. 1920.

162. Lloyd George Papers, F/40/3/4, Montagu to Lloyd George, 15 Apr. 1920; ibid., F/40/3/5, Lloyd George to Montagu, copy, 25 Apr. 1920 – memo encl. Montagu Papers, AS-IV-6, 893 (1–2), Philip Kerr to Montagu, 3 May 1920.

163. *Hansard*, 5th Ser. 1920, vol. 127, cols. 661–2. Ibid., vol. 128, col. 1474.

stated. The British Cabinet agreed that 'the best solution' for Armenia would be the acceptance of a mandate by the United States. But they realised that the prospects for this were diminishing.[164]

At one time the prospect had been good. Colonel E.M. House, President Wilson's influential adviser, had privately told Hankey that he thought the United States would accept a mandate, although he could not come out in the open and say so. Soon, however, hopes faded. According to Senator Henry Cabot Lodge, the Republican leader in the Senate, under no circumstances would the United States accept any mandate in Turkey or, its late territories. In August 1919 the British military attaché stated that absolutely no military preparations for any action in Turkish Armenia were being made or even contemplated by the United States War Department.[165]

The decision of British withdrawal from the Caucasus and the fact that no mandatory was as yet visible had emboldened the Tatars and Turks, both within the Republic of Armenia and in the surrounding regions where they were preparing for attack. The Armenians were sending 'piteous' appeals to Paris. Khatisian, the Prime Minister, had 'almost wept' when the British flag was lowered at Erevan.[166] Appeals to postpone the withdrawal came from all sides including one from Arthur Henderson, the Secretary of the Labour Party. He forwarded to Lloyd George a resolution unanimously carried at the Lucerne (Socialist) International Conference which

. . . profoundly moved by the recommencement of the massacre of the Armenian populations, . . . asks the allied governments to maintain the British army of occupation in Armenia until the League of Nations decides in favour of its withdrawal.

This was in response to the desperate pleadings made by Boghos Nubar, Avetis Aharonian, other Armenians and Albert Thomas, the French Socialist leader, that the part played by the British troops in the Caucasus was of a humanitarian nature and should not be identified with intervention in Russia; that withdrawal would bring in the attack of Tatars and Turks and would result in catastrophe.[167] In the House of Commons protests against withdrawal were made by British Armenia Committee members in particular. T.P. O'Connor remarked that there had been a great division of

164. CAB 25/118, S.W.C. 365, Supreme War Council Milit. Reps., 5 Feb. 1919. Lloyd George Papers, F/89/3/3, memo. by Balfour, 4 July 1919; ibid., F/89/3/13, Philip Kerr, to PM, 30 July 1919. CAB 23/12, War Cabs. 617 and 618, 19 Aug. 1919 (morning and afternoon).
165. Lloyd George Papers F/23/4/28, Hankey to Lloyd George, 1 Mar. 1919; ibid., F/89/2/33, Philip Kerr to PM 26 Feb. 1919; ibid., F/89/3/4, Kerr to PM, 16 July 1919 reporting on letter Lodge to Col. Lawrence; FO 371/3659/120555, Lindsay, Washington, to FO, 25 Aug. 1919.
166. Lloyd George Papers, F/89/3/12, Kerr to Lloyd George, 29 July 1919. FO 371/3659/129090, Wardrop to FO, 12 Sept. 1919.
167. FO 371/3668/11067/120100, min. by A.C. Kerr, 16 Aug. 1919. Lloyd George Papers, F/27/3/36, Henderson to Lloyd George, 12 Aug. 1919. Labour Party LSI. 3/291/302/298/289, dtd 5 Aug., 14 Aug., 13 Aug., 3 Aug. 1919 respectively.

opinion in the country with regard to British intervention in Russia, but there had been no such division with regard to keeping British troops in the Caucasus. In fact, Lord Robert Cecil, Conservative, Aneurin Williams for the Liberals and Neil Maclean, Labour MP for Govan, had all joined in the appeal to keep British troops temporarily in the Caucasus for the protection of Armenia. Aneurin Williams asked the Under-Secretary for Foreign Affairs as a matter of special urgency over and over again what steps had been taken 'to bridge the interval' between the withdrawal of the British troops and the establishment of some other protectorate in the country. Lord Robert Cecil, no longer a member of the government, also joined his voice arguing that the case for assisting Armenia was 'really overwhelming'. He reminded the House that the 1915 massacres had been organised from Constantinople because it was thought that the Armenians were the 'friends' of the Entente. At the time when Russia went to pieces through the Revolution, no doubt these Armenians had for some months maintained the Entente cause in that part of the world. They had fought gallantly, but by so fighting they had merely exacerbated the views which obtained in that part of the world and now they were being treated there as traitors. It would be a 'great responsibility' to take away the division and a half of British troops now there, Robert Cecil maintained.[168] A memorandum in the name of the British Armenia Committee appealed to the whole of the daily press to use its influence to dissuade the government from withdrawing troops; and the Armenian United Association of London cabled both the Foreign Secretary and the King desperately appealing to them not to abandon the Armenian people.[169]

A telegram from William Haskell, the Allied High Commissioner for Relief in Armenia, also pleading that London revoke the order, was discussed by the Supreme Council. Balfour reminded the meeting that the date of withdrawal had been postponed from 15 July to 15 August and that the British could no longer continue in the Caucasus. No representative however came forward with any positive proposal; and Clemenceau, the President of the Conference, concluded:

> France could do nothing; Italy could do nothing; Great Britain could do nothing and, for the present, America could do nothing. It remained to be seen whether, as the result of this, any Armenians would remain.[170]

In the United States, some sections of public opinion apparently felt especially strongly for Armenia. James W. Gerard, formerly American ambassador to Germany and now Chairman of the American Committee for

168. See *Hansard*, 5th Ser. 1919, vol. 119, cols. 1304–5, 1676, 2034–5, 2058, 2061, 2065.
169. *BAC Minutes*, 18 Aug. 1919. FO 371/3668/11067/11569/116229, tels. to Foreign Minister and King, 13 Aug. 1919.
170. DBFP vol. I, pp. 389–90, Supreme Council, 11 Aug. 1919.

Independence of Armenia, twice cabled Balfour asking him to press at the Peace Conference for an independent Armenia with big boundaries. In March 1919, forty State Governors, 250 college and university presidents, 85 bishops and 20,000 ministers and priests had petitioned President Wilson in this respect.[171]

But if the Americans actually felt so strongly, why did not they assume some responsibility for the security and protection of Armenia, the British government apparently asked. They were a nation of 100 million people, owning almost all the fluid wealth of the world. Philip Kerr hoped the British government would take the line of saying to the Americans that this was 'their responsibility and the responsibility of nobody else'.[172] Balfour's views were similar. He sternly told Gerard that Britain found the utmost difficulty in carrying out the responsibilities she had already undertaken. She could not add Armenia to their number. The United States with her vast population and undiminished resources and without fresh responsibilities derived from the war, was much more fortunately situated. But charity unsupported by political and military assistance was quite insufficient to deal with the unhappy consequences of Turkish cruelty.

The crux from the British point of view was put by Balfour most clearly:

> Great Britain has no interest whatever in Armenia except the interest of humanity which she shares to the full with the United States.[173]

The British interests in Armenia were 'purely sentimental'. There was 'no practical interest' of any kind, Hankey in his turn had written in a confidential memorandum. (Hankey had given his views on Armenia after several talks with the Prime Minister in Normandy at the beginning of September 1919.[174]) He stated that Britain should act before the Armenians were massacred out of existence, because 'strong feeling, in their favour existed in many circles in the British Empire. It would be callous to withdraw the British forces at the very moment when massacres were reported to be in progress. From a military point of view it would seem that the only nation which could intervene in time was Britain. Moreover, a small British force might probably accomplish as much as a large force from other nations because of the great prestige which the British were said to have acquired. On the other side, the withdrawal from the Caucasus had been undertaken in response to an overwhelming desire to get quit of all Russian territory, especially since the maintenance of this force was 'extremely costly'.

---

171. FO 371/3658/74847, Gerard to Balfour, 17 May 1919; Balfour Papers, Add. MS. 49749 ff.184–95, Balfour to Gerard [16 Feb. 1920]; Gerard cable 15 Feb. [1920].

172. Lloyd George Papers, F/89/3/12, Philip Kerr to Lloyd George, 29 July 1919.

173. Balfour Papers, Add. MS 49749, ff. 186–91, Balfour to Gerard, first draft, [16 Feb. 1920]; ibid., ff.192–5, second draft, with minor corrections.

174. Lloyd George Papers, F/24/1/10, Hankey to Lloyd George, 4 Sept. 1919. Hankey Papers, HNKY 1/5, diaries, entry for 4 Sept. 1919.

National economy was vital to Britain which had no practical interests of any kind in Armenia: this was not the time to undertake quixotic adventures. Moreover, once committed to action in Armenia, there was no knowing when the British would be able to withdraw. Britain could not undertake this adventure single-handed, nor could she sustain the whole cost. The man-power and the cost should be divided among the Allied Powers.[175] This was the conclusion of Hankey's memorandum which apparently also reflected the Prime Minister's views.

Thus it seems that it became British policy to try and pass the responsibility for Armenia on to other countries. Stephen Bonsal characterised this attempt as 'passing the buck'. For Sir Henry Wilson it was an attempt by the Allied Frocks at 'carting' President Wilson.[176]

It was Bonar Law who actually tried to shift the responsibility onto other powers. He simply tried 'to sell' the Armenian problem first to the United States and then to France. Referring to withdrawal, he stated that the British could not be responsible for securing good order in Armenia, with which they had 'no connection at all'. This was 'an American problem rather than a British'. Their interests there were greater. If the United States were officially to ask the British government to hold on until the Americans made arrangements, the British would certainly do their best. Otherwise he could hold out no hope of keeping troops there any longer. Bonar Law's statement was forwarded to the American ambassador in London.[177]

In September 1919, the French proposed to land a 12,000-strong force at Alexandretta which would then proceed to help the Armenians in the Caucasus. The War Office suggested that the proposal was not practicable. The War Cabinet was suspicious, and in the end they decided to invite the French government to despatch their force through the Black Sea ports.[178] Bonar Law, as astute as ever, pointed out that acquiescence to the French proposals would not 'save' the British from responsibility if a massacre should happen. Seizing the opportunity to strike a sound bargain for formally throwing off any British responsibility for Armenia, he wrote to Balfour in Paris:

> If you could get Clemenceau to make a public declaration that he would undertake the responsibility of protecting the Armenians, then I think that would be a good thing whether or not he was able in reality to do so.[179]

175. Lloyd George Papers, F/24/1/10, Hankey to Lloyd George, 4 Sept. 1919.
176. Bonsal, *Suitors and Suppliants*, p. 192, entry for 3 Mar. 1919. Callwell, *Wilson*, II, p. 235, entry for 24 Apr. 1920.
177. *Hansard*, 5th Ser. 1919, vol. 119, cols 2086–7; FO 371/3659/119103, Curzon, copy, 19 Aug. 1919.
178. CAB 23/12, War Cab. 621, min. 1, 2 Sept. 1919.
179. Bonar Law Papers, 101/3/142, Bonar Law to Balfour, copy, 4 Sept. 1919. Another copy in Lloyd George Papers, F/31/1/8.

Thus, Bonar Law was not so much concerned whether Clemenceau 'in reality' could protect the Armenians, but in his making a 'public declaration' for undertaking the responsibility. The following day, he expanded his somewhat 'cynical' views — as he himself put it — to the Prime Minister. He emphasised that the Alexandretta proposal would not help Britain 'out' of her difficulties unless the French would accept 'the full responsibility publicly' for looking after the interests of the Armenians.

> If they would do this and let us get away, though this is rather a cynical thing to say, I would not much care if they propose to help them from Mars instead of Alexandretta.[180]

It is evident that the British government at least felt some moral responsibility for the Armenians. Instead of effectively helping them, however, they tried to 'get away' and throw this responsibility onto other powers.

The French went back on their offer and never landed troops at Alexandretta or the Black Sea ports for Armenia. Hankey's proposal that the manpower and the cost of protecting the Armenians should be divided among the Allies was very reasonable from the British point of view, and indeed in every respect. Armenia was not, after all, an exclusively British concern. Where Britain's diplomacy markedly failed was in her inability to carry the other Allied powers with her and to make some political and financial arrangement with a view to helping Armenia in her first difficult years of existence. Pro-Armenian humanitarian feeling was substantial in France, Italy and the United States. But Hankey himself knew that these Allies had been alienated by British manoeuvring in the former Ottoman Empire. Britain had secured for herself alone the richest and strategically the most important parts of the Ottoman territories. Influenced by Admiral Slade, Hankey was convinced, even before the end of the war, that Britain 'ought' to make it a 'first class war aim and peace aim' to acquire oilfields in Persia and Mesopotamia. It was supremely important for the future of Britain to get this oil, and he had written so to Balfour.[181] In Paris, taking a 'very intransigent attitude', Lloyd George had wanted to go back on the Sykes-Picot Agreement in order to get Palestine and Mosul for Britain. At the peace negotiations during the first half of 1919, Lloyd George had succeeded in establishing an increasing ascendancy and in the end had 'always got his way'. The French talked of 'La Paix anglaise' — the English Peace — recorded Hankey.[182]

---

180. Lloyd George Papers, F/31/1/9, Bonar Law to Lloyd George, 5 Sept. 1919. Copy in Bonar Law Papers 101/3/143.

181. Hankey Papers, HNKY 1/5, diaries, entries for 29 July, 1 Aug. 1918. Cecil Papers, Add. MS 51094, f. 16, Hankey to Balfour, 12 Aug. 1918, transm. to Cecil.

182. Hankey Papers, HNKY 1/6, diaries, entry for 6 Oct. 1918. Ibid., HNKY 1/5, diaries, entry for 2 July 1919.

In Paris, it was felt that since Britain was securing the best of the world, she could not much hope for co-operation from the Allies for humanitarian purposes. Likewise, some Americans 'very' strongly felt that the British withdrawal from the Caucasus was an attempt to 'force' the hands of the United States government and to see that only the 'poorest' parts of the territories were eventually assigned to mandatories.[183]

Moreover, the Americans apparently resented the fact that, whilst during the war the British leaders had issued a Blue Book and made many statements promising liberation and protection, they were now trying to pass the responsibility onto the United States. According to Stephen Bonsal's diary, Sir William Wiseman, the Adviser on Anglo-American Affairs in the British Delegation in Paris, who often acted as a messenger for Lloyd George, had dropped in on 2 March 1919, and after a few minutes had asked Bonsal:

> I wonder if you could tell me, and through me, the P(rime) M(inister) , confidentially of course, when the President is planning to bring the Armenian question before the Council for final adjustment.

To the surprise of Wiseman, Bonsal had replied that possibly the President thought he should not interfere with the British plans 'in this quarter'; and to the further surprise of Wiseman, had shown him a copy of the Prime Minister's speech made at the Guildhall in 1916, which with 'malicious purpose' he had kept on his desk for some weeks. As Wiseman seemed to shy away, Bonsal had read aloud:

> 'Britain is resolved to liberate the Armenians from the Turkish yoke and to restore them to the religious and political freedom they deserve and of which they have been so long deprived.'

On his own part, Bonsal had told Wiseman:

> It seems to have been your job, and you accepted it at least a year before we entered the war. Why should the President barge in? *Après vous, messieurs les Anglais!*

Bonsal commented in his diary that as the extreme difficulty of the task became apparent, both France and Britain earmarked the job for 'Simple Simon, that is, for Uncle Sam'.[184]

During the first months of 1920 the Supreme Council occupied itself with the Turkish treaty. It 'unanimously' accepted the proposition that Armenia, in accordance with the 'pledges repeatedly given' by the Allies during the

---

183. FO 371/3668/11067/120100, min. of convers. betwn Aneurin Williams/Clark Kerr, FO 16 Aug. 1919.

184. Bonsal, *Suitors and Suppliants*, pp. 191–2, entry for 3 Mar. 1919.

war and since its conclusion, be constituted a free and independent state. Yet still no power was willing to accept responsibility for Armenia. So Curzon, on behalf of the Supreme Council, cabled the Council of the League of Nations to know whether the League would be disposed to accept the obligation to protect the future Armenian state.[185]

In reply, the Council of the League of Nations regarded the establishment of an Armenian state upon a safe and independent basis as 'an obligation of humanity'. But, its memorandum went on, the League of Nations was not a state. It had as yet no army and no finances. The stipulations of Article 22 did not contemplate the League itself accepting a mandate. On the contrary these stipulations required the League to supervise the execution of mandates entrusted to a specified power.[186]

Next, the Supreme Council gallantly and formally turned to the United States despite the fact that 'all' Americans had told the British privately, as the knowledgeable Hankey scribbled, that the Senate would 'never' agree to a mandate.[187] Addressing President Wilson in late April 1920, the Supreme Council expressed their conviction that the only great power qualified alike by its sympathies and its material resources to undertake the mandate 'on behalf of humanity' was America. The prospect of creating an Armenia which should include Cilicia had for long been abandoned as impracticable. There remained the questions, what portions of the *vilayets* of Erzerum, Trebizond, Van and Bitlis, still in the possession of the Turkish authorities, could safely be added to the existing state of Erevan, and what means of access to the sea should be provided to the new state. The Supreme Council appealed therefore to President Wilson for the United States to accept a mandate for Armenia; whatever might be the answer of the United States government on the subject of the mandate, the President should accept the honourable obligation of arbitrating on the boundaries of Armenia to the west and south. Finally, the Supeme Council called the sympathetic attention of the United States government to the possibility that an American loan of a few millions sterling for both the provision of military forces and the constitution of an orderly administration, might be the means of setting Armenia at once on her feet. There might also be 'universal emulation' in responding to an appeal than which no more deserving could have been addressed to the 'heart and conscience' of mankind.[188]

But the rhetoric could not transfer the responsibility onto American shoulders. Yet the heavy responsibility remained:

The Government are very anxious to mention something about the

185. Lloyd George Papers F/206/4/22, 'Armenia, Wilson and the Supreme Council', Curzon to Derby, Paris, for President, League of Nations (no. 325 v. urg.) 12 Mar. 1920.
186. Ibid., memo. by Council of League of Nations (A.J.156), 11 Apr. 1920.
187. Hankey Papers, HNKY 1/5, diary, entry for 16 Oct. 1919. See also DBFP vol. IV, p. 797, fn. 3, Grey tel., 10 Oct. 1919.
188. Lloyd George Papers F/206/4/22, Supreme Council to President Wilson, 26 Apr. 1920.

Armenians. They will want to assure the British and American publics
that something has been done to assure that the Armenians are being well
treated . . . ,

Admiral Calthorpe had told Raouf Bey in October 1918 when discussing the
draft clause concerning the Allied prisoners and Armenian internees.[189]
Likewise, in May 1920, the War Cabinet itself had referred to

> . . . the intentions and promises in regard to the independence of
> Armenia . . . and the promises of so many statesmen in regard to that
> country . . .

when discussing the proposed withdrawal from Batum.[190] The government
could not go back on the promises made by British statesmen. Nor could
they completely disregard the pro-Armenian pressure of the humanitarian
groups who pinned down the British political leaders to their own statements
and resolutions. 'Armenia — we are doing our best', Curzon wrote to the
Archbishop of Canterbury in 1919. 'I shall never in any settlement with
Turkey lose sight of Armenian interests', he would tell Aneurin Williams
later. He was even more forthcoming to the Archbishop of Canterbury:
'You may rely on me to spare no effort for the safety of these unhappy
people'.[191]

But Britain could not solve the dilemma of reconciling the pledges she had
given for the liberation of Turkish Armenia with her inability to assume
responsibility for making liberation effective. The argument that her control
of Constantinople would give security to Armenia never prevailed. Nor did
British attempts to shift the responsibility for Armenia onto France or the
League of Nations, or the United States succeed.

In the end, Lloyd George's government decided to solve the dilemma in
its own way by sticking to its promises to liberate Armenia. By the Treaty of
Sèvres of 10 August 1920, a very substantial part of the ancient territory of
the Armenian people — to be delimited by President Wilson — was formally accorded to Armenia. The Treaty was signed by the representatives of
the governments of Erevan, Constantinople and the European powers.[192]

The British government could now wash their hands of the matter.

Across the borders, however, the Bolsheviks had already taken control of
Baku and Azerbaijan in April. Erevan itself was considered to be in the
danger zone. In May the British Cabinet had taken note of the War Office

189. FO 371/5259/E5732, notes of actual negotiations of armistice, Oct. 1918.
190. CAB 23/21, Cab. 24/20, min. 1, 5 May 1920.
191. Davidson Papers, Box on Armenia, Curzon to Archbishop, 18 Aug. 1919; Curzon
Papers, MSS Eur. F112/232 f.44, Curzon to Williams, copy, 6 Dec. 1921; Davidson Papers, Box
on Armenia, Curzon to Archbishop, 23 Nov. 1921.
192. PP. 1920, vol. LI, *Treaty of Peace with Turkey*, articles pp. 88–93, in pp. 633–4.

view that it was 'unjustifiable' to send British officers, 'even those who volunteered, to Armenia' where in certain eventualities they might run grave risk of being cut off from all possibility of assistance.[193] As regards Turkish Armenia, the Geneal Staff had in March pointed out that the extent of the front from the Black Sea to Lake Van, close on 300 miles, was a task 'quite beyond the capacity' of the Armenian forces. In addition, Turkey was 'fully armed' and Armenia 'unarmed'. Armenian soldiers lacked 'everything', even uniforms.[194]

The Treaty of Sèvres was indeed the consummation of the British and Allied pledges for the liberation of Armenia and the response to humanitarian public opinion — on paper.

193. CAB 23/21, Cab. 30 (20) min. 3, 21 May 1920.
194. DBFP vol. XIII, p. 35, Gen. Staff, WO, memo. 15 Mar. 1920. Callwell, *Wilson*, II, p. 234, entry for 20 Apr. 1920. Rep. of Arm. Archives, File 335/5, Boghos Nubar and Aharonian to Marshal Foch, 20 Jan. 1920.

5   Illusions: From Sèvres to Lausanne

The Treaty of Sèvres, the first peace treaty signed between the Allied and associated powers on the one hand,[1] and Turkey on the other, was, and is, a document of historic importance as regards its Armenian clauses. By according territory in the *vilayets* of Erzerum, Trebizond, Van and Bitlis to Armenia, the Allied powers took the decisive step of removing from Turkish rule lands which had constituted the national home of the Armenian people since the dawn of history: lands where they had lived from biblical times and for indisputably longer than the Turkish people had been in Anatolia. The Treaty of Sèvres was the recognition of the rights of the Armenian people over the Eastern Provinces. The Treaty was particularly significant because it acknowledged, at a time when these lands were completely and cruelly depopulated of their native inhabitants, their ownership by the Armenian people.

Earlier, in February 1920, Lord Curzon had stated at the First London Conference[2] of Allied representatives that the 'Allies were pledged to constitute an independent Armenia'. He was putting forward the general principles of the forthcoming treaty of peace with Turkey, which, he thought, 'were accepted by all the Allies'. Francesco S. Nitti, the Italian Prime Minister, agreed. Philippe Berthelot, the French Foreign Minister, also agreed. 'Everything must be done to compensate the Armenians for the atrocities from which they have suffered' he argued, although he believed that the problem presented very grave difficulties, since 'all' Armenians in Great Armenia had been 'massacred or deported'.[3]

In April 1920, at the Conference of San Remo,[4] where the representatives of the Allied powers finalised the peace treaty with Turkey, Curzon once again repeated that the freeing of Armenia had been 'one of the most often proclaimed Allied war aims'. The Allies had, therefore, 'a heavy moral responsibility' upon them, he insisted. The Conference of Foreign Ministers and Ambassadors in London, over which he had presided, had recommended a rather large Armenia which should include Erzerum. The United States had been particularly anxious that the port of Trebizond should be

1. British Empire, France, Italy, Japan, Armenia, Belgium, Greece, the Hedjaz, Poland, Portugal, Romania, the Serb-Croat-Slovene State and Czecho-Slovakia; see PP. 1920, vol. LI, p. 612.
2. 12 Feb. to 10 Apr. 1920. DBFP, vol. VII, pref.
3. Ibid., p. 43, 14 Feb. 1920; ibid., pp. 81, 83, 85: Meeting of Allied Reps., London, 16 Feb. 1920.
4. 18–26 Apr. 1920, DBFP, vol. VIII, pp. 1–252.

granted to Armenia, but this would be impossible if Erzerum were left in the hands of Turkey, Curzon added, he too favouring a large Armenia. During these San Remo discussions, Berthelot always warmly supported the inclusion of Erzerum where, although there had not been an Armenian majority, there had been an extensive Armenian colony, most of whom had been massacred. There were, therefore, strong 'moral' grounds for giving that city to Armenia, Berthelot believed. Moreover, it was a powerful fortress, the centre of the region and the focus of all its roads. Were it to be left in Turkish hands, Armenia would be entirely denied any possibility of access to the sea. It would be almost impossible, Berthelot added, to build up a new Armenian state without that city. The problem was most difficult but it was a point of 'honour' for the Allied powers, *vis-à-vis* the whole world, to settle it. Neither the Armenians nor public opinion in the world, particularly in America, would be content without the place, Berthelot insisted.[5]

Thus, considerations of past pledges, moral responsibility, honour and public opinion, especially in the United States, induced the representatives of the Allied powers to decide on the transfer of territory in the Eastern *vilayets* to the Republic of Armenia. Later, Woodrow Wilson, the President of the United States, was also guided by similar considerations. When giving the result of his arbitration on 22 November 1920, he stressed that he had examined the question, as he put it, with a mind 'to the highest interests of justice' and in the light of the 'most trustworthy' information available.[6] He decided that 42,000 square kilometres of territory should be added to the Republic of Armenia from Turkish Armenia.

Avetis Aharonian, as President of the Peace Delegation of the Republic of Armenia at Paris, was first to append his signature to the Treaty of Sèvres immediately after the representatives of Britain, France, Italy and Japan, the major Allied powers. Armenia was first in alphabetical order among the Associated powers. On 15 August, a thanksgiving service was held in the Armenian Church of Paris and then a reception at the Delegation's centre to celebrate 'the great national day'. In Armenia too, celebrations were held on the occasion of the signing of the Treaty of Sèvres.[7] Armenians were vibrant with patriotism all over the world. Kajaznuni would, a few years later, comment with the wisdom of experience:

The Treaty of Sèvres had dazzled the eyes of all of us, restricted our power to think, clouded our consciousness of reality.[8]

5. Ibid., p. 49, Meeting of Supreme Council, San Remo, 20 Apr. 1920. Ibid., pp. 109–11, 138, 22, 23 Apr. 1920.
6. *Foreign Relations of the United States* (Dept. of State), 1920, vol. III, p. 796; see also, pp. 790–804.
7. Aharonian to Minister of For. Affairs, Erevan, 19 Aug. 1920, quot. in Simon Vratsian, *Hayastani Hanrepetutiun* (The Republic of Armenia) (Paris, 1928), pp. 397–8.
8. H. Kajaznuni, *H.H. Dashnaktsutiune Anelik Chuni Aylevs* (Dashnaktsutiun Has Nothing To Do Any More) (Vienna, 1923), p. 42.

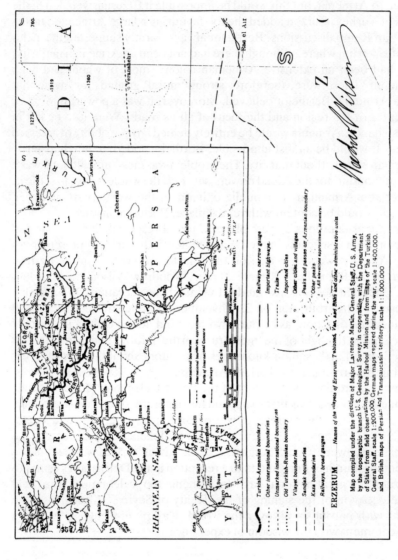

Map 8: President Woodrow Wilson's Award

The Treaty of Sèvres, drafted by the victorious Allies, the mightiest powers in the world, pinned all Armenian hopes on far-away Paris.

But the position of these powers as regards the Armenian clauses was somewhat false. That position was fatally based on an illusion of power and authority when in reality the Allies lacked the effective means – the will and the forces — to implement the Treaty of Sèvres. Even before the Peace with Turkey, it was clear that they could spare neither money nor arms to turn the clauses of the Treaty into reality.

At the request of Lloyd George, the military and naval representatives of the Allied powers were summoned by Marshal Foch, the supreme military adviser, even before the Conference of San Remo, to consider the question of the military means to be employed for enforcing the execution of the Treaty of Peace upon Turkey, should the Turkish government refuse to carry it out. According to their report, the Allies needed for such a task 27 infantry divisions in all, while they only had on the spot 19 divisions. In more detail, they stated that the territory of the future Armenian state was occupied 'by 4 Turkish infantry divisions, with large stocks of military materials', and that these divisions could be reinforced by large numbers of irregulars. On the other hand, Armenia, in view of the 'feeble strength' at her disposal — 15,000 men, insufficiently armed and without war material — was 'not in a position' to establish her sovereignty and to resist possible attacks from Turkey or Azerbaijan. It would, therefore, be indispensable to give her immediately the assistance of an Allied force of at least '4 infantry divisions' and, in addition, to furnish her as quickly as possible with instructors, armament and war material. The representatives concluded that the execution of the Treaty could not be assured in its entirety, and more especially in eastern Turkey-in-Asia without the intervention of Allied forces in greater strength than that at present available.[9]

This conclusion was supported by the General Staff of the War Office, who pointed out that there were no reinforcements available and, indeed, British military resources were 'strained to a dangerous extent' in meeting existing commitments. The General Staff concluded that the British government could enforce the proposed peace treaty, only if it was prepared to face 'a further call for troops'.[10] But to answer a call for troops was an impossibility. After the war to end all wars, even the existing armies were only too impatient to return home. In 1919 there had been open riots at some military camps to protest against the slowness of demobilisation. Nothing, it was thought by the authorities, was more likely to produce a revolution in Britain than an attempt to keep the men in the army longer than was absolutely necessary. In addition, military expenditure became a major

9. CAB 24/103, C.P. 1035, Annex, no. II, Report, n.d., encl. in Foch to Lloyd George, 30 Mar. 1920.
10. Ibid., C.P. 1014, Gen. Staff Memo., 1 Apr. 1920.

target for economies. In consequence, in 1920, expenditure on the armed forces was reduced by more than half, from £604 million to £292 million, and over the next two years it was reduced by more than half again to £111 million. The result was further demobilisation and 'a shrunken British Army to handle on a shrunken British budget'.[11]

Under such circumstances, the General Staff of the War Office pointed out that they were unable to contemplate the Allied plan for the formation of an Armenian state as a practicable policy.[12] But the politicians persisted in their task.

At San Remo the territory to be transferred to the Republic of Armenia from the Eastern *vilayets* was discussed at twelve meetings.[13] The crux of the difficulty was the irreconcilability of policy *vis-à-vis* strength.

According to Marshal Foch there could be no question that the Turks had a great quantity' of arms in the interior of Anatolia, and they were in a position to give the Allies an enormous amount of trouble. He could see 'no possibility' of sending Allied help to Armenia. It would, therefore, be 'exceedingly difficult' for Armenia to constitute the new state and to build up an army, surrounded as she was 'by hostile elements'. On 23 April 1920, the Allied military experts once again provided the Supreme Council with a note pointing to the existing difficulties, the inaccessibility of Armenia and the unavailability of Allied forces: the only land-link for despatching arms to the Armenians was that of Batum-Tiflis, the use of which could not be depended upon. On the other hand the governments had decided that no Allied force should be sent to Armenia. Under these circumstances it seemed, therefore, that the Armenians would be 'incapable' of taking possession of Turkish Armenia and in particular Erzerum.[14]

Access to Erzerum by the British forces was discussed in great detail by Colonel F.R. Maunsell and was also set as a 'problem for the Staff College, Camberley'.[15] The difficulties were summarised by the General Staff of the War Office: the route to Erzerum from the railhead at Sarikamish was impracticable owing to the hopelessly bad condition of the 400 miles of railway from Batum to Sarikamish. The only other possible way from the sea was by road from Trebizond, a distance of 196 miles. The gradients were 1 in 10 and the passes reached a height of 8,200 feet. Trebizond itself was an open roadstead and ocean-going vessels could not come alongside.

Moreover, Marshal Foch maintained that

11. Michael Howard, *The Continental Commitment* (London, 1972), pp. 72, 78. See also C.J. Lowe and M.L. Dockrill, *The Mirage of Power* (London, 1972), II, pp. 350, 362, 378; Kenneth O. Morgan, *Consensus and Disunity: The Lloyd George Coalition Government 1918–1922* (Oxford, 1979), p. 289.
12. CAB 24/103, C.P. 1014, Gen. Staff, Memo., 1 Apr. 1920.
13. DBFP, vol. VIII, nos. 4, 6, 7, 9–16, 20.
14. Ibid., pp. 56, 60, Supreme Council, San Remo, 20 Apr. 1920. Ibid., p. 131 (A.J.173), Note of Military Experts, 23 Apr. 1920.
15. WO 106/64 Col. Maunsell, 'Proposed Movement Inland from Trebizond', 31 Mar. 1920; ibid., Problem for Staff Coll., Camberley, n.d.

. . . the Armenian nation had been oppressed for centuries. It had at present no administrative organisation, nor did it possess a military organisation of any value. The immediate future of Armenia, therefore, was not roseate.

Turkey, on the other hand, could still emerge again as a considerable military state. She possessed the elements of an administration, and what he would describe as a 'nervous system'.[16]

The Allied political leaders, however, were willing to agree to the transfer of a substantial extent of territory to the Republic of Armenia in the peace treaty. Apparently they could then show their public that they were keeping their promises. But the difficulty was providing the means to carry out their policy. France could neither guarantee loans nor give military help in view of French commitments elsewhere, Millerand, the French Prime Minister, stated, referring to Armenia. Nitti likewise intimated that the situation was very much the same for Italy. She could not offer any military forces, and in the present state of her exchange she could not consent either to give advances or to guarantee loans. Lloyd George was not far behind. 'As to troops, Great Britain could certainly supply none' he remarked.[17]

The deadlock resulting from the conflict between the often declared policy of the Allies — the liberation of Turkish Armenia — and their unwillingness to provide money or men for a region which was neither of strategic nor economic importance led to various compromises and expedients. Lloyd George was against the inclusion of Erzerum in the future state of Armenia: the creation of a Larger Armenia would make for 'bad feeling' among the Moslems in India. It was also indefensible on 'ethnological' grounds. Moreover, he thought that it was not right for the Great powers to negotiate treaties which they knew they could not, and had no intention to, carry out. He strongly deprecated encouraging illusory hopes among the Armenians when the Allied powers were perfectly aware that they could not justify those hopes. Nitti agreed; Armenia had better not have Erzerum in her own interests. But Curzon and Berthelot, the Foreign Ministers, disagreed: the arguments against leaving Erzerum in the hands of the Turks were 'much more powerful'.[18]

The difficulty was not solved. It was simply evaded in an ingenious way. It had been recognised that to make the treaty effective in the case of Armenia, the Allies had to undertake both 'military and financial' responsibilities. Berthelot, cleverly simplifying the problem, argued that essentially there was only one question which dominated all the rest: the financial. After every war there always were large numbers of officers and men, who,

16. DBFP, vol. XIII, p. 36, Gen. Staff Memo., 15 Mar. 1920; ibid., vol. VIII, p. 122, Supreme Council, San Remo, 23 Apr. 1920.

17. Ibid., pp. 48–9, 20 Apr. 1920.

18. Ibid., p. 145, 24 Apr. 1920; and pp. 109–12, 22 Apr. 1920.

trained in arms, would be quite prepared to enlist so long as they received good and regular pay. Seizing on this quickly, Lloyd George perceived the United States as the source of the money required. He had been told that Armenia would need a loan of about £10 million. Who was prepared to advance such a sum? Why did not the League of Nations appeal to America? He believed that such an appeal would be successful. At least it might have the effect of 'stopping' President Wilson from addressing any further notes to the Supreme Council on behalf of Armenia.[19] As referred to in Chapter 4, the Supreme Council finally appealed to President Wilson, asking that the United States should accept the mandate for Armenia and he himself should arbitrate on the boundaries. Lloyd George saw 'a great advantage' in this appeal as the United States would be 'forced' to take a definite interest in Armenia's future. A few days before, on 20 April 1920, Lloyd George had already expressed the view that the Allies 'ought' to put the Washington government in a position in which it must either agree to assist or refuse. America should be informed that the Allied powers now had an 'impossible burden' on their shoulders. She should take a share of that burden. If she refused, let her refusal be 'definitely placed on record'. Then she could not continue to complain of the inability of the Allies to protect Armenia.[20]

Lloyd George simultaneously devised another scheme: the Allies should find equipment for the Armenians who should be armed and given a chance of fighting their own battles. If they were not in a position to defend their own frontiers, then he thought that there was 'no use for a nation of that kind in the world'. Surely, not one of the Allied governments would send 'even a single battalion', he added. Sir Henry Wilson and Marshal Foch were present at the meeting of the Supreme Council on 20 April, which the CIGS considered as the 'most incompetent, impotent, cynical meeting' of all the hundreds he had been present at. He was especially critical of Lloyd George's view that if the Armenians were not in a position to win, then they were not worth saving. He regarded it as 'absolutely cynical'. Not much mention of small states, of the 'brutality' of the Turk, of the 'poor' Christians massacred by Moslems, he pointed out — in his diary. Foch and himself had agreed that this was the most *'pitoyable'* (pathetic) of any meeting they had been present at; and Foch's comment had been: *'La politique à deux sous'* (cheap policy).[21]

Was then the policy of the Allied powers and especially of Britain towards Armenia cynical? The decimated Armenians, the people of 'the land soaked with the blood of innocence', certainly could not regain their territories in eastern Turkey without effective assistance. Yet the powers had drafted a treaty, for the implementation of which, as regards the Armenian clauses,

---

19. Ibid., pp. 50, 62, 20 Apr. 1920, 11 am. and 4 p.m.
20. Ibid., p. 157, 24 Apr. 1920; ibid., pp. 61, 63, 20 Apr. 1920, 4 p.m.
21. Ibid., p. 58, 20 Apr. 1920, 4 p.m.; C.E. Callwell, *Field-Marshall Sir Henry Wilson: His Life and Diaries* (London, 1927), II, pp. 233–4, entry for 20 Apr. 1920.

they would spare neither a single battalion nor any money. Were the attitudes, then, of the pro-Turkish General Staff and Montagu more realistic and more honest? According to the General Staff, the 'best interests' of Armenia demanded that her existence as a self-contained state, if she desired to absorb any formerly Turkish territory, could only be guaranteed under Turkish suzerainty.[22] Montagu in his turn advised the Cabinet to adopt a completely different course. It was now 'certain that no Power will accept a mandate for Armenia'. It was therefore essential that the new republic should be on friendly relations with her western neighbour. These conditions were possible only if the frontier of Armenia was drawn east of Erzerum, Montagu maintained. Any other alternative would provoke continuous warfare in a region in which the Allies could not be expected to operate.[23]

Attributing deliberately cynical motives to British politicians as regards the Armenian clauses, would mean taking too simplistic a view and would certainly be incorrect. It seems that it was their misplaced belief in Britain's authority, prestige and power which was erroneous. The British wrongly thought that they could somehow impose the treaty.

The break-up of the German, Austro-Hungarian, Russian and Turkish Empires, the defeat of the Central powers and the withdrawal of the United States from Europe in 1919 had created for the victorious Allies, and especially for Britain, a vast political vacuum.[24] The Allied and especially the British leaders suddenly found themselves with unprecedented world-wide responsibilities shaping the destinies of millions of people and settling the frontiers of a host of countries. The result was an exaggerated sense and awareness of immense power and prestige. Thus, during the London Conference of the Allied Representatives in February 1920, when the Kemalists attacked the French forces in Cilicia and massacred between 15,000 and 20,000 Armenians, Curzon was outraged. He told an Allied meeting that it was 'impossible' for the Allies to tolerate this 'insulting defiance' by the Turks, and that all three powers should join in exacting 'the appropriate penalties'. Likewise, Lloyd George expressed his grave concern about the 'prestige' of the Allies throughout the Turkish Empire and the 'dignity' of Great powers.[25] But with her armies melting fast, Britain's military strength was shrinking. British authority, prestige and power, unsupported by military capability, were illusory, and certainly insufficient to impose the Turkish Treaty in its entirety. The British leaders had yet to adjust themselves to the disproportion between Britain's suddenly expanded post-war

22. CAB 24/103 C.P. 1014, Gen. Staff Memo. on Turkish Peace Treaty, 1 Apr. 1920.
23. Ibid., C.P. 1046, Memo. by S.S. India, 9 Apr. 1920.
24. For a discussion of British power in the Near East after the First World War, see Albert Hourani, *A Vision of History* (Beirut, 1961), pp. 124–5.
25. DBFP, vol. VII, p. 298, Meeting of Allied Reps, London, 28 Feb. 1920; ibid., p. 417, 5 Mar. 1920.

prestige and her contracting armed forces.

But perhaps the Armenian clauses, inserted from considerations of humanitarian public opinion, were meant not so much to be carried out as merely to exist in the treaty. It seems that Lloyd George, an amateur, aware of the popular distrust of 'old' and 'secret' diplomacy, and having usurped the powers of the Foreign Office, showed a tendency to conduct foreign policy which was rather 'opportunist and hand-to-mouth'.[26] Holding peripatetic conferences with the other Allied leaders and engaged in elaborate talks under the white glare of publicity, he was above all keen 'to *seem* to have achieved positive results'.[27] The Armenian clauses of the Treaty of Sèvres were the response to past public pledges and the debt paid by both the Allied leaders and Lloyd George to that part of public opinion which was deeply sympathetic with Armenia and believed in the principle of nationality. These clauses would show that the government was caring for Armenia. They might also serve as a distraction to those idealists who felt aversion to the grabbing policies pursued by the Great powers in the Middle East — in Syria, Palestine and especially Mesopotamia.

The insistence of Lloyd George on forcing the Armenian question onto the United States of America, despite common knowledge that there was not much hope, reflected political expediency which was irresponsible to no small extent. It was not constructive statesmanship. What would actually happen to Armenia were the United States to refuse responsibility? His argument that if they refused, then their refusal should be 'definitely placed on record' was a commonplace device to share out the blame for a probable failure. It was not a solution for Armenia.

In June 1920 the American Senate decisively rejected the Armenian mandate. President Wilson, however, consented to arbitrate on the boundaries. As stipulated in the Treaty of Sèvres, Turkey, Armenia as well as the other High Contracting Parties agreed 'to accept' the President's decision.[28] But by the time the result of his arbitration was made known in November, the Kemalists had already reached Erevan in Russian Armenia.

The Treaty of Sèvres, based on an illusion of power by the Allies and Britain, and expediency, in its turn created an illusion among the Armenians. A small people, they saw in the Treaty, drafted by world leaders, an evidence of the friendship of great nations. The Treaty pinned their faith and hopes on the remote European powers who were promising so much. But the Treaty provided no arrangements whatsoever for the security of Armenia. On the contrary, by offering the prospect of extensive Armenian frontiers, it infuriated the Turks. They saw Armenia inflated but

---

26. *Hansard*, 5th Ser. 1920, vol. 127, col. 697 (Lt. Col. A.C. Murray).

27. Gordon A. Craig, 'The British Foreign Office from Grey to Austen Chamberlain' in G.A. Craig and F. Gilbert (eds.), *The Diplomats 1919–1939*, 2nd edn. (Princeton, 1960), pp. 28–9.

28. PP, 1920, vol. LI, p. 633: *Treaty of Peace with Turkey*, article 89.

totally helpless and isolated. Thus the Treaty of Sèvres, for which Armenians held thanksgiving services, became a document of provocation for the Nationalist Turks. They not only did not cede any territory from Turkish Armenia, but even crossing the pre-war Russian frontier occupied the greater part of Russian Armenia. The Treaty in the end became Armenia's doom.

If the position of Britain and the Allies was quite false in Paris, it was no less brittle in the Caucasus. Britain's irreconcilable dilemma between policy and strength was also manifest as regards the Caucasian republics. The British government clearly aimed at keeping the Caucasus and Persia out of the reach of Bolshevik influence. But it could not, or was not willing to, use the necessary force. Even some members of the British Cabinet recognised this situation. Thus it was significantly 'urged' and admitted with reference to the Persians, that the government's attitude was a 'false' one:

> We ought to recognise that we had not the military forces available to enable [the Persians] to keep the Bolsheviks out. As we could not do this, we ought to encourage the Persians to conclude some arrangements with the Bolsheviks. Up to the present we had rather deterred them from doing so.[29]

The case as regards the Caucasus was similar. To the end the British government, or rather the Foreign Office under Curzon, used its authority to induce the Caucasian republics to withstand the spread of Bolshevik influence — without however providing the requisite means and effective assistance to enable them to do so.

Reference has already been made to the conditions under which the Republics of Armenia, Georgia and Azerbaijan were given *de facto* recognition. It was only after the defeat of Denikin's army by the Bolsheviks, in Jnauary 1920, that the Allies recognised them, on the recommendation of the British government, as independent states. This recognition, however, was not suggested by the principle of national self-determination. It was merely based on the argument that since the 'White' Russian armies had collapsed, and as neither the British, nor the French nor the Italian governments could 'spare' any forces in the Caucasus, these republics should be encouraged and helped — by arms, ammunition and foodstuff — to oppose Bolshevism. They should 'resist' the Bolsheviks, defend the Caucasus and especially 'garrison' Baku. Explaining his reasons for suggesting the *de facto* recognition of Armenia, Curzon told the Allied Representatives:

> . . . the Armenian State is prepared to join in the defence of the Trans-

29. CAB 23/21, Cab. 30(20) min. 3, 21 May 1920.

caucasian States against the Bolsheviks. Consequently, I think it would be just and wise to give it recognition . . .

In addition to recognition, Lloyd George also proposed providing these states with material help, but

> . . . on the express condition that the Caucasian States will resist the Bolsheviks and garrison Baku with all their strength.[30]

Thus, the British and Allied recognition of Armenia as a *de facto* republic was functional, and the help to be given, conditional.

Soon after, under instructions from Paris and with a view to arming and equipping the Armenian army, Captain H. Court, the British Intelligence Officer in Erevan, urgently asked the Armenian Prime Minister as well as the Minister of War, in his strictly secret and confidential letter, to put 'all [military] information' at his disposal. He 'assured' them that by so doing 'you will be acting in the interests of the Armenian Republic and that of the Allies'.[31] Armenia, with the other Caucasian republics, was simply meant to become, on the side of the Entente powers, a pawn in the struggle to contain Bolshevism.

The decision was political. The independence of the Caucasus would prevent an alliance between the Bolsheviks and the Kemalists and would also serve as a barrier against Bolshevik advance on Persia, a great 'key position' in British Imperial defence. It was on this argument that the Cabinet agreed to retain in Batum two British battalions 'as long as possible', even after the withdrawal of the British forces from the Caucasus in August 1919. Owing to the collapse of the 'White' Russian armies of Kolchak and Denikin, the Caucasus had become a 'bridge' which should be defended by the Allies to prevent the union of the 'two hordes' — the Bolsheviks and the Moslems. Curzon was a particularly strong advocate of the retention of this region as a 'barrier' against Bolshevik advance. He stressed that its collapse might have 'very far-reaching' consequences. His views were fully shared, or faithfully echoed, by Oliver Wardrop, the British High Commissioner in the area.[32]

Even after the takeover of Azerbaijan by the Bolsheviks in April 1920, and the withdrawal of British troops from Batum in June, and as late as September 1920, the Foreign Office vigorously and relentlessly urged the 'independence'[33] and anti-Bolshevik attitude of the Caucasus. Instructing

30. DBFP, vol. II, pp. 923–5, 19 Jan. 1920; ibid., pp. 725, 796–7, 10 Jan. 1920.

31. Rep. of Arm. Archives, File 334/4, Court, Erevan, true copy, 25 Jan. 1920.

32. CAB 23/21, Cab. 30(20), min. 3, 21 May 1920; DBFP, vol. II, p. 926, note by Br. Deleg. Paris, 12 Jan. 1920; ibid., vol. XII, p. 560, 9 Feb. 1920; ibid., p.604, Curzon to Adm. de Robeck, 6 May 1920; ibid., p. 574, Wardrop to Curzon, 15 Mar, 1920.

33. Rep. of Arm. Archives, File 335/5, Tilley to Aharonian, orig., 20 May 1920; 'independence' in Foreign Office phraseology apparently meant anti-Bolshevism. Neither Armenia nor Azerbaijan were ever granted *de jure* recognition. Georgia was granted it in January 1921. See DBFP, vol. XII, p. 664.

Colonel C.B. Stokes of the British High Commission in the region, Curzon gave the following 'broad lines of policy':

    a. The maintenance of the independence of the Caucasian States.
    b. The rescue, if possible of the Republics of Azerbaijan and Erivan from the influence of the Soviet Government.
    c. The moral support of Georgia while she maintains her present friendly and anti-Bolshevik attitude.[34]

Thus, to the end, the British government tried to deter the Caucasian peoples from coming to a comprehensive agreement with Soviet Russia.

But the British policy regarding the Caucasus did not rest on a solid foundation. No effective help was ever given to the republics; the policy was supported by statements and exhortations only.

British military power had flowed out into the Caucasus in late 1918 to fill in the apparent vacuum caused by the collapse of Russia in 1917 and the defeat of Germany and Turkey in 1918. Thus, British involvement in the Caucasus had been shaped more by chance than by design.[35] The withdrawal of the bulk of British troops in 1919 — mainly for financial reasons[36] — was followed by the gradual recovery and revival of Russian — now Bolshevik — power. In 1920, therefore, British authority in the Caucasus was only based on her name as a Great power. Britain, then, was in the position of contriving to give guidance but could provide no protection.

The collapse of Denikin's armies was an event of major significance in the shaping of British policy. While British politicians generally tried to build up the Caucasus with Allied arms, as a barrier against Bolshevism, the soldiers and the War Office lost, it seems, their interest and hope in the region and resigned themselves to the fact that sooner or later it would once again come, as of old, under the control of Russia — this time Bolshevik Russia. By early 1920 information from various sources indicated that the Bolsheviks were gaining ground. During a secret interview, Enver, the former Turkish War Minister, who had lately been in Russia, told Major Ivon Hedley of the British Military Mission in Berlin that the Bolsheviks 'will not be beaten'. Enver had seen both Denikin's and the Soviet armies at close quarters. On Denikin's army he had spoken contemptuously; but with the 'highest praise' for the Soviet armies.[37] Although the position of the Bolsheviks was improving, Britain could not undertake full-scale resistance against them in the Caucasus. When on 3 January 1920 Wardrop cabled

34. Ibid., p. 635, Curzon to Stokes, 13 Sept. 1920.
35. Briton Cooper Busch, *Mudros to Lausanne: Britain's Frontier in West Asia, 1918–1923* (New York, 1976), pp. 5, 390.
36. FO 371/7729/E 8378, pp. 13, 17.
37. Lloyd George Papers F/206/4/10, Hedley, Berlin, 'Notes on an Interview with Enver Pasha', 6 Jan. 1920.

Curzon about the possibility of the complete collapse of Denikin and the urgent need of at least a division of thoroughly equipped troops at Batum, Churchill, the Secretary for War saw 'of course no possibility' for such a measure. Even the withdrawal of the British troops there must soon be considered, he wrote.[38]

Sir Henry Wilson argued that as it was 'impossible' to employ two divisions to keep the command of the Caspian Sea, it was an 'impossibility' for Britain to stand on the forward lines in defence of India. The only possible line was the railheads of the systems of Palestine, Mesopotamia and India. He therefore insisted that British policy should be adjusted to this possible line of defence — thus discarding the Caucasus. The Treasury was relentlessly pressing for economy and the Cabinet had taken the decision to allow only a total of £75 million to both the War Office and the Air Ministry. But to keep in the Caucasus the effective two divisions would cost £50-60 million per year. Therefore Sir Henry Wilson insisted that:

> . . . what is essential is *concentration* of forces in theatres vital to us, viz. England, Ireland, Egypt, India, Mesopotamia, in that order.

He was convinced that if Denikin fell, the Bolsheviks 'would certainly take Baku'. It was useless, he believed, to arm the Caucasian states since all the arms would become presents to the Bolsheviks. As Britain and the Allies were not able to exercise effective power, he was reconciled as early as January 1920, to the Caucasus, 'Georgia and Azerbaijan [going] Bolshevik'. Britain would even have to clear out of Persia, he believed.[39]

Thus, after the defeat of Denikin, and from the beginning of 1920, the CIGS clearly saw no hope whatsoever that the Caucasus could withstand the advance of Bolshevism without the presence there of two Allied divisions. Marshal Foch agreed.[40] But neither the Cabinet nor the War Office could spare two divisions for the Caucasus.

Even some Cabinet members admitted that the decision of British military withdrawal from the Caucasus and later from the Caspian had rendered inevitable the loss of British and Allied control throughout these regions and it was better to recognise this inevitable march of events. It was pointed out that once the Bolsheviks had taken command of the Caspian Sea, the whole situation had changed: the limited British forces only remained in North Persia 'on sufferance of the Bolsheviks'.[41]

Therefore, starting in January 1920, the CIGS and at least some members

---

38. Curzon Papers, MSS Eur. F 112/279, Wardrop to Curzon, 3 Jan. 1920; ibid., Churchill to Curzon, n.d. [Jan. 1920].
39. Callwell, *Wilson*, II, pp. 221–2, 224, entries for 12, 19 Jan. 1920. Ibid., p. 208, Aug. 1919, (n.d.); ibid., p. 253, entry for 15 July 1920.
40. Ibid., p. 224, entry for 19 Jan. 1920.
41. CAB 23/21, Cab. 24(20), min. 1, 5 May 1920; ibid., Cab. 30(20), min. 3, 21 May 1920.

of the Cabinet were convinced that the fall of the Caucasus to Soviet rule was inevitable.

Nevertheless, the Foreign Office under Curzon rigorously exhorted its political representatives in the Caucasus to urge the republics to resist Bolshevik influence as long as possible; and the British representatives followed their instructions over-zealously. The republics should be made to act as a barrier. But Lloyd George's proposal and the decision of the Supreme Council of January 1920, to provide the Caucasian states with arms, ammunition and foodstuff, remained mostly ineffectual. Around mid-April the Allies had still not sent any arms or other military supplies to Armenia. It was indeed found that the arms available for the three republics were 'very limited'. Britain could therefore furnish only a comparatively small proportion of the total required, Curzon cabled. It was recognised, however, that the need of Armenia was greatest as she would also have to defend herself against the Turks.[42]

If surplus arms were not available in abundance, neither was money. Armenia's request for a loan of £1 million sterling was turned down by Curzon. The Treasury was not prepared to ask Parliament to sanction any loan to the Caucasian republics. Neither flour nor arms could be sent to the Caucasus because the three republics had no sterling credit. 'Everything is dependent on and held up by [the] financial question' Lord Hardinge cabled Curzon at San Remo. Both the Treasury and the War Office were insisting on previous payments with 'interest' and were refusing future credits based on exports. The Foreign Office had been in communication with the War Office 'for two months' regarding the despatch of officers to the Caucasus. But it would express no opinion about military advisers for Armenia pending 'full information' as to the funds available there to cover the expenditure incurred. Only on 20 April the War Office had stated that it had no objection to providing officers for the Caucasus provided 'no expenses fall on Army funds'.[43]

Thus, neither arms nor military advisers were despatched to the Caucasus until late April 1920; and the Cabinet was fully aware of this state of affairs.[44] Financial stringency overshadowed all aspects of policy, especially as regards an area which the military authorities believed was not vital for the defence of the Empire.

But during all this time the Caucasian republics were being urged incessantly by British politicians to resist Bolshevism. Bonar Law, the Leader of the House of Commons, publicly stated, on 24 February 1920, that if Soviet Russia attacked her border states — whose independence or *de facto*

42. DBFP, vol. XII, pp. 590–1, Curzon to Wardrop and to Derby, 12, 13 Apr. 1920.
43. Rep. of Arm. Archives, File 334/4, Tilley to Malcolm, orig., FO, 26 Feb 1920; DBFP, vol. XII, p. 572, Curzon to Wardrop, 3 Mar. 1920; ibid., pp. 595–6, Hardinge to Curzon, 22 Apr. 1920.
44. CAB 23/21, Cab. 24(20), min. 1, 5 May 1920.

autonomy the Entente powers had recognised — 'the Allies will give them every possible support'.[45] Referring to this statement, Wardrop cabled Curzon:

> I do not believe Georgian and Azerbaijan Governments will come to an agreement with Soviet if Allies fulfil pledge given on February 24th . . .
>
> If this pledge is unfulfilled, policy I have been endeavouring to carry out, believing it to be that of Your Lordship, will have ended in failure . . .

On 18 April, the Foreign Minister of Azerbaijan called on Wardrop and expressed his grave fears of Bolshevik attack. Wardrop referred to the statement of 24 February when 'every possible support' was promised by the Supreme Council.[46] Yet Curzon cabled in no uncertain words:

> There is no question of our giving Georgia and Azerbaijan active military support in case of an attack on them by Soviet forces, and you should be careful not to put any such interpretation on Mr. Bonar Law's statement of February 24th.

Again, when General Milne directly asked whether the Allies were going to try 'to prevent' the advance of the Reds into Georgia by force of arms, the Foreign Office replied:

> . . it is not part of the policy of H[is] M[ajesty's] G[overnment] to prevent by force of arms the advance of the Bolsheviks into Georgia.[47]

In April, Bolshevik troops entered Azerbaijan.

Evidently, Bonar Law's public promise of 'every possible support' did not mean effective help.

The Georgians and the Armenians increased their requests for arms. But Curzon cabled Commander H.C. Luke, the Acting British High Commissioner in the Caucasus — for his 'own information' — that among the difficulties in complying with the request was the question of payment: Parliament and public opinion would not support the gift of arms. Curzon added:

> We cannot definitely promise but if you think effect would encourage the Government and people you are authorised to state that we are doing all we can.[48]

---

45. *Hansard*, 5th Ser. 1920, vol. 125, cols. 1501–2.
46. DBFP, vol. XII, pp. 583, 593, Wardrop to Curzon, 1 Apr., 18 Apr. 1920.
47. Ibid., p. 599, Curzon to Wardrop, 27 Apr. 1920; ibid., p. 585, Milne to WO, 4 Apr. 1920 and fn. 8, FO to WO, 14 Apr. 1920.
48. Ibid., p. 605, Curzon to Adm. Webb for Luke, 10 May 1920.

Thus, the representative of the British government in the Caucasus was authorised 'to encourage' — by statements — without however 'definitely' making any promise for arms.

Britain's dilemma between maintaining her control and influence in the Caucasus, and, the necessity of retrenchment, was manifest over Batum. It was recognised in the Cabinet that its retention, as long as possible, was desirable in order to avoid an alliance between the Kemalists and the Bolsheviks and to prevent Georgia becoming Bolshevik. It was also needed as a port for the passage of arms to Armenia. Batum was, in the first half of 1920, a symbol of the British and Allied interest in the Middle East. On the other hand, however, the Cabinet was well aware of the 'popular dissatisfaction' with Britain's expenditure on military adventures in the various centres in the Caucasus, at a time when economy was urgently necessary and when Britain was very much in need of troops for Ireland. It was also admitted in the Cabinet that it might be possible to hold Batum for a few weeks more without 'disaster', but sooner or later it would have to be evacuated.[49]

Both France and Italy had promised to send one battalion each to Batum. But France sent, late in the day, an Algerian, instead of the promised white battalion. Italy absolutely declined to implement her promise.[50]

On 28 June 1920 the British authorities handed over Batum to the Georgians and started to withdraw their two battalions. One of the considerations for this decision was the Bolshevik advance to the Caspian and their seizure of Baku. In late May the Cabinet had accepted the military advice that Britain should no longer hold the forward defence lines of India.[51] British presence in the Caucasus was not feasible any more.

The withdrawal of the British garrison from Batum meant severing the last link between Armenia and the West.[52] No Allied or British forces were left in the region. The presence of the Entente powers in the Caucasus became, therefore, nominal from the end of June 1920.

The sudden and unannounced departure of William Haskell, the Allied High Commissioner for Relief, from the Caucasus further added to the sense of abandonment in Armenia. Certain sections had concluded that the Allies were deserting Armenia, the Reverend H.W. Harcourt (the Anglican Chaplain in Transcaucasia, 1920-4 and agent of the Armenian Refugees (Lord Mayor's) Fund in Armenia), reported from Erevan. However, Haskell's departure was connected with relief. He had been diverting 'all' the available flour earmarked for Armenia to the government of Azerbaijan 'in return for cash payment'. When he had learnt of the impending visit of

---

49. CAB 23/21, Cab. 30(20), min. 3, 21 May 1920; ibid., Cab. 24(20), min. 1, 5 May 1920; ibid., Cab. 33(20), conclusions of meeting of Cab., min. 5, 7 June 1920.
50. Ibid., Cab. 30(20), min. 3, 21 May 1920.
51. Ibid.
52. A.J. Toynbee, *The Western Question in Greece and Turkey* (London, 1922), p. 368.

auditors, he had apparently removed all his records and tried to smash the whole organisation in order to make any inquiry impossible. Referring to this sudden decision, Commander Luke also believed it was not a little embarrassing that Haskell should have evacuated his staff without any notice to the Allied Missions.[53]

In the meantime, while British and Allied power was definitely ebbing in the Caucasus, that of Soviet Russia was rising. One of her main targets was Baku, on whose oil, as motive power, her industries were largely dependent. G.V. Chicherin, the Commissar for Foreign Affairs, had referred to it as one of the most important cities of the Russian republic and had renounced the Treaty of Brest-Litovsk immediately after the Turks had seized it in September 1918. 'Does not Soviet Russia need Baku oil as man needs air?' one of her leaders would ask in 1921.[54]

From mid-January 1920 the Bolsheviks had been gradually consolidating their position in this region. They had first occupied Trans-Caspia, and then had captured Derbent on the Caspian Sea. On 28 April their troops entered Baku. The new Soviet administration declared all relationship with the Entente to be at an end.[55] On the same day Commander Luke wired Captain G.F. Gracey, the Chief Commissioner's representative in Armenia, to be ready to leave Erevan if necessary.[56] As seen above, in June 1920 the British authorities withdrew from Batum.

Thus, by the summer of 1920, Soviet Russia was clearly poised to become the potential master of the Caucasus. According to H.A.L. Fisher, then President of the Board of Education, all the indications were pointing to a steady increase in the 'weight and authority' of the Soviet government in Russia. As to Soviet military power in the Caucasus, the General Officer Commanding-in-Chief, Mesopotamia, reported, referring to the 11th Bolshevik Army, that the discipline, equipment and the clothing of the troops were very good. The army officers, however, were untrained. The Bolsheviks had taken over large consignments of arms recently sold by the Italians to Azerbaijan.[57] Thus, when British forces finally withdrew in the summer of 1920, the Russians were ready to step into their place in the Caucasus.

53. FO 371/4942/E7619, Harcourt, Erevan, 21 May 1920. Harry C. Luke, *Cities and Men* (London, 1953), II, p. 146 quot. diary, entry for 5 May 1920; For Hubert Wm. Harcourt, see Crockford's *Clerical Directory*, 1910–33.

54. WO 106/1396, Milne to CIGS, 6 Feb. 1919; Jane Degras (ed.), *Soviet Documents on Foreign Policy* (Oxford, 1951), I, p.110, Chicherin to Turkish F. Minist., 20 Sept. 1918; X.J. Eudin and R.C. North, *Soviet Russia and the East 1920–1927: A Documentary Survey* (Stanford, 1957), p. 57, Ordzhonikidze, Tiflis, Dec. 1921.

55. WO 106/330 no. 186, Gen. Staff, Jan. 1920, n.d.; WO 106/349, 25th ser. no. 28, 16 Apr. 1920; ibid., 26th ser. no. 3, 5 May 1920.

56. Luke, *Cities and Men*, II, p. 139, quot. diary entry for 28 Apr. 1920.

57. Lloyd George Papers, F/16/7/56, Fisher to Lloyd George, 26 May 1920. FO 371/4942/E7446/E7588, GOC Mesopotamia to WO, copy, 24 June 1920, and Army Council to FO, 1 July 1920.

The earlier vacuum in the Caucasus, created by the collapse of Russian power following the October Revolution, had only been filled 'in form' by the newly-born independent local republics: 'in reality' by the military power first of Germany and Turkey, and then of Britain.[58] Neither were these republics able to fill the new vacuum created by the British withdrawal. Divergences of interest and a morbid nationalism made even an elementary agreement impossible between them and contributed to their weakness.

After the British withdrawal, therefore, Soviet Russia and a reviving Turkey were the only two powers which could fill that vacuum. But somehow, Armenia could not come to an accommodation with either of these states, which alone had a real presence around her. Between Armenia and Turkey there stood the spectre of the Treaty of Sèvres; and between Armenia and Soviet Russia there hung Armenia's illusory hope of support from the Allies.

On their part the British authorities never stopped providing guidance and advice to Armenia, even when they completely lacked any solid basis of actual power and when they could give her no protection whatsoever. They encouraged Armenia to rely on Britain, and indirectly — sometimes directly — deterred her from coming to terms with Soviet Russia. Thus on the very day that the agreement finalising the evacuation of British troops from Batum was signed, Colonel Stokes recommended to Curzon that the British government should give 'hard-pressed' Armenia and Georgia some sign of encouragement lest the evacuation be interpreted as their final abandonment by Britain. Colonel Stokes requested, with the entire concurrence of the Chief British Commissioner, that:

> A communication be made to Armenian and Georgian Governments that His Majesty's Government continue to take keenest interest in welfare of two Republics and will afford them all possible moral and political support.
>
> ....
>
> That *de jure* recognition be granted to Armenia and Georgia forthwith.

The above suggestions would 'encourage' the two states ' to hold out (? to the last) against Bolshevism'. Stokes concluded in a revealing note: 'They entail no call on British exchequer'. In his reply Curzon authorised that the suggested announcement be made to the Armenian and Georgian governments. The question of *de jure* recognition would be discussed by the Allies.[59]

This was the so-called British policy against the spread of Bolshevism in the Caucasus: providing 'moral' support without any call on the British 'exchequer' as evidence of 'keenest interest'. Such a policy completely

58. E.H. Carr, *The Bolshevik Revolution 1917–1923* (London, 1950–3), I, p. 345.
59. FO 371/4942/E7467, Luke to FO, encl. report from Stokes, 28 June 1920; DBFP, vol XII, p. 630, Curzon to Hardinge, 4 July 1920.

disregarded the fundamental changes in the bases of power taking place in the Caucasus. But it also contributed to Armenia's illusions and to her actual — and fatal — isolation.

The withdrawal of the British troops from the Caucasus had marked the renewal of hostilities between Azerbaijan and Armenia over Karabagh and the other disputed territories of Zangezur and Nakhichevan. Fighting had again broken out along the frontier in April 1920. All the efforts of the Allied representatives had been so far without result. So, a few days later when Azerbaijan became a Soviet republic, the new rulers sent an ultimatum to Armenia demanding the withdrawal of the latter's regular troops within three days from Karabagh and Zangezur. Failing compliance, the Soviet Azerbaijani troops would invade Armenia. But such a move would endanger the security of Persia, as Commander Luke reported to the Foreign Office. Armenia rejected the ultimatum and again applied to the Entente for assistance. At long last munitions were shipped for her by the War Office to Batum. But Armenia was also being hampered from inside. Tatar bands were active on the Julfa-Erevan railway, which was only kept open by patrols. According to the General Staff, it was feared that the attack on Armenia from the north by the Bolshevik and Azerbaijani troops would be carried out in conjunction with a Turkish attack from the south.[60]

Such action by the two outcast powers, Turkey and Soviet Russia, was a possibility.

Since October 1919 Mustafa Kemal had set himself, in defiance of the Ottoman government, in the district of Erzerum, to organise resistance to all forms of foreign interference, and chiefly to the formation of an independent Armenian state within 'Turkish boundaries'.[61] According to Lieutenant-Colonel A. Rawlinson, who was a prisoner in Erzerum from March 1920, when the Supreme Council at San Remo made known that certain portions of eastern Anatolia were to be given to Armenia, preparations for a 'military offensive' were evident. Recruits, conscripted from all parts of the country, constantly arrived at the fortress of Erzerum and machine-gun practice and drill of all kinds were carried on every day from sunrise to sunset.[62]

Nationalist Turkey was determined to sabotage the Peace Treaty being imposed by the Entente.

The Nationalist movement was 'created' by the Greek landing in Smyrna in 1919, Toynbee wrote after his eight months' study trip to Greece and

60. WO 106/330/200, Gen. Staff, 22 Apr. 1920. Ibid., no. 202, Gen. Staff, 6 May 1920; DBFP, vol. XII, p. 602, Luke to Curzon, 1 May 1920; WO 106/330/203, Gen. Staff, 13 May 1920.
61. WO 106/349, 22nd ser. no. 37, 'Summary of Intelligence', 27 Oct. 1919.
62. A. Rawlinson, *Adventures in the Near East 1918–1922* (London, 1923), pp. 295–6.

Turkey in 1921. 'We must let the Greeks occupy Smyrna', Lloyd George had proposed and President Wilson and Clemenceau had agreed to use the Greek forces for frustrating the Italian designs in Anatolia and also for controlling the Turks. The Greeks would substitute the forces which the Allies were neither able nor willing to send themselves.[63] In return the Allies, and especially the British Prime Minister, wished to support the Greek territorial claims. Lloyd George firmly believed that a friendly Greece dominant in the eastern Mediterranean at the expense of Turkey, and flanking the main communications through the Suez Canal with India and the Far East, would be an invaluable advantage to the British Empire. Lloyd George's dislike of the Turk was unalloyed: he argued that the Turk was a continual source of trouble in Europe and Asia. Britain and France had kept the 'wretched' Turkish Empire alive again and again. But as soon as the war broke out the Turks had betrayed them shamefully.[64]

On 16 March 1920 strong British forces occupied Constantinople in the hope of crushing the nationalist agitation. It was at this stage that Kemal showed his astute abilities in diplomacy. He perceived and exploited in a masterly way the rivalry and the differences of policy between Britain, France and Italy over the Middle East and the greater chasm that separated the Western powers from Soviet Russia. Kemal would negotiate alternately with Russia and the West, or simultaneously with both; and he would use any advantage that he won on one side to force concessions on the other.[65] Turkey's unequalled strategic position was of course, as always, a tremendous asset.

Kemal swiftly reacted to the British occupation of Constantinople by formally disowning the authority of the Turkish government in Constantinople, and by calling for elections to a Grand National Assembly which proclaimed him head of government. Soon after, on 26 April, it was Kemal who sent a note to the Soviet government expressing

. . . the desire to enter into regular relations with it and to take part in the struggle against foreign imperialism which threatens both countries.[66]

Soviet Russia was another power equally determined to undermine the Entente which had tried to strangle her through intervention and economic

---

63. Toynbee, *Western Question*, p. 312; P. Mantoux (ed.), *Les Délibérations du Conseil des Quatre* (Paris, 1955), I, pp. 60, 485–6, quoted in R.A.C. Parker, *Europe 1919–45* (London, 1969), pp. 36–7.

64. Winston S. Churchill, *The World Crisis – The Aftermath* (London, 1929), p. 391. DBFP, vol. VIII, pp. 446, 846.

65. Roderic H. Davison, 'Turkish Diplomacy from Mudros to Lausanne' in Craig and Gilbert (eds.), *The Diplomats* (2nd edn.), p. 173.

66. Quot. in Carr, *Bolshevik Revolution*, vol. 3, p. 248; WO 106/349, 26th ser. no. 19, 'Summary of Intellig.' quot. Chicherin acknowledging Kemal's letter. See also, Mustafa Kemal, *A Speech Delivered by Ghazi Mustapha Kemal, President of the Turkish Republic, October 1927* (Leipzig, 1929), p. 396.

blockade. Hostility against the Entente was, therefore, a common interest which would bring the two powers closer together. For Turkey the co-operation of Soviet Russia would be a morale-booster. She might also hope for munitions from Russia in the same way as the Greeks were receiving them from the Allies.[67] Moreover if the Soviets supported her, Kemalist Turkey would feel secure on her northern and north-eastern frontier while she fought the Greeks and the Allies to her south and west. At a time when there were still French troops in Cilicia, Greek troops in south Anatolia and British and Allied forces in Constantinople, Kemalist Turkey simply could not afford to have a hostile Russia on her north. In August 1920 a confidential British military intelligence report stated:

> The Angora Nationalists, as a result of the Greek successes, are becoming more ready to treat with the Bolsheviks . . .

> The Nationalist move *re* Mosul and increasing pro-Bolshevik propaganda are probably intended to draw the Bolsheviks to their assistance.[68]

It was certainly Kemal's own brilliant doing that he was not left in diplomatic isolation. He simply made use of the political power of Turkey's northerly neighbour.

Soviet Russia, on her side, would benefit from supporting Turkey. Co-operation would ensure the expulsion of Allied and mainly British influence from both the Black Sea and Transcaucasia, influence which had been used for equipping the 'White' Russian armies. Russia was also willing to back Turkey against Greece in order to deter her from purchasing the backing of any of the Western powers who were Russia's enemies. Above all, by supporting Turkey, Soviet Russia tried to assume the role of champion of Islam — a role left vacant by Britain. After the Russian defection in the war following the Revolution Britain was suddenly left as the protagonist fighting Turkey and conspicuously the chief Empire still possessing dominion over Islamic peoples. Soviet Russia could now exploit that situation. In her diplomatic war against the Entente, and especially Britain, she tried to undermine the foundations of British imperialism among the Islamic peoples in Mesopotamia, Persia, Afghanistan and India by revolutionary propaganda. She did this with the help of Islamic Turkey.[69] Furthermore, Turkey and Soviet Russia needed, and sought, each other's co-operation, to help consolidate their position in the Caucasus, a region left with a power

67. Toynbee, *Western Question*, p. 313.
68. WO 106/349, Directorate of Milit. Ops. and Intellig. 27th ser. no. 14, 27 Aug. 1920.
69. A.J. Toynbee and K.P. Kirkwood, *Turkey* (London, 1926), pp. 65, 122; Toynbee, *Western Question*, p. 42; See R.G. Hovannisian, 'Armenia and the Caucasus in the Genesis of the Soviet-Turkish Entente', *International Journal of Middle East Studies*, vol. 4 (1973), pp. 129–47. See also, FO 371/4959/E10734, Arm. Dipl. Rep. Tiflis, to Luke, 14 Aug. 1920, encl. in Luke to Curzon, 16 Aug. 1920.

vacuum after the British withdrawal.

Both countries gained from their mutual co-operation since it gave them a position of additional importance for bringing pressure to bear on the Entente. Both could extort some kind of recognition from the West. Thus, concessions to Turkey, aimed at detaching her from Bolshevik Russia, were strongly urged on the British government both by the Secretary for War and the Secretary for India. On the other hand the Cabinet, recognising the 'difficulties' the Bolsheviks were making for the British all over the East, agreed that advantage should be taken of the forthcoming conversations with Krassin, of the Soviet Trade Delegation in London, to clear up the position in the Middle East.[70]

In 1920 both Soviet Russia and Kemalist Turkey probably considered the Caucasian republics, forming a wedge between them and enjoying the patronage of the Supreme Council, as potential centres of hostile foreign influence. According to a Foreign Office paper, the Soviet government could not have failed to deduce that the republics were meant as a buffer between Bolshevism and the East, since the Allies had recognised their independence only after the definite failure of the 'Russian reactionary movements'.[71] Soviet Russia, therefore, would naturally work with Turkey to see the influence of the Entente removed from the Caucasus, including Armenia.

But, this co-operation was not unqualified. As Arnold Toynbee maintained in 1922, Soviet Russia also 'backed' to a limited extent the Armenian Republic of Erevan

. . . against both Turkey and Azerbaijan, as a barrier between possible Turkish 'Pan-Turanian' ambitions and the oil-fields of Baku.[72]

Evidently, Moscow and Angora co-operated together in excluding all Western powers from the settlement of the Caucasus, but at the same time they 'competed' in extending their own control in the area. Some such competition between the two contestants for power in the region was bound to happen naturally. Rivalry was 'still very much alive'; Russia would not willingly allow a Turkish hegemony extending from Anatolia to the Black and Caspian Seas. Thus, on 9 October 1920, Lenin referred to Turkey's attack on Armenia and to its aim at acquiring Batum and Baku and advised maximum precaution. On 21 November he considered the situation in the Caucasus very complicated and contemplated the possibility of 'war'; and on 10 December 1920 Chicherin, the Commisar for Foreign Affairs, clearly

70. CAB 24/117, C.P. 2387, memo., 16 Dec. 1920. Lloyd George Papers F/40/3/2, Montagu to Lloyd George, 20 Jan. 1920. CAB 23/21, Cab. 30(20) min. 3, 21 May 1920.
71. Carr, *Bolshevik Revolution*, III, p. 248; FO 371/7729/38378, Childs and McDonnell, 'Outline of Events in Trans-Caucasia . . . ', pp. 21–2, FO, 31 May 1922.
72. Toynbee, *Western Question*, p. 42.

indicated that the acquisition of Batum by Turkey was 'unacceptable'.[73] A British intelligence report for November 1920 also stated that the temper of the Russians towards the Kemalists 'is in any case one of covert distrust'. One of the major objects for Soviet Russia's recovery of Baku, at a time when she was fully occupied with her war against Poland, but which admitted of no delay, seems indeed to have been the 'destruction of the Mahommedan *bloc,* in process of formation under Turkish guidance . . .' a Foreign Office paper, in its turn, claimed.[74]

Could the Armenian leadership make use of this undercurrent of power struggle within the Caucasus? If it did not, perhaps British diplomacy was partly to blame. It seems that Armenia's attempts to come to terms with her neighbours remained half-hearted at all times.

Armenia had of necessity to come to terms with Soviet power, especially after the sovietisation of Azerbaijan. She wholly depended on the fuel oil from Baku for her trains. The change of administration had resulted in a total stoppage of services, including the failure of electricity throughout Armenia. In addition, Soviet Azerbaijan had sent, as seen above, an ultimatum to Armenia demanding the withdrawal of her regular troops from both Karabagh and Zangezur. It seems that Moslem Azerbaijan, with her newly acquired power, was keen on settling her old territorial scores. Moreoever, these two districts were the only obstacles preventing an alliance between the Bolsheviks and the Turkish Nationalists.[75] According to Toynbee, it was especially desirable for Turkey to have an overland route for communication with Soviet Russia for the purpose of obtaining munitions for her struggle against Greece. The sole 'barrier' was the Erevan republic.[76] The Black Sea was under British control. So Armenia was under pressure from Moslem-inhabited provinces on all sides of her border.

On 30 April 1920, a three-man delegation left Erevan for Moscow. Levon Shant, the author and playwright, was the leader of the delegation, whose other members were Levon Zarafian and Hambardzum Terterian. It was authorised to sign a treaty by which Soviet Russia would (a) recognise the independence of Armenia, including Karabagh, (b) accept at least in principle the notion of the annexation of Turkish-Armenian provinces by Armenia and (c) refrain from intervention in the internal policy of Armenia, either directly or indirectly.[7]

73. Davison, 'Turkish Diplomacy . . . ', p. 186; Carr, *Bolshevik Revolution*, vol. III, p. 248; also ibid., I, p. 346, J.S. Kirakosian (ed.), *Hayastane Mijazcayin Divanacitutyan ev Sovetakan Artakin Kaghakakanutyan Pastateghterurm, 1828–1923* (Armenia in the Documents of International Diplomacy and Soviet Foreign Policy, 1828–1923 (Erevan, 1972), pp. 455-6, 460, 465.

74. CAB 24/117, C.P. 2352, Directorate of Intellig. 'A Monthly Review of Revol. Movements', no. 25, p. 30, Nov. 1920. FO 371/7729/E8378, p. 22.

75. Luke, *Cities and Men*, II, p. 178. Kajaznuni, *H.H. Dashnaktsutiune*, p. 67. WO 106/349, 26th ser. no. 3, 'Summary of Intellig', 5 May 1920.

76. Toynbee, *Western Question*, p. 313; Toynbee and Kirkwood, *Turkey*, p. 124.

77. Vratsian, *Hayastani Hanrapetutiun* p. 406.

During the first meeting with the delegation, Chicherin stressed, according to Terterian, that Russo-Turkish co-operation was a matter of life and
death for Soviet Russia. Turkey was prepared to attack the Allies but was
afraid that Armenia would strike her in the rear. Hence the Soviet government desired to reconcile Armenia to Turkey. At another meeting in June,
Chicherin on 'behalf of Soviet Russia' 'promised to satisfy the Armenians' by
annexing to Armenia certain territories of Turkish Armenia and securing for
her an exit to the Black Sea. As to the question of the boundary with
Azerbaijan: Zangezur and Nakhichevan would be declared Armenian territories but Karabagh's legal status would be decided after a referendum.
Armenia would also receive gratis from Soviet Russia about ten locomotives
as well as a sum of 2½ million gold rubles as an aid. This oral agreement was
to be put in writing. But the signing of the treaty was postponed.[78]

Internal feuds in Armenia prevented any real improvement in Soviet-
Armenian relations. On 1 May, just after the sovietisation of Azerbaijan,
Armenian Communists made an abortive attempt in Alexandropol to take
over the country. The Armenian government 'executed seventeen ring-
leaders'.[79] Those who escaped to Baku were trying to defeat the Russo-
Armenian negotiations in Moscow, according to Terterian, by their reports
of persecution in Armenia.[80]

Towards the end of June the Armenian delegation was presented with
another proposal: Karabagh would go to Azerbaijan, Nakhichevan to
Armenia, while Zangezur would be a disputed territory, its final fate to be
decided later. This would have assured, first, the Soviet's official recognition
of the independence of Armenia, and second, Nakhichevan's becoming a
part of Armenia. Zarafian and Terterian wanted to sign the Armeno-
Russian friendship treaty 'at once', and regarded the disputability of
Zangezur and Karabagh as temporary. They feared that if the matter
'dragged on', they would lose 'a golden opportunity'. But they failed to
persuade Levon Shant,[81] and referred to Erevan for advice.

The draft agreement was soon prepared and the treaty would be signed
'the minute' the Armenian government gave its assent. But the reply from
Erevan was 'delayed'. After a 'long waiting', the delegation finally received
two telegrams. It was instructed to protest to the Soviet government at the
brutal murder by Bolsheviks in Goris, Zangezur, of two members of the
ruling Dashnak party who were also members of the Armenian Parliament.
The other telegram instructed the delegation in 'no uncertain tones' 'to

78. H. Terterian, 'The Levon Chanth Mission to Moscow', Part I, *Armenian Review*, vol. 8
(June 1955), pp. 8, 13.

79. Luke, *Cities and Men*, II, p. 154, quot. diary entry for 15 June 1920. Vratsian, *Hayastani
Hanrapetutiun*, gives the number of those condemned to death as 'not over ten' on p. 369, and
as 'three' on p. 406.

80. *Armenian Review*, vol. 8 (June 1955), p.13 (Terterian); see also Vratsian, ibid., pp. 406,
409.

81. *Armenian Review*, vol. 8 (June 1955), pp. 14–15 (Terterian).

insist' not only on the annexation of Mountainous Karabagh but also of Lower Karabagh. The claim to Lower Karabagh was, according to Terterian, 'a new issue', and the members of the delegation were 'greatly surprised' by this 'novel' instruction. They finally came to the conclusion that the victorious Allies must have given Armenia 'definite assurances as regards the Bolsheviks'; and that the Armenian government by raising the issue of Lower Karabagh wanted 'to drag out' the conversations with Moscow. The delegation left the Russian capital on 10 August without concluding any agreement.

A Turkish delegation, headed by Bekir Sami, the Commissar for Foreign Affairs in Kemal's government, and representing the Turkish National Grand Assembly, was likewise in Moscow at the same time as the Armenian delegation. It was also trying to negotiate a friendship treaty with Soviet Russia. Zarafian and Terterian considered it desirable that their delegation should have some special interviews with the Turkish delegation with a view to settling their mutual disputes. But Levon Shant vigorously opposed the idea.[52] Thus up to the summer of 1920 it had not been possible for Armenia to come to an understanding either with Soviet Russia or with Turkey: the very states surrounding her, with one or both of which, good relations were imperative.

When the Turkish delegation left Moscow, they too had not signed a treaty: most significantly, the main obstacle had been the Soviet insistence on Turkish concessions to Armenia.[83]

Terterian rightly thinks that the prospect of the definitive peace treaty caused such enthusiasm among the leaders in Erevan that they ignored the presence of the Red divisions in the Caucasus and 'underestimated' the role of Russia in the solution of the Armenian question. Thus, exaggerated Armenian hopes in far-away Allies, ill-feeling between the Dashnaks and the Bolsheviks, the passionate belief of the British officers in the Caucasus that horrors and misery accompanied Bolshevism,[84] and their exhortations to the Armenian government to resist concessions to Soviet Russia, all contributed to the failure of an early Armeno-Soviet understanding. Terterian has also pointed out that certain government and party circles in Armenia were misled by Armenia's purchase — in July — of British arms into underrating Kemal's military power. They believed that in a clash the Armenian divisions could easily occupy Erzerum.[85]

In the meantime, events marched on in the Caucasus. When Armenia

82. Ibid., pp. 20–1 and 11–12 (Terterian).
83. Mustafa Kemal, *A Speech*, p. 415; Kirakosian, *Hayastane Pastateghterum*, p. 481; Davison, 'Turkish Diplomacy . . . ', p. 185; Carr, *Bolshevik Revolution*, III, p. 250.
84. *Armenian Review*, vol. 8 (Sept. 1955), p. 97 (Terterian, Part II); FO 371/4942/E7467, Stokes in Luke to FO, 28 June 1920.
85. The reference is to the Armenian government and the ruling Dashnak party. *Armenian Review*, vol. 8 (Sept. 1955), p. 97 (Terterian, Part II).

rejected, as seen above, the ultimatum from Soviet Azerbaijan to withdraw her forces from both Karabagh and Zangezur, the Soviet troops marched in, and the Armenians suffered a series of military reverses. The Armenian government was forced to stop the hostilities. An agreement, signed in Tiflis on 10 August 1920 between A. Jamalian and A. Babalian on behalf of the Republic of Armenia, and B.V. Legrand, the representative of Soviet Russia, provided for the 'provisional' occupation by the Soviet Russian troops of Karabagh, Zangezur and Nakhichevan — described in the Text as 'the regions under dispute'. According to Article 3, this temporary occupation was to be undertaken by the Soviet Russian Republic in order to create favourable conditions for the peaceful solution of the territorial disputes between Armenia and Azerbaijan. Article 5 specified that the railway line between Shakhtakhti and Julfa was to be controlled by the Armenian government on condition that it would not be used for military purposes.[86]

Why had Russian Bolshevik troops moved in — provisionally — to Karabagh, Zangezur and Nakhichevan? Perhaps it was in order to effect an alliance with the Kemalists; or to stop the inter-racial hostilities between the Armenians and the Azerbaijanis, although the Armenian diplomatic representative in Tiflis dismissed these preventive measures as a pretext.[87] Most probably the Soviet troops moved in to bring pressure to bear on Armenia and to conclude with her a peace treaty as soon as possible. It seems that Soviet Russia was anxious to wean Armenia away from the Entente and herself to arbitrate on the territorial disputes in the Caucasus. Thus, Article 3 of the Agreement explicitly referred to creating the conditions for resolving the territorial disputes on the bases of the peace treaty, which should be concluded between Soviet Russia and the Republic of Armenia 'as soon as possible'.[88] The provisional occupation of the provinces was meant to be an exertion on, and an inducement to, Armenia to reorientate her policy. Could she do this?

Ironically, the Tiflis Agreement was signed on 10 August: the very day Aharonian in Paris signed the Treaty of Sèvres — the treaty which promised so much to Armenia.

In the Caucasus, therefore, there was strong pressure on Armenia from Soviet Russia which seemed anxious to establish her power in the region as quickly as possible. But pressure was also brought to bear from the British side: Britain seemed equally anxious to retain her power for as long as possible.

The Armenian representatives in Tiflis tried in vain to explain to Com-

---

86. FO 371/4959/E10726, French transl. of 'Text of Agreement bet. Armenian and Soviet Govts. respecting Provisional Occupation of Karabagh, Zangezur and Nakhichevan by Russian Bolshevik Troops', encl. 2 in no. 1, Luke to Curzon, 11 Aug. 1920; also in ibid., E11703, encl. 2 in no. 1, Gracey to Luke, 19 Aug. 1920.
87. Ibid., no. E10734, Arm. Rep. to Luke, 14 Aug. 1920, in Luke to Curzon, 16 Aug. 1920.
88. Ibid., no. E10726, French transl. of text, encl. in Luke to Curzon, 11 Aug. 1920.

mander Luke that the agreement with Soviet Russia was only signed because Armenia was for the time being at the end of her powers of resistance. They also pointed out that Armenia was retaining Shakhtakhti with access to Persia, together with her control of the railway as far as Julfa near the Persian frontier — of interest to Britain. But in Erevan, Captain Gracey, the Chief Commissioner's representative, told Dr Hamo Ohandjanian, the Prime Minister and Minister for Foreign Affairs, that the agreement would be received 'very unfavourably' in Britain.[89] Commander Luke was particularly severe. He considered the agreement as a betrayal of trust on the part of Armenia and an act of treachery against Britain. As he reported to Curzon, he had referred

> . . . in strong terms to the painful impression which this act on the part of Armenia, amounting in effect to a betrayal of trust, was bound to make on His Majesty's Government, who would . . . feel that they had been ill repaid for their help to Armenia in the matter of munitions and otherwise.

Again, he had stressed that

> . . . the Armenian Government's consent to the Bolshevik occupation of Nakhichevan, which opened their road into North-West Persia and into Turkey, almost amounted to an act of treachery against Great Britain, and was especially deplorable at the time when Armenia had just received a large consignment of British munitions.

Significantly, the Armenian representatives had to affirm, in reply, 'the continued loyalty of Armenia to the *Entente.*' They further claimed that the time which they hoped to gain by the negotiations to be continued in Erevan, would enable them 'to organise resistance' should the Bolsheviks fail to keep their promise ultimately to evacuate Nakhichevan.[90] In Erevan, an official of the Armenian government 'confidentially' told Captain Gracey that they had yielded temporarily. Moreover, he 'assured' the latter that the Armenian government

> . . . will form an anti-Bolshevik bloc with Georgia and the Khan of Maku of Persia to repel the Bolshevik forces from Transcaucasia.[91]

Armenian and British officials might well talk about plans to repel the

89. Ibid., no. 1, Luke to Curzon, 11 Aug. 1920; ibid., no. E11868, Gracey, Erevan, to Luke, 25 Aug. 1920.

90. Ibid., no. E10726, Luke to Curzon no. 1 (tel. 256), 11 Aug. 1920; ibid., encl. 1 in no. 1 (tel. no. 355), 11 Aug. 1920.

91. Ibid., no. E10733, Gracey, Erevan, to Luke, 12 Aug. 1920.

Bolshevik forces from the Caucasus. But the stark reality was that in the summer of 1920 the position of Armenia was very far from hopeful. The surrounding military forces were tightening their grip more strongly day after day. There were no friendly troops for her to turn to.

Prime Minister Ohandjanian reminded Captain Gracey — probably with bitterness — that it was the decision of the British Military Command in the past to transfer Armenian Karabagh to Azerbaijan and not to allow the Armenian occupation of Zangezur which had first struck a blow to the defence of his country; and it had eventually opened up the way for the alliance of the Bolsheviks and Turkish-Azerbaijanis. Moreover, his government had for a long time stressed the necessity of urgent military help to Armenia, but the promised armaments had not reached her even in June. General T. Nazarbekian, the Commander-in-Chief of the Armenian armed forces, also considered the late arrival of British arms as one of the causes of Armenia's military reverses.[92]

Armenians were being attacked on all sides, by the Azerbaijanis, the Turkish Nationalists, the Russian Bolsheviks, and, within the disputed territory, by the Molokans and the Kurds. Moreover, Armenia was hampered by lack of financial resources, of fuel, and of means of transport for the army. The loan of a few million dollars by the British government to Armenia would save her from an impossible situation, the Armenian Diplomatic Representative in Tiflis wrote to Luke; and Ohandjanian told Captain Gracey very decisively that the life of Armenia entirely depended upon the good-will of Europe and her diplomatic assistance.[93]

But besides the misleading Treaty of Sèvres, the Allies could give neither real good-will nor effective diplomatic assistance. In the summer of 1920 Armenia was fatally isolated in the Caucasus.

The Allies did absolutely nothing to show the Turks that they meant to implement the provisions of the Treaty of Sèvres regarding Armenia. According to General Milne, affording the Armenians armed assistance at present, either in the shape of a demonstration at Trebizond or otherwise to enable them to occupy the valley of Alashkert, on the Armeno-Turkish frontier, was impracticable. He even suggested a word of 'warning' to be given to the Armenian government as regards Colonel Katheniotes, an officer in the Greek army. According to Katheniotes' plan, volunteers would be raised among the Greeks of the Black Sea coast to help Armenia occupy Trebizond, in return for the ultimate grant by Armenia of some sort of autonomy to the Greeks in such parts of the coast which might come under Armenian sovereignty. The warning to Armenia was duly given by Commander Luke who believed that the plan merely seemed a device to

92. Ibid., no. E11868, Luke to Curzon, 6 Sept. 1920, encl. Ohandjanian (no. 4884) to Gracey, 21 Aug. 1920, and Nazarbekoff (no. 01126) to For. Minister, Erevan, 20 Aug. 1920.
93. Ibid., no. E10734, Arm. Dipl. Rep. Tiflis, to Luke, 14 Aug. 1920 in Luke to Curzon, 16 Aug. 1920. Ibid., no. E11868, Gracey to Luke, 25 Aug. 1920 in Luke to Curzon, 6 Sept. 1920.

resuscitate the Pontine Republic — a Hellenistic state which had existed in the Old Ages. Any action on the part of Katheniotes was considered 'inopportune'.[94]

Thus, Armenia was urged not to make concessions to the Soviets. But from nowhere in the Allied camp did she receive even diplomatic help.

Neither could Armenian relations with Soviet Russia improve. Very soon after the Tiflis agreement, Ohandjanian wrote to Legrand strongly protesting against the execution of thirteen 'eminent' members of Dashnaktsutiun in Karabagh, the destruction of about thirty Armenian villages in Zangezur and the penetration by Soviet troops into the district of Aksibar. These acts were, according to Ohandjanian, a direct violation of the agreement of 10 August.[95]

As to Kemalist Turkey, the summer of 1920 was for her a period of watching the victorious powers and balancing their unity of purpose and determination to implement the Peace Treaty against, on the other hand, securing any possible support from Soviet Russia. When, however, the American Senate decisively rejected the Armenian mandate and the Allied powers showed no intention whatsoever of backing up the Armenian clauses of the Treaty of Sèvres which they had themselves drafted, and when Armenia herself was somehow unable to come to an agreement either with her Caucasian neighbours or with Soviet Russia, Kemalist Turkey felt herself in a position to act in complete freedom.

In a note sent to Kemal on 2 June 1920, Chicherin had expressed the 'satisfaction' of the Soviet government at the decision taken by the Grand National Assembly to leave to 'Turkish Armenia', to Kurdistan, to Lazistan . . . the duty of 'fixing their own fate'. The note added:

> The Government naturally mean by that that free representation shall take place, in which will take part refugees and emigrants obliged previously to leave their country for reasons independent of their own will, and who, moreover, will have to be repatriated.

The Soviet government hoped, Chicherin concluded, that the frontiers between Turkey on one side, and Armenia and Persia on the other, would be established by diplomatic *pour-parlers*. They were ready, 'if invited to do so by the interested parties, to accept the duty of mediation'.[96] Kemal's response, according to E.H. Carr, was somewhat ambiguous. By his note of 20 June 1920, Kemal 'gladly' accepted the offer of mediation. He added that

94. Ibid., E10728/E10731, Luke to Curzon, 12, 14 Aug. 1920.
95. Ibid., no. E11868, Ohandjanian to Legrand, 22 Aug. 1920, encl. in Luke to Curzon, 6 Sept. 1920. FO 371/4960/E12813, Ohandjanian to Bekzadian, 21 Sept. 1920.
96. WO 106/349, 26th ser. no. 19, Directorate of Milit. Ops. and Intellig. 'Summary of Intellig', 15 June 1920 quot. a wireless message from Paris; see also Degras, *Soviet Documents*, pp. 187–8; Rep. of Arm. Archives, File 47/1, extr. from *l'Humanite*, 24 June 1920.

the Turkish government had postponed military operations in the provinces of Kars, Ardahan and Batum on receipt of Chicherin's note, but complained of Armenian provocations. Carr has concluded in a footnote that clearly Kemal's intention was politely to reject the Soviet offer of mediation. Carr has also pointed out that the move against Armenia was made at a moment when the Red army had its hands full with the Wrangel offensive in southern Russia, although it may have been a coincidence.[97]

In June 1920 Armenian troops moved into Olti, a district rich in coal, on the Russian side of the pre-war Russo-Turkish frontier, as a preliminary step towards the Treaty of Sèvres. Bekir Sami claimed that Olti formed part of the Ottoman Empire under the Treaties of Brest-Litovsk and Batum. He therefore requested the withdrawal of the Armenian troops 'without any delay'. The Armenian government, however, rejected both treaties as bases for the relations between the two countries. The district of Olti was an incontestable part of the Armenian republic. Having signed the Peace Treaty with Turkey, Armenia would await the decisions of the President of the United States and was not crossing the former Russo-Turkish frontier.[98]

Thus, in the summer of 1920, Armenia based her claims on the Treaty of Sèvres; Kemalist Turkey on the Treaties of Brest-Litovsk and Batum although Brest-Litovsk had been renounced by Soviet Russia in the autumn of 1918.[99]

In September 1920, Commander Luke reported to the Foreign Office that at least four battalions of Kiazim Karabekir's troops had crossed the 1914 Russo-Turkish frontier, and by a surprise attack had driven the Armenians back thirty versts east of Olti. The Armenians had suffered heavily. Having captured Olti, the Turks were advancing in large numbers towards Kars with the object of seizing that district. In the meantime it seemed that the Bolsheviks were using the provided opportunity: Armenians were being pressed by the Bolsheviks towards Karakilisa on the Dilijan front. Although the Foreign Office Staff were of the view that there was really no concerted action,[100] Armenia was certainly being squeezed by anti-Allied powers: Turks attacking on the west, Bolsheviks pressing on the north and a hostile Azerbaijan manoeuvring on the east.

In her desperate plight Armenia turned to her only allies: the powers of

97. Carr, *Bolshevik Revolution*, III, pp. 249–50, 295. See also Kirakosian, *Hayastane Pastateghterum*, p. 480.

98. FO 371/4959/E11703, Bekir Sami to For. Minist. Arm., translat. of true copy, 8 July 1920, encl. in Luke to Curzon, 24 Aug. 1920. Ibid., no. E11868, Ter-Akopian, FO Armenia, to Bekir Sami, 28 July 1920 in Luke to Curzon, 6 Sept. 1920. See also Rep. of Arm. Archives, File 75/2; Vratsian, *Hayastani Hanrapetutiun*, pp. 373–5, 413.

99. Degras, *Soviet Documents*, I, p. 110, Chicherin to Turkish For. Minist., 20 Sept. 1918. Kirakosian, *Hayastane Pastateghterum*, pp. 439–41.

100. FO 371/4960/E11896/E12108/E12216, Luke to FO 25 Sept. 1920; GHQ Constant. to WO, 29 Sept. 1920, 1 Oct. 1920. Mins. by R. McDonell, 5 Oct. 1920 and by D.G. Osborne, 4 Oct. 1920.

the Entente. On 30 September 1920 the Armenian government in Erevan cabled Admiral Sir J. de Robeck, the British High Commissioner in Constantinople, about the exceedingly serious situation caused by her lack of fuel. It also requested Ferdinand Tahtadjian, the Armenian chargé d'affaires to the Allied High Commissioners, to apply immediately to Eleutherios Venizelos, the Greek Premier, asking him that pressure be brought to bear on the Greek front by every possible means. A Greek advance would mean a Kemalist retirement, Curzon explained in the Foreign Office. Khatisian, the former Prime Minister, personally proposed to Admiral de Robeck that a Greek force should occupy Trebizond. It seems that de Robeck clearly favoured the idea. He cabled the Foreign Office that in view of British information regarding the use of Trebizond as a source of supplies and as a base for operations against the Caucasus, he was of the opinion that its early occupation by the Allies was the most effective means of giving assistance to Armenia. These views of the British High Commissioner in Constantinople were decisively and strongly supported by both Colonel Stokes, now the High Commissioner in the Caucasus, and by the Admiralty in London.[101] In addition, a memorandum by the British Armenia Committee, transmitted by Lord Bryce to the Prime Minister, urgently asked for a more vigilant patrol of the Black Sea by the British navy.[102]

In the meantime, Armenia sent urgent appeals for help in every direction. A telegram on behalf of the government in Erevan to Avetis Aharonian in Paris repeated the case about the complete lack of fuel for the railways. It asked him to appeal to all the Allied powers to lodge an immediate protest against the 'violation' by the Turks of the Treaty. The cable, transmitted through Colonel Stokes and Lord Derby, urged the necessity for military pressure to be brought to bear upon other Turkish fronts.[103] In similar notes addressed to the British, French, Italian, Japanese and United States governments, Aharonian pointed to the Turkish objective of securing the provinces of Kars and Batum with a view to bringing about an alliance with the Bolsheviks. He appealed for the Allied occupation of Trebizond which would be the most effective means of neutralising such a plan.[104]

The British military authorities, however, had long since abandoned hope for the Caucasus. The British Cabinet favoured the independence of the Caucasus as against the Bolsheviks and Turkish Nationalists, but it was reluctant to give any substantial help. So the assistance thought of in the

101. Ibid., nos. E12108/E12109, de Robeck to FO, 2 Oct. 1920; Curzon, min., 4 Oct. 1920. Rep. of Arm. Archives, File 75/2, Tahtadjian to Aharonian, 5 Oct. 1920. FO 371/4960/E12836, Stokes to Curzon, 7 Oct. 1920. Ibid., Flint, Admiralty to FO, 7 Oct. 1920. DBFP, vol. XII, p. 635fn.2: Stokes took over the Mission from Luke on 29 Sept. 1920.
102. Lloyd George Papers, F/5/7/4, Bryce to Lloyd George, 26 Nov. 1920, encl. memo. by BAC of 23 Nov. 1920.
103. FO 371/4960/E12270, Bekzadian, Tiflis, to Aharonian, 29 Sept. 1920, transm. by Stokes/Derby to FO, 3, 4 Oct. 1920.
104. Ibid., E12478, Aharonian to Derby, 5 Oct. 1920 in Derby to Curzon, 7 Oct. 1920.

Foreign Office was less than half-hearted.

'I doubt if we can, or want to, occupy Trebizond but we should control traffic to the port', D.G. Osborne minuted at the Foreign Office. Lord Hardinge deprecated a Greek occupation on political grounds; and Curzon authoritatively cabled Admiral de Robeck in reply to his queries:

> Allied occupation of Trebizond is impracticable and Greek occupation is considered undesirable.

There was 'no question' of military support at Trebizond or elsewhere: this was also the decision of the Inter-Allied Commission.[105]

But on his own initiative, Admiral de Robeck in Constantinople requested the Admiral commanding the Mediterranean to despatch sufficient oil to Batum for Erevan when Khatisian described to him the desperate situation in Armenia. Railway transport had entirely ceased. Besides fighting the Turks, Armenia had to meet riot from Moslems within her frontiers. Kurds were fighting in the district of Igdir. Soon an agreement was concluded on the despatch of, and the method of payment for, 1,000 tons of fuel oil. But this provision of fuel, it seems, was not made without a sound bargain: Armenia should repatriate her refugees in Mesopotamia.

> If we can assist in supply of fuel necessary for railways, Khatisian agrees to receive in Armenia over 14,000 Armenian refugees now at Basra,

Admiral de Robeck reported.[106]

On 5 October 1920 Colonel Stokes visited both Erevan and Kars and saw the Armenian Prime Minister and the Minister of War. He cabled his impression that the Armenian government and the people were united in their determination to defend their country. The troops were 'well equipped' with the munitions and uniforms received from Britain in July. General mobilisation of men aged up to 35 was in progress and volunteers had 'flocked' to the colours. But the danger which threatened Armenia was 'very serious'.[107]

Surely the position of Armenia, as a pro-Entente enclave, would be untenable were she not to have effective external help. Soviet Azerbaijan was hostile. The Russian Bolsheviks were gradually closing in. Having established their supremacy in the Caspian Sea, they were now engaged in the Crimea and on the Black Sea coast. In the meantime the Turkish Nationalists were advancing relentlessly.

105 Ibid., E12109, mins. 4 Oct. 1920; FO to de Robeck, 6 Oct. 1920. DBFP, vol. XII, p. 643, Curzon to Stokes, 29 Oct. 1920.

106. FO 371/4960/E12423/E12836, de Robeck to FO, 8 Oct. 1920; Stokes, 7 Oct. 1920. Ibid., no. E12465, C.-in-C. Medit. to Admiralty, copy, 9 Oct. 1920; ibid., no. E12423, de Robeck to Curzon, 8 Oct. 1920.

107. Ibid., no. E12836, Stokes to Curzon, 7 Oct. 1920.

Despite her many internal difficulties and severe shortcomings, it seems that Armenia initially presented a bold face. Colonel Stokes commented on the 'very creditable' manner in which she was doing her 'utmost' to meet the very serious danger threatening her.[108] Captain Gracey, stationed in Erevan, personally told Sir John Tilley of the Foreign Office about 'a good deal of constructive ability' that the Armenians had shown.[109] But the Foreign Office easily found the justification needed for explaining Britain's unwillingness and inability to help Armenia effectively. William Haskell had, as seen above,[110] left Armenia before the arrival there of auditors. On his way back home to the United States he had called at the Foreign Office to tell D.G. Osborne that:

> The country is a desert and the people nothing but professional beggars . . . There is no administrative or political capacity in the country, no money, and no resources to develop. Foreign Armenians who have amassed fortunes . . . will neither contribute nor return to the national home.

He had, in the meantime, emphasised that he was 'speaking *unofficially*' —a clever move indeed.

What is of interest is the way these allegations were received in the Foreign Office: 'I wish Col. Haskell could meet and talk to Mr. Aneurin Williams', D.G. Osborne minuted. C.H.S. went even further:

> It is a pity that we cannot show it to Aneurin Williams, as it will indicate to him that we are really not to blame for the state of affairs in Armenia, and that his attacks on the French and ourselves are really not justified.[111]

It seems that Haskell's words had come as a relief to the Foreign Office saving them from their moral responsibility towards Armenia: she herself was to blame and it was 'a pity' that the hopelessness of Armenia and the Armenians could not be publicised.

When the Foreign Office was informed through General J. Bagratuni, the unofficial Armenian representative in London, that Avetis Aharonian would come to London to depict personally the 'desperate' position of his country, Osborne prepared a brief for his seniors. It was worthwhile to point out, he wrote, that

> H[is] M[ajesty's] G[overnment] is not a charity organization and that instead of perpetual appeals for foreign pity and assistance we should like

108. Ibid.
109. FO 371/4963/E14033, min. of interv. with Gracey by Tilley, FO, Nov. 1920.
110. See above, pp. 195–6.
111. FO 371/4960/E12174, mins. by Osborne, 29 Sept. 1920; by C.H.S., 14 Oct. 1920.

to see evidence of some self-reliance and political ability in Armenia; that the continued existence of Armenia as an autonomous state is dependent on Armenian efforts and capacity and cannot be based on foreign armies and foreign money . . .

On 12 November Aharonian called on Sir John Tilley at the Foreign Office and after expressing his 'warmest' thanks for the arms and fuel oil Britain had supplied, described 'the terrible situation' in which Armenia found herself. He said their 'only hope' was in armed intervention by Britain. Tilley told him 'that was entirely out of the question'. Aharonian then suggested the formation of an army of Armenian volunteers from different parts of the world concentrating at a base on some Greek island. That too was 'wholly impracticable', Tilley told him. Aharonian later suggested an army of peace with volunteers from all parts of the world. Tilley rejected that too. Aharonian then asked how the powers contemplated executing the Turkish Treaty. Tilley told him that the powers could execute immediately that which related to Constantinople and the Straits. Then they would organise 'Turkish' forces with which they hoped it would be possible gradually 'to pacify Anatolia'.[112]

So, the Treaty of Sèvres, regarding the Armenian clauses and the Eastern *vilayets,* would only be carried out through pacifying Anatolia by 'Turkish' forces.

When Aharonian urged how important it was for Britain to prevent the Turks and Russians joining hands, Tilley replied he was afraid 'he [Aharonian] must expect nothing'. Referring to the above interview, he recorded on another page:

I made it quite clear that it was "wholly out of the question" that H[is] M[ajesty's] G[overnment] should send any military aid of any kind or accept a mandate or do anything whatever to render assistance — even the sending of arms being now precluded by the Turkish advance.[113]

Earlier, referring to one of Aharonian's numerous letters asking for effective help, Lord Curzon had expressed the view that 'no reply need be returned'.[114]

Meanwhile, the Turkish armies were sweeping deep into pre-war Russian Armenia. Appeals were sent to King George V by the Catholicos at Etchmiadzin, and to the Speaker of the House of Commons on behalf of 25,000 Armenians in California. In their desperation the Armenians and their friends also tried to mobilise the League of Nations. The Allied

112. FO 371/4963/E14033/E14103, Osborne to Tilley, min. 9 Nov. 1920; min. by Tilley, 12 Nov. 1920.
113. Ibid., mins. by Tilley, both 12 Nov. 1920.
114. FO 371/4960/E12478, Tilley to Derby, copy, 19 Oct. 1920.

powers, however, opposed any discussion. Thus, M. de Fleuriau, the French ambassador, told Sir J. Tilley on 9 November 1920 that his government agreed with the point of view of the Foreign Office, namely that

> . . . no useful discussion was possible while the boundaries were still unsettled & Armenia was an unknown quantity.

M. de Fleuriau hoped, therefore, that the Foreign Office would instruct the British delegate 'to discourage' any attempt to raise the Armenian question in the League of Nations. Tilley concurred with him. He concluded his minute:

> I do not feel that it is a matter we want to hear very much about: & whatever may have been expected of us originally we intend to do as little as we can for Armenia either in men or money.

Curzon read the minute and initialled it. He did not argue against it.[115]

In a similar mood a Conference of British Ministers agreed, on the advice of the Chancellor of the Exchequer, that Britain should not offer to participate in any financial guarantee to be given to Armenia by the members of the League of Nations. H.A.L. Fisher, now a member of the British Empire Delegation to the first Assembly of the League of Nations, wrote to the Prime Minister from Geneva that there had been a great deal of talk about Armenia, but what could be done? 'I am sure I don't know.' On 2 December 1920 he cabled that René Viviani, a former Prime Minister of France, and Lord R. Cecil were 'trying to rush Armenia into [the] League'.[116] A Conference of British Ministers was of the view that the admission of Armenia to the League would involve an undertaking, under Article 10, to preserve her territorial integrity and existing political independence against external aggression. But it was pointed out that the League would be incapable of fulfilling such an undertaking. The Treaty of Sèvres was not yet ratified. Moreover, the boundaries of Armenia, just defined by President Wilson, were so extended that the powers could hardly accept, under existing conditions, the responsibility to guarantee them. The admission of Armenia was also discussed at a Conference with the French and Italian representatives. Opposition was unanimously agreed on;[117] Armenia was refused membership of the League.

115. FO 371/4964/E14571/E14539, 19, 22 Nov. 1920 respectively; FO 371/4963/E14026, min. by Tilley, 9 Nov. 1920. Curzon initialled, n.d.

116. CAB 23/23, Cab. 59(20), min. 7, App. V, Conclusions of Conf. of Ministers held 18 Oct. 1920. Cab. 3 Nov. 1920 took note of. Lloyd George Papers, F/16/7/63, Fisher to Lloyd George, 21 Nov. 1920. DBFP, vol. VIII, p. 856, note 5, Fisher, 2 Dec. 1920.

117. CAB 23/23, Cab, 70(20), min. 4, App. III, Conclusions of Conf. of Ministers, 2 Dec. 1920. CAB 24/116, C.P. 2238, App. II tel. to Balfour, n.d. [3 Dec. 1920]. Same in DBFP, vol. VIII, no. 99, App. 1, pp. 856-7; ibid., pp. 841-2; 848-50.

At the same time, M. Hymans, the President of the Council of the League of Nations, cabled the British government asking whether they would be disposed either alone or conjointly with other nations, to undertake, on behalf of the League, the humanitarian mission of stopping the hostilities between Armenia and the Kemalists. The response was negative. At a Conference of Ministers on 2 December 1920, it was pointed out that:

> Armenia, with scant resources, with little apparent capacity to defend herself and almost cut off from the outside world, was ground between the Turkish Nationalists and the Bolshevist Russians, who themselves appeared to be rapidly drifting into a state of hostilities. In these circumstances Armenia would probably make her own terms or have terms forced on her.

> It was generally felt that, in view of our immense preoccupations elsewhere, it would not be desirable for Great Britain to volunteer to undertake this intervention.[118]

Earlier, on 19 November, the Army Council wrote to the Foreign Office that it would no longer serve any useful purpose to forward munitions to Armenia.[119]

Thus, the abandonment of Armenia was total and complete in respect of protection and help: but not in respect of advice and guidance. Britain had neither the power nor the will to protect Armenia and the Caucasian republics. Nevertheless, she discouraged them from coming to terms with either Soviet Russia or Kemalist Turkey, the only states with real power in the Caucasus. After his visit to that region in October-December 1920, C. Leonard Leese, the Organising Secretary of the British Armenia Committee and special correspondent of the *Manchester Guardian,* revealed that an offer by Kemalist Turkey in the spring of 1920, to negotiate directly with Armenia, was declined by the latter 'after consultation with the British Chief Commissioner for Transcaucasia'.[120] Above all, Britain discouraged Armenia from coming to a feasible understanding with Soviet Russia, an understanding which alone might have saved her from dismemberment by Turkey. 'Armenia is helpless unless the Bolsheviks help her', Montagu wrote in November 1920. If there was to be a military solution, 'Russia alone had forces at hand to intervene', Arnold Toynbee, back from his long trip in the East, told a meeting.[121] Britain could not help Armenia: but to the end,

---

118. CAB 23/23, Cab. 70(20) min. 4, App. III, Conclusions of Conf. of Ministers, 2 Dec. 1920.

119. FO 371/4964/E14649, WO to FO, 24 Nov. 1920 ref. letter of 19 Nov. 1920.

120. Bryce Papers, UB 65, Leese, 'Political Cross-Currents in the Nr. East', 3 Jan. 1921. According to Kajaznuni, *H.H. Dashnaktsutiune,* pp. 41-2, the Kemalists offered to negotiate with Armenia in Sept. 1920. The offer was turned down.

121. Montagu Papers, AS-IV-6, 903(2), 22 Nov. 1920. *BAC Minutes,* 21 Oct. 1921.

her representatives aimed at keeping her within the orbit of the Entente powers. In his telegram to the British Armenia Committee, Chicherin alleged that the Allies systematically prevented the government of Armenia from taking a more moderate attitude towards Soviet Russia and even stopped sending food supplies when it opened negotiations with its northerly neighbour. And Armenia rejected all Soviet Russia's proposals of mediation to fix her frontiers with her neighbours and, in particular, the frontiers of 'Turkish Armenia', Chicherin claimed.[122] As can be seen above, British policy in the Caucasus was based on confused and confusing illusions. To the end, the British representatives faithfully tried to carry out Curzon's instructions:

> The rescue, if possible, of . . . Erivan from the influence of the Soviet Government.[123]

Generally well informed about Armenia's foreign relations and naturally favouring mainly British interests, they prevented Armenia from seeing the latent power struggle between Turkey and Soviet Russia and discouraged the Armenians from coming to an agreement with the latter, which was probably inevitable, before it was too late.

On 7 October 1920, Colonel Stokes cabled Curzon that Bolshevik representatives at Kuban had offered the Armenian representative to arrange Turkish withdrawal to the 'Russian frontier of 1914' if Armenia would 'sever all connection with *Entente.*' Similarly, in Moscow, the Soviet Assistant Foreign Minister told the Armenian delegate that Russia was in a position to stop the Turkish advance and perhaps even to arrange for the evacuation of one part of Armenian territory in Turkey. But Armenia should temporarily hand over the Shakhtakhti-Nakhichevan railway so that Russia could help Turkey 'against the Entente'.[124] In mid-October, Tigran Bekzadian, the Armenian representative in Tiflis, also cabled the Armenian Delegation in Paris that the Bolsheviks had offered to arrange the withdrawal of the Turks 'to 1914 frontier' provided the Armenian government officially declared that it had 'nothing in common with the Entente'. Bekzadian added: 'The offer rejected'. According to E.H. Carr, even a proposal of Soviet military aid was made.[125]

It seems that as the Turkish armies advanced, Soviet Russia became increasingly nervous and anxious to mediate. But her offers were rejected by

122. Rep. of Arm. Archives, File 336/6, Chicherin to BAC, copy, 12 Nov. 1920; also in Files 334/4, 335/5, 371.
123. DBFP, vol. XII, p. 635, Curzon to Stokes, 13 Sept. 1920.
124. FO 371/4960/E12836, Stokes to Curzon, 7 Oct. 1920; FO 371/4964/E14902, Eghiazariantz to Arm. Govt, 5 Oct. 1920, in Court to Stokes, 22 Oct. 1920.
125. FO 371/4961/E12869, Bekzadian to Arm. Deleg. (no. 4449), n.d., in Stokes to Derby desp. from Constant. 18 Oct. 1920; Rep. of Arm. Archives, File 17/17, Bekzadian to Arm. Deleg., 20 Oct. 1920; Carr, *Bolshevik Revolution*, III, p. 295.

the Armenian government with the knowledge — and perhaps the advice — of the British representatives.

A report sent by Captain H. Court, the British Intelligence Officer and Political Representative in Erevan, to Colonel Stokes, is particularly revealing and significant. It was dated 22 October 1920, at the very time when Britain was opposing a financial guarantee by the members of the League of Nations. According to Captain Court, the reply of the Armenian government as drawn up by Ruben Ter-Minasian, the Minister for War, and 'as seen by the Chief British Commissioner on 16th October at Erivan' had been presented to Legrand, the representative of Soviet Russia, with the exception that the claim for Armenia's western frontier was further extended to include Trebizond, Erzinjan and Kharput. Court had been informed by the Armenian government that, 'contrary to all expectations', Legrand was considering the proposals set forth by Ter-Minasian and that 'he appears more than willing to accede to almost all of them'. Legrand would be shortly leaving Erevan for Baku, where he would submit these proposals to the Soviet government of Azerbaijan and get in touch with Mustafa Kemal. Court went on with the crucial revelation:

These negotiations will, it is estimated, take at least one month, a delay which will be of the greatest assistance to Armenia as it will give her time to train and organize her forces . . .

The Armenian Government have informed me that in any case they do not intend to come to a definite understanding with Legrand until they have received the decision of the Georgian Government regarding the alliance of the two states against the Bolsheviks.[126]

Thus, contrary to all expectations Legrand appeared 'more than willing to accede' to the proposals of the Armenian government, which however 'in any case' did 'not intend' to come to a definite understanding with him. It seems that by making excessive territorial claims and by using delaying tactics, the Armenian government were naïvely — and dangerously — playing for time. Encouraged by the British, the Armenian leadership was following a frightening policy of illusion.

Within the next twenty days Armenia lost almost everything to the Turks. On 7 November an armistice was signed between the Armenian government and Kiazim Karabekir on the latter's terms. Karabekir had perceived, since 1919, that British power was ebbing in the Caucasus, and had argued, with a chilling realism, that no assistance whatever would come to Armenia.[127] On 9 November he presented a new ultimatum with harsher conditions. The

126. FO 371/4964/E14902, Court, Erevan, to Stokes, 22 Oct. 1920.
127. Kâzim Karabekir, *Istiklâl Harbiniz* (Our War of Independence) (Istanbul, 1960), pp. 71, 20, 23.

fighting was resumed, but the Armenian government had finally to sue for a fresh armistice on 18 November.[128] Alexander Khatisian was appointed to negotiate the peace with the Kemalists. Still without realising that Britain had ceased from being a Caucasian power, Armenia to the last looked to her. On 18 November, before the negotiations, and actually on the day of the armistice, Khatisian visited Colonel Stokes in Tiflis. He told him that the Armenian people were 'in a fog'. The Armenian government realised that it was obliged to make peace either with the Turks or the Bolsheviks. It would be 'preferable to make peace with the Turks' and he inclined to the belief that the British government would also prefer this. Khatisian asked whether Britain could be a party to the negotiations with Turkey. The Bolsheviks assured the Armenians that they could settle the Turkish trouble immediately if Armenia '(?will) (?denounce)' the Turkish Peace Treaty. The Armenian government wanted to adopt a course which would, so far as possible, meet with the 'approval' of Britain.[129] Replying, Curzon stated that Britain could not be a party to a treaty with the Nationalists, but considered that the alternative of a treaty with Soviet Russia was 'doubtless worse'. Earlier, two members of the Foreign Office had similarly indicated that a peace with the Turks was 'clearly preferable'.[130]

Before the arrival of Curzon's reply, Simon Vratsian, the new and last Prime Minister of the Republic of Armenia, also asked Stokes, in late November, for his 'advice' whether to accept the Turkish claim for a treaty assigning them large areas of territory, or the Bolshevik offer. The latter would make the Turks

> . . . abandon their demand and retire beyond old Russian frontier. They state they will do this peaceably or by force but in either case Armenia must allow Bolshevik troops to enter Armenia and establish contact with Turks.

The offer was rejected. Armenia finally agreed to the 'half loaf' left by Turkey as she believed that the 'whole loaf' offered by Bolshevik Russia would mean 'the loss of all sympathy in Europe'.[131]

Before the departure of Khatisian's delegation to Alexandropol, to negotiate with the Kemalists, the Armenian government asked Legrand and Mdivani, the Soviet representatives, to put pressure on the Turks. Accord-

---

128. FO 371/4964/E14604, note by McDonell, FO, 24 Nov. 1920. See also Vratsian, *Hayastani Hanrapetutiun*, pp. 433–5.

129. FO 371/4964/E14759, Stokes to Curzon, 18 Nov. 1920. Same in DBFP, vol. XII, pp. 648–9. See also A. Khatisian, *Hayastani Hanrapetutian Dsagumn u Zargatsume* (The Creation and Development of the Republic of Armenia), 2nd edn. (Beirut, 1968), pp. 290–1.

130. DBFP, vol. XII, p. 653, Curzon to Stokes, 28 Nov. 1920. FO 371/4964/E14759, mins. by Tilley and [Osborne], FO stamp, 26 Nov. 1920; Khatisian, ibid. p. 291.

131. FO 371/4965/E15081/E15175, Stokes to Curzon, 23, 30 Nov. 1920. FO 371/4964/E14759, R. McDonell, min., 25 Nov. 1920.

ing to Khatisian both promised to help. Legrand asked the Armenian government for permission to move two divisions of Red troops into Armenia from Azerbaijan so that he might have 'more real power to talk to the Turks'. The Armenian government, however, rejected the proposal fearing that this might lead to a military occupation of Armenia by the Bolsheviks.[132]

That there definitely was a power struggle between Turkey and Soviet Russia at this time is once again revealed by the fact that at Alexandropol Kiazim Karabekir categorically rejected the participation of Mdivani in the negotiations.[133] The Turkish delegation wanted, indeed, to have Armenia, fatally isolated and abandoned, for themselves alone to deal with.

The crushing Treaty of Alexandropol left Armenia with a territory of 27,000 square kilometres: Kars and Surmalu, including Mount Ararat would go to Turkey; Nakhichevan and Zangezur would become Azerbaijani protectorates; Armenia would be permitted to have a detachment of only 1,500 soldiers equipped with 20 machine-guns and 8 cannons; compulsory military service was forbidden. All these matters could be inspected at any time by a Turkish political agent resident in Erevan. Moreover, Turkey would have the right to supervise goods entering Armenia. Finally, Armenia would declare the Treaty of Sèvres null and void; the representatives of the Allies should leave.[134] The only Armenian state permitted by Karabekir was a tiny protectorate wholly dependent on Turkish goodwill.

The renunciation of the Treaty of Sèvres by Armenia had been the pre-condition for Turkish negotiations. But it had also been the only major condition asked by Soviet Russia in return for her mediation in securing for Armenia the pre-war Russian frontier. She had in addition agreed to recognise her independence. The offer was rejected.[135] Had it been accepted, Kars and Surmalu might have been within Armenian territory, the war might have ended earlier and Karabekir's troops would not have wrought death and destruction as thoroughly as if they were committed to annihilation.

In a paper written after his return to Britain, Dudley S. Northcote, an agent of the Armenian Refugees (Lord Mayor's) Fund resident in Erevan from 1921 to 1925, referred to the massacres in Kars, to the crazed flight of the remaining population, and to a valley in Armenia known as 'Death Valley'. A group of about 4,000 refugees followed by Turkish soldiers tried

132. Khatisian, *Hanrapetutian Zargatsume*, p. 295.

133. Ibid., p. 301; Vratsian, *Hayastani Hanrapetutiun*, p. 436; FO 371/4965/E15290, Stokes to Curzon, 3 Dec. 1920.

134. The Treaty was signed on 3 Dec. at 2.00 a.m. See Christopher J. Walker, *Armenia: The Survival of a Nation* (London, 1980), pp. 317–22; Zaven Messerlian, *Yerek Dashnagirer* (Three Treaties) (Beirut, 1979), pp. 70–88, 146–51; Khatisian, *Hanrapetutian Zargatsume*, pp. 294–311; Vratsian, ibid., pp. 437–8; Sh. Toriguian, *The Armenian Question and International Law* (Beirut, 1973), pp. 195-7.

135. Vratsian, ibid. p. 411.

to flee beyond Alexandropol towards the little town of Karakilisa. At a certain point four or five miles from the former town there was a break in the hills, a small valley which ended in a cul-de-sac. Believing that the valley would provide them with a short cut, the whole party left the road and went down to it.

> But it led nowhere, soon the Turkish troops came up, the people were trapped, and every single one of them, men, women, and children, were slaughtered.[136]

The complete devastation of the districts of Alexandropol and Kars was accompanied by murder, rape and deportation. Even the animals were not left behind; the Turks herded them in droves towards Erzerum. Colonel Rawlinson has described at first-hand a few of the Armenian prisoners who were being used as labourers in the latter town. It was then midwinter, the snow lying deep everywhere, with arctic winds:

> . . . yet those miserable spectres were clothed, if the word can be applied to their condition, in the rottenest and filthiest of verminous rags, through which their fleshless bones protruded in many places, so that it seemed *impossible* that humanity could be reduced to such extremities and live.[137]

Could Armenia have been saved from the above mentioned adversities? The republic's Delegation in Paris ascribed her downfall to three main causes: the Treaty of Sèvres was never ratified; neither her international position nor her frontiers were clearly defined; and finally she never received adequate military and material assistance essential for her survival.[138] Certainly, the Treaty of Sèvres made Armenia a prey to Turkish attack. It provided her with wide boundaries at the expense of Turkey, but not with the means of defence. On the other hand, a Foreign Office paper, as if to counter the charge of Armenia's abandonment by the Allies, blamed the 'internal dissensions' between the Dashnaks and the 'Democrats'; and Lord Curzon angrily referred to the reluctance of wealthy Armenians to help their country financially.[139] It was pointed out that the administration in Erevan, besides its unavoidable lack of experience, suffered also from the

136. Northcote Papers, Add MS 57560, 'Armenia', p. 30, 1926.

137. FO 371/6266/E1713, Note by Soviet Arm. Govt. to Angora, 18 Jan. 1921, in Stokes to Curzon, 4 Feb. 1921; E.K. Sarkisian and R.G. Sahakian, *Vital Issues in Modern Armenian History* (trans. E.B. Chrakian) (Watertown, Mass., 1965), p. 55. A. Rawlinson, *Adventures in the Near East 1918-1922* (London, 1923), p. 307.

138. Bryce Papers, UB 65, Bureau d'Information de la Délég. de la Rép. Arm., No. 1, Paris, 15 Sept. 1921.

139. FO 371/7729/E8378, McDonell and Childs, 'Outline of Events in Transcaucasia', p. 29, 31 May 1922; Curzon Papers, MSS Eur. F. 112/232 ff.43–4, Curzon to Williams, copy, 6 Dec. 1921; FO 371/6267/E12699, Curzon min. 16 Nov. 1921; DBFP, vol. XII, p. 637 fn.5.

'blight of [a] narrow party outlook' which made the formation of a national-coalition government impossible. Thus it failed to draw on the support of all sections and classes and especially could not attract Armenian capital from the diaspora.[140] According to Aneurin Williams, it was the 'universal' opinion in Britain that Armenia was very much weakened by the fact that her government represented one party only; and the problem which the Armenians evaded was that they had no resources in men or money, a member of the Foreign Office minuted.[141] Moreover, although there was often much provocation on the part of the Tatar population within the frontiers of Armenia, the administration was at times unable to prevent Armenian bands from committing excesses in Moslem villages. The result was their alienation and an increase in the hostility of both Azerbaijan and Turkey.[142] However, important as these shortcomings were, they were certainly not central to the survival of the republic. The administration was faced with a superhuman task: the task of bringing order to a decimated people in a country desolated by war and burdened with the crushing problem of refugees; and according to the Reverend H.W. Harcourt, resident in Erevan, 'in spite of all some order and progress was emerging'.[143]

The survival of the republic was greatly put at risk by the fact that, without being given protection, she was made a pawn in the power struggle of the Caucasus. Oliver Baldwin (the Prime Minister's son), fiercely anti-Bolshevik, a Lieutenant-Colonel in the Armenian army in late 1920 and early 1921, who, according to his memoirs, fully tasted the harshness of Soviet rule in its first months in Erevan, considered that agreement by Armenia to Moscow's terms would have been 'a far smaller sacrifice' than what she ultimately sustained. He maintained that Armenia could have agreed but for her faith in Britain. Significantly, Baldwin twice characterised this faith as 'blind': Armenia

> . . . held a blind, strange faith in Great Britain, who had made so many promises to help her and who had once beaten the Turks.

And again, that Armenia 'had a blind faith in England and anyone English'.[144]

Arnold Toynbee, much more sophisticated than Oliver Baldwin, partly

---

140. FO 371/6267/E8002, Harcourt, 'Transcaucasia', June 1921; Luke, *Cities and Men*, II, p. 179; Kajaznuni, *H.H. Dashnaktsutiune*, pp. 32, 38.

141. Rep. of Arm. Archives, File 337/7, Williams to Aharonian, 3 March 1921; FO 371/6266/E3010, Osborne, 9 March 1921.

142. Bryce Papers, UB 65, Harcourt, 'The Situation in Armenia', p. 4, 1 Dec. 1920; Oliver Baldwin, *Six Prisons and Two Revolutions* (London, 1924), pp. 71, 261. See also, Avetis Aharonian, 'From Sardarapat to Sèvres and Lausanne: A Political Diary', Pt. IV, *Armenian Review*, vol. XVI, no. 3–63 (Sept. 1963) pp. 52–4; Mustafa Kemal, *A Speech . . .* , p. 416.

143. Bryce Papers, UB 65, Harcourt, 'The Situation in Armenia', p. 3, 1 Dec. 1920. Orig. in Davidson Papers.

144. Baldwin, *Six Prisons*, pp. 23, 30.

blamed the 'short-sighted particularism'[145] of the republics themselves for their failure of co-operation, and partly the conspiracy and aggression of Angora and Moscow for the death of these Caucasian states. But in writing their 'epitaph', he put a 'heavy share' of the responsibility on the Allied powers, which although no longer in a position to exercise effective power in the Caucasus, attempted nevertheless to make a show of authority.

> . . . by encouraging the inexperienced and unorganised Transcaucasian Republics to look to them for a guidance and a protection which they had no intention of giving at any sacrifice to themselves, they deterred them from coming to terms before it was too late . . .

Toynbee has characterised the Allied show of authority, despite their lack of power, as 'both a moral and a political blunder'.[146]

The Reverend H.W. Harcourt, who had first-hand knowledge of Armenia and the Caucasus in those years, was also of the view that in the 'absence of any assistance' from the Allies, 'the use of Allied influence to prevent a reconciliation' between the Caucasian states and Russia was 'disastrous for them, immoral and unjust on the part of the Allies'. He was 'firmly convinced that favourable terms' could have been obtained from Russia during the summer of 1920, and Armenia 'should have been left free by the Allies to make peace'. The process of the negotiations showed an 'evident' desire on the part of the Russian delegates for 'a strong buffer state between Moslem-Russia and the Turks'. T.P.C. Evans, the Secretary of the British Armenia Committee, likewise attributed Armenia's disaster to her loyalty to Britain; and the Armenian representative in Tiflis to her fidelity to the Allied cause.[147]

It seems that Britain's illusion of power and prestige — the result of the disproportion between her world influence and shrinkage of military strength — , her reluctance to relinquish her authority in the Caucasus and her persistence in giving guidance to Armenia contributed in their turn to Armenia's illusions. Britain was slow in recognising the stark reality of the recuperating power of Soviet Russia and Kemalist Turkey; and Armenia followed her example until it was too late. Moreover, Armenia's illusion of having mighty friends in the West was prolonged by the delay in President Wilson's decision as regards her boundaries — given only in late November

---

145. Kazemzadeh has written about the 'myopic mediocrity' of their statesmen. Even Harold Buxton pointed to the absence of 'a few men of judgment and sangfroid', capable of subordinating their petty national jealousies to the larger issues of common interests and common defence. See Firuz Kazemzadeh, *The Struggle for Transcaucasia* (New York/Oxford 1951), p. 274; H. Buxton, *Trans-Caucasia* (London, 1926), pp. 28–9.

146. A. J. Toynbee, *Survey of International Affairs 1920–1923* (Oxford, 1925), pp. 369, 373–4.

147. FO 371/6267/E8002, Harcourt, 'Transcaucasia 1920–1', June 1921; *Westminster Gazette*, letter, 16 Nov. 1920, cutting in Rep. of Arm. Archives, File 334/4; FO 371/4963/E14145, Stokes to FO, 6 Nov. 1920.

1920 when she already was in her death throes. All this time she was left in a fatal state of expectation. It was the dream of prospective support from the European powers to recover Turkish Armenia — stipulated in the Treaty of Sèvres — which prevented the Armenian government from coming to an accommodation with Soviet Russia. They believed that the Allies would never 'annex the Turkish-Armenian provinces' were Armenia to come under the Soviet sphere. As late as 11 November 1920 the Armenian government were prepared 'to postpone [the] negotiations with Soviet Russia' in expectation of a British reply for help.[148] Thus, the Treaty of Sèvres, promising so much, became for Armenia, in Kajaznuni's words, 'a kind of blue bird', 'intangible and inaccessible'.[149] Yet Armenia's commitment to the Allies did not give her protection; on the contrary it provoked the suspicion of both Soviet Russia and Turkey and exposed her to reprisals. Both powers saw Armenia as the satellite of Britain, their most dangerous enemy. It would be easy to blame Armenia for her illusions. But it was perhaps humanly impossible for her to renounce what the victors of a world war were nominally giving her. Yet the new reality in the Caucasus centred on the power of Turkey and Soviet Russia, co-operating if need be against their common enemies and competing with each other for a place in the region. Only in 1921 would Curzon realise that Britain was 'not in a position to exert effective influence either at Moscow or at Angora'; and Aharonian would sadly admit that 'the protection of Armenia was of no interest' to the European powers and that all wanted to avoid it.[150]

In the meantime (in late November and early December 1920), while the Turks, having excluded Mdivani from the negotiations, were imposing their terms unfettered in Alexandropol, Soviet Russia acted swiftly by taking over the government in Erevan. The Treaty of Alexandropol was never ratified. It was signed by the Delegation of the Republic of Armenia when the government it represented had actually ceased to exist.

Was there collusion between Kemalist Turkey and Soviet Russia to overthrow the Armenian government? Vratsian believed there was: Soviet Russia 'helped' Turkey 'to attack and crush little Armenia'.[151] Both Kajaznuni and E.H. Carr maintain that a belief in such collusion was widespread in Armenia at that time. Carr twice rejects the idea, maintaining that the anti-Bolshevik circumstantial stories of the period do not rest on reliable evidence. Moreover, he quotes Lenin, who on 20 November 1920 anxiously contemplated the possibility that 'war may be forced on us

148. Rep. of Arm. Archives, File 140/39, [Aharonian] to Hamo [Ohandjanian], no. 1714, copy, 14 May 1920; FO 371/4963/E14514, Ohandjanian to C-in-C. Medit. 11 Nov. 1920 in de Robeck to Curzon, 14 Nov. 1920.
149. Kajaznuni, *H.H. Dashnaktsutiune*, p. 51.
150. FO 371/6266/E3476, Curzon to Bagratuni, copy, 29 March 1921; same in Rep. of Arm. Archives, File 337/7; Rep. of Arm. Archives, File 337/7, Aharonian to Williams, copy, 27 Aug. 1921.
151. Vratsian, *Hayastani Hanrapetutiun* pp. 441, 401.

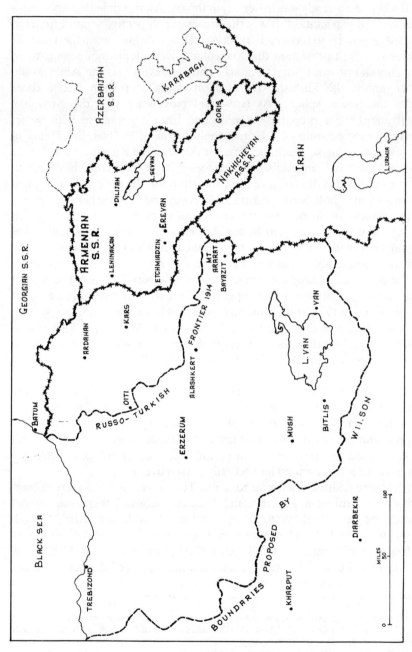

Map 9: Armenia: Boundaries Proposed by President Wilson in 1920; also Boundaries of Soviet Armenia

from one day to the next'. In addition, Carr has argued that had such collusion existed, more favourable results might have been expected for Soviet Russia. Kajaznuni has also stated that 'there is no positive evidence'.[152]

The Armenian government, generally believing in collusion, could not make diplomatic use of the rivalry between Armenia's two neighbours. But rivalry there certainly was. On 16 November 1920, when the Kemalists were sweeping forward in Armenia, T.P.C. Evans of the British Armenia Committee, called at the Russian Trade Delegation in London. Referring to a telegram from the Caucasus, Evans asked M. Klishko

. . . what truth there was in the idea that between Kemalists & Bolsheviks there was rivalry for Azerbaijan. M. Klishko replied that they had very serious grounds for suspecting the Kemalists, & that they were very much on their guard.[153]

British Intelligence was aware of this rivalry. An Admiralty Intelligence Summary referring to Turkish demands for 'a large portion of Armenia', and the Bolshevik offer to compel the Turks 'to retire beyond the old Russian frontier' stated:

Reports from various sources indicate that the Kemalist-Bolshevik Entente is not running smoothly.

The Bolsheviks were 'nervous' of Turkish intentions and 'evidently aiming at preventing Turks entering Azerbaijan'.[154] The strongest reference about such rivalry, as revealed over the sovietisation of Armenia, came from no less a person than the Secretary of State for War who wrote most significantly: 'The evidence in our possession appears to warrant the conclusion' that the Nationalist Turks though still anxious to secure Russian help, had found such assistance 'a double-edged weapon':

The Russians, who feared a junction between the Nationalists and the Azerbaijanis, as a result of Kiazim-Karabekir's rapid advance into Armenia in November, 1920, retaliated by Bolshevising what was left of Armenia . . .

While maintaining an outward semblance of unanimity of purpose, the Russians and both militant Turkish parties appear jealous of each other.[155]

152. Lenin, *Sochineniya*, XXV, 487, quoted in Carr, *Bolshevik Revolution*, vol. III, p.296 (see also fn.); ibid., vol. I, p. 347 (see also fn.), Kajaznuni, *H.H. Dashnaktsutiune*, p. 44.
    153. *BAC Propaganda Sub-Committee Minutes*, 23 Nov. 1920.
    154. CAB 24/116, C.P. 2255, Admiralty Weekly Intelligence Summary, no. 22. 4 Dec. 1920, Part II, 'Azerbaijan' and 'Turkey-Armenia'.
    155. CAB 24/120, C.P. 2608, memo., 19 Feb. 1921.

Thus, according to the Minister of War, the sovietisation of Armenia in November 1920 was an act of retaliation against Karabekir's advance.

British policy was to make increasing use of this rivalry and the Foreign Office would support the Turks against the Bolsheviks under pressure from both the War Office and the India Office especially after the collapse of the Caucasian republics. Yet, it discouraged Armenia from perceiving this rivalry between the two Eastern powers and from coming to terms with at least one of them. Arnold Toynbee, however, strongly favoured a pro-Russian orientation for Armenia since Turkey was passing through a period of 'rabid nationalism'.[156]

Referring to one of Aharonian's letters soliciting assistance and addressing 'a supreme appeal' to the principal Allied powers some time before Armenia's collapse, D.G. Osborne had minuted airily:

> We receive a 'supreme appeal' from the Armenians about once a month. We are usually unable to do anything, but Armenia continues to exist.[157]

After 3 December 1920 he would no longer be able to write so: one part of Armenia was sovietised; and Turkey had not only forced on Armenia the renunciation of the Treaty of Sèvres and of her historic provinces in eastern Anatolia, but had also occupied a considerable extent of territory in Russian Armenia. It was the victory of sheer force. British policy had conspicuously failed. With it, Armenia failed.

In a contemptuous mood, Sir Henry Wilson blamed, as usual, the politicians for the failure of policy in the Middle East. There was 'absolutely no connexion whatever' between the policy of Britain, which he considered did 'not exist' and the armed forces of the Empire which practically did not exist either. Referring to the Supreme Council, he maintained that the 'Four Immortals' at the Paris Conference had decided in their wisdom first to disarm themselves and then had proposed to their enemies that they should disarm next.[158] What Henry Wilson pointed out was not far from truth in this case. Turkish power in Anatolia had been allowed to grow into a reality.

In February 1921 the Dashnak government was re-established in Erevan following an uprising which was provoked by the prevailing harsh economic conditions, incited by Turkish Nationalist and French agents in the Caucasus and led by Dashnak Party members. Vratsian passionately appealed to the 'conscience' of civilised humanity and asked for help in every direction. But from nowhere was there any effective response. Trying to win the goodwill of the Turks, he telegraphed the British Foreign Office and asked that the decisions of the Second London Conference do not bring about 'reciprocal

156. *BAC Minutes*, 21 Oct. 1921.
157. FO 371/4960/E12478, 13 Oct. 1920. Ibid., Aharonian to Derby (copy 2645), 5 Oct. 1920, encl. in Derby to Curzon, 7 Oct. 1920.
158. Wilson Papers, 73/1/13, File no. 37/16, Wilson to Gen. Milne, 2 June 1920.

distrust' between Turkey and Armenia. He also cabled Chicherin stating
that the forthcoming Moscow Conference had no legal authority to examine
the question of Armenia. He even requested military help from Kemalist
Turkey. It was a desperate move based on illusion. The Turks would not
openly support anti-Bolshevik rebellion. Shrewdly keen on obtaining good
terms from Soviet Russia in Moscow, they would not risk Soviet hostility.
On the other hand Armenia did not attend the Moscow Conference held in
March 1921, although she had earlier been invited to it by Chicherin.[159] The
Bolsheviks re-entered Erevan in April 1921.

But Soviet Russia apparently also had its fair share of illusions. Russia's new
rulers had appealed to the Moslems of the East for 'sympathy and support' in
the work of 'regenerating' the world.[160] In early 1921 Lenin told Soviet
Armenian representatives that although he was prepared to provide
Armenia with supplies and money, he would not, and could not fight for the
inclusion of Kars in Armenia. He had hopes of a rising among the Turkish
peasantry:

> We are temporarily compelled to sacrifice the interests of the Armenian
> labour classes to those of the World Revolution,

he argued.[161] Furthermore, having experienced during the civil war the
results of the unimpeded access of foreign warships to the Black Sea and
being anxious to exclude the influence of the Entente from there, Russia was
keen to have Turkish co-operation over the Straits. By the Treaty of
Moscow the two powers agreed to entrust the elaboration of an international
statute for the Black Sea and the Straits to a special conference of 'the littoral
countries'. Kars and Ardahan were left to Turkey and both parties agreed
that Nakhichevan should form 'an autonomous territory under the protection of Azerbaijan'.[162] Thus Soviet Russia did not claim Armenian territory

159. FO 371/6266/E3476, Vratsian, 7 Mar. 1921; FO 371/6267/E3698, Vratsian to FO, 26
Mar. 1921; Kirakosian, *Hayastane Pastateghterum*, p. 464. For different views about the causes
of the February uprising see: Northcote Papers, Add. MS. 57560, Northcote, 'Armenia', pp.
31–3, 1926; Kajaznuni, *H.H. Dashnaktsutiune*, pj 46; Avetis Yapujian, *Ov Kazmakerpets
Petervarian Arkatsakhendrutyune ev Inch Eghav Anor Hetevanke* (Who Organised the
Adventure of February [1921] and What Was Its Consequence) (Cairo, 1969), pp. 68–94; G.A.
Galoyan, *Patmutyan Karughinerum* (At the Crossroads of History) (Erevan, 1982), pp. 363–
79.
160. Degras, *Soviet Documents*, I, p.17, Council of People's Commissars to Moslems of East,
3 Dec. 1917.
161. FO 371/6266/E2303, intercepted tel. conversation bet. Al. Bekzadian and Mravian of
Arm. Govt. and Attabeckof, Arm. Repr. in Azerbaijan, 26 Dec. 1920, in Stokes to Curzon, 2
Feb. 1921. See also ibid., no. E1712, Stokes to FO 28 Jan. 1921.
162. Degras, *Soviet Documents*, I, pp. 238–9, Treaty betw. RSFSR and Turkey, 16 March
1921; see also an unsigned paper, *Moscow and Angora* [1921], in Rep. of Arm. Archives, File
75/2.

because of her illusory belief in peasant risings in Turkey and in Turkish goodwill over the Straits. In the meantime, Turkey received substantial moral and material help from Russia against Greece. However, once she had defeated the Greeks, Turkey supported not the Russian but the British proposal over the Straits at the Conference of Lausanne. Vessels sailing under Russian flag were forbidden to enter the port of Constantinople. 'Ungrateful' Turkey had 'forgotten all that Russia did for her at a time when she was in great difficulties', Zalkind, the Soviet representative in Constantinople reported in 1923. Moreover, Mustafa Subhi, the Turkish communist leader and fourteen of his companions were mysteriously — and conveniently — drowned at Trebizond. Still, despite all Angora's manoeuvring, the withdrawal of Turkish troops from the Alexandropol region in Armenia was due to Soviet Russia's threats.[163]

In Britain, a comprehensive unity of policy towards Turkey and the Caucasus was also gradually becoming an illusion. If on the one hand the politicians at Paris were sometimes genuine and sometimes simply loud in their statements on the principle of national self-determination and the rights of small states, the sentiments of many high-ranking generals in responsible positions betrayed immense contempt towards the inexperienced and unorganised peoples of the Caucasus. After his visit to the region in 1919, George F. Milne, the General Officer Commanding the Army of the Black Sea with jurisdiction over Anatolia and the Caucasus, could not see that these republics would 'ever be able to stand on their own'. He had never seen a more miserable country or people. The world would not 'lose much' if the whole of the inhabitants cut each other's throats. About a year later he wrote:

> There will be no peace in Trans-Caucasia so long as these petty republics are allowed to continue . . .

Sir Henry Wilson absolutely agreed. This Balkanising of Europe and Russia, agreed at Paris, was a 'perfectly mad and insensate arrangement', certain to breed eternal wars.[164] The Chief of the Imperial General Staff was 'determined to make love to the Turk' and 'to Kemal' in order to get peace for Britain in the East and in order to make the Turkish nation a buffer against Russia. Writing in 1921, Wilson insisted that Britain should have a

---

163. FO 371/9158/E5286, encl. Zalkind to Moscow, copy, 24 Apr. 1923. George S. Harris, *The Origins of Communism in Turkey* (Stanford, 1967), p. 91; Kirakosian, *Hayastane Pastateghterum*, pp. 507–10, quot. Chicherin's notes to Turk. ambassad., Moscow, 6, 8 Apr. 1921.

164. Wilson Papers, 73/1/13, File 37/5, Milne to H. Wilson, 22 Jan. 1919. Ibid., Files 37/11, 37/12, Milne to H. Wilson, 16 Dec. 1919, Wilson to Milne, copy, 29 Dec. 1919, respectively.

strong and friendly Turkey 'stretching from Smyrna to Baku . . .' on her side.[165]

Evidently there was no room for Armenia in his plan.

With such views prevalent among the General Staff, what were the arms sent to Armenia in the summer of 1920? H.W. Harcourt wrote on 1 December 1920:

> . . . the utility of the shipment was largely destroyed by the fact that the War Office took this opportunity to unload on the Armenians the Canadian Ross rifles — marksmen's rifles — which had been tried in France and proved useless for general field service.

For Harcourt it was not too much to say that the Ross rifle had much to do with the degeneration of the Armenian army. The matter was also raised in Parliament by Lord Robert Cecil.[166]

A demand for the revision of British government policy towards Turkey increasingly grew stronger after the resurgence of Nationalist power in Turkey, the sovietisation of the Caucasus, unrest in the Empire and after awareness of the diverging attitudes of Britain's allies. A pro-Turkish orientation was considered more profitable for Britain. Even before the final collapse of Armenia, Bonar Law wanted to revise the Treaty of Sèvres in favour of the Turks. According to Hankey, the supposed advantage would please the Mohammedan world, and for Britain less trouble in India and Egypt. Montagu also favoured a revision: under the existing Turkish Treaty of Peace the situation in the East looked like 'prolonged warfare'.[167] The War Office in its turn advocated concessions in the 'territorial terms' of the Treaty in order to 'induce the Turkish Nationalists to break with the Russian Soviet Government'. Such a policy might 'wean' them from the Russian Bolsheviks, recreate Turkey as a buffer state between the Entente powers and Russia and also remove some of the underlying causes of unrest throughout the British dominions. A British officer in Turkey had strongly advised that the Turk should be induced to 'eat out of our hand' since he was 'the *only* means' of arresting the advance of Bolshevism to the south and east. Where else could one find, he asked, human war material which was so 'ready made and cheap' — as the Turkish soldiers who were enduring, required little and had a natural amenity to discipline?[168] Finally,

165. Ibid., 73/1/8, File 12E/7, Wilson to Gen. Sackville West, 11 Oct. 1919; ibid., 73/1/9, File 13B/41, Wilson to Gen. Lord Rawlinson, 23 Nov. 1920; ibid., 73/1/14, File 46B/45, Wilson to Sec. for War, 19 Dec. 1921.

166. Davidson Papers, Box on Armenia, Harcourt, 'The Situation in Armenia', n.d.; same, in Bryce Papers, UB 65, 1 Dec. 1920. *Hansard*, 5th Ser. 1922, vol 151, col. 1125.

167. Hankey Papers, Diary, HNKY 1/5, entry for 28 Nov. 1920; Montagu Papers, AS-IV-6, 903(2), paper circ. by Montagu, 22 Nov. 1920.

168. CAB 24/120, C.P. 2608, memo, by Sec. for War, 19 Feb. 1921. Wilson Papers, 73/1/9, File 13B/23, Col. Rawlinson to Gen. Rawlinson, 13 Feb. 1920, transmit. by latter to H. Wilson, 24 Feb. 1920.

worries regarding British trade with Turkey were expressed by the Department of Overseas Trade. The Kemalists had brought trade between Britain and Turkey 'virtually to a standstill' by almost completely interrupting the communications with the interior. The value of the stranded British goods in Turkish ports was estimated at between £5,000,000 and £12,000,000. The Prime Minister was also reminded that the value of pre-war British exports had amounted to £8,500,000. Even the King found the proposals of his Minister of War, advocating an attitude of friendship towards Kemalist Turkey and an immediate withdrawal of all British troops from Turkish territory, as 'very sound' and made his view known to the Cabinet.[169]

As to Armenia, the problem of giving her effective help, always considered difficult by Britain, owing to her total lack of interest in the region, was further complicated by the sovietisation of the country. Annexing territory to Armenia was now viewed by the Foreign Office as extending Soviet territory and was, therefore, undesirable:

> . . . it would seem that the attempt to give them [the Armenians] the Wilson frontier would merely be to bring Russian influence nearer Const'ple, — which neither we nor the Turks want.[170]

Moreover, after the collapse of the Caucasian republics, Turkey was considered the only possible barrier in the east against Soviet Russia. So weaning her away from Moscow became the main preoccupation of the Western powers for that region. Armenia might be ignored. When the Soviet Armenian government complained to Angora about the complete devastation by the Turkish troops of the district of Alexandropol and the province of Kars and demanded by its note of 18 January 1921 their withdrawal from these regions,[171] Lord Chelmsford, the Viceroy of India, cabled about suggestions that the 'dissension' between Moscow and Angora 'be emphasised' in the press. D.G. Osborne minuted:

> The ruining of Turkey by Russia is a point we might make in our discussions with the Turks. Their choice is between the Allies and Russia.[172]

---

169. Lloyd George Papers, F/206/4/25, 'Note on Trade with Turkey', unsigned, n.d. but ref. to communic. by Dept. Overseas Trade, 2 Feb. 1921; ibid., F/25/2/42, Stamfordham to Thomas Jones, 12 Nov. 1921, and memo by Sec. of State for War, C.P. 3474, 9 Nov. 1921.
170. FO 371/6266/E1712, Osborne, 8 Feb. 1921.
171. Ibid., no. E1713, Stokes to F.O., 4 Feb. 1921; see also Kirakosian, *Hayastane Pastateghterum*, pp. 485–9.
172. FO 371/6266/E1885, Chelmsford to India Office, copy, 9 Feb. 1921; ibid., minute, Osborne, 14 Feb. 1921.

Thus, policy regarding Armenia, which had been mostly confined to pronouncements only, became of necessity more complicated. When discussing the revision of the terms of the Treaty of Sèvres to be proposed, the Cabinet approved in December 1921, Curzon's advice, with regards to a 'Home' in Cilicia, that:

> . . . an enclave should be created in the South near the sea where, under guarantees of protection all the remaining Armenians should be congregated.

Amidst the confusions of policy Curzon admitted that it was worth trying to do 'something' for the Armenians as to whose fate public opinion in Britain was 'much exercised'. Three months later, however, he had to put another proposal to the Cabinet as he thought that there was no chance of the Turks accepting the scheme in Cilicia. Curzon despaired of doing much for the Armenians. But the Soviet Armenian republic was 'safe' for the moment:

> He would like to persuade the Turks to increase the size of this state.[173]

However, the British government's intention generally to treat Turkey as a defeated country, which, unprovoked had joined the enemy, closed the Straits and committed so many crimes, was veritably sabotaged by both Italy and France.

The unity of the Entente powers, especially as regards Turkey, was another illusion.

Italy backed Kemalist Turkey because Britain was supporting Greece, and because, frustrated of what she deemed her due in Paris, she looked for prospective economic concessions in Anatolia. France, too, backed Kemalist Turkey against Britain because she felt that the latter had let her down over the Rhine. Berthelot was quite open about it:

> He said that if we would support the French move on the Rhine, France would help us a great deal more in the East . . .[174]

In addition, French financiers, having heavily lost in Russia following expropriation by the revolutionaries, were particularly anxious not to lose also in Turkey. From the very first, therefore, French politicians took a propitiatory line towards Turkey in order to safeguard their country's 'material and moral' interests there. For example, both Clemenceau and

---

173. CAB 23/27, Cab. 93(21) App. III, Conclusions of a Conf. of Ministers, min. 3, 21 Dec. 1921. CAB 23/29, Cab. 19(22), min. 2, 20 Mar. 1922.
174. Quot. in Lowe and Dockrill, *Mirage of Power*, vol. 2, p. 367.

Berthelot favoured leaving Constantinople to the Sultan. Berthelot maintained that France still possessed the great majority of capital in both the railways and public and private enterprises where, before 1914, she had invested over three milliards.[175]

However, what poisoned the relations of the Allies, encouraged the Turks, increased their spirit of defiance and made the power of the victorious Allies a mere illusion, were the secret dealings of both France and Italy not with the legal government of Turkey in Constantinople — which they probably considered to be under British influence — but with the Kemalists. The position of the Italians in Constantinople was 'idiotic', General Milne wrote from that city. They were 'frankly' with the Nationalists and acted 'as their spies'. He had evidence that the Italian member of the Turkish War Office Commission attended Nationalist meetings. Neither the Italians nor the French wanted the Treaty of Sèvres carried out and they were 'encouraging the Nationalists to resist'.[176]

'A nice savoury disclosure' wrote W. Thwaites, the Director of Military Intelligence, in a covering note in 1920, forwarding to the CIGS the reproductions of ten cipher telegrams dealing with various interviews between the Nationalists and the French authorities. They were obtained secretly and deciphered by the British Army of the Black Sea.[177] François Georges Picot, the French Commissioner Extraordinary for Syria and Armenia, had, on his way to the Paris Peace Conference, a special interview with Mustafa Kemal at Sivas in December 1919. Kemal had strongly protested against the French occupation of Cilicia and against the 'atrocities committed by the French and Armenians'. In reply Picot had stated that in exchange for securing 'economical advantages' in Adana, the French might 'probably evacuate' Cilicia and endeavour 'to remove the occupation' by other governments. Kemal added:

> The opinion I have formed from this interview is that the French consider it more favourable to [one or two words missed. Tr.] in favour of TURKEY.

According to another intercepted telegram, Major Brissod, the French Intelligence Officer at Brusa, told Bekir Sami, on behalf of Franchet d'Esperey, the French High Commissioner in Turkey, in February 1920:

> The Turks are living in an important and delicate period. They must endeavour not to lose the favourable public opinion of the French who are their only friend in the world . . .

175. Lloyd George Papers F/206/4/7, Berthelot, note of 12 Dec. 1919, App. to Minutes of First Meeting, Anglo-French Conf. on Turkey, 22 Dec. 1919.
176. Wilson Papers, 73/1/13, Files 37/17, 37/14, 37/17, Milne to Wilson, 26 June, 22 May, 26 June 1920, respectively.
177. WO 106/64, Thwaites to CIGS, 30 July 1920.

Contact by the French with the Nationalists at this time meant 'a political advantage of the highest importance' — admitted Mustafa Kemal himself.[178]

Similar reports of secret dealings between the Italians and the French on the one hand and the Turks on the other came from various sources. According to Réchad Halise Bey, the former Turkish Minister in Berne, it was Italy who first began intriguing following the Greek occupation of Smyrna. She provided Turkey with money and munitions of war. In his turn Sir Adam Block, in Constantinople, reported that it was very sad there were 'traitors' in the Allied camp.[179]

Thus even before the first Peace Treaty, the Turks could fully enjoy the 'savoury' spectacle of a divided Allied front. If the Allies could not agree on matters of importance, surely there would be no prospect at all for their agreeing to support far-away, inaccessible Armenia. In 1922 no less a person than Lord Curzon alleged at a Cabinet meeting[180] that there was reason to believe the British views were being passed on to the Turks by the French. Perhaps the Turks knew in advance in 1920 that Armenia would receive no effective help whatsoever from the Allies. No wonder that they not only did not hand over any land in Turkish Armenia — as stipulated by the Treaty of Sèvres — but also in absolute defiance of the signatory 'Allies' marched into Russian Armenia.

The French were the first to demand the revision of the Treaty of Sèvres. But before this could be done, and while officially peace negotiations were still going on between Turkey and the Allied powers, they concluded the Franklin-Bouillon Agreement on 20 October 1921. According to an infuriated Curzon a territory of 10,000 square miles in Cilicia and containing the military approaches to Mesopotamia was handed over to the Kemalists. The Christian population was thus left to the 'tender mercies' of the Turk. The French had 'stolen a march' on their Allies and had by 'underhand' methods obtained preferential treatment for their 'interests'. Curzon was emphatic that

> The action of the French Government had done more than anything else to improve the moral and increase the prestige of Mustapha Kemal and so made it most difficult to reach a peaceable settlement.[181]

In a Note annexed to the Agreement, Yussuf Kemal Bey told Bouillon that in return for French assistance in solving 'all the questions relating to the independence and sovereignty of Turkey', concessions would be granted to

178. Ibid., GHQ Gen. Staff 'Intelligence' Constant., no. 4578/16 'I' no. 7, Mustafa Kemal to Kiazim Bey, 6 Dec. 1919, repeated 17 Dec. 1919; ibid., no. 8, Bekir Sami, Brusa, to Mustafa Kemal, 8 Feb. 1920. Mustafa Kemal, *A Speech* . . . , p. 391.
179. Curzon Papers MSS Eur F/112/197 ff.24–6, Derby, Paris, to Curzon, 30 Jan. 1920. Ibid., no. 215, ff.55–8, Block to Curzon, 12 June 1920.
180. CAB 23/29, Cab. 19(22), min. 2(iv), 20 Mar. 1922.
181. CAB 23/27, Cab. 88(21), min. 2, 22 Nov. 1921.

a French group for the exploitation of iron, chrome and silver mines in the Karshut valley. In addition, the Turkish government would examine with 'utmost goodwill' other requests for 'concessions for mines, railways, ports and waterways'.[182] Thus, the Allied front was formally broken up and the spiral for concessions was set going. Not a few influential Englishmen and Americans, motivated mainly by financial and economic considerations, also urged concessions to their governments.[183]

The British Cabinet soon agreed to propose to the Allies that the Kemalists should be invited 'unconditionally' to a Conference; and if necessary, Angora might be informed that on a satisfactory settlement being reached, Britain would be prepared to consider favourably the grant to Turkey of financial assistance for rehabilitation.[184]

The French and Italian policy of winning the favours of Turkey continued unabated. In March 1922 Curzon referred in the Cabinet to information received from the Italian ambassador: that the Turks had given Italy 'concessions for railways, mines, etc.' — probably in return for support. Curzon considered his task of negotiating a new peace treaty with Turkey very difficult and the prospect of achieving success remote, recalling the 'consistent and almost treacherous' attitude of the French:

> There was reason to believe that all the British views, if communicated to the French Government, were passed on to the Turks, and General Pellé and the French Foreign Office had practically thrown themselves into the arms of the Turks.[185]

These relations were not improved at the Conference of Lausanne, where the Allies met the representatives of Turkey to make peace for the second time. Curzon complained to Barrère, the principal French representative, about the daily attacks upon him that appeared in quarters in close touch with the French Delegation. Sir W. Tyrrell of the Foreign Office felt furious at the treatment Curzon had received at the hands of the 'so-called allies'. Lausanne was a shocking chapter of 'treachery & ineptitude', he remarked.[186] Thus, on the one hand the Allies were divided among themselves; on the other they were wooing Turkey, who was also enjoying now the advantage of her victory over Greece. An entry in a diary kept during the

182. PP. 1921, vol. I (session 2), p. 128.
183. See PRO Oliphant Papers, FO 800/253, Tu/22/8 and Tu/22/49, memo. by Waugh encl. in H. Rumbold to Oliphant, 25 Feb. 1922, Rumbold to Oliphant, 13 Nov. 1922; See also Bonar Law Papers, 111/12/57, 111/12/61, about the interests of Walter Long, a former Cabinet Minister and other MPs.
184. CAB 23/27, Cab. 88(21), min. 2, 22 Nov. 1921.
185. CAB 23/29, Cab. 19(22), min. 2, 20 Mar. 1922. See also Bonar Law Papers, 111/12/61, Curzon to Bonar Law, 25 Jan. 1923.
186. Curzon Papers, MSS Eur F 112/283, Curzon to Barrère, copy, 21 Jan. 1923. Ibid., F 112/284, Tyrrell to Curzon, 5 Feb. 1923.

Conference has referred to Barrère and Garroni, the French and Italian representatives, who

> . . . toady Ismet, bawling 'Excellence' at him at every sentence, shouting 'ami et cher collègue'. This makes Curzon sick with disgust . . . He rose from his chair and did an imitation of Garroni addressing Ismet Pasha, fondling him, stroking him, cooing endearments . . .[187]

Allied unity was an illusion. This was not the scene of an alliance of victors imposing or negotiating a peace in unity but perhaps a spectacle nearer prostration. Bonar Law, now Prime Minister, was well aware of the situation. He warned Curzon:

> . . . there are two things which seem to me vital. The first is that we should not go to war for the sake of Mosul, and second, that if the French, as we know to be the case, will not join us, we shall not by ourselves fight the Turks to enforce what is left of the Treaty of Sèvres. I feel so strongly on both these points.[188]

Under such conditions Ismet hardly made any concessions to the Allies and absolutely none at all as regards Armenia. Lord Curzon did refer, at Lausanne, to the 'cruel sufferings' which the Armenians had endured for generations and pleaded for a national home for them. He bluntly asked Ismet how was it that the 3,000,000 Armenians formerly in Asia Minor had been reduced to 130,000? 'Had they killed themselves, or had they voluntarily run away?' Why were hundreds of thousands of Armenians now fugitives in every country in the world? Why was this Armenian question one of the great scandals of the world?[189] It was useless. Curzon's indictment remained a statement. And to quote Churchill's words, in the Treaty of Lausanne 'history will search in vain for the word "Armenia" '.[190]

From Sèvres to Lausanne: during this fluid period of illusions, political instability and intense power struggle, it seems that neither Armenia, nor Britain and the Allies, nor even Russia had adjusted their aspirations and objectives to the realities of their resources. Kemal Ataturk alone had measured all too exactly the immense strategic strength of his country and knew precisely what actual power he could achieve. Armenia was the greatest loser in 1923, Turkey the beneficiary.

187. Nicolson, *Curzon*, p. 319, quot. diary entry, 22 Dec. 1922.
188. Bonar Law Papers, 111/12/57, Bonar Law to Curzon, copy, 8 Jan. 1923; also in Curzon Papers MSS Eur F 112/282.
189. PP. 1923, vol. XXVI, pp. 178–9, 211–12, Conf. of Lausanne, 12, 13 Dec. 1922.
190. Ibid., 1923, vol. XXV, pp. 533–782, Treaty of Lausanne, signed on 24 July 1923. Churchill, *The Aftermath*, p. 408.

6   The Disappointment of Pro-Armenian Humanitarians After 1918

It has already been seen, in Chapter 2, that the war brought a convergence of attitudes towards Armenia in both the pro-Armenian humanitarian groups and the Establishment. The latter considered it of national interest, during 1914-18, to arouse sympathy with the sufferings of the Armenian people. The former, on the other hand, never ceased from working with total devotion for the cause they had adopted, both during the war and throughout the whole period covered by this study. They organised relief and, especially after their bitter disappointment with the Armistice of Mudros, they vigorously pressed the government to secure the liberation of Turkish Armenia and the return and protection of the thousands of refugees.

At a public meeting organised to express sympathy with the Armenian cause and held at Central Hall, Westminster, on 19 June 1919, G.P. Gooch[1] moved the resolution earnestly appealing to the generous British people for funds for the relief of the Armenian refugees. Earlier, the Chairman of the meeting, Lord Herbert John Gladstone, had read a telegram from the Prime Minister of the Armenian republic in Erevan, stating that about 150 were dying daily from starvation and disease. The contents of the telegram were confirmed by Dr Paul S. Leinbach, Secretary to the eighteen members of the American Commission for Near East and Armenian Relief, who were on their way back home after their visit to Armenia, Mesopotamia and various parts of Turkey. Dr Leinbach had told the meeting about their heart-breaking experiences: about the 250,000 orphans, many of them with horrible tattoo marks on their faces and about the 50,000 Armenian children and women who were still captives in Moslem houses. Gooch asked support for his resolution 'in the name of the greatest sufferings' of modern, or perhaps of any, period of history. The Armenians were the 'most gifted' race of the Middle East;

> . . . there are not many of them left, but they are quite enough to repair the disasters of the past. They are the trustees of unborn generations and I ask you to support this Resolution in memory of those who are dead and in the interests of the generations to come . . .

Through another resolution the meeting trusted that the new Armenian

---

1. Historian and editor of *Contemporary Review*. See Alexandre Rossman, *Contemporary Review*, vol. 213, no. 1234, (Nov. 1968), p. 229.

state would embrace all the Armenians who dwelt within the limits of the ancient Armenian kingdom, including those in Cilicia and in Transcaucasia. When E. Harrison Yelverton, the American Vice-Consul in London, moved the vote of thanks to the Chairman, Lord Gladstone stated that he needed no vote of thanks. The last public speech his father had made was at Liverpool in 1896 on behalf of Armenia and he had felt it one of his first duties to come to the meeting. He added that the British owed a great deal to Armenia, not so much for what the Armenians had done for the British, but for what Britain, with its wealth and power had not done for them which she ought to have. The meeting was also addressed by Lord Bryce, Ronald M. Burrows (Principal of King's College, London), the Reverend Dr John Clifford, T.P. O'Connor, Noel Buxton, Aneurin Williams and other Armenophiles. Those who had sent letters of apology and sympathy included Lord Sydenham, Lord Weardale, Lord Tenterden, J.L. Garvin (the editor of the *Observer*), John Galsworthy, who had contributed £1,000 towards the Armenian-Syrian Relief — the net profit resulting from his lecture tour in the United States — and the historians Dr Holland Rose and G. Lowes Dickinson of Cambridge and Professor Henry Spencer Wilkinson of Oxford.[2]

Early in January 1920 a memorial was also drafted, on the suggestion of Bryce, Noel Buxton, T.P. O'Connor, Arnold Toynbee, the Reverend Silas Hocking and Dr F.B. Meyer, to urge upon the British government 'the fulfilment of [the] pledges'. The draft, as sent to the Archbishop of Canterbury, was addressed to the Prime Minister and the Secretary of State for Foreign Affairs. It asked that:

1. The rule of the Ottoman Turks over the subject races . . . ought now at last to end wherever there is a non-Turkish majority.

2. [The Armenian] republic should be at once recognised, and that there should be added to it an extensive zone of the Armenian territory hitherto subject to Turkey, including a suitable port on the Black Sea.

3. In wide areas the Armenians and other Christian races have been in part massacred and in part driven into exile. We ask that these districts be dealt with on a pre-war basis, so that no recognition be given to the policy of turning a majority into a minority by means of massacre.

The Archbishop expressed his willingness to have his name appended to the memorial. Most of the other signatories also represented the Churches.[3]

---

2. Aram Raffi (ed.), *Armenia and the Settlement* (Report of Public Meeting to Express Sympathy with the Armenian Cause, held at the Central Hall, Westminster, 19 June 1919) (London, 1919), pp. 3–7, 12–13, 16–17, 26, 34–5, 38–40.

3. They included among others, W.T.A. Barber (President, Wesleyan Methodists), John H. Barlow (Clerk of the Yearly Meeting, Society of Friends), Hugh Falconer (Moderator, Presbyterian Church of England), Arthur T. Guttery (President, National Free Church Council), H. Marnham (President, Baptist Union). There were also W.B. Selbie (Principal, Mansfield College, Oxford) and Alfred E. Garvie (Principal, New College, London). See Davidson Papers, Box on Armenia, draft memorial, encl. in Williams to Archbishop of Canterbury, 2 Jan. 1920; Archbishop to Williams, copy, 6 Jan. 1920.

However, as already seen, no territory of the Armenian provinces in Turkey was added to the Republic of Erevan, and the Armenian refugees could never return to their homes. In late 1920 the existence of the republic itself was threatened by the Kemalists. On 12 November, Gevorg V, the Catholicos of all the Armenians, made a statement from Erevan. It read:

> Weakened, famished, suffering, the Armenian people sees itself abandoned at the present hour to the enemy which desires their total destruction . . . In the name of the Saviour I appeal to Christian humanity to save the rest of my people in Armenia.[4]

The statement was published in the January issue of the *Friend of Armenia* in 1921. It was too late.

The pro-Armenian humanitarians were bitter. When the Erevan republic became Soviet, strong blame was placed on the 'neglect' of the powers to give it proper protection against the attacks of the Turkish forces.[5] In 1922 the discussion of 'Item J', brought forward by the Supply Committee of the House of Commons, initiated a passionate discussion in the House. It had been noted that in 1920 the Erevan republic had been furnished by the Royal Navy with fuel oil estimated at £16,368. The sum had been discharged by the Admiralty which now asked to be reimbursed, and the Supply Committee advised:

> The claim has been noted for presentation to any future stable Government of Armenia.

Referring to the words 'any future stable Government of Armenia', Aneurin Williams stated that the existing government in Armenia was, as a matter of fact, the most stable they had ever had, but it was a government hostile to Britain, and that was the net result of the 'poltroon policy' of the government which had abandoned these people. Lord Robert Cecil reminded the House that 'Item J' had brought up painful memories of one of the most 'discreditable' and unfortunate chapters in recent history. He asked what had been done to discharge an 'obligation of honour' that the British and the French had undertaken during the war. These people had been told officially and unofficially that if they assisted the Allies in the war against the Turks, the Allies would take care that they would have national independence and would be protected. Almost nothing was done. G. Barnes, a former member of the War Cabinet, did not think that the government had stood behind these people as it should have done. The

---

4. *Friend of Armenia*, no. 79 (Jan. 1921), p. 6.
5. *Hansard*, 5th Ser. 1920, vol. 136, col. 14 (T.P. O'Connor).

only objection that O'Connor would raise in regard to this particular item, would be that it was 'so small'.[6]

As mentioned earlier, there was reluctance to help Armenia effectively. This was mainly caused by considerations of economy and a general suspicion on the part of the public towards foreign ventures together, in some quarters, with concern for Mohammedan feeling and arguments in favour of economic interests. The pro-Armenian groups were aware of a resurgence of Turkophile sentiment in Britain, even immediately after the armistice. T.P. O'Connor asked whether its cause was money or international finance. He had never seen a more lavishly financed, or a more artificial agitation than this concern for Mohammedan feeling in India.[7]

For pro-Armenian pressure groups, it was clear that concern for Armenia had nothing to do with feelings towards Moslem religion. The Archbishop of Canterbury stressed over and over again that he had never protested against the rule of Islam in itself. He did not denounce the faith of Islam but the oppression and cruelties of Turkish rule.[8]

It seems that the Church, various religious denominations and some intellectuals and educational establishments felt that concern with Mohammedan feelings in India was simply being used as a pretext for financial interests and Turkophilism. They fought as hard as they could, sometimes independently, sometimes with the British Armenia Committee. A leaflet signed by the Reverends H.J. Fynes Clinton and J.A. Douglas on behalf of the Anglican and Eastern Churches Association and the Society of Faith was sent to all churches and chapels in England with a request that telegrams should be sent to the Prime Minister and to the local Member of Parliament insisting that Armenians, Syrians and other Christians of the Turkish Empire be set free from every semblance of the Sultan's rule. 'Confused issues and materialistic influences' were prevalent, the leaflet noted. British opinion was being inoculated with the absurdity that Islam was identified with the Turkish Empire, and that while the Sultan's flag might be safely hauled down in Moslem Mesopotamia, Egypt, Palestine and elsewhere, the Moslem world would be stung to fury by its ceasing to fly over Christian lands, the leaflet added.[9]

The Reverend F.B. Meyer, a member of the British Armenia Committee, reported in December 1919 that the Council of the Free Churches had issued to 1,000 of their branches a resolution in support of the claims of Armenia, which they were asked to pass and send to the government.[10]

6. Ibid., 1922, vol. 151, cols. 1178, 1124, 1177, 1168.

7. Raffi (ed.), *Armenia and the Settlement*, p. 23. *Hansard*, 5th Ser. 1920, vol. 125, col. 1983.

8. *BAC Minutes*, 4 July, 2 Aug. 1921. Davidson Papers, Box on Armenia, Archbishop of Canterbury to Lord Mayor of London, copy, 10 Dec. 1921. Ibid., Archbishop to M. Zaven, Arm. Patriarch, Const., copy, 16 Nov. 1921.

9. Ibid., leaflet, 6 Jan. 1920.

10. *BAC Minutes*, 18 Dec. 1919.

A memorial signed by a few resident members of Oxford University was also sent by Canon A.C. Headlam of Christ Church, the Regius Professor of Divinity, to the Foreign Minister. The signatories expressed their grave anxiety at the threatened restoration and strengthening of Turkish rule over the subject Christian population. They could not admit in any way the claim made by the Turkish nation 'to the whole' of Asia Minor. The Turks were invaders from central Asia. It had also been stated that the rights of subject populations would be respected under Turkish rule. This did not conform to experience. The policy of the Turks in Anatolia, as in Armenia, had 'obviously been one of deliberate deportation or massacre' wherever opportunity had occurred. The signatories were convinced that the claims of Indian Mohammedans were being used to paralyse the action of Britain. The signatories assured the Foreign Secretary that in any steps which he might feel able to take to prevent this, he would have the support of an influential and widespread educated opinion. The signatories included Herbert E.D. Blakiston, President of Trinity and a Pro-Vice Chancellor; Francis Pember, Warden of All Souls and a Pro-Vice Chancellor; Reginald W. Macan, Master of University College; Herbert Warren, President of Magdalen College; W.A. Spooner, Warden of New College; B.J. Kidd, Warden of Keble College; A. Cowley, Bodleian Librarian; Charles Oman, All Souls' College, Chichele Professor of Modern History and Burgess of the University.[11]

It was the Archbishop of Canterbury, however, who, on the eve of the Conference of Lausanne, wrote an exceptionally strong-worded letter to Bonar Law, the Prime Minister, claiming to express, together with his own views, those of the Church and of the 'thoughtful' people of the country. Uninformed newspaper writers and some less uninformed politicians were talking airily about 'economic' grounds for Britain's ridding herself of any responsibilities towards the Christian peoples and churches of Turkey. The Archbishop was profoundly conscious of the ramifications of this question, and of the effect upon Mohammedans in India of British relations to Islam in the Near East. He wished, however, to say to the Prime Minister, how widespread among earnest and thoughtful people in England and Scotland would be the sense of 'unutterable shame' were it to be announced that Britain was 'ignoring solemn pledges' and leaving great Christian populations to the sword of a merciless foe. The Prime Minister ought to be aware of the strength of religious opinion which would support him if he affirmed that

> . . . our pledged word cannot be broken or ignored. Such breach would be regarded by tens of thousands of religious people when informed of the facts as nothing short of infamous.[12]

11. Curzon Papers, MSS Eur F. 112/284, Headlam to Curzon, 20 Mar. 1922. Memorial originally meant for Prime Minister.
12. Bonar Law Papers, 112/10/1, Archbishop of Canterbury to Bonar Law, 24 Oct. 1922.

As an aftermath to this letter, the Archbishop and Curzon, the Foreign Secretary, had an interview and on the latter's 'instructions' a draft reply was prepared for Bonar Law to sign. It stated that the question of protecting Christians under Turkish rule had been profoundly modified in that the Turks had 'practically eliminated' the Christian elements in Turkey. According to recent American reports there were now 'practically no Armenians left in Turkish Armenia' nor Greeks on the coast of the Black Sea. So, the elaborate minorities provisions of the Treaty of Sèvres would be pointless in any new peace treaty with Turkey. But the Archbishop should also realise that the British government were not free agents in this matter. They were dependent on the support of their Allies.[13]

The draft letter, with all Curzon's strange candour, was not sent. Apparently it would have laid the British government open to the charge that it was accepting the *fait accompli* solution in Turkey, achieved by the policy of eliminating native populations by force. Instead Bonar Law, the shrewd businessman from Glasgow, produced an anodyne reply. He promised the Archbishop that 'the most earnest attention' would be given to his views, and then blamed dependence on the Allies for his failure to commit Britain.[14]

Cilicia had its own tragedy. After the war thousands of Armenian refugees from the Syrian deserts had returned there with the specific encouragement of the Allied powers, and when it was known that France would be its mandatory. Early in 1921, after the Kemalist occupation and the sovietisation of Armenia, the creation of a 'safety-zone' in Cilicia, where Armenians could be temporarily settled in security, was seriously considered. The discussions, held by the British Armenia Committee, were attended by Boghos Nubar and Avetis Aharonian as the Armenian representatives, and by Dr James L. Barton and G.R. Montgomery, as the pro-Armenian American representatives. But the practicability of the 'safety zone' in Cilicia depended on the provision of American financial aid and especially on the consent of France to remain in this region. The proposal was put before the Foreign Office, but the Chairman of the Committee had the impression that the Foreign Office did not endorse it.[15]

In 1920 the French had suffered some reverses in Cilicia at the hands of the Kemalists and in the summer of 1921 they made it clear that they might withdraw. Replying to T.P. O'Connor, Aristide Briand, the Prime Minister, expressed the inability of France to spend financial or military resources on the protection of the Armenians. This occupation of Cilicia had cost the country six thousand lives, he told a special British deputation composed of

13. Ibid., 112/10/1, draft for Bonar Law's signature to Archbishop of Canterbury, initialled by E. Crowe, 27 Oct. 1922.
14. Ibid., 112/10/2, Bonar Law to Archbishop of Canterbury, copy, 31 Oct. 1922.
15. *BAC Minutes*, 21, 28 Feb. 1921.

Lord Bryce, O'Connor and two clergymen representing the Bishop of London and the President of the Free Church Council. The British humanitarians were unremitting and undaunted in their efforts. The British Armenia Committee unanimously adopted the resolution that

> . . . having learned that the situation in Cilicia is becoming extremely critical owing to the evacuation of the province by French troops . . . , [it] urges H[is] M[ajesty's] Government to send warships to Mersina to give protection to the Armenians, who were our Allies in the War . . . The Committee again reminds H.M. Government that large numbers of Armenians were, after the Armistice, sent back to Cilicia by the British authorities under promise of protection.

In addition, the Chairman undertook to write officially, on behalf of the Committee, to eminent Frenchmen — to Raymond Poincaré, the former President of the Republic, J.C.G. Leygues, former Prime Minister, Victor Bérard, President of the Senatorial Commission on Foreign Affairs and to the Cardinal Archbishop of Paris among others.[16]

But, by the Franklin-Bouillon Agreement of October 1921 when France agreed to evacuate Cilicia, the Armenians, who had supported the Allied cause and fought with the Allies, were left in the lurch. In an article, described by the Archbishop of Canterbury as having produced a 'profound impression', Lord Bryce sternly asked what right the French government had to depart from the mandate by leaving to the tender mercies of the Turks people whom the Allied powers had by mandate committed to her charge. But Britain also had her share of responsibility. When retiring from Aleppo she had 'required the refugees' to return to Cilicia. Moreover, Britain was a party to the Covenant of the League of Nations which had assigned the mandate to France. Bryce asked again what was to become of these peoples. In what country were they to find refuge. Giving the story of the Eastern Christians and especially the Armenians since the war, Bryce grimly concluded:

> Bickerings between the Allied Powers, and 'diplomatic checks' given or received, are small matter compared with the honour and good name of England, and with the fate of the unfortunate peoples who have put their trust in her.[17]

The Armenian Patriarch and Church Dignitaries in Constantinople, and Dr Abel Nazarian, the religious leader of the Armenians in London, des-

16. Ibid., 4 July, 15 Nov. 1921; Curzon Papers MSS Eur F 112/221 (b) ff.148–9, O'Connor to Curzon, 24 Dec. 1921.

17. Davidson Papers, Box on Armenia, Archbishop of Canterbury to Curzon, copy, 23 Nov. 1921. *Manchester Guardian*, 19 Nov. 1921, p. 8, cols. 6–7.

perately pleaded with the Archbishop of Canterbury for help. Archbishop B. Sarajian of the diocese of Cilicia, cabling from Cyprus, appealed to Great Britain, as the personification of justice, the protectress of the unprotected, to have mercy on this nation, who wanted 'nothing else but a hearth' where they could live and breathe freely.[18]

The Archbishop of Canterbury wrote to Curzon about the steadily growing sense of resentment against the very idea of Britain's 'acquiescing' in what was apparently French policy, the abandonment of these Christian populations to the very foes who had been most ruthless hitherto in their cruelty. Curzon replied that he was also 'terribly concerned' and had addressed the French in the strongest terms.[19]

But at Mersina, in Cilicia, thousands of unsheltered Armenians were waiting to be moved to safe quarters. On 26 November 1921, Bishop Torgom in Egypt cabled that the French authorities in Syria and the British authorities in Palestine, Egypt and Cyprus were refusing to accept the Armenian refugees. The British government now stated that they could not 'afford' to give the Armenians an asylum in British territory. A few who had even reached Alexandria in Egypt were not allowed to disembark. At a loss, Aneurin Williams argued that the British government had made public and repeated promises to the Armenians during the war that they would be delivered from Turkish rule. On the strength of these promises, the Armenians had taken the side of Britain and had lost innumerable lives. Williams asked who was going to trust England in any future emergency.[20]

The government, however, thought otherwise. It believed it was a practical impossibility to accommodate the refugees in Cyprus, Egypt, Mesopotamia or Palestine, and there was no money to defray the very heavy expenses of their maintenance. The government could not accept financial responsibility on such a scale, when it had refused to raise the unemployment allowance in Britain in respect of children.[21] It was impossible for the government, repeated Curzon, to accept financial responsibility for tens of thousands of 'alien' refugees in foreign lands.[22]

In the post-war period, financial considerations were necessarily a matter of concern for the government especially in areas which were not of national interest, or which would not materially benefit British citizens and com-

18. Davidson Papers, Box on Armenia, Bezjian-Nazlian Zaven, Dr. A. Nazarian and Archb. Sarajian, to Archbishop of Canterbury, 13 Nov., 16 Nov., 11 Nov. 1921 respectively.

19. Ibid., Archbishop of Canterbury to Curzon, copy, 23 Nov. 1921; Curzon to Archbishop 23 Nov. 1921.

20. Ibid., Archbishop Tourian, Smyrna and Bishop Torgom to Archbishop of Canterbury, 27, 26 Nov. 1921, respectively; ibid., Williams to Archbishop of Canterbury, 29 Nov. 1921.

21. Ibid., Sir Eyre Crowe to Rev. Bell, Chaplain to Archbishop of Canterbury, E13267/-800/44, 2 Dec. 1921.

22. Curzon Papers, MSS EUR F112/232 ff. 45–6, Curzon to Williams, copy, 6 Dec. 1921.

panies. Curzon proudly pointed to the achievements of the British in the southern part of Mesopotamia, since the British occupation of that area in 1917, and in Palestine and Syria. More had been done, he maintained, in two years than had been done in the five preceding centuries.[23]

But these British authorities were naturally not happy at all that they alone should care for over 50,000 refugees at Bakuba camp near Baghdad. The Archbishop of Canterbury asked for the 'practical, strong, and substantial aid' of the Americans for sharing responsibilities towards these Eastern Christians and solving their problems. The British government was spending £1,000 a day for their upkeep, the Archbishop added. Curzon was more specific. The refugees at Bakuba numbered about 53,000, of whom 12,000 were Armenians, the rest being Assyrian Christians. These refugees had been in the camp since September-October 1918. The cost, Curzon believed, amounted to over £200,000 per month, or £2,500,000 per year when the camp was being run by the military authorities (it meant over £6,600 a day — more than six times the figure given by the Archbishop). Curzon hoped, however, that the expense would be reduced by a civilian administration. Still, he stressed, the British government had never been quite able to see why this expenditure, as indeed most of the expenditure of the war in the East, had fallen upon Great Britain alone.[24]

The letters of Lieutenant Dudley Stafford Northcote, beginning in December 1918 and regularly written to his parents and sister, give an intimate and first-hand picture of the life of the Armenian refugees at Bakuba camp, 30 miles north-east of Baghdad. With the end of the war in 1918, Northcote, a grandson of the Earl of Iddesleigh (Chancellor of the Exchequer and Foreign Minister in the 1870s and 1880s), educated at Winchester and Trinity College, Cambridge, had left his regiment in order to work with the refugees. At Bakuba he had 1,300 Armenian refugees to look after and a staff of five British 'Tommies' to help. There were 'heaps more' refugees, he wrote, but each batch of 1,300 or so had an officer. They had one section composed 'entirely of orphans', that is children under 14 whose parents and relatives were 'all' killed during the recent massacres.[25]

In February 1919 Northcote had signed on for another year of service with the refugees. He had also taken another section over and had as many as 2,700 Armenian refugees to look after at Bakuba. He could soon write, however, that everything was going along quite well in the camp. The people were 'very quiet and docile' and gave 'very little trouble'. But it was very different in the early days when fresh hordes of refugees were arriving daily, 'all absolutely helpless and on the verge of starvation'. In those days about 80 died every day. But now, a year later, the death rate had fallen remark-

23. *Hansard*, 5th Ser., 1919, XXXIII, 261–2.
24. Ibid., 1919, XXXVIII, 287, 289–90.
25. Northcote Papers, Add. MS 57559, 1/1, 1/2, 1/3: 3, 10, 11 Dec. 1918, respectively.

ably. Evidently he was also pleased that in seven months he had learned to speak Armenian quite well.[26]

On 11 August 1920 the Arabs in the region had rebelled and had taken control of Bakuba, which, however, had later been recaptured by the British. As soon as the way to Baghdad was properly reopened, orders had come that the camp should be cleared as quickly as possible. The Armenians had to go to Nahr-Umar camp near Basrah and the Assyrians to Mosul. The refugees had accordingly been transferred.[27]

In the summer of 1921, the British government gave orders that the Armenian camp should be closed. Apparently, Northcote had revolted against this decision, resigned and written a memorandum, in the sincere belief that the government at home would not allow this if they knew all the facts of the case. There was 'not one' of the British staff at Nahr-Umar camp who would drive 'women and children out of their tents' into the hot sun, and they had all said so.[28]

Northcote's memorandum stated that he had been engaged in looking after the Armenian refugees in Mesopotamia for two-and-a-half years, and therefore he 'knew something' about them. The number of refugees in Nahr-Umar camp was approximately 11,500 and the majority came from the vicinity of Lake Van and practically all were peasants. It was always intended to repatriate these Armenians to their republic in the Caucasus. For that reason 'no attempt' was made for a very long time to settle them permanently to work. They had been sent to Nahr-Umar, close to Basrah, to wait for ships. In December 1920, however, the Armenian republic in the Caucasus had collapsed. It could not possibly be considered the fault of the refugees that they had remained a burden on the shoulders of the British taxpayer. They had been 'discouraged' from looking for work. It was not as if they had been tried and failed, Northcote added. On 9 July 1921, definite orders had been given that the evacuation of able-bodied men and their families should begin during the week ending 18 July and continue at the rate of 1,400 persons a week; and that fourteen days' rations and Rs 13 should be issued to each refugee leaving the camp. Northcote protested that the refugees were mostly penniless. This was the hottest time of the year and they would not be able to stand the heat if they camped out under the boiling sun. The camp was literally 24 miles away from anywhere. Moreover, there was scarcely any demand for unskilled labour at the present time and the rent of a single room in Basrah was at least Rs 25 per month. Northcote concluded his memorandum by stating that, if the public at home really knew all the facts, they would probably be willing to do something better for these people, who had had more than their fair share of suffering as a direct

26. Ibid., 1/6, 1/7, 2, 17 Feb. 1919; 1/8, 7 Mar. 1919; 1/14, 13 Sept. 1919; 1/11, 5 July 1919.
27. Ibid., 2/4, 3 Oct. 1920; 2/3, 28 Sept. 1920.
28. Ibid., 2/6/1, 2 July 1921.

result of their having taken the Allied side during the war.[29]

It seems that the British Armenia Committee in due course had access to this memorandum. It had also learnt that the Colonial Office, responsible for the administration of Mesopotamia, was about to issue to the press a communiqué in which the cessation of government relief would be announced, and justified on the grounds that the recipients were 'lazy and inefficient'. Accordingly, the British Armenia Committee asked Northcote, now back home in England, if his evidence could be published. Bishop Charles Gore, the Acting Chairman, believed this evidence to be 'most valuable'.[30]

Whatever the wrangle, the Mesopotamian camp was closed by the British government, not in the summer as was planned, but later in 1921. The bulk of the Mesopotamian refugees would be transferred to Erevan, now in Soviet Armenia. However, this was also the time when, following the Franco-Turkish Agreement of 20 October 1921, thousands of Armenians from Cilicia were seeking asylum. In Britain, the relief agencies continued their efforts. The Armenian Refugees (Lord Mayor's) Fund and the Friends of Armenia undertook a 'Joint Campaign' in the winter of 1921-2 under the experienced Captain George F. Gracey, DSO,[31] formerly the British Chief Commissioner's representative in Erevan.

In October 1921 the Reverend Harold Buxton, the Honorary Secretary of the Armenian Refugees (Lord Mayor's) Fund, signed an agreement by which Northcote would go to Erevan to work under the general direction of the Reverend H.W. Harcourt, the agent of the Fund in Armenia.[32] Immediately afterwards, Northcote and Harold Buxton set out for Erevan, to meet the Armenian refugees from Mesopotamia. The Armenian government had undertaken to transport the refugees to Erevan and provide accommodation in the villages, but had told Buxton that food supplies were 'absolutely lacking'. In a cable from Erevan, Buxton and Harcourt said that they had seen Askanaz Mravian, the Commissar for Foreign Affairs, and others in responsible positions. The refugees would be condemned to death by starvation unless the British government made a further allocation. They added significantly:

> Original agreement to send instalments one thousand at certain intervals unfulfilled. Erivan Government powerless to cope with 9000 additional refugees during winter . . .[33]

29. Ibid., 2/6/2, memo. by Northcote, 19 July 1921.

30. Ibid., 2/7, 2/9/1, C.L. Leese, Sec., BAC to Northcote, 23, 26 Sept. 1921.

31. Bryce Papers, UB 65, two leaflets by Arm. Ref. (Lord Mayor's) Fund and Friends of Armenia, dated 31 Aug. 1921 and Aug. 1921.

32. Northcote Papers, Add. MS 57559, 3/2/1, 27 Oct. 1921 and 3/2/2, H. Buxton to Northcote.

33. Davidson Papers, Box on Armenia, Buxton, Tiflis, to Graves, Br. High Commis. Const., copy, 17 Dec. 1921. A. Williams as Chairman had asked Sec. of Fund to send copies of all important despatches as to Basrah refugees to Chaplain to Archbishop of Canterbury. See ibid., Williams to Rev. Bell, 25 Jan. 1922. Ibid., Buxton and Harcourt to Fund, 26 Dec. 1921.

On 21 December 1921, the steamship *Dara* had arrived carrying 3,000 refugees. Northcote also maintained that the Armenian authorities claimed that they had consented to accept the refugees at the rate of 1,000 per fortnight. They had been unable to handle as many as 3,000 at once owing to the great lack of accommodation in Batum and the great shortage of railway wagons and engines.[34] There was a deficiency of 3,500,000 *poods* or 56,000 tons of foodstuffs on the basis of 'half rations' for the whole population of Armenia until harvest. The Armenian government was at the 'end' of its realisable resources. Buxton and Harcourt reported that there were about 500,000 destitute persons and large numbers were actually starving as they themselves had witnessed. The advent of the Basrah refugees during winter was 'deplorable'.[35]

During his stay in Erevan, Buxton had come into close contact with several of the Commissars, and they had been most helpful. They had none of the oratory of diplomats but had a keen sense of responsibility. They worked like Trojans and lived spartan lives. Moscow was 'generously disposed' towards these Caucasian republics, but its own difficulties made any large assistance impossible. Anxious to see as much as possible, Buxton had also visited the countryside. Near Etchmiadzin he had talked to a group of refugees looking 'starved and miserable' as they had shuffled along the frozen road in their 'scanty rags'. 'Scarecrows' like the crowd at Ashtarak, Buxton had never seen. These were the immigrants from Turkey. Thousands of starved and half-naked children were herded together in these villages, 'roaming the fields and lanes for refuse to eat'. In Ashtarak for instance, a typical village, there were ten houses set apart for children containing about 70-80 each. In one or two of these homes the children received a regular though scanty food supply. Others seemed to be merely empty barracks where the children, huddled together, slept on the floor and

> . . . spent their days in hunting and robbing for food, or fighting one another for a crust of bread, driven crazy with hunger.

Buxton ended his statement by adding that help should come quickly if it was to be of much use.[36]

Another report about the famine conditions in South Caucasus, submitted in 1922 to Fridtjof Nansen, High Commissioner for Relief in Russia, specified that the condition of Armenia was worse than that of both Georgia and Azerbaijan, because a large section of its territory remained under

34. Northcote Papers, Add. MS 57559, 3/7, 'Report for Jan. 1922', copy, Northcote, Erevan, 31 Jan. 1922.
35. Davidson Papers, Box on Armenia, Harcourt and Buxton, Erevan, to Lord Mayor's Fund, copy tel., 1 Jan. 1922.
36. Ibid., Buxton, Erevan, Report on Situation of Rep. of Armenia, copy, 3 Jan. 1922.

Kemalist occupation and because it was isolated from the sea and could be reached only from Batum by traversing nearly 400 *versts* of Georgian territory. In addition, Armenia was burdened with an 'enormous' number of refugees, who were unable to return to their homes, owing to the fact that there still was no settlement with Turkey.[37]

The situation relating to the Mesopotamian refugees was explained by E. Carlile, the joint Secretary of the Armenian Refugees (Lord Mayor's) Fund, during an interview in late January 1922 with the Reverend G.K.A. Bell, the Chaplain to the Archbishop of Canterbury. The first two shiploads of refugees had arrived at Batum where they were refusing to land as there were no food supplies for them on shore. The British government had now granted £35,000 — its first offer had been £5,000 — on condition that 'guarantees' were given by the Armenian government that the first two boats would be cleared and that the third and last boat, which would shortly be on its way, would be cleared 'immediately' on arrival. This grant of £35,000 backed by the promises made to provide a further £10,000 to this Fund if necessary, should, Carlile believed, relieve the position and give these refugees time to be absorbed into the country on a self-supporting basis. Thus, the contribution made by the British government to the Armenian Refugees (Lord Mayor's) Fund for the settlement of these Meso-potamian refugees did in fact amount to £45,000.[38]

But the famine in Armenia was worsening every day, as Northcote wrote to his mother, and every day one saw more and more 'destitute and aban-doned children and almost naked men and women lying about in the streets, just waiting for death'. He did not think the position of Armenia had ever been blacker than it was then, regarding both the internal famine and her complete abandonment by the Allies. The situation was made worse by the attitude of the Georgian government, which was proving most troublesome and unsympathetic to famine-stricken Armenia, Northcote added. When food worth £10,000 for Armenia was due to arrive, Harcourt, as usual, had once again hurried off to Tiflis and Batum for negotiations in order to fool 'the beastly' Georgian government and stop it from 'stealing' half of it in the form of 'heavy taxes'. In this connection, commenting on the information he had heard on very good authority that a Federation of Armenia, Georgia and Azerbaijan was likely to be established very shortly, Northcote wrote: 'if this should take place it will greatly help Armenia'.[39]

The report about the famine conditions in the Caucasus, submitted in 1922 to Nansen, specified the work done by the relief agencies. The British Funds, grouped under the heading of the British Relief Mission, were in

37. Toynbee Papers, Box on Armenia, Report on Transcaucasia, copy, 10 Feb. 1922.

38. Davidson Papers, Box on Armenia, Carlile to Rev. Bell, 26 Jan. 1922; H. Buxton, *Trans-Caucasia* (London, 1926), p. 55.

39. Northcote Papers, Add. MS 57559, 3/9, 3/10/1, Northcote, Erevan, 20, 28 Feb. 1922, respectively.

1922 feeding and clothing 9,000 refugees at Gamarlu in the Araxes Valley, besides maintaining orphanage work in Erevan and distributing food and clothing wherever the need was most urgent. The American Near East Relief Committee, however, was the largest relief agency at work in the Caucasus. It maintained over 20,000 orphans in its own institutions and gave daily rations to 50,000 destitute and starving persons. Of the orphans maintained and looked after by the Near East Relief, 11,000 were at Leninakan in Armenia: probably 'the largest number' to be found assembled 'anywhere', according to Nansen.[40]

A year later, in February 1923, Northcote reported that apart from the 600 children that his Fund was keeping at Erevan and Gamarlu, just over 2,000 were being fed in the Fund's feeding stations in Erevan, Gamarlu, Etchmiadzin, Oshakan, Ashtarak and Bashgarni. He also added that there was no doubt about the fact that the situation in Armenia was much improved owing to the large quantities of flour imported into the country from Russia. This was being sold 'very cheaply' by the Russian State Bank.[41]

After being an administrator of relief in Transcaucasia and especially in Armenia for three-and-a-half years, Northcote wished to come home and resigned in the summer of 1925. Both Harold Buxton and Harcourt had been 'exceedingly' pleased with the 'admirable' work he had done, under difficult circumstances. He had shown a real capacity for organisation and zeal for the highest interests of the children.[42]

In July 1923, the Joint Council of British Armenian Societies representing the British Armenia Committee, the Friends of Armenia and the Armenian Refugees (Lord Mayor's) Fund, addressed an appeal to Lord Curzon, reminded him that in Greece and the Islands, in Syria and Palestine, in Caucasian Armenia and elsewhere, there were scattered three-quarters of a million Armenian refugees and pressed for 'a solution'.[43]

At the Conference of Lausanne, however, the hopes for a 'National Home' for these Turkish-Armenian refugees were dashed to the ground. Instead, a policy of uprooting a whole native population was adopted. Turkey was left as absolute master of Turkish Armenia — the land whose native Armenian inhabitants it had finally eliminated during the war. Since the refugees could not return to their homeland, the Council of the League of Nations approved in September 1923, at the request of the Armenian National Delegation, a Scheme for the land settlement of 50,000 Armenian

40. Toynbee Papers, Box on Armenia, Report to Nansen, 10 Feb. 1922. Fridtjof Nansen, *Armenia and the Near East* (London, 1928), p. 175.
41. Northcote Papers, Add MS 57559, 3/16, Northcote to Sec. of Fund, 26 Feb. 1923.
42. Ibid., 3/12, Carlile to Mrs. Northcote, 8 May 1922, quot. from Harcourt of 12 and 20 Apr. 1922; ibid., 3/18, Buxton, ref., 24 Mar. 1926.
43. Arm. Nat. Deleg. Papers, microf., reel 8C/14517-8; *Friend of Armenia*, no. 89 (fourth quarter 1923), inside front cover, Armenians and the Treaty of Lausanne.

refugees in the little Republic of Soviet Armenia in the Caucasus.[44] The governments of France, Italy and Belgium and others, authorised the setting up of National Committees to collect subscriptions. In 1924, the British government nominated the Committee of the Armenian Refugees (Lord Mayor's) Fund to deal with this question.[45] On 26 September 1924, the leaders of the two main opposition parties in Britain, H.H. Asquith, the former Prime Minister, and Stanley Baldwin, a future Prime Minister, presented an extremely remarkable memorial to Ramsay MacDonald, the Prime Minister. The signatories argued that the British government should respond to the letter from the Secretary-General of the League of Nations, dated 24 March 1924, and support the work of assistance to the Armenian people by 'a substantial contribution' to the Scheme for the following reasons:

1. Because the Armenians were encouraged by promises of freedom to support the Allied cause during the War, and suffered for this cause so tragically . . .
2. Because during the War and since the Armistice, statesmen of the Allied and Associated Powers have given repeated pledges to secure the liberation and independence of the Armenian nation . . .
3. Because in part Great Britain is responsible for the final dispersion of the Ottoman Armenians after the sack of Smyrna in 1922 . . .
4. Because the sum of £5,000,000 (Turkish gold) deposited by the Turkish Government in Berlin, 1916, and taken over by the Allies after the Armistice, was in large part (perhaps wholly) Armenian money. After the enforced deportation of the Armenians in 1915, their Bank accounts, both current and deposit, were transferred by order to the State Treasury at Constantinople. This fact enabled the Turks to send five million sterling to the Reichsbank, Berlin . . . this sum, by a Convention between the Allies, dated 23rd November, 1923, will shortly (probably during October, 1924) be distributed among Allied nationals having claims in Turkey. The Armenians as a community are not permitted to claim compensation for their losses out of this sum. But our responsibility cannot be forgotten . . .
5. Because the present conditions of the refugees are unstable and demoralising; and constitute a reproach to the Western Powers.

Asquith and Baldwin recognised that it was impossible now to fulfil the pledges given by Britain to the Armenians. They maintained, however, that there was another method of expressing their sense of responsibility. The most appropriate territory for the settlement of the remnant of Turkish

44. Arm. Nat. Deleg. Papers, microf., reel 1C/000001, G. Noradounghian to Arm. Reps., London, Manchester, Geneva, Belgium, Italy, 5 Oct. 1923.
45. Buxton, *Trans-Caucasia*, p. 62.

Armenians would surely be Russian Armenia. Facilities were offered by the local government, and the Armenian leaders in Europe approved this plan, which, put forward by the Council of the League of Nations, called for an expenditure of about £1 million sterling. In France, the government had opened the subscription list with a substantial sum, and in Britain, well-to-do Armenians had already promised about £14,000. Asquith and Baldwin concluded their memorial by saying that the Scheme had no political implications and as some compensation for unfulfilled pledges was 'morally due' to the Armenians, the British government should 'forthwith make an important grant'.[46]

Shortly afterwards the minority Labour government of Ramsay Mac-Donald fell from power. Baldwin became the new Prime Minister commanding 419 seats out of 615 in the House of Commons. But no grants whatsoever came from his government either for the settlement of the refugees in Armenia or even for their settlement in Syria.[47]

In the Greek Islands thousands of Armenian refugees had taken shelter. But after the sacking of Smyrna and the consequent flight of the native population onto the Greek mainland, there was no room for the Armenians any more. Greece felt that she had been the only power to accept the Armenian refugees. The Allies had used her as a 'dumping ground' but had not assisted her financially, reported Captain George F. Gracey, now the General Secretary of the Friends of Armenia. On 12 June 1924, the Greek delegate at the League of Nations Council Meeting in Geneva asked for the immediate evacuation of the Armenian refugees from Greece, and offered up to £60,000 for transportation assistance.[48]

Under such conditions the Armenian Refugees (Lord Mayor's) Fund warmly supported the League of Nations Scheme. As reasons for supposing that Armenia was now capable of absorbing refugees, it specified the progress made by the republic during the last few years, Russia's great need of cotton, and the advantage of settling Armenians in a country whose population was 94 per cent Armenian and which contained Etchmiadzin. It also stressed that Armenia was now under the protection of a Great power which could defend her from the Turks, and could help her to live with Georgia and Azerbaijan on terms of friendliness. Miss Magda Coe, the Organising Secretary of the Fund, had written an enthusiastic report on her visit to Armenia, where she had stayed for seven weeks during April to June 1925. Preferring to interpret events in the light of the conditions that gave rise to

46. Toynbee Papers, Box on Armenia, 'Memorial', 26 Sept. 1924.
47. A.J.P. Taylor, *English History 1914–1945* (Oxford, 1965), p. 220. Edith M. Pye, 'The Present Position of the Armenian Problem', *The World Outlook,* no. 44 (5 Aug. 1927), p.60. Also Rel. Soc. of Friends, MS Vol. 174, *Armenia Commit. Minutes*, 3 Feb., 31 March 1927.
48. Toynbee Papers, Box on Armenia, Gracey, 'Notes on Report to Exec. Commit. Friends of Arm.', copy, 25 Nov. 1925. Orig. in Davidson Papers, Box on Armenia. Arm. Ref. (Lord Mayor's) Fund, *Armenian Settlement* (Nov. 1924), p. 4.

them, she had pointed to the 'excellent progress' made in the public and private lives of the Armenians. They were now for the first time 'free' from terrible massacre and worse. But everywhere there was the ever present need of money, she had maintained.[49]

At the request and under the instruction of the Council of the League of Nations, Nansen, now the League's High Commissioner for Refugees, went to Armenia, in the summer of 1925, personally to make the necessary investigations on the spot. He was accompanied by a team of distinguished experts. Formerly a scheme had been put forward for the irrigation and cultivation of the Sardarabad 'desert', but Nansen and his team preferred instead the irrigation of the Kirr districts, and the drainage and irrigation of the Kara-su region, an area of about 81,000 acres. The whole irrigation scheme and the settlement of refugees would cost about £1 million sterling.[50]

Nansen proposed that the League should raise a loan among the member states. The Armenian government in Erevan, the federal government of Transcaucasia and Soviet Russia successively agreed to guarantee the loan.[51] On 12 September 1925, Nansen laid his cause before the Assembly of the League of Nations and pointed out that if the Sixth Assembly could launch the scheme, by that alone it would live in history, for it would have made a first move to right what everyone in the Chamber believed to be a great international wrong. Lord Robert Cecil, the Duchess of Atholl, Albert Thomas, the French director of the International Labour Bureau, and the International Near East Association representing 23 phil-Armenian organisations, all supported Nansen's general proposals. However, Winston Churchill, the Chancellor of the Exchequer, telegraphed to the Duchess of Atholl, forbidding her as a British delegate, to commit Britain to any financial assistance. This sudden withdrawal of British support virtually blocked all advance. In addition, the security given by the Soviet State Bank was not considered by the financial committee of the League sufficient to ensure the successful flotation of a loan on the open market.[52]

After this dismal failure of Nansen's Scheme of settlement in Armenia, the relief agencies fell on the Syrian Settlement Scheme, organised by the International Labour Office at the request of the Assembly of the League of Nations. The British members of the special sub-committee set up by the International Labour Office were Alfred E. Backhouse and Edith M. Pye. The refugees in Syria, numbering about 100,000, were the largest remaining body, gathered in camps, in the Near East. Although the Armenian

49. Ibid., p. 11; ibid., *The Story of the Armenian Nation* (Dec. 1926), p. 6. Toynbee Papers, Box on Armenia, 'Report' by Magda Coe, 17 June 1925; see also Nansen, *Armenia and the Near East*, p. 60.

50. Ibid., pp. 5–6, 217–18. For details of the Scheme of Sardarabad, see Arm. Nat. Deleg. Papers, microf., reel 1C.

51. Arm. Ref. (Lord Mayor's) Fund, *The Story of the Armenian Nation* (Dec. 1926), p. 7.

52. Joseph Burtt, *The People of Ararat* (London, 1926), pp. 160–4; Arm. Ref. (Lord Mayor's) Fund, ibid., pp. 7–8.

Refugees (Lord Mayor's) Fund emphasised that schemes of settlement in lands other than the republic of Erevan were 'not the ideal' solution to the problem of the Armenian refugees, from 1926 onwards they applied all their resources to the Scheme of the Syrian Settlement. Transport and settlement would cost less than in Erevan. In addition, Syria was under the mandate of France, a Western power, and the French government had already made a contribution.[53]

According to Nansen, who acted as President of the Armenian Commission appointed by the International Labour Office, over 400,000 Armenian refugees had emigrated to Russian Armenia and the Caucasus from Turkey. The total number of Armenian refugees who had fled abroad, he estimated at 'between 300,000 to 400,000'. They were scattered in countries including Greece, Bulgaria, Cyprus, Palestine, Syria, Mesopotamia.[54]

Armenians themselves had not been backward in assisting their unfortunate countrymen, despite the loss, as a community, of the greater part of their wealth. According to the figures laid before the League of Nations in September 1925, by Levon Pashalian of the Central Committee of the Armenian Refugees, 260 million francs had been contributed by Armenians from, especially, America and France. As to Russia, in 1915 alone the All Russia Urban Union had granted about £110,325 to meet the urgent needs of the Armenian refugees and the Russian government had contributed important sums, Consul Patrick Stevens reported from Batum. The Americans, in their turn, had been most generous. By the beginning of 1921 they had contributed not less than $50 million through the Near East Relief. Not until 1929 was the Near East Relief officially terminated. During its fourteen-year existence since 1915 it had raised and expended $85 million.[55]

Certainly, the British relief agencies also worked very hard. By the beginning of 1922, the Armenian Refugees (Lord Mayor's) Fund had collected, since its formation in 1915, £300,000, and £50,000 during the last six months. At Easter 1927, a 'combined appeal' by the British relief agencies, with a broadcast by Lord Hugh Cecil, brought in £3,229.[56] If it appears that the public response was bigger in the United States than in continental Europe and Britain, one could argue that the latter were deeply involved in war when the greatest of the Armenian tragedies occurred. The World War was indeed, at the beginning, a European War. In a way the Armenian holocausts were lost in the tumult of 1914-18. According to one

53. Rel. Soc. of Friends, MS Vol. 216, Edith M. Pye to Marshall Fox, copy, 4 Nov. 1926; Arm. Ref. (Lord Mayor's) Fund, ibid.. pp. 7–8; Burtt, ibid., pp. 168–9.

54. Rel. Soc. of Friends, MS vol. 216, 'League of Nations, I.L.O. Report by F. Nansen . . . ', copy, 28 July 1925.

55. Burtt, *The People of Ararat*, p. 149; FO 371/2768/10980, Stevens to Grey, 3 Jan. 1916; see also, ibid., no. 52366, Stevens to Grey, 25 Feb. 1916; Bryce Papers, UB 65, Walter George Smith, Pres. Armenia America Soc., to Bryce, 17 Jan [1921], wrongly dated 1920. Howard M. Sachar, *The Emergence of the Middle East 1914–1924* (New York, 1969), pp. 344–6.

56. Davidson Papers, Box on Armenia, E. Carlile, interview with G.K.A. Bell, 13 Feb. 1922. Rel. Soc. of Friends, MS vol. 174, *Arm. Commit. Minutes*, 5 May 1927.

historian, a period of profound peace is apparently needed to bring home the horrors of a great massacre. It was during a rather peaceful time that Gladstone's famous pamphlet on Bulgarian horrors had rung through Britain, yet the victims totalled only some thousands.[57] But during the Great War there had been so many claims on Britain's sympathy and means. Looking at random at the notices in the press, one could read about tens of special 'Funds' all making urgent appeals for help.[58] Thus the Armenian tragedy seemed only *one* of the horrors of the war.

The British relief agencies inevitably pursued a semi-political line since only a political solution could have eased the crushing Armenian refugee problem. They reminded the government over and over again of its war-time pledges and, deeply disappointed, blamed its failure to give effective help to Armenia on 'political expediency'.[59] One leaflet maintained that the British were very hearty in their condemnation of defaulting countries in the financial sense, but asked whether 'the default' of the Western nations in respect of their promises to the Armenian people was any less deplorable. The agencies were especially grieved at the lack of response from the government after the presentation of Asquith's and Baldwin's memorial. Britain, the greatest empire in history, argued a relief worker, had refused its 'paltry share'. Nansen was puzzled by Asquith's and Baldwin's memorial, and the latter's refusal to contribute when he came to power. Was it 'mere empty words', he asked?[60] On his part Harold Buxton prayed that Europe and America might experience 'a moral uplift' and move the question of Armenia onto a 'higher plane' so that statesmen could be compelled to redeem the pledges they had so solemnly made.[61]

As to Emily Robinson, she not only continued her work in relief, but also exerted herself to secure the liberation of Armenian women and children forcibly detained in Turkish harems since 1915. She maintained in the *Slave Market News* that the armistice terms with Turkey had provided for the return of *all* prisoners of war. Yet only male prisoners had been released and that 'about 100,000' Armenian women and children remained '*captives still*'.[62] As one result of her efforts, the League of Nations appointed in 1920 three Commissioners to enquire into the conditions of these detainees. In

57. H. Temperley in A.J. Grant and H. Temperley, *Europe in the Nineteenth and Twentieth Centuries 1789–1938*, 5th edn. (London, 1939), p. 569.

58. See for example *The Times*, 10 Mar. 1916, p. 1, cols. 6–7, ibid., p. 6, cols. 1–6; ibid., p. 7, cols. 3–4.

59. Arm. Ref. (Lord Mayor's) Fund, *The Story of the Armenian Nation* (Dec. 1926), p. 5; see also ibid., *Armenian Settlement* (Nov. 1924), p. 6; ibid., *The Armenian Problem* (June 1929).

60. Ibid., *The Story of the Armenian Nation* (Dec. 1926), p. 8; Burtt, *The People of Ararat*, pp. 164–5. Nansen, *Armenia and the Near East*, p. 323.

61. Rel. Soc. of Friends, MS. vol. 216, Papers of Marshall N. Fox, Buxton to M.N. Fox, 7 Sept., 20 Oct. 1924.

62. E. Robinson, 'Facts about Armenian Refugees and Slaves', *Slave Market News*, vol. 1, no. 3 (Dec. 1924), pp. 4–5.

1921, the Assembly of the League approved with one accord, in her presence, the Reports of that Commission and decided that its work should continue. In 1923, however, in reply to her queries, the Foreign Office had written to tell her that the Turks at Lausanne 'refused to allow the work of the Commission to continue'. She was outraged. This meant, she wrote to Canon J.A. Douglas, another Armenophile, that the Turks had flouted the decision of the League and that they had been upheld by the victorious powers. White slave traffic was a crime in Britain, but it seemed it had only to be conducted on a wholesale scale and by Turks to be permissible, she protested. Grieved that the Allies would go to any length to secure concessions for themselves, instead of carrying out their pledges to liberate Turkish Armenia, she bitterly wrote that Admiral Colby M. Chester and his American company were arranging to run railways and dig mines 'in the property of *Armenians*'. The Turks had thus been 'allowed' by the Allies to deport and kill the Armenians and then sell rights over their property to Americans. She was sorrowful:

By betraying Armenia the Allies have destroyed not only faith in themselves but in other things as well.[63]

By 1926, after nine years, her health had broken down so badly from overwork that the doctors advised her to leave London. She could no longer take up Committee work, but she maintained that she was still interested in 'everything' that was done for Armenia which needed 'justice not charity'.[64] Thus, the more prominent relief workers were not happy at all at the British government's failure to bring about a desirable and feasible solution to the Armenian question.

It has been suggested in this study that pro-Armenian sentiments and interest among humanitarian Britons were not confined to mere statements. They were often expressed in concrete form such as the organisation of relief. One has also to record that among these humanitarians there were a few so wholly dedicated to the idea of the Armenian nation's survival that for them it transcended every other consideration and even ordinary relief work. They realised too well that total extinction could have been the alternative to an even harsh existence. To this ideal of survival, therefore, they committed themselves deeply and resolutely and were cheered at any sign of vitality.

Despite their disappointment and gloom, these humanitarians were partly relieved by the knowledge that even after the ordeal they had been through, the Armenians both in the diaspora and in Armenia had 'never abandoned

63. Douglas Papers, vol. 61, ff.105–7, 109, Robinson to Douglas, 3, 12 June 1923.
64. Rel. Soc. of Friends, MS. vol. 174, *Arm. Commit. Papers*, Oct.–Dec. 1926, Robinson to J.P. Fletcher, 8 Nov. 1926.

hope'.[65] Marshall N. Fox, of the Friends Foreign Mission Association, who had been prominent in the work done towards the housing of the homeless Armenians in Lebanon and Syria through the Nansen Office, quoted from Report A.24, presented to the League of Nations in 1932, testifying that the Armenian refugees had given splendid proof of their 'traditional qualities of work and economy'. In 1925 the Society of Friends had sent Joseph Burtt on a journey of some six thousand miles covering the various Armenian centres in order to investigate the conditions of the refugees. His conclusions were not totally pessimistic:

> Although today the story of almost every family is a tragedy . . . the terrible days through which they are passing seem to have strengthened the determination to make the best of things. With faces towards the future they struggle for a decent life . . . and when they can, grow sunflowers outside their huts . . .[66]

Captain George F. Gracey, in his turn, pointed out with some satisfaction, when referring to the Armenian refugees in Greece, that he had 'not known a people who will sacrifice so much for education'.[67]

Reference has already been made to a few historians who were also concerned, along with humanitarians, about the suffering and fate of the Armenians. Another such historian was Harold Temperley, Cambridge Professor, President of the International Historical Congress in 1933 and 1934 and an 'outstanding' intellectual and personality of 'great strength'. He had referred to the Armenian question in the supplementary chapters to the fourth edition of the popular *Europe in the Nineteenth and Twentieth Centuries 1789-1932* by A.J. Grant and himself. His integrity and independence is revealed in the fact that, entrusted by the Foreign Office to select and edit with G.P. Gooch the *British Documents on the Origins of War,* he had so often threatened to resign, if asked to suppress any document regarded as vital, that Austen Chamberlain, the Foreign Secretary, had commented:

> Mr. Temperley is as difficile than [sic] a Prima Donna, and as argumentative, disputatious and litigious as the occasional terrors of the Law Courts.[68]

With his almost unrivalled experience in the handling of historical docu-

65. Nansen, *Armenia and the Near East*, p. 324.
66. Rel. Soc. of Friends, MS. vol. 216, Papers of Marshall N. Fox, 'Friends and Housing . . . of Homeless Armenians, 1924', by Fox, 31 Oct. 1935; Burtt, *The People of Ararat*, pp. 97, 130.
67. Toynbee Papers, Gracey, 'Notes on Report to Exec. Commit. Friends of Arm.', copy, 25 Nov. 1925; orig. in Davidson Papers.
68. Frank Eyck, *'Clio and the State: G.P. Gooch and the Foreign Office',* (Edmonton, June 1975, typescript for Canadian Historical Association), pp. 23 and 14.

ments, and his first-hand knowledge of the Peace Conference at Paris, Temperley certainly did not flinch from passing judgement on the Armenian question. On the nationalist Turks he laid the blame of massacres and cruelties 'such as authentic witnesses' had 'never before related'. The Enver-Kemal attempt 'to exterminate' a whole nation was a crime 'absolutely unparalleled in history'. Apparently Temperley too was grieved that the British government had refused to contribute to the Armenian Refugee Loan, believed that the Bolsheviks deserved 'real credit' for helping Armenia, and above all shared in full the relief of the humanitarians that 'the purpose of the plot was defeated . . . by the superhuman constancy of the Armenian nation'.[69]

Another point of consolation for these humanitarians was that, after all, the Armenians still had a national home, even though it was 'red'. Their commitment to their survival was so absolutely total, that without any consideration whatsoever of their own personal and political likes or dislikes, and despite misgivings, they were relieved that the Armenians had at last gained 'a respite from the Turk' and were not 'continually threatened' with massacre and physical extermination as in the 'terrible days of 1918-1921'.[70] Standers-by on the quayside at Batum had sworn loudly in 1921 at Harold Buxton and his party as 'the fat bourgeois'.[71] Still, with a remarkable integrity and independence in the best traditions of Englishmen, the unremitting honorary secretary of the Armenian Refugees (Lord Mayor's) Fund, this 'perceptive' clergyman of the Church of England with 'a very clear and incisive mind' (who would soon become Archdeacon in Cyprus, Bishop of Gibraltar and later Rector of Launton in Oxfordshire[72]), stressed the 'important and dominating fact' that '*an* Armenia' existed; and that the Soviet Republic of Armenia was 'a national home'. Well over one million Armenians were already established there. It included Etchmiadzin, the ancient seat of the Armenian Patriarchs, and Armenian was the language spoken everywhere. And he concluded:

The group of men who threw Armenia into the arms of Russia in the winter of 1920-21 undoubtedly did a real service to their country; at a great cost, no doubt — and at the sacrifice of many cherished traditions and ambitions, and in defiance of public opinion in Europe. Yet it is true that they saved their country from extinction, by the only means available.[73]

Northcote, in his turn, would always dislike the 'crude materialism' of the

---

69. Grant and Temperley, *Europe in the Nineteenth and Twentieth Centuries*, pp. 567–71.
70. Northcote Papers, Add. MS. 57560, Northcote, 'Armenia', ff.73, 85, strict. confid., 1926.
71. Buxton, *Trans-Caucasia*, p. 35.
72. I owe this information to Mrs Sarah Hogg and Mr Ronald de Bunsen, given on 3 Nov. 1979, 23 Nov. 1979, respectively; *Who Was Who*, 1976.
73. Buxton, *Trans-Caucasia*, pp. 52–3, 56.

Bolshevik creed. But he repeated over and over again, that in late 1920, in the darkest days of Armenia, when even the 'last remnants' of the race were threatened with extermination, 'no sign of any help' had come from Europe. Now, following a few years of 'peace and tranquillity' the position was 'very much better'.[74] The whole nation, he claimed, had shown a disposition to make the best of things, 'to roll up its sleeves, and get down to work'. He wrote in 1926 that plans already existed for the pulling down of Erevan and for its entire reconstruction on ambitious lines. Situated in the very heart of Armenia, within easy distance of the ruins of previous capitals of the race, such as Vagharshapat, Artaxias, Dvin, and Ani, Erevan would itself in turn become the capital. Why should it not? asked Northcote. It lay in a wealthy agricultural district, was potentially rich in hydro-electric power and was inhabited by an intelligent and hard-working race. Despite his evident pride, Northcote would nevertheless experience a certain feeling of 'sadness' at the passing away of the old Erevan in which he had 'worked so hard' and which he 'knew so well'.[75]

One cannot write enough about at least a few of these humanitarian Britons who certainly worked not only very hard to organise relief but even identified themselves with the cause of Armenia: both with her plight and her aspirations during the most critical period of her history.

When discussing the devotion of pro-Armenian humanitarian individuals, groups and relief organisations and, on the other hand, their disappointment with the British government at the inadequacy of help given to Armenia, one cannot but consider whether their pressure failed completely.

It does not seem that the authorities ignored pro-Armenian opinion. As seen above,[76] Lord Curzon repeatedly gave his word that he would do his best for Armenia. 'I can promise you' he told Aneurin Williams in 1921, referring to the security of Armenians in Cilicia, that 'I shall lose no opportunity at Constantinople or Paris of assisting these unfortunate people'.[77] In well-argued pamphlets like *The Case for Armenia* printed in 1921 and reprinted in 1923 and distributed to the public and the government, and in their memorandum to the government headed 'Armenia and the Turkish Settlement',[78] the British Armenia Committee pinned down the British politicians to their own statements and promises. Lord Bryce, a member of three former governments, and someone who was more than a statesman, also reminded the administration of the 'dishonour' which would

74. Northcote Papers, Add. MS. 57559, 3/9, Northcote to mother, 20 Feb. 1922. Ibid., 57560, Northcote, 'Armenia', f.77, strict. confid., 1926. See also ibid., ff.32–3; ibid., 57559, 3/17, 'Soviet Armenia', very strict. confid., n.d. [1925–1926].
75. Ibid., 57560, Northcote, 'Armenia', ff.73, 80–1, strict. confid. 1926.
76. See p. 178.
77. Williams Papers, Curzon to Williams, 11 July, 1921.
78. Bryce Papers, UB 65; ibid., 'Arm. and the Turk. Settlement', proof, 29 Dec. 1919; Arm. Nat. Deleg. Papers, microf. reel 8C/14686–93, 14598–610; Toynbee Papers, Box on Armenia.

rest upon Britain if the government abandoned innocent peoples to whom they had promised liberty and protection.[79] Pro-Armenian pressure was substantial in Britain. Between 1908 and 1923, about 44 different Members spoke in the House of Commons in favour of helping Armenia, on different occasions, many of them on more than one occasion.

The government responded to this pressure by *showing* that they were caring for Armenia. Thus the Treaty of Sèvres promised everything the Armenians dreamed of. Even later, when the Turkish Nationalists had not only disregarded this Treaty but had almost swept away Caucasian Armenia, some members of the government responded by making further statements as a substitute for effective help. Thus a letter on behalf of Curzon to the Archbishop of Canterbury, argued, referring to the future of the Cilician Armenians:

> . . . it is difficult to believe that the Nationalist authorities would disregard their solemn pledges to the French Government and affront the conscience of the entire world by any fresh exhibition of that brutality which has hitherto kept Turkey without the pale of civilization.[80]

But would the Nationalists mind affronting 'the conscience' of the world since it was Turkey who had been exhibiting brutality?

Perhaps the government might have been forced to help the Armenians effectively had public opinion and pressure been stronger.

The greatest handicap, however, to the success of the pressure groups was that they could not and did not have clear aims to pursue in Britain; and because they, like the British government, did not consider the Armenian question as an exclusively British concern, although they believed that Britain had a certain duty to see to the liberation of Armenia. In early 1919 Bryce held that the United States was the only power which could be trusted with the responsibility for Armenia since, as he put it, Britain's hands were already full. Later, in 1921, Aneurin Williams and his British Armenia Committee colleagues insisted that the United States government should also do its part both in money and men.[81] Thus, the pro-Armenian groups lacked clearly defined aims because under the swiftly changing political conditions, the Armenian question was not a simple issue exclusively depending on Britain. Accordingly, their pressure suffered.

Within Britain, sympathy with the Armenian cause was almost universal and unanimous. It fatally lacked, therefore, the excitement and the passion of a keenly fought party contest that had marked the agitation over the

79. H.A.L. Fisher, *James Bryce*, (London, 1927), II, pp. 330–2; James Bryce, 'The Revision of the Turkish Treaty: Armenia', *Contemporary Review*, vol. 119 (May 1921), p. 581.

80. Davidson Papers, Box on Armenia, E. Crowe to G.K.A. Bell, 2 Dec. 1921.

81. Fisher, *Bryce*, II, p. 211, quot. Bryce to M. Storey, 20 Feb. 1919; Bryce Papers, UB 65, Williams to Bryce, 22 Feb. 1921; see also *BAC Minutes*, 21 Feb. 1921.

Bulgarian atrocities in the 1870s. According to Lloyd George, there was not a British statesman of 'any party' who did not have it in mind that after the war Armenia should be redeemed for ever from Turkish misrule. T.P. O'Connor believed, even as late as December 1921, that opinion about Armenia, and indeed about the desirability of liberating every Christian race from the domination of Turkey, was 'as unanimous, and as strong, even vehement as ever'.[82] It seems, however, that this almost universal and unanimous sympathy, cutting across party lines, ironically remained only a general, vague and diffused humanitarian feeling.

One may also point out that the pro-Armenian pressure groups did not include shrewd politicians of the first rank. The post-war pro-Armenian agitation, for example, did not have a personality comparable to Gladstone, who had led the Bulgarian agitation. Most of the protagonists of the Armenian cause were idealists, intellectuals and clergymen, and not hard-headed politicians. Lord Bryce was first an intellectual and only secondly a politician. According to his biographer, he was considered too academic in Parliament, and Joseph Chamberlain used always to allude to him as 'Professor'. Aneurin Williams was conspicuous for 'self-effacement', and Noel Buxton was not 'scintillating and dynamic' and he lacked the 'gift of speech'.[83] In addition, many of the leaders of the pro-Armenian groups were ageing and died before or soon after the Treaty of Lausanne in 1923. (Lord Bryce died in 1922, Aneurin Williams in 1924, Lady Frederick Cavendish in 1925 and Sir Edwin Pears in 1919.) T.P. O'Connor was about seventy-five years old in 1923. Moreover, he and Lord Robert Cecil were taken up by the League of Nations movement. Indeed, it may be argued that the latter movement became an alternative outlet for British idealists. Many of the members of the British Armenia Committee were ardent adherents of the League of Nations idea and naturally there was some diversion of time and energies.

The liberation of the subject Christian nationalities had essentially been a nineteenth-century humanitarian movement associated with Gladstonian Liberalism, and perhaps some sections in British society viewed it as an anachronistic piece of antiquated sentimentality which had not much bearing on twentieth-century problems. Social historians have pointed to the fact that the carnage of the Great War had certainly given a blow to human 'sensitivity' and to that broad humane liberalism which for two centuries had been one of the most vital elements in British politics. O'Connor blamed the 'paralysis' which had come over Britain through the war.[84] The Armenian

82. Lloyd George, *Peace Treaties*, pp. 1257–8; Curzon Papers, MSS Eur F.112/221(b), f. 149, O'Connor to Curzon, 24 Dec. 1921.

83. Fisher, *Bryce*, I, pp. 174–5; N. Buxton and H. Buxton, *Travel and Politics in Armenia* (London, 1914), p. 126; G.P. Gooch in Foreword to Mosa Anderson's *Noel Buxton: A Life* (London, 1952), pp. 5, 9–10.

84. Arthur Marwick, *Britain in the Century of Total War* (London, 1968), pp. 113–14; Curzon Papers, MSS Eur F.112/221(b), f. 149, O'Connor to Curzon, 24 Dec. 1921.

holocausts had taken place, unlike the Bulgarian atrocities, during the traumatic experience of the first total war: an experience which had drained dry almost all sympathy with the sufferers. For, as it has been argued, neither in this nor in any other regard is man's capacity unlimited.[85] Thus, evidently, there was not much room left for sympathy with Armenian suffering after 1918.

Although the post-war dislocation suffered in Britain was on a far smaller scale than in most other countries, she had never before been through a world war and therefore had never experienced a post-world war period with its host of momentous changes and new complex problems. The landed class, one component of the political elite of Edwardian times, was largely replaced by the class of businessmen. Aristocrats like Lord Henry Bentinck deeply regretted that the Conservative Party was being, as he put it, 'thoroughly commercialized'. The members of the first post-war House of Commons were described by Baldwin as 'hard-faced men' who had done well out of the war, and by Austen Chamberlain as 'a selfish swollen lot'. At the other extreme, the majority of the Labour Members elected were trade union officials, whose main anxiety was to consolidate the gains their movement had made during the war through the expansion of industry. The movement was narrowly focused on industrial unrest. At another level, the ordinary soldiers, war-wearied and infected with pacifism were anxious to get home. Yet on another plane, the conclusion of the war was accompanied in Europe by the crushing of thrones. One diarist recorded the view — though exaggerated — that men of property were 'everywhere secretly trembling'; and that Edward Grey was fearful in 1919 of the imminence of revolution in Britain.[86]

Clearly the problems facing post-war Britain were completely different from those in the nineteenth century, when Gladstonian Liberals had felt it their humanitarian duty to think of, and work for, the liberation of Christian populations.

Although sympathy with the Eastern Christians and Armenia had cut across party lines, it had mainly and traditionally been a concern of the Liberals, described by Lord Robert Blake as the party of moral conscience. During the war members from all the three main political parties, represented in the Coalition government of Lloyd George, had strongly supported the cause of Armenia, some out of liberal sympathies with her sufferings and others, as already seen, for reasons of national interest in order to stimulate the war effort. After the war, however, Armenia did not serve any particular national purpose. Moreover, the 1918 Coupon election proved to be disastrous for the cause. The great Liberal Party of the

85. T.P. Conwell-Evans, *Foreign Policy from a Back Bench 1904–1918* (Oxford, 1932), p. 11.

86. H. Bentinck, *Tory Democracy* (1918), pp. 2–3, quoted in Marwick, *Britain*, pp. 166–8; Taylor, *English History*, p. 129; Margaret I. Cole (ed.), *Beatrice Webb's Diaries 1912–1924*, (London, 1952), pp. 136, 164: entry for 11 Nov. 1918, 14 July 1919, respectively.

nineteenth century was shattered and almost annihilated. The new government of Lloyd George, therefore, had a strong Conservative bias. But then, the Conservatives, according to Lord Blake, were, 'by a long tradition dating from the days of Disraeli, pro-Turk'.[87] In the post-war period, according to Hankey, Bonar Law, the Leader of the party, had

> . . . gone back to the old Tory fondness of the Turks and wants to revise the Treaty of Sèvres in favour of the Turks.[88]

The two main exceptions in the party were Balfour and Lord Robert Cecil.

The Labour Party had done better than the Liberals in 1918 and had become the Opposition.[89] But the militants, because they were also the pacifists, had been ousted from Parliament, including Ramsay MacDonald, Philip Snowdon and even Arthur Henderson. In her cutting way Beatrice Webb remarked that out of the 59 Labour members, 25 were miners — 'for general political purposes dead stuff'. She added, moreover, that the party in Parliament was led by the respectable but 'dull-witted' Adamson.[90] Thus, the Labour Party, weak within Parliament, and always occupied by industrial and organisational problems outside, was not in a position to exert, despite its professed sympathies with the Armenian question, the necessary pressure on the government to induce it to help Armenia effectively.

In its memorandum on War Aims, printed in 1917, the Labour Party and the Trades Union Congress had condemned the

> . . . handing back to the universally execrated rule of the Turkish Government any subject people. Thus, whatever may be proposed with regard to Armenia, Mesopotamia, and Arabia, they cannot be restored to the tyranny of the Sultan and his Pashas.[91]

Later, in February 1920, the Labour Party's Advisory Committee on International Questions[92] passed a 'Resolution on Armenia', protesting 'against the treatment of Armenia by the Allied Powers'. During the war, the resolution claimed, the Ottoman government had once for all forfeited any right to rule the Armenian provinces of Turkey by the 'deliberately organised' attempt 'to exterminate' the Armenian population. The evidence was 'abundant and conclusive' and the British government had published it

87. Robert Blake, *The Conservative Party from Peel to Churchill* (London, 1970), p. 196; Robert Blake, *The Unknown Prime Minister* (London, 1955), pp. 446, 487; see also Winston S. Churchill, *The World Crisis – The Aftermath* (London, 1929), p. 391.

88. Hankey Papers, Diaries, HNKY 1/5, entry for 28 Nov. 1920.

89. See Taylor, *English History*, p. 128.

90. Cole, *Beatrice Webb's Diaries*, p. 141, entry for 10 Jan. 1919.

91. Labour Party and Trades' Union Congress, *Memo. on War Aims* (1917), p. 5.

92. The members included at various times in this period: Prof. D.R. Beazley, Dr Ethel Bentham, G.D.H. Cole, Arnold Toynbee, D. Mitrany, Noel Buxton, C. Roden Buxton, E. Burns and L.S. Woolf. See *Labour Party*, LP/IAC/1/91 and ibid., no. 170.

in a Blue Book and used it for discrediting Turkey and indirectly Germany. Yet, in negotiating the armistice with Turkey, when the Turkish armies had been shattered, the Allied governments had left the Armenian provinces under the Turkish authorities, while Turkish rule was 'immediately' terminated in the Arab provinces. The penetrating and incisive resolution claimed that:

> . . . the policy of the Allied Governments since the Armistice lays them under the suspicion that they intend to detach from Turkey and attach to themselves under the form of mandates conferred by the League of Nations all those provinces of the Ottoman Empire where they have financial economic or strategic interests, while no provision is being made for Armenia, the one region of Turkey which unquestionably ought to be released from Turkish sovereignty.

In a draft memorandum, this same Committee further argued that the case for a mandate in Armenia was immensely stronger than in any other part of the former Turkish Empire, though, just because it would be 'onerous and not lucrative', it seemed unlikely to be accepted by any Great power.[93] Written in November 1919, the memorandum proved to be only too accurate a prediction.

In 1921, when apropos Armenia the Treaty of Sèvres had dismally failed, the Labour Party's Advisory Committee on International Questions claimed that the Treaty (of Sèvres) and the 'Tripartite' Agreement between Britain, France and Italy had endeavoured 'to carve up' the Turkish Empire both territorially and economically, and strongly blamed the Allies for having sacrificed the Armenians to their own interests. Had they followed 'a wise foreign policy' by meeting the just claims of Turkey with fairness,

> . . . if they had been prepared to give up their own policy of plunder — they could have obtained all that could reasonably be demanded including that freedom for Armenia which they had promised to secure. They have sacrificed the Armenians to their own self-aggrandisement.

The Committee proposed that the Treaty of Sèvres should be revised and a new bargain be made with Turkey: an 'independent Armenia' should be recognised, while in return Turkey should receive back Thrace and Smyrna, and should be freed from the humiliating control of the Financial Commission and from the occupation of Constantinople. Greece should give up her claim to Turkish territory and receive the Greek territories of Cyprus and the Aegean Islands from Britain and Italy respectively.[94]

93. *Labour Party Advis. Committ. on Internat. Quests.*, no. 129 a, Feb. 1920; ibid. no. 103, Nov. 1919.

94. Ibid., no. 228a, 'Draft Pamphlet on For. Policy', pp. 13–14, 21 Mar. 1922; ibid., no. 226, p. 9, Nov. 1921. See also Arthur Henderson, *Labour and Foreign Affairs* (London [1922]).

However, there is not much evidence that the above views were vigorously pressed on the government. Still, in 1922, the indefatigable Noel
Buxton, now Labour MP for Norfolk North, asked the government to
confer with the powers, including Russia at Lausanne, with a view to
obtaining an accession of territory to the Armenian republic, in return for a
cession of territory to Turkey in northern Mesopotamia. Later, he pointed
out once again that the only feasible suggestion had come from the Labour
Party: in order to get a concession for the Armenians to some territory in the
north-east of Turkey, some sacrifice had to be made. If it lay between
adhering to oil rights at Mosul or carrying out pledges to Armenians, honour
stood first. The government ought to put principle before profit, Buxton
insisted.[95]

It should be stressed, however, that besides a few such statements professing a genuine sympathy, Labour, a comparatively new party, did not bring
enough pressure to bear on the government or mount agitation for effective
help to Armenia. The British Armenia Committee in vain expressed the
desire that the Labour Party should join a proposed deputation to the Prime
Minister. On another occasion they indicated that they would like to get
some Labour Members of Parliament to act with their Committee. But
nothing concrete came out of these efforts. Even a letter was written to Tom
Shaw, MP, expressing the wish that a trade union element should be introduced into the British Armenia Committee. Tom Shaw however regretted
that he 'could not find time himself', but would try to discover some other
Labour man.[96]

Thus, the Armenian question, while commanding general and sometimes strong humanitarian sympathies, did not become a point of keen party
political contest and did not arouse controversial passions. It did not have a
solid basis of power and support.

The resignation of Lord Robert Cecil, a strong supporter of the Armenians, from the government in 1918, was also unfortunate. Described by Lord
Beaverbrook as a man highly respected and greatly admired for his sturdy
qualities. he was the champion in Britain of the League of Nations and the
self-determination of peoples. President Wilson considered him the greatest
man in Europe — the greatest man he had ever met.[97] In late November
1920, during the darkest days of the Kemalist invasion of Armenia, he
desperately and almost single-handed tried to rally support in the League of
Nations Assembly, where he represented South Africa. He even summoned
General F. Maurice to Geneva, to advise the League as to military action in

95. *Hansard*, 5th Ser. 1922, vol. 159, col. 2375; ibid., 1923, vol. 160, cols. 212–13.
96. *BAC Minutes*, 23 Jan., 27 May 1920; 24 Jan., 7 Feb. 1921.
97. Lord Beaverbrook, *Men and Power 1917–1918* (London, 1956), 'Biographies',
p. xiii; James Headlam-Morley, *A Memoir of the Paris Peace Conference 1919* (London, 1972)
p. 16, extract from diary, entry for 25 Jan. 1919.

support of Armenia — ignoring and thus offending the British General Staff, according to Hankey.[98] It was hopeless.

Whether more pleading by a greater number of idealists and humanitarian groups would have made much difference is doubtful. Lieutenant-Commander J. Kenworthy, the Radical Member for Kingston-upon-Hull, Central, implied cynically but with brutal frankness that helping the Armenians — 'not aristocrats' — would not have in any way furthered the material interests of the influential ruling classes, who, however, had wholeheartedly supported intervention in Russia. This had cost the country around £115,000,000 and therefore the government had apparently nothing left now for the Armenians, to whom it was pledged 'to the hilt'. Yet it was attracted by the oil and natural riches of Mesopotamia, Kenworthy maintained. But there was 'no cotton or oil in Armenia'.[99] Oliver Baldwin also believed that the desertion of Armenia would not have taken place had the Mosul oil wells been situated at Karakilisa. This view was generally shared by many humanitarians such as Dr Fridtjof Nansen and Joseph Burtt, author of *The People of Ararat.*[100]

In the turbulent and confused Britain of the post-world war period, pro-Armenian pressure groups could not achieve much besides arousing among the public a sentimental and humanitarian interest in Armenia. They could not force the government into giving effective help to a country which did not particularly serve British national interests. Perhaps their passionate devotion even had negative effects indirectly. It introduced a factitious element into policy. By their constant pressure they induced the British political leaders to *show* that they felt for Armenia. Thus they aroused among the Armenians hopes and expectations which would not be realised, and contributed to the fact that the Armenians depended exclusively on Allied support instead of trying to follow a more realistic policy of accommodation with their neighbours in the Caucasus — the Georgians, the Tatars of Azerbaijan, the Russians and even the Turks: peoples with whom they were bound to live together. Still, the statements and writings of the members of these pressure groups, despite their disappointment, testify to this day to their faith in a worthwhile cause: the right of an ancient but small people desperately anxious to survive. These advocates, who thought, like Aneurin Williams, that recognising 'majorities made by massacre' was absolutely intolerable; who believed, like Emily Robinson, that to know of a

98. See *The Times*, 18 Nov. 1920, p. 11, col. 3; ibid., 23 Nov. 1920, p. 11, col. 1; ibid., 27 Nov. 1920, p. 9 col. 3; ibid., 3 Dec. 1920, p. 11, col. 2; Hankey Papers, Diaries, HNKY 1/5, entry for 4 Dec. 1920 (for last 3 days).

99. *Hansard*, 5th Ser. 1919, vol. 119, col. 1306; ibid., 1920, vol. 127, col. 711; ibid., 1920, vol. 129, col. 1671.

100. Oliver Baldwin, *Six Prisons and Two Revolutions* (London, 1924), p. 260; Fridtjof Nansen, *Armenia and the Near East* (London, 1928), p. 324; Joseph Burtt, *The People of Ararat* (London, 1926), p. 84.

crime and to be a party to hushing it up was in itself 'a crime'; or who insisted like the Archbishop of Canterbury that whatever else happened, the 'pledged word' of Britain could not be 'broken or ignored';[101] all these certainly reflected the moral conscience of Britain at its best.

101. *Hansard*, 5th Ser. 1920, vol. 128, col. 1491 (Williams); *Ararat* (London), vol. 1, no. 2 (Aug. 1913), pp. 40–2 (Robinson); Bonar Law Papers, 112/10/1, Archbishop of Canterbury to Bonar Law, 24 Oct. 1922.

Conclusion

The Armenian people were drawn to Britain from 1878 onwards, for she secured by the Cyprus Convention in that year, the Sultan's promise 'to introduce necessary reforms' into the eastern territories of Turkey. Britain was also instrumental in drafting the Berlin Treaty which made the Sultan undertake to carry out reforms 'in the provinces inhabited by the Armenians'. Soon after, British military consuls were sent to these regions to report back. In the 1880s and 1890s Britain above any other power pressed for reforms. The Armenian people felt particularly close to her when Gladstone took up their cause during the massacres of the 1890s. The beautifully illuminated Armenian Gospel at Saint Deiniol's Library, Hawarden and both the solid silver chalice and the 'Armenian Window' at Hawarden Parish Church, all bear witness, to this day, of their deep affection and 'undying gratitude' towards that British statesman.[1] In 1916 it was the British Foreign Office which issued in a Blue Book the data available for a 'full and authentic record' of what had occurred in 1915. During the war very sympathetic statements were made by British political and religious leaders, from Asquith and Lloyd George, to Balfour, Curzon and the Archbishop of Canterbury. In 1918 Curzon believed that were the Armenian population polled about a protectorate, both in their homelands and in the diaspora, in all probability they would 'opt' for Britain.

However, Britain was somewhat unable to help Armenia effectively either before, or after, the war.

In the nineteenth century her interest was centred on the Armenian territories, which, her statesmen believed, controlled the strategic head of the Persian Gulf by way of the Euphrates and Tigris valleys. These territories should on no account come under the influence of Russia, her major rival power in the east. Britain remained committed, up to 1914, to the integrity of the Ottoman dominions in Asia. Thus Britain's interest in Armenian territory far outweighed her concern about the Armenian people. The result was that no security whatever was asked for, or given, for reforms. No effective pressure was put on Turkey for their implementation. Consequently, while the stipulations and the constant reminders about reforms aroused, on one hand, the hopes of Armenians, they laid them

---

1. The Gospel was presented to Gladstone by the Caucasian Armenians in 1895; the chalice by the Armenians of London and Paris in 1894, on his 85th birthday; and the 'Armenian Window' was dedicated to him in 'undying gratitude' by Arakel Zadouroff of Baku, in 1897.

267

open, on the other, to the hostility and reprisals of the Turks, and helped to cause successive massacres.

The war radically changed the direction of Britain's interest in Armenia. As she was opposed to Turkey, she did not care about Ottoman integrity any longer. She was prepared to satisfy the territorial desiderata of her Allies, Russia and France, over Armenia. Moreover, having secured by arms and agreements the certainty of her predominance in the Persian Gulf, she lost almost all her interest in Armenian territory. The war, however, brought a dramatic increase of interest in the Armenian people. Britain had to use all her material and moral forces to win the war. So, she used the Armenian holocausts of 1915 to discredit her enemies, Turkey directly and Germany indirectly, in order to wean American sympathy from the Central powers, to show to her Moslem subjects the nature of the Turkish government they were being urged to fight, and in order to stimulate the war effort at home by indicating that the conflict was against cruelty, oppression and injustice. Britain also made use of Armenian manpower, both in the Near East and in the Caucasus: especially in the Caucasus, to reinforce that disintegrating front after 1917. But in order to stimulate the Armenians, Britain had to 'pledge' herself to the liberation of Armenia, an expression which was also used to counter the charges of the pacifists at home about the war being fought for greed. What was 'imperialistic' in wishing to see Armenia freed from Turkey, Balfour asked. At the end of the war, then, Britain was in the position of having made, in Harold Nicolson's words, the provision of a 'National Home' for the Armenians, one of the 'most loudly advertised' of her war aims.[2] The British government itself had contributed to building up public opinion which expected, and demanded, the liberation of Armenia. But British sympathy with the Armenian people had flowed out of war conditions, and, however genuine, was bound to wane after 1918. More inauspiciously, interest in, and sympathy with, the Armenian people was not matched by a corresponding interest in their territory.

Thus, Britain was unable to solve after 1918 the dilemma of reconciling her sympathetic statements and wartime pledges with her reluctance to assume responsibility on behalf of Armenia, a country where she had no territorial interests at all. She tried several expedients — for example, passing the responsibility for helping Armenia to other powers — all of which in the end failed. Moreover, the public statements and the Treaty of Sèvres given to vindicate these statements, again aroused hopes among the Armenians — as the stipulations of reform in the nineteenth century had done — and laid Armenia yet again open to the hostility of Turkey and now also to that of the other Caucasian states. The Treaty of Sèvres, unaccompanied by real help, exposed Armenia to reprisals and in the end proved to be her doom.

Thus, Britain failed to help Armenia effectively both after 1878 and after

2. Harold Nicolson, *Curzon: The Last Phase 1919–1925* (London, 1934), p. 316n.

1918. Yet it seems that the diplomatic failure was more marked after 1918 because in the former period Britain had committed herself — rightly or wrongly — to Ottoman integrity in Asia. She had no such restrictions after 1918, although the difficulties which she faced were certainly great. Extended British responsibilities in the Near East, financial stringency and shrinking armies at home, the inaccessibility of Anatolia and the depopulation of the Armenian Provinces were problems which could not be disregarded. Furthermore, the post-war diplomatic relations between the 'Allies' were often tense and strained. Mixed motives resulted in a complexity of aims. France was obsessed by the need of security and of having the Rhine frontier as her bulwark against Germany. Italy's main preoccupation was the provision for herself of spoils with a view to exorcising socialism. At the Peace Conference the Italians behaved like 'sulky children' with delaying and obstructing tactics — in order to obtain 'fat plums' and keep quiet, Harold Nicolson recorded. On the other hand the tragedy of the American Delegation in Paris was that President Wilson possessed 'a one-track mind' and after the Congressional Elections in November 1918 it did not represent what America was feeling.[3] There was certainly an atmosphere of suspicion and resentment. Still, one wonders whether the creation of a viable Armenian state was a task beyond Britain: never had her voice counted for more, as rightly said by Curzon, in determining the future destinies of mankind.[4]

But Armenia was not an exclusively British responsibility. It was never supposed that Britain herself should necessarily be the mandatory. Where Britain failed was in her diplomatic efforts to bring about a feasible arrangement for Armenia. Balfour told the Assembly of the League of Nations that the question of Armenia could only be solved if they found some power willing to become the mandatory: 'You cannot find a mandatory unless the other States are prepared to guarantee it with money, men and munitions'.[5] Could not have Britain taken the initiative in finding a mandatory under the League, and together with other countries guaranteed it with money, men and munitions? Reference has already been made to her international diplomatic prestige, to her 'ascendancy' in Paris and to the French talking of 'La Paix anglaise' (the English Peace).[6] British military standing was equally high in the east. According to Captain Jerome Farrell, an officer in the Caucasus in 1919,

> British prestige was such that a solitary subaltern with only a batman, a groom and a riding crop could impose peace and order on naturally turbulent and mutually hostile tribes.[7]

3. Harold Nicolson, *Peacemaking 1919* (London, 1933), pp. 65, 291, 66, 266, 52, 58–9.
4. See above, p. 141.
5. *The Times*, 23 Nov. 1920, p. 11, col. 1.
6. See above, p. 175.
7. St Antony's College, Mid. E. Centre, Farrell Papers, 'Switch to the Caucasus', p. 5, n.d.

Moreover, mobilising European opinion for help to Armenia under the League of Nations would not have been impossible, considering the prevailing substantial sympathy in many countries, from the United States, France, Italy and Switzerland to Canada. Money, civilian adminstrative advisers, volunteer military officers and arms could have been provided for a limited number of years.

But Britain did not have her own policy towards Armenia. Lloyd George's argument that once the Allies were in Constantinople they could do what they liked as regards Armenia, or his insistence that if the United States refused to accept responsibility the refusal should be recorded, or Balfour's assumption that the Turks would not be so 'foolish' as to do foolish things in Armenia or in the Caucasus, or the War Office view that the pacification of Asia Minor and the repatriation of Armenians should be left to the mandatory power when there was still no shadow of such a power,[8] all point to a complete want of foresight and statesmanship.

Neither the Armistice of Mudros, after the Turkish armies had been shattered, nor the intervening period up to the Treaty of Sèvres, were used to prepare the requisite groundwork and the preconditions for the creation of an Armenian state. While Turkey was allowed to consolidate her power in the Armenian provinces and build up her forces, the Erevan republic was not even provided with the necessary means for her defence and was overburdened with thousands of discontented Turkish-Armenian refugees. The Treaty of Sèvres, played to a pro-Armenian audience,[9] became a factitious document under these circumstances, and further exacerbated the situation. It confirmed the position of Armenia as a satellite of the Allied powers and especially of Britain but gave her no protection. When Kemal decided to challenge the Treaty, he inevitably chose for attack the Armenian republic, 'the line of least resistance'.[10]

Lord Bryce was probably harsh in describing the men in power in Britain as ignorant and wanting in wisdom. One would agree, however, with him when he described Britain's post-war policy towards Armenia as a failure marked by a lack of foresight and energy.[11] It seems that what was basically at fault was that the Foreign Office did not have a strong Foreign Secretary at its head able to think policy through to the end, responsible both, that is, for making decisions and for their execution. On the contrary, the Foreign Office often allowed itself to be superseded by Lloyd George's ever-ready, superficial improvisations and to be manoeuvred out of the way by the

8. See above, pp. 129, 186, 129, 164.

9. On democratic diplomacy, see M.S. Anderson, *The Eastern Question 1774–1923* (London, 1966), p. 210; and Nicolson, *Curzon*, pp. 5, 391–8.

10. *Labour Party Advis. Committ. on Internat. Questions*, no. 175, Krassin during interview about Armenia with Geo. Lansbury, Sidney Webb and W. Gillies, 23 Nov. 1920.

11. Bryce Papers, UB 25, Bryce to Lord Fitzmaurice, 4 Aug. 1920; *Contemporary Review*, vol. 119 (May 1921), p. 580.

pro-Turkish policy of appeasement relentlessly pressed by both the War Office and the India Office.

If towards Turkish Armenia the attitude of the Foreign Office was marked by indecision and weakness, in the Caucasus it was marked by an illusion of power. Under world conditions — the break-up of Empires and the withdrawal of the United States from Europe — Britain was at the height of her prestige. But under domestic pressures her power was shrinking. The Foreign Office was slow to see this fatal disproportion between influence and power and did not adjust its policy to the available resources. It could not give effective help to Armenia and was unable to control the events in the Caucasus, but to the last discouraged her from coming to terms with Turkey or Soviet Russia, the only two states whose power was real. The Armenians — with little experience in statecraft since the end of the fourteenth century and, moreover, having been 'terribly stricken' in the loss of their leaders by the holocausts of 1915[12] — were fatally dragged behind this illusory policy. They not only did not gain control of the Armenian provinces in Turkey, but also lost lands in pre-war Russian territory.

However, weakness of policy or illusion would not have prevailed if only Britain had had interests in Armenia. But she did not. Thus Armenia was the only one not liberated, from among the list of Ottoman territories, 'Arabia, Armenia, Mesopotamia, Syria and Palestine', which the British Cabinet had agreed and Lloyd George had announced, would be 'impossible to restore' to Turkey.[13] Britain's interests in the Armenian people were not matched by a corresponding interest in their territory. Before the war Britain was interested in Armenian territory, which, she was determined, should on no account fall under Russian influence. During the war she was interested in the Armenian people, but not in their territory, for which she was not prepared to make any sacrifice in money or men. Thus, despite quite genuine sympathy, British policy was never a rounded whole in which both sympathy and strategic interest found their places.

By 1923, having at long last shed its illusions about controlling the Caucasus, the Foreign Office apparently recognised that 'history, geography and economy all point to some sort of connection with Russia'.[14] As to Armenia itself, it seems it realised the hard way, when abandoned by the Entente and Britain, that its 'only chance of existence was to adapt itself to the wishes and policies of the peoples by whom it was surrounded on all sides'.[15]

12. FO 371/3659/104621, James L. Barton, Presid. Americ. Commit. for Relief in Nr. East, to Bryce, 27 June 1919, in Bryce to Sir R. Graham, 14 July 1919.
13. See above, p. 113.
14. FO 371/8185/N1170, E.G. Forbes Adam, min., 8 Feb. 1922. See also: ibid., R. McDonell, memo., 7 Feb. 1922; FO 371/7873/E1229, D.G. Osborne, min., 6 Feb. 1922.
15. Northcote Papers, Add. MS. 57560, 'Armenia', p. 34, 1926.

Bibliography

A. Manuscript Sources

1. Private Papers

Bodleian Library, Oxford:

  Asquith Papers
  Bryce Papers
  Fisher (H.A.L.) Papers
  Milner Papers
  Toynbee Papers
  Wardrop Papers

Bristol University Library:

  British Armenia Committee Minutes, Feb. 1921-May 1924

British Library:

  Balfour Papers
  Cecil (Robert) Papers
  Northcote Papers

Churchill College Library, Cambridge:

  Hankey Papers

House of Lords Record Office:

  Bonar Law Papers
  Lloyd George Papers

Imperial War Museum:

  Wilson (Henry) Diaries (microfilm)
  Wilson (Henry) Papers

India Office Library:

  Curzon Papers

Labour Party, London:

Advisory Committee on International Questions, Minutes
and Memoranda, 1918-23
Berne and Lucerne Socialist International Congress
Papers, 1919

Lambeth Palace Library:

Davidson Papers
Douglas Papers

Private Possession:

Buxton (Noel) Papers
Hodgkin Papers
Williams Papers

Public Record Office:

Cecil (Robert) Papers
Oliphant Papers
Ryan Papers
Sykes Papers

Religious Society of Friends:

Armenia Committee Minutes, 1925-33
Fox (M.N.) Papers

Rhodes House Library, Oxford:

British Armenia Committee Minutes, Oct. 1915- Feb. 1921
British Armenia Committee Propaganda Sub-Committee
Minutes, June-Nov. 1920

St Antony's College, Oxford, Middle East Centre:

Everett Papers
Farrell Papers
Hamilton Papers
Price (Philips) Papers
Sykes Papers

Trinity College Library, Cambridge:

Montagu Papers

2. Official Papers

Archive Centre of Dashnaktsutiun, Boston, Mass., USA

Republic of Armenia, Archives. Files:

331/1
332/2
333/3
334/4
335/5
336/6
337/7
338/8
339/9
340/10
17/17
47/1
75/2
107/6
140/39
371

Armenian General Benevolent Union, Saddle Brook, NJ, USA

Armenian National Delegation Papers, 1912-24 (microfilm).
The Delegation was presided over successively by Boghos Nubar and Gabriel Noradounghian

Public Record Office, London:

Volumes and Files in the following classes:
CAB 23   :   Minutes of the War Cabinet
CAB 24   :   Papers circulated to the War Cabinet
CAB 25   :   Supreme War Council
CAB 27   :   Cabinet Committees
FO 371   :   Foreign Office Political Correspondence
FO 608   :   Peace Conference Correspondence, 1919-20
WO 106   :   War Office Directorate of Military Operations and
                   Intelligence

B. Printed Sources

1. Primary Sources

(i) Parliamentary Debates and Papers:

Hansard, 5th Series, 1913-23

Parliamentary Papers:
  1877: XC, XCII
  1878: LXXXII, LXXXIII
  1881: C
  1889: LXXXVII
  1895: CIX
  1896: XCV, XCVI
  1916: XXXIII
  1920: LI
  1921: I (Session 2)
  1922: XXIII
  1923: XXV, XXVI

(ii) Published Documents, Speeches and Diaries.

Aharonian, Avetis, 'From Sardarapat to Sèvres and Lausanne: A Political Diary', Parts 1-13, *Armenian Review,* vol. XV, no. 3-59 to vol. XIX, no. 2-74 (Sept. 1962-summer 1966)

[Armenia], Délégation de la République Arménienne à la Conférence de la Paix, *La République Arménienne* (Paris: 1920)

Armenian Bureau (London), *Leaflets*, nos. 1-11, June 1920-Jan. 1921

Armenian National Delegation, ·*Memorandum on the Armenian Question* (Paris: 1918)

Armenian Refugees (Lord Mayor's) Fund, *Armenians: Saving the Remnant* (London: 1917)

——*Armenian Settlement* (London: 1924)

——*The Story of the Armenian Nation* (London: 1926)

——*The Armenian Problem* (London: 1929)

——*Armenia's Charter* (London: 1918)

Bailey, John (ed.), *The Diary of Lady Frederick Cavendish*, 2 vols. (London: 1927)

Bonsal, Stephen, *Suitors and Suppliants: The Little Nations at Versailles* (New York: 1946)

[Bryce, J. and A. Toynbee], *The Treatment of Armenians in the Ottoman Empire* (London: 1916)

Callwell, C.E., *Field-Marshal Sir Henry Wilson: His Life and Diaries*, vols. I-II (London: 1927)

Cole, M.I. (ed.), *Beatrice Webb's Diaries 1912-1924* (London: 1952)

Degras, Jane (ed.), *Soviet Documents on Foreign Policy,* vol I, 1917-24 (Oxford: 1951)

Eudin, X.J. and R.C. North, *Soviet Russia and the East 1920-1927: A Documentary Survey* (Stanford: 1957)

Foreign Office, Historical Section — Handbooks (London: 1920)

Anatolia (no. 59)
Armenia and Kurdistan (no. 62)
Caucasia (no. 54)
Mohammedan History (no. 57)
Turkey in Asia (no. 58)
Turkey in Europe (no. 16)

Gooch, G.P. and H. Temperley (eds.), *British Documents on the Origins of the War 1898-1914*, vols. V, IX (i) and X (i) (London: 1928-38)

Harbord, James G., *Report of the American Military Mission to Armenia* (Senate document no. 266, Washington, DC: 1920)

Hendrick, Burton J., *The Life and Letters of Walter H. Page* (London: 1924)

Hertselt, Edward, *The Map of Europe by Treaty* (London: vol. II, 1875; vol. IV, 1891)

Kemal, Mustafa, *A Speech Delivered by Ghazi Mustapha Kemal, President of the Turkish Republic, October 1927* (Leipzig: 1929)

Kirakosian, J.S. (ed.), *Hayastane Mijazcayin Divanacitutyan ev Sovetakan Artakin Kaghakakanutyan Pastateghterum, 1828-1923* (Armenia in the Documents of International Diplomacy and Soviet Foreign Policy, 1828-1923) (Erevan: 1972)

[The] Labour Party and the Trades Union Congress, *Memorandum on War Aims* (London: 1917)

Lazian, Gabriel, *Hayastan ev Hay Date (Vaveragrer)* (Armenia and the Armenian Question, Documents) (Cairo: 1946)

Léart, Marcel, *La Question Arménienne à la Lumière des Documents* (Paris: 1913)

Middlemas, K. (ed.), *Thomas Jones, Whitehall Diary* (London: 1969), vol 1

Moberly, F.J. (comp.), *The Campaign in Mesopotamia* (based on official documents), 4 vols. (London: 1923-7)

Naim Bey, *The Memoirs of Naim Bey: Turkish Official Documents Relating to the Deportations and Massacres of Armenians* (London: 1920)

Nicolson, Harold, *Peacemaking 1919* (London: 1933)

Poidebard, A., 'Le Transcaucase et la République d'Arménie dans les Textes Diplomatiques du Traité de Brest-Litovsk au Traité de Kars 1918-1921', *Révue des Études Arméniennes*, vol. III (1923), vol. IV pt. 1 (1924)

Raffi, A. (ed.), *Armenia and the Settlement* (Report of Public Meeting to Express Sympathy with the Armenian Cause, held at the Central Hall, Westminster, 19 June 1919) (London: 1919)

Riddell, Lord, *Intimate Diary of the Peace Conference and After 1918-1923* (London: 1933)

Seymour, Charles, *The Intimate Papers of Colonel House*, 4 vols. (London: 1926)

Temperley, H.W.V., *A History of the Peace Conference of Paris* (London: 1920-4)

Temperley, Harold and Lillian M. Penson, *Foundations of British Foreign Policy* (Cambridge: 1938)

[Turkey], *The Armenian Aspirations and Revolutionary Movements*, Albums I and II (no date)

[Turkey], *Verité sur le mouvement révolutionnaire arménien et les mesures gouvernementales* (Constantinople: 1916)

United States, Department of State, *Foreign Relations of the United States, 1920, vol. III* (Washington, DC: 1936)

Woodward, E.L. *et al.* (eds.), *Documents on British Foreign Policy 1919-1939*, 1st Series, vols. I, II, IV, VII, VIII, XII, XIII, XVIII (London: 1947-)

Besides the *Dictionary of National Biography*, Directories such as *Burke's History of the Peerage . . . ; Crockford's Clerical Directory; DOD's Parliamentary Companion; Foreign Office Civil List;* and *Who Was Who* have been used.

(iii) Newspapers and Periodicals.

Ararat (London), 1918-20
Contemporary Review, 1915-23
Friend of Armenia, 1900-24
The Times, 1913-23

(iv) Unpublished Theses and Papers in Typescript.

Arslanian, A.H., 'The British Military Involvement in Transcaucasia 1917-1919' (University of California, PhD thesis: 1974)

— — 'Britain and the Transcaucasian Nationalities during the Russian Civil War (Paper read at a Conference on 'Nationalism and Social Change in Transcaucasia' in the Wilson Centre, Smithsonian Institution Building, Washington, DC, April 1980)

Eyck, Frank, 'Clio and the State: G.P. Gooch and the Foreign Office' (typescript prepared for Canadian Historical Association, Edmonton: 1975)

Turner, J., 'Lloyd George's Private Secretariat 1917-1918' (University of Oxford, DPhil. thesis: 1976)

White, S., 'Anglo-Soviet Relations 1917-1924' (Glasgow University, PhD thesis: 1972)

2. Secondary Sources

Biographies, Memoirs and Studies.

Adelson, Roger, *Mark Sykes: Portrait of an Amateur* (London: 1975)
Adonz, N., *Towards the Solution of the Armenian Question* (London: 1920)

Aghayan, Ts. P., *Hay Zhoghoverdi Azatagrakan Paykari Patmutyunits* (From the History of the Liberation Struggle of the Armenian People) (Erevan: 1976)

Aharonian, Gersam (ed.), *Hushamatian Meds Yegherni, 1915-1965* (Memorial Volume of the Great Atrocity, 1915-1965) (Beirut: 1965)

Ahmad, Feroz, 'Great Britain's Relations with the Young Turks 1908-1914' *Middle-Eastern Studies,* vol. 2, no. 4 (July 1966), pp. 302-29

— — The Young Turks (Oxford: 1969)

Allen, W.E.D. and P. Muratoff, *Caucasian Battlefields: A History of the Wars on the Turco-Caucasian Border 1828-1921* (Cambridge: 1953)

Anderson, Mosa, *Noel Buxton: A Life* (London: 1952)

Anderson, M.S., *The Eastern Question 1774-1923* (London: 1966)

[Anon], *Les Turcs et les Révendications Arméniennes* (Paris: 1919)

Argyll, Duke of, *The Eastern Question,* 2 vols. (London: 1879)

— — *Our Responsibilities for Turkey* (London: 1896)

Arslanian, A.H., 'British Wartime Pledges, 1917-18: The Armenian Case', *Journal of Contemporary History,* vol. 13, no. 3 (July 1978)

— — 'Britain and the Question of Mountainous Karabagh', *Middle Eastern Studies,* vol. 16, no. 1 (Jan 1980a)

— — 'Dunsterville's Adventures: A Reappraisal', *International Journal of Middle East Studies,* vol. 12 (1980b), pp. 199-216

Baldwin, Oliver, *Six Prisons and Two Revolutions* (London: 1924)

Bayur, Yusuf Hikmet, *Türk Inkilâbi Tarihi* (History of the Turkish Revolution), vol. III, pt. 3 (Ankara: 1957)

Beaverbrook, Lord, *Politicians and the War 1914-1916* (1st edn: 1928-32) (London: 1960)

— — *Men and Power 1917-1918* (London: 1956)

— — *The Decline and Fall of Lloyd George* (1st edn: 1963) (London: 1966)

Beylerian, A., 'Les origines de la question Arménienne du traité de San Stéfano au Congrès de Berlin', *Revue d'Histoire Diplomatique* (Paris: 1973)

Blaisdell, D.C., *European Financial Control in the Ottoman Empire* (New York: 1929)

Blake, Robert, *The Unknown Prime Minister* (London: 1955)

— — *The Conservative Party from Peel to Churchill* (London: 1970)

Boyajian, Dickran H., *Armenia: The Case for a Forgotten Genocide* (New Jersey: 1972)

Bryce, James, *Transcaucasia and Ararat* (1st edn: 1877), 4th edn (London: 1896)

— — 'The Revision of the Turkish Treaty: Armenia', *Contemporary Review,* vol. 119 (May 1921)

Burney, Charles and D.M. Lang, *The Peoples of the Hills* (London: 1971)

Burtt, Joseph, *The People of Ararat* (London: 1926)

Busch, Briton Cooper, *Mudros to Lausanne: Britain's Frontier in West Asia,
   1918-1923* (New York: 1976)
Buxton, Harold, *Trans-Caucasia* (London: 1926)
Buxton, Noel and Harold Buxton, *Travel and Politics in Armenia* (London:
   1914)
Carr, E.H., *The Bolshevik Revolution 1917-1923,* vols. I, II, III (London:
   1950-3)
Churchill, Winston S., *The World Crisis — The Aftermath* (London: 1929)
—— *Great Contemporaries* (London: 1937)
Conwell-Evans, T.P., *Foreign Policy from a Back Bench 1904-1918*
   (Oxford: 1932)
Cooper, Roger, 'Armenian Aspirations', *Spectator,* 28 Aug. 1982
Craig, Gordon A. and Felix Gilbert (eds.) *The Diplomats* (1st edn: 1953),
   2nd edn (Princeton: 1960)
Cruttwell, C.R.M.F., *A History of the Great War 1914-1918* (1st edn: 1934),
   2nd edn (Oxford: 1936)
Cumming, H.H., *Franco-British Rivalry in the Post-War Near East* (Oxford:
   1938)
Darwin, J.G., 'The Chanak Crisis and the British Cabinet', *History,* vol. 65,
   no. 213 (Feb. 1980)
Davison, Roderic H., 'The Armenian Crisis, 1912-1914', *American
   Historical Review,* vol. LIII, no. 3 (April 1948)
—— 'Turkish Diplomacy from Mudros to Lausanne' in Craig and Gilbert
   (eds.), pp. 172-209
Der Nersessian, Sirarpie, *Armenian Art* (London: 1978)
Djemal Pasha, *Memories of a Turkish Statesman — 1913-1919* (London:
   1922)
Douglas, Roy, 'Britain and the Armenian Question 1894-7', *Historical
   Journal,* vol. 19, no. 1 (1976)
Dugdale, Blanche E.C., *Arthur James Balfour* (London: 1936)
Dunsterville, L.C., *The Adventures of Dunsterforce* (London: 1920)
Dyer, Gwynne, 'Turkish "Falsifiers" and Armenian "Deceivers": Historio-
   graphy and the Armenian Massacres', *Middle Eastern Studies,* vol. 12,
   no. 1 (Jan. 1976), pp. 99-107
Edib, Halidé, *The Turkish Ordeal* (London: 1928)
Egremont, Max, *Balfour: A Life of Arthur James Balfour* (London: 1980)
El-Ghusein, Fâ'iz, *Martyred Armenia* (London: 1917)
Emin, Ahmed, *Turkey in the World War* (Yale/Oxford: 1930)
Fieldhouse, H.N., 'Noel Buxton and A.J.P. Taylor's "The Trouble
   Makers" ' in Martin Gilbert (ed.), *A Century of Conflict: Essays for
   A.J.P. Taylor* (London: 1966)
Fisher, H.A.L., *James Bryce,* 2 vols. (London: 1927)
Galoyan, G.A., *Patmutyan Karughinerum* (At the Crossroads of History)
   (Erevan: 1982)

Gibbons, Herbert Adams, *The Blackest Page of Modern History* (New York: London: 1916)

Gidney, James B., *A Mandate for Armenia* (Ohio: 1967)

Gooch, G.P., 'Lord Bryce', *Contemporary Review,* vol. 121 (March 1922), pp. 304-13

— — 'British War Aims, 1914-1919', *Quarterly Review,* vol. 280, no. 556 (April 1943)

Gottlieb, W.W., *Studies in Secret Diplomacy during the First World War* (London: 1957)

Grant, A.J. and H. Temperley, *Europe in the Nineteenth and Twentieth Centuries,* 5th edn (London: 1939)

Grenville, J.A.S., *Lord Salisbury and Foreign Policy: The Close of the Nineteenth Century* (London: 1964)

Grey of Fallodon, *Twenty-Five Years 1892-1916,* vols. I, II (London: 1925)

Guinn, Paul, *British Strategy and Politics 1914 to 1918* (Oxford: 1965)

Hamilton, Mary Agnes, *Remembering My Good Old Friends* (London: 1944)

Hankey, M.P.A., *The Supreme Command 1914-1918* (London: 1961)

Hardinge of Penshurst, Lord, *Old Diplomacy* (London: 1947)

Harris, George S., *The Origins of Communism in Turkey* (Stanford: 1967)

Hart, Liddell, *The War in Outline 1914-1918* (London: n.d.)

Headlam-Morley, James, *A Memoir of the Paris Peace Conference 1919* (London: 1972)

Henderson, Arthur, *Labour and Foreign Affairs* (London: [1922])

Herbert, Aubrey, *Ben Kendim* (London: 1923)

Heyd, Uriel, *Foundations of Turkish Nationalism* (London: 1950)

Hinsley, F.H. (ed.), *British Foreign Policy under Sir Edward Grey* (Cambridge: 1977)

Hodgkin, Lucy Violet, *George Lloyd Hodgkin 1880-1918* (Edinburgh: 1921)

Hourani, Albert, *Syria and Lebanon* (London: 1946)

— — *Minorities in the Arab World* (London: 1947)

— — *A Vision of History* (Beirut: 1961)

Housepian, Marjorie, *Smyrna, 1922: The Destruction of a City* (London: 1972)

Hovannisian, R.G., *Armenia on the Road to Independence, 1918* (Berkeley/ Los Angeles: 1967)

— — 'The Allies and Armenia, 1915-18', *Journal of Contemporary History,* vol. 3, no. 1 (Jan. 1968)

— — *The Republic of Armenia, Vol. I. The First Year 1918-1919* (California: 1971)

— — 'Armenia and the Caucasus in the Genesis of the Soviet-Turkish Entente', *International Journal of Middle East Studies,* vol. 4 (1973), pp. 129-47

Hovannisian, R.G., S. Shaw and I. Shaw, 'Forum: The Armenian Question', *International Journal of Middle East Studies*, vol. 9, no. 3 (Aug. 1978), pp. 379-400

Howard, Harry N., *The Partition of Turkey: A Diplomatic History 1913-1923* (New York: 1966)

Howard, Michael, *The Continental Commitment* (London: 1972)

Kajaznuni, H., *H.H. Dashnaktsutiune Anelik Chuni Aylevs* (Dashnaktsutiun Has Nothing To Do Any More) (Vienna: 1923)

Karabekir, Kâzim, *Istiklâl Harbimiz* (Our War of Independence) (Istanbul: 1960)

Kayaloff, Jacques, *The Battle of Sardarabad* (The Hague/Paris: 1973)

Kazemzadeh, Firuz, *The Struggle for Transcaucasia* (New York/Oxford: 1951)

Kedourie, E., *England and the Middle East: The Destruction of the Ottoman Empire 1914-1921* (London: 1956)

— — *Nationalism* (London: 1960)

— — *The Chatham House Version and Other Middle-Eastern Studies* (London: 1970)

Kent, Marian, *Oil and Empire* (London: 1976)

Kerr, Stanley E., *The Lions of Marash* (Albany, NY: 1973)

Khatisian, A., *Hayastani Hanrapetutian Dsagumn u Zargatsume* (The Creation and Development of the Republic of Armenia), 2nd edn (Beirut: 1968)

Kirakosian, J.S., *Arajin Hamashkharhayin Paterazme ev Arevmtahayutyune* (The First World War and the People of Western Armenia) (Erevan: 1965)

Klieman, A.S., 'Britain's War Aims in the Middle East in 1915', *Journal of Contemporary History*, vol. III, no. 3 (July 1968)

Korganoff, Général G., *La Participation des Armeniens à la Guerre Mondiale* (Paris: 1927)

Lang, D.M., *A Modern History of Georgia* (London: 1962)

— — *Armenia: Cradle of Civilization* (London: 1970)

— — *The Armenians: A People in Exile* (London: 1981)

Langer, William L., *The Diplomacy of Imperialism 1890-1902* (1st edn: 1935), 2nd edn (New York: 1956)

Lee, Dwight E., *Great Britain and the Cyprus Convention Policy of 1878* (Cambridge/Harvard: 1934)

Leslie, Shane, *Mark Sykes: His Life and Letters* (London: 1923)

Lewis, B., 'Islamic Revival in Turkey,' *International Affairs*, vol. 28 (Jan. 1952)

— — *The Emergence of Modern Turkey* (Oxford: 1961)

Lloyd George, D., *War Memoirs*, 6 vols. (London: 1933-6)

— — *The Truth About the Peace Treaties* (London: 1938)

Lowe, C.J. and M.L. Dockrill, *The Mirage of Power*, vols. II, III (London:

1972)

Ludendorff, General, *My War Memories 1914-1918*, vols. I, II, 2nd edn (London: n.d.)

Luke, Harry C., *Cities and Men*, vol. II (London: 1953)

Lynch, H.F.B., *Armenia: Travels and Studies*, vols. I, II (London: 1901)

MacDonell, Ranald, ' . . . *And Nothing Long*' (London: 1938)

McLean, D., 'English Radicals, Russia, and the Fate of Persia 1907-1913', *English Historical Review*, vol. XCIII, no. 367 (April 1978), pp. 338-52

Mardiganian, Aurora, *The Auction of Souls* (London: 1920)

Marwick, Arthur, *Britain in the Century of Total War* (London: 1968)

Masis, Antranik, *The Question of the American Mandate Over Armenia* (Nicosia: 1980)

Matossian, Mary Kilbourne, *The Impact of Soviet Policies in Armenia* (Leiden: 1962)

Maurice, F., *The Armistice of 1918* (Oxford: 1943)

Mayer, Arno J., *Politics and Diplomacy of Peacemaking* (London: 1968)

Mears, E.G., *Modern Turkey* (New York: 1924)

Medlicott, W.N., *British Foreign Policy since Versailles 1919-1963* (1st edn: 1940), 2nd edn (London: 1968)

Mejcher, Helmut, *Imperial Quest for Oil: Iraq 1910-1928* (London: 1976)

Messerlian, Zaven, *Haykakan Hartsi Masin* (About the Armenian Question) (Beirut: 1978)

— — *Yerek Dashnagirer* (Three Treaties) (Beirut: 1979)

Millman, Richard, *Britain and the Eastern Question 1875-1878* (Oxford: 1979)

Monroe, Elizabeth, *Britain's Moment in the Middle East 1914-1956* (London: 1963)

Morgan, Kenneth O., *Consensus and Disunity: The Lloyd George Coalition Government 1918-1922* (Oxford: 1979)

Morgenthau, Ambassador Henry, *Secrets of the Bosphorus* (London: 1918a)

— — *The Tragedy of Armenia* (London: 1918b)

Nalbandian, Louise, *The Armenian Revolutionary Movement: The Development of Armenian Political Parties through the Nineteenth Century* (Berkeley/Los Angeles: 1963)

Nansen, Fridtjof, *Armenia and the Near East* (London: 1928)

Nicolson, Harold, *People and Things* (London: 1931)

— — *Curzon: The Last Phase 1919-1925* (London: 1934)

Niepage, Martin, *The Horrors of Aleppo* (London: n.d.)

Paléologue, Maurice, *An Ambassador's Memoirs*, 3 vols. (London: 1923-5)

Papazian, K.S., *Patriotism Perverted* (Boston: 1934)

Parker, R.A.C., *Europe 1919-45* (London: 1969)

Pasdermadjian, H., *Histoire de l'Arménie* (Paris: 1949)

Pears, Edwin, *Turkey and Its People* (London: 1911)

— — *Forty Years in Constantinople* (London: 1916)

— — *Life of Abdul Hamid* (London: 1917)

Pipes, Richard, *The Formation of the Soviet Union* (1st edn: 1954), revised edn (Harvard: 1964)

Platt, D.C.M., 'Economic Factors in British Policy during the "New Imperialism" ', *Past and Present*, no. 39 (April 1968)

Poincaré, Raymond, *The Memoirs of Raymond Poincaré*, 4 vols. (London: 1926-30)

Price, Philips M., *War and Revolution in Asiatic Russia* (London: 1918)

Pye, Edith M., 'The Present Position of the Armenian Problem', *The World Outlook*, no. 44 (5 Aug. 1927), p. 60

Raffi, Aram, 'Armenia: Historical Background' in Buxton and Buxton

Ravitch, Norman, 'The Armenian Catastrophe', *Encounter*, vol. LVII, no 6 (Dec. 1981)

Rawlinson, A., *Adventures in the Near East 1918-1922* (London: 1923)

Robbins, Keith G., 'Lord Bryce and the First World War', *Historical Journal*, vol. X, 2 (1967), pp. 255-77

Robinson, Emily J., *The Truth about Armenia* (London: 1913)

— — *Armenia and the Armenians* (London: 1916)

— — 'Facts about Armenian Refugees and Slaves', *Slave Market News*, vol. 1, no. 3 (Dec. 1924), pp. 4-5

Ronaldshay, *The Life of Lord Curzon*, vol. III (London: 1928)

Rothwell, V.H., *British War Aims and Peace Diplomacy 1914-1918* (Oxford: 1971)

Rowntree, Maud A., *In the City of the Sultan* (The Work of the Friends' Armenian Mission, Constantinople) (London: 1917)

Rustem, Ahmed, *La Guerre Mondiale et la Question Turco-Arménienne* (Berne: 1918)

Ryan, Andrew, *The Last of the Dragomans* (London: 1951)

Sachar, Howard M., *The Emergence of the Middle East 1914-1924* (New York: 1969)

Sanders, Liman von, *Five Years in Turkey* (Annapolis: 1927)

Sarkisian, E.K. and R.G. Sahakian, *Vital Issues in Modern Armenian History* (transl. E.B. Chrakian) (Watertown, Mass.: 1965)

Sarkissian, A.O., *History of the Armenian Question to 1885* (Urbana: 1938)

— — 'Concert Diplomacy and the Armenians, 1890-1897' in A.O. Sarkissian, *Studies in Diplomatic History and Historiography* (London: 1961)

Saul, S.B., 'Britain and the World Trade 1870-1914', *Economic History Review* (1954-5)

Sazonov, Serge, *Fateful Years 1909-1916* (London: 1928)

Schemsi, Kara, *Les Turcs et la Question d'Arménie* (Genève: 1918)

Seton-Watson, R.W., *Disraeli, Gladstone and the Eastern Question* (1st edn: 1935), 2nd edn (London: 1971)

Sforza, Carlo, *Makers of Modern Europe* (London: 1930)

Shahan, *'Verstin Havelvads' Alexandropoli Dashnagri 'Inchpes'n u 'Inchu'n* (Another Appendix, the 'How' and 'Why' of the Treaty of Alexandropol) (Boston: 1955)

Shannon, R.T., *Gladstone and the Bulgarian Agitation 1876* (London: 1963)

Shaw, S.J. and E.K. Shaw, *History of the Ottoman Empire and Modern Turkey*, vol. II (Cambridge: 1977)

Sonyel, Salahi Ramsdan, *Turkish Diplomacy 1918-1923* (London: 1975)

Storrs, Ronald, *Orientations* (London: 1937)

Suny, Ronald Grigor, *The Baku Commune 1917-1918* (Princeton: 1972)

Swartz, Marvin, *The Union of Democratic Control in British Politics During the First World War* (Oxford: 1971)

[Talaat], 'Posthumous Memoirs of Talaat Pasha', *Current History*, vol. XV, no. 2 (Nov. 1921), pp. 287-95

Taylor, A.J.P., 'The War Aims of the Allies in the First World War' in R. Pares and A.J.P. Taylor (eds.), *Essays Presented to Sir Lewis Namier* (London: 1956)

— — *The Trouble Makers* (London: 1957)

— — *Politics in the First World War* (London: 1959)

— — *Lloyd George: Rise and Fall* (Cambridge: 1961)

— — *English History 1914-1945* (Oxford: 1965)

Tchobanian, Archag, *The People of Armenia* (transl, G.M. Gregory) (London: 1914)

Terrell, Charles D., *Historical Sketch of the Friends' Armenian Mission from 1881 to 1926* (London, n.d.)

Terterian, Hambardzoum, 'The Levon Chanth Mission to Moscow', parts I and II, *Armenian Review*, vol. 8 (June and Sept. 1955)

Toriguian, Shavarsh, *The Armenian Question and International Law* (Beirut: 1973)

Toynbee, A.J., *Armenian Atrocities: The Murder of a Nation* (London: 1915)

— — *The Murderous Tyranny of the Turks* (London: 1917a)

— — *Turkey: A Past and a Future* (London: 1917b)

— — *The Western Question in Greece and Turkey* (London: 1922b)

— — 'Great Britain and France in the East', *Contemporary Review*, vol. 121 (Jan. 1922a)

— — 'Angora and the British Empire in the East', *Contemporary Review*, vol. 123 (June 1923)

— — *Survey of International Affairs 1920-1923* (Oxford: 1925)

— — *Acquaintances* (London: 1967)

Toynbee, A.J. and K.P. Kirkwood, *Turkey* (London: 1926)

Trevelyan, G.M., *Grey of Fallodon* (1st edn: 1937), 2nd edn (London: 1940)

Trumpener, Ulrich, *Germany and the Ottoman Empire 1914-1918* (Princeton: 1968)

Ullman, Richard H., *Anglo-Soviet Relations, 1917-1921. I. Intervention and* the War. II. Britain and the Russian Civil War. III. The Anglo-Soviet Accord (Princeton: 1961; 1968; 1972)

Uras, Esat, *Tarihte Ermeniler ve Ermeni Meselesi* (The Armenians in History and the Armenian Question) (Ankara: 1950)

Vansittart, Lord, *The Mist Procession* (London: 1958)

Varandian, M., *H.H. Dashnaktsutian Patmutiun* (History of Dashnaktsutiun) (Vol. I, Paris: 1932; vol. II, Cairo: 1950)

Vratsian, Simon, *Hayastani Hanrapetutiun* (The Republic of Armenia) (Paris: 1928)

Walker, Christopher J., *Armenia: The Survival of a Nation* (London: 1980)

Wheeler-Bennett, John W., *Brest-Litovsk: The Forgotten Peace, March 1918* (London: 1938)

Williams, Aneurin, 'Armenia, British Pledges, and the Near East', *Contemporary Review*, vol. 121 (April 1922), pp. 418-25

Williams, W. Llewellyn, *Armenia's Tragic Story* (London: 1916)

Winkler, Henry R. 'The Emergence of a Labour Foreign Policy in Great Britain, 1918-1929', *Journal of Modern History* (Sept. 1956)

Woodward, Llewellyn, *Great Britain and the War of 1914-1918* (London: 1967)

Yapujian, Avetis, *Ov Kazmakerpets Petervarian Arkatsakhendrutyune ev Inch Eghav Anor Hetevanke* (Who Organised the Adventure of February [1921] and What Was Its Consequence) (Cairo: 1969)

— — *Hay Zhoghovurdin Ankakhutyan Paykare Kilikio Mej 1919-1921 TT.* (The Independence Struggle of the Armenian People in Cilicia 1919-1921) (Cairo: 1977)

Young, Kenneth, *Arthur James Balfour* (London: 1963)

Index

Abbott, Ernest 27
Abdul Hamid II, Ottoman Sultan 12, 40
Abedine, Pasha 17
Abovian, Khachatur 16
Adam, Eric Graham Forbes 165
Adana 61, 139, 232; massacres 21-2
Afghanistan 29
Aharonian, Avetis (President of the
    Republic of Armenia Delegation to
    Paris) 50, 142, 153, 155, 171, 181, 210,
    212-13, 223, 241
Ahmed Emin 26, 28, 32
Ahmed Rustem 19
Aidin 27
Aintab 124, 134, 139
Akhalkalak 155
Alashkert 6, 10, 207; Valley, proposal to be
    ceded by Turkey 122-3
Aleppo 128
Alexandretta 149, 174-5
Alexandropol 140, 149, 218, 220, 223, 228,
    230; Treaty of 219, 223
Allen, W.E.D. 101, 106
Allenby, General E. 126, 128; and
    Armenians in the victory in Palestine
    115
Allied powers 163, 170, 175, 185, 222; and
    Armenia: an impossible burden 186,
    liberation of a war-aim 116, 180,
    promise of autonomy 110, protection of
    142, sympathy with 109; Armenian
    suffering as result of association with
    246; de facto recognition of Caucasian
    republics 153; written declaration to
    respect integrity of Turkey in return for
    neutrality in war 68-9
American Board of Commissioners for
    Foreign Missions 120
American Commission for Near East and
    Armenian Relief 236; see also Near East
    Relief
American Committee on Armenian
    Atrocities, report 76
Anatolia 8, 12, 26
Andranik, General (Ozanian) 50; British
    Foreign Office and War Office views on
    106; denounces Treaty of Batum 106; in

Zangezur 156
Anglican and Eastern Churches
    Association 239
Anglo-Armenian Association 45
Anglo-Russian Convention 25
Angora 222-3, 230
Ani 258; cathedral and ruins of 39
Arabia, liberation from Ottoman rule 111,
    122, 137
Ararat (Mount) 142, 219; Bryce on 36-7;
    Lynch on 39
Araxes, river 3, 36; valley 249, drive by
    Noel Buxton in 43
Ardahan 6, 7, 209; left to Turkey 227;
    Turkish proposal to cede 122
Argyll, Duke of 9, 10, 34-5, 44, 58
Armeni, tribes 1
Armenia 9, 247, 269; abandonment of 271;
    and Allied pledges and war aims 176,
    179-80; and armistice terms 126-8,
    131-2, 137; and British War Cabinet 99,
    120; and interest of Britons 44;
    autonomy proposals by various Turkish
    authorities 121-3; Eastern 3;
    inaccessibility of 184; liberation of and
    self-determination 111, 115; loses
    importance for Britain 117, 119; loyalty
    to the Entente 206; position 1;
    protectorate undesirable for Britain
    143; Republic of 104-5, 181, 184-5, 189;
    Russian 3, 15, emigration to from
    Turkish Armenia 16, 43; seen as satellite
    of Britain 223; Soviet 246, 257; Turkish
    3, 18, 32, British pledges for liberation
    of 178, contrast with Russian Armenia
    43; Western 3
Armenian, -s and British government
    attitude before war 8, 52; and British
    sympathy with 118, 121; characteristics
    of 21; claims in Turkish Empire before
    1914 22-3, 50-1; condition in Turkey 38;
    dispersion of 1-2; in Russian armies 95;
    lands and peasantry 25, 43; language 1;
    massacres 3, 11, 19-22, 34-5, 40, 54, 61,
    63, 70-91 passim; 143; Plateau 5, 24;
    population and elimination of 3, 5, 24-5;
    provinces 23, 111, 120, 124, 133, 136,